THE RIVER WHERE
AMERICA BEGAN

THE RIVER WHERE AMERICA BEGAN

A Journey Along the James

BOB DEANS

ROWMAN & LITTLEFIELD PUBLISHERS, INC.
Lanham • Boulder • New York • Toronto • Plymouth, UK

ROWMAN & LITTLEFIELD PUBLISHERS, INC.

Published in the United States of America
by Rowman & Littlefield Publishers, Inc.
A wholly owned subsidary of The Rowman & Littlefield Publishing Group, Inc.
4501 Forbes Boulevard, Suite 200, Lanham, Maryland 20706
www.rowmanlittlefield.com

Estover Road
Plymouth PL6 7PY
United Kingdom

British Library Cataloguing in Publication Information Available

The hardback edition of this book was previously cataloged by the Library of
Congress as follows:

Deans, Bob.
    The river where America began : a journey along the James / Bob Deans.
        p. cm.
    Includes bibliographical references and index.
    ISBN-13: 978-0-7425-5172-5 (cloth : alk. paper)
    ISBN-10: 0-7425-5172-5 (cloth : alk. paper)
    ISBN-13: 978-0-7425-5173-2 (pbk. : alk. paper)
    ISBN-10: 0-7425-5173-3 (pbk. : alk. paper)
    eISBN-13: 978-0-7425-6489-3
    eISBN-10: 0-7425-6489-4
    1. James River (Va.)—History. 2. James River Valley (Va.)—History. I. Title.
F232.J2D43   2006
975.5'4—dc22
                                                    2006025056

Printed in the United States of America

∞™ The paper used in this publication meets the minimum requirements of
American National Standard for Information Sciences—Permanence of Paper for
Printed Library Materials, ANSI/NISO Z39.48-1992.

For my father

CONTENTS

ACKNOWLEDGMENTS

In the time-feathered edges of my earliest memory I am standing by a creek with an Indian name, a tributary of the James River, anxiously clutching a fishing rod in both hands and listening to the voice of my father. He's a broad-shouldered man in faded khakis, looming large among the saplings along the muddy bank. He thinks he's teaching me how to fish. Really, he's beginning to hand over to me his lifelong love for water and words, a gift I would continue to unwrap, one golden morning at a time, in the hallowed hours we would spend together during treasured years that followed, on mist-shrouded rivers, creeks, and ponds with names like Chickahominy, Tuckahoe, and Powhatan. That's where, for me, this story began.

It would never had grown into a book, though, without the able hand of my agent, Zoe Pagnamenta, who took a more or less raw idea, helped nurture it through the proposal process, and found it the perfect home with Rowman & Littlefield, where it came under the care of Laura Roberts Gottlieb, Niels Aaboe, and Andrew Boney. Many thanks to each of you.

In telling the story, I have drawn inspiration and knowledge from many and varied streams, beginning with the friends and colleagues I've been privileged to work with during the course of my newspaper career. Special mention is owed to James Harding, Ken Bacon, Steve Weisman, April Ryan, Jay Branegan, and Suzanne Malveaux, who took time to talk with me about the book from its inception, helping me to form its guiding ideas.

My colleagues at Cox Newspapers provided vital support and I thank you all. I owe a special debt to my bureau chief, Andrew Alexander, who has led my career for two decades with his can-do spirit, his demanding professional ethic, and his unfailing good humor, and to Cox political writer Scott Shepard, who shared with me his own insights and sensibilities from the beginning of this project to the end. My cousin and life-long mentor, the Richmond journalist David Burton, whose gift for storytelling and passion for Virginia history have enriched my world since I was a child, generously shared his deep knowledge, allowed me to peruse his personal library, and read over the manuscript word for word, suggesting numerous edits that added immensely to the readability of the book.

In completing this book, I drew strength from the encouragement of many friends, including Randy Wright, who has both enlightened and re-assured me with his steady companionship; Pete Myers, whose own love for American waters is mirrored in a poet's soul; and Captain Sandy Vermont, the naturalist and storyteller laureate of the South Carolina low country. David Smith read the manuscript, found hidden jewels in the story, and helped me polish them. Bob Gorman and Tom Ruby pushed me to explore themes I might have otherwise overlooked.

Every retelling of the Jamestown story owes a deep debt to Philip Bar-bour, the late author who placed the life and writings of Captain John Smith into context through his own intellectually heroic body of work. Any serious look at the Powhatan people of Virginia draws heavily from the scholarship of Helen Rountree, who has devoted a distinguished career to the wide-ranging and meticulous study that has enabled her to piece to-gether the lives of people who left behind no written record of their world. And anyone interested in the river's natural and historic course can be grateful for the work of William Trout III and the Virginia Canals & Nav-igations Society.

For the most current estimates concerning the transatlantic slave trade I am grateful to Emory University historian David Eltis, who generously shared with me data he and several colleagues have prepared for a forth-coming publication by the Cambridge University Press. Many thanks are due the patient and professional staffs of the Library of Congress, the Li-brary of Virginia, and the Valentine Richmond History Center. And I am indebted to Rebecca Wrenn of the Omohundro Institute of Early Ameri-can History and Culture for drawing the splendid maps that illustrate the river's path for this book.

For taking time from busy schedules to usher me along vital portions of the James, I thank Randolph Turner, Powhatan Owen, David Harbor, and Mike Gorman. For opening a window into the lives of contemporary native Virginians, I am deeply grateful to Karenne Wood. And for intro-ducing me to the world of Virginia archaeologists I thank Harry Jaeger.

I am also indebted to my sister Susan Blanding, a devoted Virginia educator who challenged me to childhood biography contests during which we would huddle with flashlights in the seclusion of closets on rainy weekends spent rummaging through the lives of Jefferson, Washington, Henry, and others. My sister Robin Deans has been a lifelong source of wonder and love, never more so than in these recent months, when she has been at my side in spirit to impel me forward with her enthusiasm for this story. And our mother, Evelyn Deans, who has led our family with quiet strength, irrepressible courage, and abiding grace, used cornmeal and pepper to turn stringers of bluegill and bass into the most magical dinners of my boyhood, and continues to nourish me every day of my life through her deep reservoir of judgment and faith.

My wife Karen has patiently abided my incessant discussion of water and suppressed her better instincts to allow a morass of books, journals, maps, and scribblings to take over our bedroom for months. She has provided encouragement and an endless stream of hot tea and honey when both the backing and the beverage were needed most: in the pre-dawn hours when most of the writing got done. Far more than her forbearance and support, Karen has pressed and challenged me through her own intellectual and artistic quests, her love for life and the deep spiritual center at the heart of who she is. Thank you, Kindall, for being you.

I am grateful to each of our three children, all of whom have passed wistful summer hours bobbing alongside me over quiet stretches of water in black inner tubes rented from James River Runners. I am particularly thankful to Emily, who employed the uniquely insistent nature of a firstborn child to remind me of the jagged cultural shoals imperiling this journey and to squeeze out as much of my ethnocentric prejudice as was humanly possible, even as she skillfully prepared the bibliography; to our son, Robby, who has remained awake as I worked through concepts out loud during marathon drives to Key West and who offered the midnight epiphanies and everyday votes of confidence only a teenager can be counted on to muster; and to Maisy, who inspired this book with the wisdom of a child and cheered long hours of research and writing by simply appearing unscheduled at my bedroom door.

At last my thanks drift back to those who helped forge the deeply personal bonds that tie my own life to the eternal course of the James: Jack Grubbs and Mark Hayward, boyhood soul mates who shared with me countless and unmeasured days in every season, walking the river's shoreline, wading its muddy waters, and fishing its creeks and shallows; Charlie

Eskridge, my high school football teammate, who was taken by the river in the bloom of his life in a springtime swimming accident that blew a hole in our youthful world and terrified us with the mystery, caprice, and unforgiving force of the James; and, finally, my father, who launched this journey many years ago, a big man with a rich mind and fathomless faith in troublesome boys, before he crossed the clear and ancient waters of the Great River, where he waits for me on the other side.

Bethesda, Maryland
February 2007

INTRODUCTION

Racing along the rivers of cement that crisscross the United States or soaring in airliners high overhead, it's easy for modern and mobile Americans to forget that, until just the past century or so, it was water that tied this country together. The story of the James River reprises those beginnings, taking us back to our headwaters as a nation.

This is a biography of sorts, a tale of the most historic waterway in America, the place where Africans, English, and Native Americans first came together four centuries ago to form the beginnings of a new civilization that would change the world. The story is ugly in places. Seldom is it fully just or fair. It is, though, a fully American story, the story of the river where America began.

The drama that has played itself out along the shores of the James is as powerful a tale as has ever been told, a sweeping saga of astonishing moments narrated by as vivid a cast of characters as appear anywhere in the annals of history: pirates and tobacco barons, slave traders and thieves; evangelicals and turncoats, patriots and spies; redcoats and rebels, smugglers and knaves; soldiers of fortune, leaders of insurrection and peddlers of doom; Powhatan and Pocahontas, Patrick Henry, John Smith, Jefferson, Washington, Lincoln, and Lee. Their voices testify to the rawest ingredients of nation-building: accomplishment and ruin, charity and greed, selfishness and sacrifice, revolution, independence, and civil war, all within earshot of this river's watery spine. And, for all its celebrated triumph and glory, the river has also witnessed hatred, betrayal, heartache, and loss on a scale and along a timeline unsurpassed anywhere else in the country.

The story is at times so horrifying, in fact, it's a wonder the entire haunted landscape wasn't abandoned long ago by people who simply wanted to wash their hands of its terror and purge their souls of all memory of this bloodstained topography of grief.

And yet, this American cradle has not only endured; it has been redeemed through the long-running drama that ties Native American dreams to European ambitions and the power of African people who came to this country in chains and somehow kept faith through the long nightmare of slavery with their unfathomable will to be free.

Strangely, it seems, the cartography of our national origins has rendered the James River's contribution in muted tones of low relief, thin and sketchy lines across some faded map of our collective past, as if we as a people slipped briefly and all but unnoticed through its turbid waters. This book arose from an impulse to restore that part of the map.

Placing the past on the land is a powerful reminder of where we come from and who we are. Few landscapes anywhere echo with the force of remembering quite like the banks of the James.

After coursing through fifteen thousand years of American Indian life, the river ushered in this country's first English settlers and African slaves. From that riverside clash of civilizations sprang the origins of epic conflicts that shaped the nation: the struggle between native people and Europeans, the tragic rise and violent fall of American slavery, and the search for a new form of governance for a new kind of nation in which the aspirations of its people were king. The river followed those conflicts through revolution, the building of the country, and even civil war, until Abraham Lincoln himself journeyed up the James, using its symbolic and strategic importance to reaffirm American unity and purpose in the final days of his life.

As a boy growing up in Richmond, the Virginia capital built at the falls of the James, I came to understand how this river has endured on the strength to be found in all of its waters, the rich confluence of mountain springs, piedmont creeks, and tidewater tributaries that churn and roil and sometimes cloud its deep channels, even as they constantly replenish and revive this great stream and power it along its ancient course. I first encountered the river's story in muddy rivulets as well. They painted a meandering portrait like ink trickled upon water, a blurred and unsteady image whose features could simply vanish into a fog of illusion and myth. In time, I found that the more I filled in the portrait, the more I learned about this magnificent river and what has transpired along its shores, the better I understood the nation's larger story. I have tried here to tell that tale unbroken, consulting the most authoritative sources available, then doing my best to bear honest witness to each account.

As with any great journey, this story transformed itself as I traveled into the river's own past. Finally, the James became, for me, not only the stage along which so much of our essential history has played out but a living metaphor for who we are as a diverse and democratic republic rushing from the tributaries of varied cultures into a single stream held in its channel by the national story, shared inheritance, and common purpose that gather the American people as one.

Certainly no single region anywhere can rightly claim to be the nation's sole place of birth. This country's beginnings are spread out instead across Plymouth Rock, Charleston, Boston, Philadelphia, Washington, D.C., New Orleans, and New York, as well as Bunker Hill, Lexington, Yorktown, and many other places. Even that list, moreover, little more than hints at the making of America. A democracy is built, after all, one citizen at a time and is ever a work in progress, in every community, city, and back road where the public resides, and in every corner of the world the nation touches. Ours is a land of immigrants, and our true ancestral headwaters are to be found as much across the broad plateau of Central Asia, the bone-bleaching savannah of West Africa, and the rain forests of Latin America as in Western Europe or the plains of North America, just as the James itself finds its true origins not in a single confluence of streams but in an intricate web of distant waters springing from beneath porous limestone beds laid down many hundreds of millions of years ago.

And yet, it is from this majestic river, along the muddy banks of the James, that our country got its start four centuries ago. It was into these waters we first waded—red, white, and black—and from them emerged as one. It is here, in that sense, our national story begins.

1

HEADWATERS

IRON GATE—The Fourth of July had come and gone in this quiet mountain hamlet, leaving only the hottest part of summer to scorch the corn and sorghum fields along the gravel lane that snaked over the railroad tracks and up to the red brick farmhouse where Clyde Gibson presides over a national treasure.

"Yeah, we let people go back there and see it," he said, nullifying with a wave and a shrug the stark "No Trespassing" signs lining the dust-choked driveway that links Gibson's place to a two-lane state road and the world beyond.

Bearing the measured gait of a man who's lived beyond middle age off the toil of the land, Gibson gestured to a shaded footpath rambling through the forested edge of the property he owns with his brother Charles. "Just walk right through there, look up to your left, and you'll see it."

I hauled my young daughter up onto my shoulders, beyond the reach of the copperheads that favor the tall grass and soft mud running alongside Gibson's lush tomato vines. As we ambled forth, the tree line opened, the path gave way to smooth stones of brown and gray, and, suddenly, there it was, the junction of two mountain streams, wedded beneath spires of birch and sycamore to form the beginnings of the James River.

Cool air off the water broke the summer heat. Maisy climbed down from my shoulders, slipped out of her sandals, and waded into a clear, shallow pool at the river's edge.

"I'm taking a drink," she explained, crouching low enough to dip into the water and make a cup with her hands. "Now I will always have the spirit of the James in me."

As the country pauses to mark the four-hundredth anniversary of the first permanent English settlement in America, about 280 miles downstream

1

at Jamestown, a child reminds us that, whether we drink from the river literally or figuratively, all Americans carry within them something of the spirit of the James, the birthplace of the nation and the very headwaters of American history.

From its unheralded origins behind Gibson's modest farm, the James River cuts a meandering course three hundred and forty miles through the heart of Virginia, its verdant piedmont pastures and rolling farms, its quiet tidewater villages and vibrant ports and towns, before flooding the Chesapeake Bay. There, it tunnels into the great Susquehanna River, the mother channel of the Chesapeake, and empties into the Atlantic Ocean, scattering the sediments and sands of its ancient riverbed far out to sea along the continental shelf.

At each bend along the way, there is something of this unassuming waterway possessed by no other river anywhere in the world. For it is along this river that African, English, and Native American peoples—each largely alien to the others—first came together to form the beginnings of a new civilization that would change the world.

In the four centuries since those tenuous beginnings, the United States has become the mightiest democratic trade and military power in history.

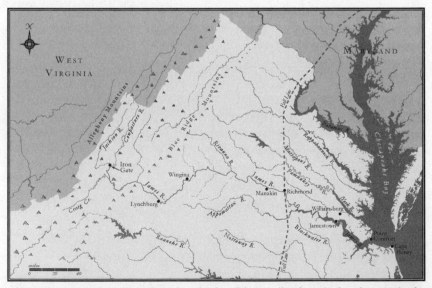

The James River runs about three hundred and forty miles from its headwaters in the Allegheny Mountains to its mouth at the Chesapeake Bay, wandering through the Virginia Piedmont heartland and spreading out into broad tidewater reaches on its journey to the sea. Map drawn by Rebecca Wrenn.

Its cradle is the James, the backbone along which American Indians once thrived, the setting for the English riverside military fort that became the seat of the first representative government in America, the landing point for the first Africans to arrive in English America in chains, and the place where the country's original cash crop, tobacco, was raised on plantations that generated the export profits that, in turn, drove one of the first major economies ever created specifically to participate in a truly global marketplace.

Today, whether we live in Atlanta or Los Angeles, in Chicago, Boston, Dallas, or Seattle, our lives would be vastly different were it not for the personalities and events that played themselves out along the wandering banks of the James. This river flows through all of us and the epic national journey we share.

"Though the James is wholly contained within the state of Virginia, it is not a local river, for it belongs to the nation; not to the native-born only, but also to those who have come from many lands to become citizens of the United States," wrote Blair Niles in *The James*, a book published in 1939 as the world drifted toward a war that pitted this country and its allies against Nazi Germany and imperial Japan and set the stage for the decades-long ideological battle that defined the cold war, the twentieth century, and modern America. "So much of significance to our country has happened in the James River watershed that this river cannot belong to one state alone," wrote Niles, "but must belong to all."

If the Atlantic Ocean divided Europe from the American continent, the James River provided English explorers with a gateway to the newfound frontier; it was the muddy umbilical cord tying the New World to the old. The English were not, it turned out, the first to get there.

At least fifteen thousand years before, American Indians had wandered along the river's shores. They were the ancient antecedents of native clans and tribes—the Appamattuck, Chesapeake, Chickahominy, Kecoughtan, Kiskiak, Monacan, Nansemond, Paspehegh, and others—that would eventually settle into scores of villages up and down the James and its tributaries, from the Allegheny and Blue Ridge mountains, across the broad Piedmont plains, to the great falls near present-day Richmond and along the river's tidewater reaches and toward the sea.

Yeokanta was the Powhatan word for river. When the English first arrived, the Native Americans there called the James the Powhatan after the paramount chief of the tribes that ranged across the eastern and coastal half of what is now Virginia. The English settlers quickly renamed the river for their king, James I, and, after listening breathlessly to native legends of the great, briny waters that supposedly lay somewhere just beyond the rock-strewn rapids of the fall line, headed upriver in search of the elusive passage to the Pacific and the short cut to Asia's riches it promised.

No matter whose chief the river was named for, it led to no great salt-water sea, unless one counts the mineral-laden Allegheny hot springs, surely the source of the Indians' reference to briny western waters. The mutual misunderstanding tumbled downstream from there. Instead of the long hoped-for passage to the Pacific, the river became the conduit for the first sustained culture clash between English settlers and indigenous groups, foreshadowing three centuries of conflict and bloodshed that resulted in the near annihilation of the Native American peoples.

In the process of imposing their ways upon those who'd gotten there first, the settlers established a crude military fort, which they also named for the English monarch. There, at Jamestown, they set up the first democratic body in the Western Hemisphere—its descendent, the Virginia General Assembly, still functions today—inaugurating a rough form of the American style of representative government that has evolved into the most widely emulated form of democracy in the world.

Learning from his Native American bride, Pocahontas, the favorite daughter of Chief Powhatan, the English settler John Rolfe raised the colony's first cash crop, leading the way to the export down the James of Virginia tobacco, the first source of profit for the fledgling foothold in what would one day become the richest trading nation in the history of the world.

It was up this river, also, that the first Africans journeyed into the harsh economy of American slavery, and it was here that their labors carved out of the forests, marshes, and fields the first English plantations in North America. A basic agrarian production scheme repeated across the antebellum American South, the tobacco plantation system along the James helped to generate the wealth that sustained a colony where the embers of rebellion would be fanned into the American Revolution.

When that time came, the colonies turned to the river culture for much of their revolutionary voice, to such figures as Patrick Henry, Thomas Jefferson, Benjamin Harrison, Peyton Randolph, and George Wythe. Giants of the American Revolution and the radical democratic form of government it spawned, each of those men spent many of their most formative and productive years alongside the James, discussing political philosophy with the likes of George Washington, James Madison, and James Monroe in the parlors of riverside plantation homes, Richmond churches and taverns, or the halls of the House of Burgesses in nearby Williamsburg, all of which were incubators of revolutionary thought.

As the young republic rose from the flames of revolution, river power drove the mills that turned wheat, corn, cotton, and iron into products and profits in the beginnings of this country's industrial revolution. And it was along the river that heavy, oaken packet boats and bateaus ferried goods between the manufacturing center of Richmond and the resource-rich farms and towns upstream, part of the great press westward that would lead a nation guided by notions of Manifest Destiny across the mountains and seemingly boundless Great Plains to extend the new country from sea to shining sea.

From these banks also arose the insurrectionist sentiments led by Gabriel Prosser, a Virginia slave, craftsman, and natural leader whose call for rebellion terrified the Southern aristocracy in a bloody prelude to the wider violence that would billow into civil war. It was alongside this river that rebels made their capital at Richmond, the strategic set piece of the war. It was over the waters of the James that the last tattered remnants of the Confederacy retreated from its fallen capital as dreams of Dixie were consumed by flames. And it was to the banks of the James that President Abraham Lincoln journeyed at the pinnacle of his career, just days before his assassination, to greet the newly emancipated slaves at war's end, bringing full circle the experience of the first African Americans, from slavery to freedom. As a fitting coda to that experience, less than two decades ago, Virginians sent to the Executive Mansion in Richmond the country's first black elected governor, L. Douglas Wilder, who was later elected mayor of Richmond.

The history that has unfolded along the banks of the James is no mere string of incidental events. These are serial and formative developments so fundamental to the making of America that it is hard to imagine a single cornerstone of our national identity—our democratic form of governance, our free market economy, our daily struggle to balance the common welfare with the rights of the individual, or the strength we take from our diversity even as we struggle still with the issue of race—without the human, political, and economic drama that played out along the James.

The forces behind these developments were global in nature: the duel between rival powers for world hegemony, the contest between government authority versus that of the church, the testing of long-established arrangements between yeomen and kings, the development of the technology and knowledge to cross oceans and build beachheads in faraway lands, the emergence of global patterns of consumption and trade, and the means to link, for the first time in history, individual status and fortune with opportunities and resources on the far side of the world.

At the James, though, in this country, those forces first converged in a lasting way, along a landscape formed over hundreds of millions of years of the river's own geomorphology, as if it had been preparing, through the eons of its own creation, evolution, upheaval, and growth, for the moment when history would leave its footprints in the muddy shallows along its shaded shore.

Following those tracks along the banks of the James, one can trace the long story of the nation, a willow-shrouded mural in granite and clay. Arguably the most historic waterway in the nation, an ancient stream whose contribution to the country has been both immeasurable and unique, this is America's river, America's treasure, a living and still evolving legacy to all her people.

"All in all, a river's story is a strangely structured drama, full of conflicts, revelations, and ironies, that is hard to replay because the script is blotted and sketchy," wrote Ann Woodlief in her 1985 book *In River Time*, a loving paean to the Virginia stream. "Nowhere else, perhaps, is this script more clearly written than it is on the James."

No boy who grows up along this river, as I did, wading through its shallows in the summer, hauling catfish from its muddy tributaries on rainy nights, or watching in awe as its floodwaters periodically raged, needs to be reminded of the historic debt this country owes to the James River. I was well into my teens before I realized that the phrase "Cradle of Civilization" refers to the Tigris-Euphrates river valley in present-day Iraq and not, as I had long presumed, to the confluence of the James and Appomattox rivers between Richmond and Jamestown. As it is, the James proudly joins its faraway counterparts—the Nile, the Ganges, the Danube, the Yangtze, and others—to take its place in the atlas of inland waterways that have forever left their mark on the world.

None of this is immediately apparent in the cool waters flowing behind Clyde Gibson's farm, where three otters rushed past, diving and surfacing in the fast-moving stream, their dark brown coats shimmering in the midday sun. Nor does it occur to Maisy, as she picked up a smooth gray stone from the creek bed, that she was toying with the product of a cataclysmic geological family breakup, rooted in the Precambrian era, that helped to shape the river's course.

SOFT PLACES IN STONE

Some twelve hundred million years ago, geologists believe, when the world was already three and a half billion years old, today's Virginia was sliding around, along with the rest of the North American land mass and, for that matter, much of the earth's slowly cooling crust. Over the next seven hundred million years or so, through a series of continental collisions and shifts, most of the earth's land came together to form a single supercontinent that geologists call Pangaea. The East Coast of what is now the United States was jammed against present-day West Africa.

The modern world got a tragic taste of the forces involved in those collisions the day after Christmas in 2004, when tectonic tensions snapped open a buckle six hundred miles long just off the coast of Sumatra in Indonesia. The break triggered an earthquake that registered 9.0 on the Richter Scale and sent shock waves hurtling through the Indian Ocean at the speed of a commercial airliner, pushing a train of tsunami waves that killed more than one hundred fifty thousand people in Indonesia, Thailand, Sri Lanka, India, and a half-dozen other countries.

The U.S. Geological Survey calculates that a force 9.0 earthquake unleashes the energy equivalent of thirty-two billion tons of TNT or, put another way, two million nuclear bombs the size of the one that destroyed Hiroshima in 1945. Replicating the force of that single tectonic clash, in other words, would require detonating a Hiroshima-type bomb every single day for some fifty-five hundred years.

Out of precisely that level of geologic violence grew the Appalachian mountain range and its local constituents, the Allegheny and Blue Ridge chains in western Virginia, some of the oldest mountains in the world.

Roughly five hundred million years ago, Virginia lay beneath the great prehistoric ocean of Iapetus, which laid down upon its bottom miles-thick deposits of calcium-rich algae, simple crustaceans, and mud, all of which were compressed over the eons into limestone, sandstone, slate, and shale. In cycles repeated millions of times, seawater evaporated, creating shallow lagoons, then rushed back, depositing thick banks of clay, sand, and salt, some of which were later covered over and capped by sediments with the shifting of the great ocean.

As the continents making up Pangaea crashed together like colossal tectonic bumper cars, those sediments folded and buckled and creased and bowed like a rug scrunched up beneath the legs of a chair. The result was the Appalachian mountain range, a giant wrinkle in the carpeted crust of the Earth stretching from northern Alabama to New England. Volcanic eruptions from beneath land and sea, meanwhile, spewed forth rivers of molten mineral and stone from deep within the Earth's core, which cooled into belts of basalt and granite and piled up over and in between successive sedimentary formations like bands of icing in some giant stratified layer cake.

Then, beginning about 160 million years ago, the continents pulled apart and shifted toward their current spots on the globe, stretching open and creating the broad and rolling Virginia Piedmont and what would become the Atlantic Ocean. As it slowly receded, the Atlantic left behind vast Mesozoic swamps, the domain of dinosaurs, giant winged insects, and primitive birds. As plants and animals died and slipped into the Jurassic ooze, their remains were pressed, heated, and converted, over millions upon millions of years, into coal belts found in the far western part of the state and the smaller pockets of coal that stretch all the way to the western suburbs of Richmond, which formed the ocean's rocky shoreline as recently as ten million years ago.

It would have been a harrowing place to own ocean-front property, particularly on the day, some thirty-five million years ago, when a comet or meteor the size of central Manhattan came rocketing in from space. Its path likely passed over modern-day Bermuda at more than fifty thousand miles per hour, before it slammed into the mouth of the James, gouging out a bowl nearly sixty miles wide that now forms the southern gateway to the Chesapeake Bay.

Perhaps the most cataclysmic single moment in the geologic history of the country, the impact cracked the crust of the Earth, triggering earthquakes that cleaved fault lines running nearly to what is now Richmond and fanning out like broken fingers across the continental shelf. It splashed a plume of water thirty miles into the air and drove tidal waves across the Atlantic, where they flooded the western coastlines of Europe and Africa. Virginia itself was swamped with seawater that rushed through mountain passes with enough force to dislodge boulders more than sixty miles inland. Waves flooded the entire eastern seaboard and scraped the coastline clean. If anything remotely resembling that strike were to occur today, millions of Americans would be killed instantly.

"The waves would have gone to the foothills of the Blue Ridge Mountains," said David S. Powars, the research geologist with the U.S. Geological Survey who discovered the impact crater in 1983 and has been studying and modeling its effects ever since. "It cleared the whole East Coast off, from Georgia to New England."

Lay on top of that already tortured topography three and a half million decades of glacial activity that crept as far south as present-day New Jersey, as well as the ebb and flow of ocean levels as global ice caps alternately froze and thawed then froze again, and combine that with the weathering and erosion of uncounted tons of rock, soil, and sand, and you're left with the modern James River basin, a watershed draining ten thousand square miles, a quarter of the Commonwealth of Virginia, and running the full length of the state.

Like a broad and unruly funnel, mountain ridges and gently sloping fields together channel an average of thirty-nine inches of snow and rain per year into the springs, creeks, streams, and swamps that flow into the James. As it takes in new waters along its downstream run, the river swells to a waterway five miles wide at its mouth, where it empties seven billion gallons of water a day into the Chesapeake Bay.

The largest estuary in the country, the Chesapeake Bay is fed from the north by the great Susquehanna, which brings waters from as far away as New York State. Those waters are augmented in Virginia by four great rivers: the Potomac, the Rappahannock, the York, and the James.

While the James River formally starts behind Gibson's farm, its true origins reach back farther still, to the beginnings of its parent streams, the Cowpasture and Jackson rivers, which converge to form the James. Those streams, in turn, begin with trickles from sinking creeks and underground wells and streams that bubble up to the surface, then disappear into the bee-hivelike tunnels that the water has carved out of the soft, soluble limestones and dolomites that form the fractious foundation of much of the western Virginia landscape.

"The modern James drainage has its rise in the valleys and mountains and Allegheny Plateau, where hollows become creeks, and creeks become streams, and streams become rivers," said David Harbor, professor of geology at Washington and Lee University in Lexington, Virginia, and probably the country's foremost authority on the geomorphology of the James.

A riverbed, in its most basic sense, is simply a low place in the ground, the path of least resistance for water flowing downhill. To Harbor, though, there's more to it than that.

On a warm autumn afternoon, from high atop Three Sisters Knobs, a series of humpbacked mountains near the Blue Ridge town of Glasgow, Harbor looked down on the afternoon sunlight glistening off the glassy sheet of water below. Hundreds of millions of years ago, the river began following a fault, a crack formed in the continental to and fro. In the un-fathomable sweep of time that followed, the river traced the fault to etch its course in stone, patiently carving out a great gorge in the mountain, cutting through seventeen hundred feet of ancient Iapetus Ocean sediment down to bedrock: a solid slab of quartzite.

A metamorphic rock nearly as durable as diamond, the quartzite began its life as sand along what was once the ocean shore. It was pressed into sandstone and then pressured and heated for hundreds of millions of years by the weight of mountains until it became the hard-as-granite table the river now flows across as it makes its way through Balcony Falls.

"Standing here I always get a good feel for what the James is up to," said Harbor. "Now the James is adjusting to the rocks it's in."

Since the first people came to the river's edge, they've been adjusting as well, their own lives linked to the past by the antiquity of stones.

"They were the Creator's first children, before we even had man on earth," said Eddie Branham, a white-haired Monacan Indian who has lived his seven decades in the foothills of the Blue Ridge Mountains, a two-day canoe trip downstream from Glasgow. "They were God's children."

A reverence for stone comes naturally to Branham, a distant descendant of the first Virginians, native people who may have followed the life-giving river in the twilight of the Ice Age and camped along its banks some fifteen thousand years before the first white men arrived.

Like many a working man near the mountains, Branham makes his living off the landscape set in place even before the cool waters of the James first rushed through. Taking the gray fieldstones and black-flecked granites left behind by the oceans and volcanoes and earthquakes, he meticulously stacks them into garden terraces and patio walls with the precision and grace of some Paleolithic Picasso. With each stone he sets, he's tracing the time-shrouded footsteps of his forebears, who skillfully engineered arrowheads, scrapers, hammers, and knives from the rich bounty of quartzite, jasper, chert, and other stones left in the river's billion-year creation wake.

"I've never seen a stone yet that wasn't beautiful to me," Branham said one Sunday morning in the shaded sanctuary of a stand of sugar maples at the river's edge, his white hair creeping from beneath a khaki ball cap embroidered with the words "Native Pride." He held out hands both delicate and thick—a mason's grip with a pianist's touch—and turned his palms skyward, his fingerprints all but vanished from skin rubbed smooth by his labors the way water cuts the land simply by searching its surface for soft places in stone.

"Most everything I do, I do without gloves," Branham said, the calm of the shallows reflected in his small, brown eyes. "To me, handling stone is like handling a little baby infant. You don't mishandle them. You handle them with respect, what I do."

A rock, explained Harbor, is as much a product of its past—where it has been and what it's been through—as of its chemical and mineral composition. "You can take very brittle, tough rocks and, at pressure and at heat and over time, turn them into Silly Putty and just bend them," he said. He gestured across the James, from a curve near its confluence with the Maury

River, toward a banded seam of sedimentary rock hundreds of millions of years old jutting out from the side of a mountain, folded over like the laminated frame of an old wooden tennis racket in a permanent exhibit of geologic torque.

With enough pressure, heat, and time, coal becomes diamond. Both are made of carbon; the difference between them lies in what each has endured, as is the case with sandstone and quartzite. Similarly, limestone, which dissolves in water, hardens over time into marble. Harbor explained that a river also takes its identity from its history, the course it follows, what lies along the banks that trace its shores, the richness of its waters, and the power of its flow.

Water first captured by topography quickly begins to reshape the land, nibbling away at its shoreline or scouring it in the raging violence of floods. The force of water sends cobbles tumbling downstream, like some great Zen god ever-raking smooth its twisting garden of stone, and ferries the mineral-rich sediments that nourish and rebuild its restless floodplain. Sketching its way through valleys and bends in the land, carving away and carrying off whatever loose soil and soft stone might give way, the river is constantly testing and renewing its banks, correcting its course and extending its range.

Reaching far into the western hollows and vast underground springs, the James drinks deeply from a constant supply of water that's steady even in summer and during long periods of drought. Its tributaries drain the damp and nutrient-laden forest floor and broad piedmont plateau, gulping down the mountain snowmelt and torrential rains that chase the river downstream. Farther east, in the low-lying marshes and swamps, water gathers after thunderstorms and hangs suspended in a deep, terrestrial sponge of sand, shaded by cypress and sweet gum trees, until the river sips from those reserves in the dry summer months on its journey toward the brackish coastal waters that sweep into its mouth with the tides—e pluribus unum within a bank of clay.

SMALL RUNDLES AND PLEASANT SPRINGS

"It falleth from rocks far west in a country inhabited by a nation they call Monacans," wrote one of the first Englishmen to set eyes on the river, Capt. John Smith, who first saw the James in 1607. "In the running downwards, the river is enriched with many goodly brooks, which are maintained by an infinite number of small rundles and pleasant springs, that disperse themselves, for best service, as do the veins of a man's body."

The river, as Smith noted, is far more than simply the sum of its streams; rather, it is the living, pulsing force that brings waters together from every part of the state, each source different from all the rest, through the determined and deliberate reach of its course. It is the diversity of those sources, Harbor explained, that gives the river its strength, the deep reservoir of power it can tap in wet seasons and in times of drought, the balanced blend of mineral and organic freight it both takes from and returns to the landscape in a perpetual union of the eternal forces of adaptation and replenishment that combine to keep the river alive.

"That's part of the reason why I think it's here," said Harbor, watching the silent spin of copper-colored leaves dancing along the surface of the river by its pebbled shore. "It's etching it out for us so we can see it."

And see it we can, even today, in the way the river's own life shaped the destiny of the first humans who would dwell along the James, of those who would settle there after them, and of those who live in the region even now.

From the ancient sedimentation and tectonic savagery came the Allegheny headwaters and the springs that leached the iron from the soil, leaving rich deposits in the mountains that would one day fuel the first iron-making furnaces in the country. There was the granite, left by Paleozoic volcanoes more than three hundred million years ago, that formed what geologists call the fall line, a long, east-facing cliff in the river's jagged middle that prevented tall sailing ships or dugout canoes from passing further upstream, setting the stage for the creation of an even broader cultural divide and laying the groundwork for the building of a rough-hewn trading depot that grew into the city of Richmond. Beneath that city's western suburbs lay the coal that would one day fire the foundries that produced nearly all the heavy weaponry in the arsenals of the ill-fated Confederate States of America, then, once those guns were silenced, made mile after mile of the steel rails that would help knit the shattered Union back together again.

And to the east, the river deposited over its broad, flat floodplain rich sediments chiseled out of the mountains and carried downstream over the eons. One spot along those tidewater reaches became the swamp-encircled rise that a small band of unwelcome visitors regarded as defense against their Spanish rivals and Native American tribes on a day in May four centuries ago, when three wooden ships—the *Susan Constant*, the *Godspeed*, and the *Discovery*—sailed up the James River and stopped at a sandy ridge and tied their ships to tall trees, a place the arriving foreigners named Jamestown.

2

YEOKANTA

WINGINA—A golden shaft of sunlight cut the ghostly tissue of dawn that hung like a timeless web of mist in the rambling thicket at the river's edge. Wild grasses, weeds, and thistles bowed low beneath the weight of an overnight dew, leaving a wet and woven mat of deep greens and October browns along the unkempt nape of a broad terrace rising from the bank. The field stretched out a hundred yards or so to a silvery stand of beech, sugar maple and yellow locust at the base of a sheer granite cliff. A songbird chattered from the forested rim of the field, drawing the soft and steady applause of water pouring over the stone and grassy shallows upstream, and seeming to repeat the ancient Tutelo word for river—*tak see ta, tak see ta, tak see ta.*

In quiet moments like this, with the sweet, ripe scent of black walnuts in the air, it's not hard to envision the river as it was some fifteen thousand years before, when Paleolithic people first wandered its banks in search of shelter, fish, and game, eventually building along the length of its serpentine spine a woodlands and coastal plain civilization as diverse and interwoven as the forests and fields that line its shores.

To those Stone Age explorers and the generations that followed, the river—or *yeokanta*, as the Powhatan Indians called it—was both the giver and taker of life, a fickle and genuinely mysterious mistress whose capricious ways could be learned and even predicted but, ultimately, never tamed. It was the source of water, provider of food, deliverer of fertile soil, the trunk line of transport and travel and trade, a hallowed and living being, honored, and perhaps even worshipped, by people for whom life without it would have been unimaginable. It was, quite simply, the beating heart of their world.

"The first thing was the river, and then the native peoples," said Wayne Johns, a Monacan Indian descended from the hunting and gathering bands thought to have lived along these very banks at least eleven centuries ago, as archaeological digs at Wingina have shown.

Long before any white man came, Johns' distant forebears grew corn and beans in the fertile flood plain, hunted turkey and deer and bear in its forested hillside flanks, raised children, took care of their lame and their old, and set up scores of villages and hunting camps linked by the path of the river and the full-flowered culture that emerged from its shores.

"You hear water trickle down, and you hear the birds, and you can imagine what the flute would sound like," said Johns, a mocha-skinned backhoe operator who has spent six decades fishing the rich river waters running through the spruce-shaded foothills of the Blue Ridge Mountains, lands his tribe has long venerated as sacred and spirit-filled ground. "You can also see people, it seems like, if you sit and meditate," Johns said. He paused, then spoke slowly, a gauzy cloud of breath marking each word in the crisp autumn air. "You can tell where they are. You can tell."

For the rest of us, the search for the first Virginians is a bit like looking for the headwaters of the James: the quest quickly leads underground and out of sight.

Americans know more about how ancient Egyptians, Persians, Greeks, and Chinese lived five thousand years ago than about the native peoples who came to this continent well before then. As many as twenty-four thousand years ago, people followed the late–Ice Age game across the broad land bridge of tundra that linked Asia to North America before the continental glaciers melted and released the waters that flooded the Bering Strait.

"Lumbering mammoths and trumpeting mastodons, herds of peppery musk oxen, clumsy ground sloths—their muddy trails must have led for centuries across some forty miles of stony shallows and flats," Virginia Eifert wrote in her 1966 book, *Of Men and Rivers,* a survey of the links between the country's history and its waterways. "The men following close behind them, they all came to the Alaskan shores and to the valley of the Yukon River. As simply as that, as significantly as that, men for the first time had arrived in North America."

In time, some made their way across the sweeping plains and mountain ranges, while others moved down the West Coast, across present-day Texas, and up from the south to what we now call Virginia.

Exactly when they came and the routes they took remain largely a mystery. For, unlike their distant, classical kin, the first Virginia Indians left

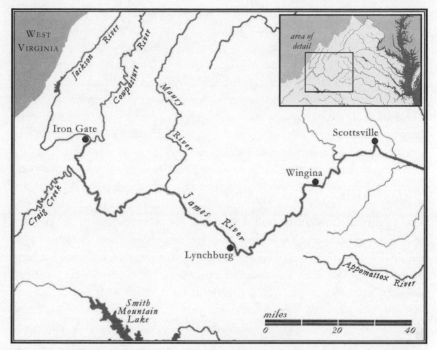

The upper James was the domain of Native American Indian tribes for thousands of years before the first Europeans arrived. Monacan Indians, of Souian descent, set up scores of villages between Iron Gate and the fall line, about sixty miles downstream from Scottsville. Map drawn by Rebecca Wrenn.

behind no written language, massive pyramids, or stone tombs as enduring testaments to their world.

They were, instead, highly mobile woodlands people who built homes of saplings, bark, and wild animal skins and enshrined their understandings and beliefs, technology, commerce, diplomacy, and law through oral traditions. The spoken word, though, grew faint, the voice of an entire civilization stilled by long centuries of silence. That voice speaks to us now only through the murmurings to be heard in small things left behind— shards of pottery, the flinty-edged remnants of stone weapons and tools, chips of bone or teeth, dried seeds, flakes of shell, the broken bits and pieces of a world that was all but swept from the landscape long ago.

"Everything that we had rotted. It all left," said George Branham Whitewolf, self-styled spiritual leader of the Monacan people near the town of Amherst in the Blue Ridge foothills. "The people weren't concerned about the future," said Whitewolf, his thin gray hair falling like Queen Anne's Lace from under the back of a white western hat festooned with a gray eagle feather. "They thought they were going to be here forever."

"Forever" is a word native Virginians use often, as if to smudge the pages left blank where their long history was never written down; as if somehow to raise the bar on those whose own past was recorded and endures in symbols and words; as if to confer a sense of permanence upon peoples grown weary of having their legacy questioned because it wasn't set down in black and white or, like the course of the river, etched into stone.

For decades, most archaeologists believed that the first humans to inhabit what we now call Virginia journeyed in from the Ohio River valley, modern-day Tennessee, or the Susquehanna River region, or perhaps all three, around twelve thousand years ago. They littered much of the state with the contents of a prehistoric tool kit: knives, scrapers, hammerheads, and drill bits made of carefully shaped bone and stone, as well as what most of us think of as arrowheads. Archaeologists call them Clovis projectile points, a more generic term for a stone that's been chipped and flaked into a point with a sort of beveled edge cut into its base that can be fitted into a notch cut into a shaft of wood. They were long thought of as this country's original warheads.

Clovis points—so named for the New Mexico town where they were first identified—were used as the tips of daggers and spears well before the bow and arrow. When these points are dug up among the organic remnants of the people who used them—bone or tooth fragments, for instance, or the charred remains of some long-ago fire—archaeologists are able to date the find with great accuracy.

All plants and animals contain carbon, a sort of crude oil of life, and its faintly radioactive isotope, carbon-14. With death, that radioactivity begins to fade from animal or plant tissue at a slow, but constant, rate. Archaeologists can measure the remaining carbon-14 content of an unearthed shinbone or pocket of dried corn like a child counts the candles on a birthday cake. That lets them peer back thousands of years into the past and reliably date that same bone fragment or seed to within several decades of its actual age, as was done with similar artifacts excavated from corn fields here in Wingina and carbon-dated to around the year A.D. 900.

All along the James River, from its mountainous headwaters to its brackish mouth, clovis tips have been found among carbon-tested artifacts commonly dating back eight hundred years or more, with some reaching back twelve thousand years. That oldest period marked the beginnings of native habitation along the James—or so archaeologists once thought.

This thinking began to change about twenty years ago, after weekend treasure hunters near the southeastern Virginia crossroads of Stony Creek began finding arrowheads in a sand hill at the end of a logging road by a river once inhabited by Nottoway Indians. Over the next decade, archaeologists discovered thousands of artifacts on the so-called Cactus Hill site, named for the prickly pear cactus locals have long called Indian fig. The findings show that people lived along the banks of the Nottoway River as early as twelve thousand years ago and were there when the Tuscarora Trail grew into a major inland artery of commerce and travel that linked what is now Virginia to the Carolinas.

As archaeologists dug deeper, however, they were astonished with what they found: triangular, stone spear tips and quartz knife blades among charcoal that was carbon-dated to thirteen thousand years before Christ, scant but solid evidence that someone had been there fifteen thousand years before.

"I was elated," recalled Howard A. MacCord, a retired archaeologist with the Library of Virginia, who first reported the Cactus Hill site to state historic resource officials in 1985. A retired army colonel who dug up his first arrowhead in 1933, MacCord has excavated five dozen Indian sites around Virginia. He's widely regarded as the dean of Virginia archaeology: Thomas Jefferson, who dug a Monacan Indian burial site at Monticello, is still considered its father. What archaeologists unearthed at Cactus Hill helped resolve a decades-old riddle for MacCord.

"I was never sold completely on Clovis springing out of nowhere," MacCord said, seated at the dining room table of his south Richmond townhouse a couple weeks after he turned ninety years old. "There had to be some antecedents. There had to be something, but we hadn't found it yet."

For Virginia's first families, the region was a very different place fifteen thousand years ago than it is today—cooler and moister, much like New England is now. It was inhabited by animals living on the razor's edge of extinction—the mastodon, for instance, or a giant beaver that grew to seven feet long and weighed more than three hundred pounds, or perhaps even the last of the short-faced bear, a fearsome predator the size of a moose.

The coastline of what we call the Atlantic Ocean, today some fifty miles from Cactus Hill, would have been at least twice as far away then; the sea rose to its current levels only after the glaciers finished melting over the next several thousand years.

Virginia is for lovers, or so the state slogan goes, but procreation was a precarious process fifteen thousand years ago. In winter and times of extended drought, malnutrition stalked the land and could barren the womb.

Harsh weather, fever, a bone-shattering accident, or a wild-animal attack could wipe out an entire family by killing or crippling its breadwinner. Native people were few and far between; they lived in temporary quarters, more like camps than villages, and traveled in small bands of a dozen or so in more or less constant pursuit of food many millennia before tribal identities began to emerge.

"You're dealing with very, very low population densities," explained Randolph Turner, director of the Tidewater regional office of the Virginia Department of Historical Resources. "You might have had a hundred to two hundred and fifty people living in all of Virginia. You're dealing with virtually no one."

Due to their sparse populations and the melt-back-into-the-forest character of their wood-and-bark homes, it's nearly miraculous that archaeologists have found any trace of the first Virginians at all. Finding evidence of people here fifteen thousand years ago also suggests that others may have been here even earlier whose remnants may never be found.

"It's not like a needle in a haystack; it's like a needle in ten or twenty haystacks," said Turner, who has spent decades cataloging archaeological sites excavated along the James River basin. "They actually found that needle at Cactus Hill."

By the time archaeologists began digging into the deep past of Cactus Hill, land in that part of Virginia's swampy Tidewater region was so cheap that a few acres could be had for the price of a new Pontiac. For the Indians who arrived fifteen thousand years earlier, however, the region could be, in summer and autumn, a sort of Paleolithic paradise, a veritable Garden of Eden lush with the rich bounty of field and stream.

Men roamed forests of white pine, maple, ash, and oak, hunting bear, turkey, and deer. Women harvested wild rice in the thick grassy marshes along the river and waded into nearby ponds and swamps, where they caught turtles and fish, snakes and frogs, for roasting and stewing back at camp. By the river's edge they gathered wild grapes. And from the moist, shaded forest floor they picked ferns, eating the raw leaves as salad greens, baking their roots like small potatoes over hot coals, and drying and grinding their stalks into the flour they used to bake a kind of bread.

If the riverside was their breadbasket, it was their medicine cabinet as well, a place where the sappy underside of watershield leaves could be used to treat skin rashes and burns, where the reddish-orange berries of the shrublike sumac could be smoked or boiled into a tea to make a mildly narcotic sedative, and where the bark of the willow could be chewed to release a powerful painkiller known today as aspirin.

"It is conceivable that they had beechnuts, hickory nuts, acorns, fruits such as cherries and raspberries," paleoecologist Lucinda McWeeney wrote in a 1997 report on the archeological work at Cactus Hill. "It appears that southern Virginia, and Cactus Hill in particular, provided a very hospitable environment."

The five-star setting at Cactus Hill would have differed little from the banks of the James, some twenty-five miles away on a northeasterly hike through flat woods and fields readily traversed by Virginia's first tourists. They almost certainly would have explored that river at about the time they were on the Nottoway River, if not before.

"Presumably the folks who are here near to the Cactus Hill site are covering a lot of ground and probably are working out of the James River drainage and other areas," said Martin Gallivan, an archaeologist with the College of William and Mary in Williamsburg, who has devoted his career to studying the native people of the James. "These are highly mobile, hunter-gatherer societies."

The past speaks softly to Gallivan; its distant echoes whisper in his basement laboratory in Washington Hall, where he stands amid a half-dozen steel-legged tables topped with heavy slabs of blond wood laminate. Across one side of the room, he's taped up a giant mural of pale green topographical maps, a cartographic mosaic of the James River and its tributaries, from its headwaters in the mountain springs to its mouth at the Chesapeake Bay.

"This is where the magic happens," Gallivan said, gesturing toward a wall of metal cabinets painted a gun-barrel gray. Each holds artifacts he and his students have dug up from Indian sites along the James—shattered fragments of clay pots and bowls, tools of bone and stone, broken shells from oysters and clams, charred seeds and wood, all meticulously labeled, cataloged, and stored in what look like heavy-duty sandwich bags.

Gallivan is a young and earnest scholar who doesn't want to be quoted speaking in a flippant vein of such serious business. Part of the archaeologists' art, though, is being able to combine skill and scholarship with the vision and even intuition it takes to bring the past alive through the broken bits and pieces of other people's lives, to listen carefully to what they're saying across the ages through the things they have left behind, and to channel their voices and somehow decipher the mysteriously coded messages contained in cast-off nubs of charred wood and time-brittled shards of clay. It's a little like taking a long-distance call from someone several thousand years away. On some level, magic isn't an altogether bad word for it.

Delicately running a finger across a dime-sized bit of brown clay, Gallivan studied the tiny dimples and almost imperceptible lines in its minutely pitted surface as if he were reading some primordial braille. The clay came from a site at Maycock's Point, a small promontory several miles downstream from Richmond, where a lush marsh filters the waters of a small creek emptying into the James. To the uninitiated, the piece of pottery looks like worthless rubble. To Gallivan, though, the simple shard narrates the past, conveying as vivid an image of long-ago riverine life as the topographical maps on his wall, a time-imbedded microchip, low-tech to be sure, with a read-only-memory downloaded in mud.

Perhaps two hundred years after the birth of Christ, he began, a woman crouched over a small pit of clay, scooped up a handful of crushed mussel or oyster shell, and kneaded it into a smooth, moist mass. She flattened it with a crude wooden roller, worked it into a slab, then used her hands to fashion it into a pot. She then picked up a wooden paddle wrapped in a coarse-fibered handwoven fabric and skillfully patted the pot round and round to give it its finished shape, pausing now and then to reflect on her work. There, on its surface, explained Gallivan, you can still see the faint imprint of the cloth in the clay, a sort of precolonial precursor to the printing press, five centuries or so before Gutenberg. In the patterns of the shell-tempered clay, in the thickness of its walls and the way it was fired, Gallivan can discern a whole way of life.

"The shell would expand and contract at a different rate from the clay," lending the pot the strength to hold up under the repeated heating and cooling of cooking over an open fire, Gallivan explained. "It serves like rubber stripping in a bridge."

And one day, perhaps when the pot was slippery from an early spring rain, when shad or herring were running thick in the shallows at the river's edge, somebody, perhaps a young girl, dropped this woman's pot. She may have been washing it in the cool water and been startled by the sudden appearance of a sturgeon twice her size, the sort of primitive giant that plied the river in those times.

The woman who made it, the young girl's mother or aunt perhaps, may have been crouched down in the nearby marsh, pulling up the waterside plant they called *tuckahoe* by its knotty root to be dried in the sun and pounded into the carbohydrate-rich flour she would later bake into bread.

She may have seen the pot shatter and let out some pre-Columbian epithet or curse and decreed in her own emphatic way that there would be no more careless handling of her wares henceforth. Sure enough, nineteen centuries later, Gallivan gently slipped the broken pieces of her handiwork back into the sandwich bag before tucking it away in the gray metal cabinet until it's time to take another call from the past.

AN OFFERING TO THE RIVER

Maycock's Point is but one of hundreds of hamlets that grew up along the length of the James and its tributaries over the thousands of years it took for roving bands of hunters and foragers to begin learning to grow corn, sunflowers, beans, and squash, adding predictability to their diet and anchoring them ever more to the land. Around three thousand years ago, this gradual shift from a migratory lifestyle to more sedentary ways led to the beginnings of tribal groupings, villages, customs, and mores, to the beginnings of Native American society along the James.

On a warm and cloudless October afternoon, in the heart of what many Americans still refer to as Indian summer, Powhatan Owen crouched at the grassy edge of water the color of cheap whiskey. He took part of a leaf of tobacco, golden brown, from his pocket, crushed it in his hands, bowed his head in reverent silence, then scattered it over the smooth surface of the quiet stream, rising to watch it drift slowly past the rounded cypress knees at the edge of Morris Creek, toward the Chickahominy River, a mile before it empties into the James.

"I make an offering to the river," he explained. "It's something that our people have done for thousands and thousands of years."

With deep olive skin and black hair streaked with gray trailing over his broad shoulders, Powhatan invites comparisons to his legendary namesake, the great chief who was once the paramount leader of perhaps fourteen thousand Indians in thirty separate tribes or clans spread along Virginia's broad eastern floodplain running east from Richmond along the width of the state to today's North Carolina line. With a lumberjack's forearms and a prizefighter's hands, Powhatan Owen, also like his namesake, is a physically powerful and deeply spiritual man it would seem unwise to cross, a Vietnam veteran with a ready smile complicated by nearly six decades of experience, a pair of ex-wives, a Purple Heart, and a 1999 Camry he's paying off by the month.

"It was almost twenty years ago," he began, patting the tobacco from his palms and motioning toward the shallow, swampy edge of the creek. "We were bottom fishing for catfish."

Pow, as he's known to his friends, was sure he'd snagged a monster when his rod doubled over and his line nearly snapped. It was no catfish, though, that he pulled from the silt-laden muck but a wooden pole as thick as a broomstick, with a charcoal gray stone the size of a man's fist shaped into a sharply pointed tip, tucked into the crudely notched end of the wooden shaft, and held into place by what looked to the old deer hunter like the sinew of a buck.

"It was just like this, just like I found it," Pow said, pulling the spear from the back of the Camry and offering the business end of it for examination. "I just thought, you know, the last hand that touched this been probably four or five hundred years old—at least—you don't know."

Precisely how much carbon-14 his treasure might contain is of little concern to Pow. There's a point in looking backward at which the hard empiricals of science give way to the heartfelt beliefs of the soul, and it's not always clear which path leads closer to truth. Perhaps Powhatan's spear is a five-hundred-year-old relic miraculously preserved under sacred ground disturbed by the same storm that churned up catfish and silt that day twenty years ago. Maybe it's a far younger reminder of a world lost to time. Either way, it connects him without question to the final century before the Europeans first came to the James.

That was a golden age of sorts for the native people along the river's shores, among them the distant forebears of Pow, whose mother, a Chickahominy Indian, married a Mohawk from upstate New York. They named their son after Wahunsenacawh, long known to English speakers as Powhatan, and raised him amid the wide fields of corn, soybeans, and cotton, the forests of oak and hickory and loblolly pine, the swamps and streams that wander the fertile land between the Chickahominy and the James. Much like his ancestors long before him, Pow spent his days fishing for herring and shad, hunting for wild turkey and deer, sitting by the riverside in a clearing so quiet that, even today, the loudest sound to be heard might be the beating of a wood duck's wings over water half a mile away.

"This was all Indian land," Pow said, casting his gaze across the deep, flat part of the James, just a few miles upstream from Jamestown. A listing barge lay rusting in the shallows, perhaps fifty yards from shore, where it lodged decades before in the sandy mud. Crabs the size of silver dollars crouched beneath the brown ripples at the water's edge. Green walnuts nearly as large as baseballs tumbled from a tall tree and bobbled downstream.

"We know people lived on this water," Pow said. "Since day one. Forever. Before you guys started keeping time. If you can picture yourself here four hundred years ago, this is what it looked like—minus that barge out there."

Long before the rusting vessel had its best days, the river was the highway, the water-paved route that guided native Virginians traveling in dugout canoes, wading along the river's shallows, or padding in buckskin moccasins over trails that traced its shoreline, the navigational equivalent of true north among woodlands people who had no compass and reckoned their way through dense forest by *yeokanta*'s constant flow from the mountains to the sea. And where that flow was interrupted by the rise of rock along the fall line, so, too, was broken the web of ancient civilization that spread along the riverside.

Sixteenth-century Virginia was inhabited by three broad groups of American Indians, each with its own language and cultural traditions, suggesting that each may have come from a different place.

East of the fall line, which roughly traces the north-south route of Interstate 95 connecting Petersburg, Richmond, Fredricksburg, and Washington, lived the Indians in Powhatan's chiefdom, a hundred and fifty villages spread out across the rich lands and along the fertile waters of the coastal plain region the Powhatan Indians called *Tsenacomoco*, or densely populated land, the bustling East Coast metropolis of its time. The tribes in Powhatan's chiefdom, which included Appamattuck, Pamunkey, Mattaponi, Nansemond, Paspahegh, Piankatank, and others, spoke an Algonquin language similar to that of American Indians ranging up the eastern part of the country as far as New England, giving rise to speculation that they migrated southward over long centuries and may have followed the Susquehanna River valley into what is now eastern Virginia.

West of the fall line were the Monacan and Manahoac people, who spoke a Souian language called Tutelo, suggesting that they might have traveled into western Virginia from the Ohio River valley. And near the present Virginia border with North Carolina were Nottoway, Meherrin, and Tuscarora, all of whom spoke a language of Iroquois extraction and could have come from further south or perhaps the territory that now makes up Tennessee.

"There are big questions we can't answer," said MacCord, the archaeologist. "How did these three language groups get here and when? And how did they stay distinct?"

It isn't known, either, how many Native Americans lived in Virginia four centuries ago. While some historians suggest the population may have approached fifty thousand, MacCord insists the archaeological evidence so far doesn't support that. "There were never a lot of Indians here," he said. "There were wide-open spaces—twenty five thousand for the whole state."

Even at double MacCord's estimate, there would have been wide-open space aplenty and more than enough room for entire villages to migrate as farmland wore out and game levels thinned. While tribes generally recognized, though frequently violated, each other's broad territorial stakes, land wasn't titled, owned, or fenced in. Still, the act of clearing an area for a camp, village, or farm was a difficult and costly undertaking for people who either chopped down trees with crude axes made of stone or set the forest afire to create open space and land for tillage.

It may sound like a conservationist's nightmare, but periodically burning parts of the forest helped the environment in some ways, improving the land and increasing its value. It encouraged the growth of a wide variety of scrub pine, sumac, sassafras, and other leafy brush that fared poorly in the deeply shaded forest but provided essential cover and food for wild animals and birds. Deer and turkey especially depended upon the plant diversity of such edge areas or transition zones, which quickly took over between forests and fields after a planned burning or the abandonment of an Indian village or farm.

In the economy of what they had—human labor, wild animals and plants, and Neolithic tools—acquiring living space was, as it is for most Americans today, one of the costliest tasks an Indian faced, short of combat. It would certainly have been the source of extensive consultation, debate, and even prayer among families and tribes, and, just as clearly, once attained, it was a resource worth fighting to preserve. Virginia's indigenous people did not need to hold a mortgage or build a fence to understand that.

Rival groups did, indeed, test and challenge each other's claim to property, frequently clashing over favored swaths of territory. For centuries, Monacan and Powhatan warriors skirmished regularly along the James River falls, which formed a demarcation line between the two groups, a kind of Native American demilitarized zone that each party ventured into—for autumn and winter deer hunts, for example—at its own risk.

"It was a hunting zone, and it was advantageous for both groups to not live there" so that game might flourish, Turner explained. "It's also a clear divide between two topographic regions—the Tidewater and the Piedmont and all that represents."

For the Powhatan, the Tidewater offered a low-lying coastal plain thick with the rich, loamy alluvial soils where Indian crops such as corn, beans, pumpkins, and squash would thrive. In the tidal reaches, clams, oysters, and crabs were easy pickings year around. And in the leanest season, early spring, when winter stores had been depleted, foraging options were few, and crop harvests were still months away, the Great Spirit sent teeming riches of shad, herring, and giant sturgeon upriver to spawn—or, for some, to feed Powhatan people gone gaunt with the travails of winter.

A year-round staple was *tuckahoe*, the starchy tuberous plant that grew wild in swamps and wetlands, areas Helen Rountree has labeled "breadbasket marshes." Rountree, professor emerita of anthropology at Old Dominion University, in Norfolk, Virginia, may be the world's leading authority on the Powhatan Indians. In thirty-five years devoted to researching them, she's delved into subjects as diverse as the foreign relations of Powhatan and the impact that women, who raised the crops, after all, and foraged for wild plants, had on such decisions as where to locate villages and camps.

A scholarly epicurean with a relish for Szechuan chicken and egg drop soup, Rountree has spent years investigating the Powhatan diet, an inquiry that's convinced her that *tuckahoe* was as important to the Powhatan Indians as rice was to their Chinese contemporaries.

"It tastes like a bee sting," she told her colleagues at a conference of the Eastern States Archaeological Federation in 2005. "You've got to sundry it to get it down."

WHEN THE *CHEAWANTA* SANG

Piedmont Indians, like the Monacans, had rich soils to work with and were adept at catching and trapping fish in basketlike weirs and in channels of stone they laid in the shallows of the James. Beyond hunting and fishing, they foraged a rich bounty of nuts and berries from the forests and fields, though they lacked the spawning fish runs or the shellfish that helped nourish the Tidewater tribes.

There was, however, one resource that apparently gave Monacans leverage with the Powhatan tribes. That was copper, which may have originated in mines near the Great Lakes and which was secured by the Monacans through trade with tribes to the west. There's evidence that the Monacans traded copper with the Powhatan Indians, perhaps in exchange for seasonal rights to the protein-rich Tidewater fisheries. Some historians have even theorized that the early English settlers were able to moderate relations with the Powhatan Indians by offering a second source of the coveted metal, undercutting what may have been, until then, a Monacan monopoly.

"Copper was viewed by the Powhatan as we view gold today," said Turner. "If you had large amounts of copper, you could buy warriors. You could buy allies. You could control people. It conveyed power."

No one appeared to understand the rough-hewn gears of power in sixteenth-century Virginia better than Chief Powhatan, who somehow managed to govern a chiefdom taking in half the state without telephones, large standing armies, or written laws. How he did it remains today as much a source of wonder as a key to the modern understanding of how the first Virginians lived.

Powhatan was born sometime around 1550, dead center between the moment when Columbus first brought Europeans to America and when Christopher Newport brought the English to Virginia. His boyhood home was on the James, a mile or so downstream from the falls at present-day Richmond in a village named Powhatan.

It's not clear exactly what the word *Powhatan* meant. English colonists translated it to something like "swift water rushing through rocks," or what we today call simply "the rapids." Linguists have associated it, however, with other Algonquin words that suggest it might instead have had to do with spiritual matters and dreams, which were closely tied to power and leadership in Powhatan's world.

Little is known of Powhatan's parents, but he inherited control over a half-dozen villages along or near the James. He expanded his chiefdom to thirty separate tribes scattered over some one hundred fifty villages during the course of his lifetime through a skillful combination of diplomacy, trade, military conquest, and naked terror.

If Powhatan was raised by the frothy rapids of the James, he's been presented to Americans ever since as ruling at the raging confluence of archaeology and history, where minds briefly meet, then quickly come to blows over interpretation, the gaps in what they know, and the chasms in what they actually understand.

In part, the mischief stems from the frailty of illusions painted from clues, some of them as subtle as a posthole stain in the woodlands soil. Some archaeologists, much like some journalists, begin to see whatever it is they go looking to find.

For historians, whose work relies heavily upon the written record, there is the equally perilous problem of culture.

Much of what we presume to know about Powhatan and his internationally famous daughter, Pocahontas, has come from the lead-inked quills of the English, who viewed the native Virginians through the lens of the European world they left behind. They understood little and misinterpreted much of what they saw and heard here. They were also hostile adversaries, invading the lands of those they sought to describe. They were not, in short, the paragons of informed and objective observation one might hope for in the authors of such a seminal chapter in our national narrative.

Not surprisingly, then, much in the life of this great chief and his people remains open to speculation, debate, and doubt. Yet, because of Powhatan's prominence at the time and in the place the English built their first permanent settlement in America, he and his dominion are the subject of some of the richest and most extensive written records available on the Native Americans as the English first found them. Those writings form the wavy-glassed window through which we peer into their lives.

As a boy growing up by the river, Powhatan would have quickly learned to fish and to swim and to bathe in its waters, as was the year-round custom of his tribe. It was a life of natural rhythms and seasonal change, with years measured according to the annual return of the leaf. The young Powhatan surely learned to welcome the sight of the *cheawanta*, or robin red breast, as an early harbinger of spring, just as he recognized the annual fall of the leaf as the forerunner of winter.

By the time he was four, a boy in Powhatan's world was typically given his first bow made of locust or witch hazel and shaped by the razor-sharp edge of an oyster shell or a blade of flaked and chipped stone. It had a string of deer gut. Young Powhatan probably first learned to use it warding off crows, raccoons, and other woodlands pests from the family corn and pumpkin plot. Like all boys of his tribe, he could later drop a deer—or a man—at forty yards with his bow, and he could be menacing with it at more than twice that range.

He spent long hours watching his elders do the backbreaking work of hauling from the forest a tree trunk nearly as wide as a man was tall and up to forty feet long before they burnt out its core. And he waited impatiently for his turn to scrape out the charred wood with oyster shells, the final stage of turning a tree into a dugout canoe.

Even as one who would inherit the chiefdom, Powhatan was expected to learn the skills necessary to take care of himself: how to boil deer antlers to make a gelatinous glue that would set up as hard as bone, how to set a fish weir of woven reeds and return to retrieve his catch when the ebb tide left shallows in the river, and how to tell the difference between a root that could heal a wound and one that could be used to poison the tip of an arrow.

Even as an old man, Powhatan took pride in demonstrating to guests his acumen at making his own moccasins, arrows, clothing, and knives.

Tribal elders passed down those things they had once been taught, and such received wisdom combined with personal experience and conjecture to form Powhatan's education. What might not be readily explained—the source of life, for example, or the cause of drought, disease, or death—was consigned to the spiritual realm. A religious hierarchy of assorted shamans, conjurers, priests, and councilors of lesser status helped the tribe navigate the dreamlike netherworld that linked the supernatural to the here and now in the seamless web of faith and knowledge that helped lend moral and social order to Powhatan's world.

There is no record of it, but almost certainly young Powhatan would have undergone the elaborate hazing through which select boys became men in sixteenth-century Virginia, a months-long ordeal of hardship and denial known as the *huskanaw*. For those boys who, through inherited status or by demonstrating exceptional promise, were selected to assume roles as tribal councilors, spiritual figures, or leaders, the *huskanaw* was the critical point in a coming-of-age process carefully followed by the entire tribe. If it takes a village to raise a child, indeed, it took that, and then some, to bring up a chief.

Powhatan would likely have undergone his *huskanaw* sometime around the age of ten. Based on what the English colonists wrote about the *huskanaw* in general, he would have risen early for a morning of ceremony, feasting, and song, after which he would have been made to run a gantlet of the warriors of the tribe, who subjected him to a hail of pummeling, whipping, jeering, and other forms of ritualized torment.

With that behind him, Powhatan was taken from his village into the wilderness by a select group of men. Under their tutelage, he was made to live outside amid stifling heat and biting mosquitoes, torrential rain, and wintry cold, denied food and sleep for extended periods, and driven to near exhaustion, very possibly near death, on arduous missions designed to force him to confront the outer limits of his own endurance.

Beyond ensuring his physical toughness and mental fortitude, the make-him-or-break-him *huskanaw* was designed to send young Powhatan into a hallucinatory state, aided by natural narcotics and herbs that would bring him, lean and spiritually purified, within reach of the various deities and spirits that would lend him the strength and wisdom to lead.

Powhatan was raised to believe he could draw power not only from the supreme god, called Okee, but also from a manitou, a lesser deity that he could connect with uniquely. He would have acquired at least one, but probably several, of these spiritual figures during the harrowing months of his *huskanaw*. The result would have been a personal pantheon of larger-than-life figures he could contact through meditation, fasting, and prayer and look to for strength and guidance in times of trial.

Securing these manitoac was essential for any priest or chief. His prestige and power were closely tethered to the mandate of the manitoac. A chief ruled, in part, by faith, the belief his people had in his personal link to the gods. His fortunes were carefully assessed. Failure in warfare or poor decision making could signal that he had betrayed the manitoac or otherwise been deserted by them. His spiritual legitimacy thus undermined, a chief could find his mandate weakened, his position in jeopardy, his job approval rating on the skids.

As chief, Powhatan was a force unto himself, the final tribal arbiter on matters of state, with the power to levy tribute, make war, and render judgment as to innocence or guilt, even to the point of sentencing offenders to death. He was the top magistrate, commander in chief, majority leader, and justice of the highest court in the land all spooled into one.

Some historians have labeled him tyrannical, even despotic. Grouping different tribes around a central leader, however, had its benefits. Powhatan, for one thing, could make timely decisions on behalf of a large group of people, then make sure those decisions were carried out, in an age when doing so could mean the difference between prosperity and annihilation by nearby foes.

However, while Powhatan's portfolio was surely broad, his authority was limited.

Personal responsibility vastly trumped the role of central government in the day-to-day workings of people's lives. The survival of Powhatan Indians, their families, and their tribes depended far more on personal knowledge, action, and skill than on some institutional machinery grinding away on behalf of the commonweal.

Even collective security was almost strictly a tribal function in a land as sparsely populated as *Tsenacomoco*, where it often made more sense for tribes to give each other space than to compete for the same land.

For those reasons, and by custom, local chiefs, called *werowances*, retained broad autonomy within Powhatan's chiefdom. They had the power to administer justice, exact revenge, or make war, for instance, while Powhatan could call upon their warriors only in extraordinary circumstances to mount a large and temporary force to confront some regional opportunity or threat.

Powhatan was not, in other words, an emperor or king. He lacked the absolute authority of a dictator, or even a sixteenth-century pope, and while his ways may have approached the despotic at times, he was not able to run roughshod over those he governed, impose broad injustice upon them, or exploit his people and their resources for personal gain.

"It was always possible, since his domain had no real boundaries, that anybody who really got fed up with the guy could move someplace else and probably be taken in," Rountree, the Powhatan scholar, said in an interview.

"So Powhatan had to make decisions that were reasonably popular, or he'd lose his people."

While the checks and balances were never codified, they were firmly in place and well understood. Powhatan had no parliament or legislature to contend with, for instance, but he was obliged to consult deeply with the shamans, priests, and councilors of his tribe. It was they who were charged with predicting the future, interpreting unusual or unforeseen events, and advising him as to his options when the road ahead was obscured in the fog of imperfect information that so frequently clouded his world.

In the four or five decades he served as paramount chief, Powhatan doubtless experienced the timeless ambiguities of power: being credited for success he played little role in securing and blamed for hardships he had no way to prevent. He learned the value of winning buy-in from those in positions of respect, a trick that required him to understand the concerns of the local *werowances* and their people.

There were, in the various Native American traditions, ways that council members or elders expressed the views and will of the members of the village or group, ways that made up a rough form, some historians maintain, of representative governance at the tribal level.

"Powhatan's authority as paramount chief was extensive, but it was as much a personal as an official authority," the anthropologist Frederic Gleach concluded in *Powhatan's World and Colonial Virginia*, an insightful study of the contrasting outlooks between the great chief and the English colonists. "He ruled with the support and advice of his people, through the republican structure of a council composed of all the chiefs and priests."

It would be going too far to suggest that government by the people was the Powhatan way—government of people who needed and got very little government seems closer to the mark. To the extent central oversight was a factor, Powhatan exercised executive authority ambitiously construed. While there were elements of popular input in the Virginia tribes, nobody would have confused his leadership with democracy, according to Rountree. "He listened to everybody and he determined what he wanted to do and then they had to follow him," she said. "He paid attention to public opinion, but he was not a democrat."

It would be wrong, also, to suggest that Powhatan built a confederacy based on mutual interests and common ideals. While some tribes seem to have recognized that there was strength in numbers, others were essentially vassal villages roped into a one-sided alliance by brute force and required to pay tribute to Powhatan in the form of corn and copper, venison and turkey, pelts and pearls.

Among regional players, only the Chickahominy managed to partner with Powhatan without becoming subservient to his chiefdom. Another tribe that resisted, the Chesapeake, appears to have been annihilated by Powhatan's warriors in the early seventeenth century, a lesson in retribution not likely lost on other area *werowances*.

It was not a moment in history distinguished by goodwill among men, in the New World or the old.

In England, Queen Elizabeth struggled to maintain her authority in a land where crown and church were in bitter and often bloody conflict. For decades the country was torn by the contest to determine whether Protestantism or Catholicism would emerge supreme—any notion that they might coexist without issue hadn't yet sunk in—and the rivalry over religion and reign gave rise to some of the most wretched forms of torture ever devised.

One center of such horror was the prison at the Tower of London, where ascribing to the wrong faith, variously described as Catholic in one decade and Protestant the next, became justification for unspeakable abuse. People were stretched out on an oaken rack until bones cracked and joints were pulled apart or stuffed into coffin-sized cells of brick and stone and left to slowly starve. Others were hanged in public, beaten deaf and blind, dragged for miles through fetid streets, slowly burned at the stake, or subjected to some macabre combination of the four.

In Powhatan country as well, such cruelty was a commonplace means of instilling fear and imposing order on durable and fiercely independent people not naturally given to a deferential respect for authority. A man of his time, Powhatan was known to send his warriors on missions to pillage and torture, to burn out an uppity village, capture for his own purposes its women and children, kill its warriors, and post their scalps as a deterrent to would-be upstarts elsewhere. A man of kindness Powhatan most certainly was not—at least, not by today's standards.

Nor would he likely be extolled for his virtues as a social progressive. Powhatan is thought to have had as many as a hundred different "wives," or, perhaps more accurately, women who bore him children. Betrothal to the chief was little more than a temporary visa granting a wife entry to his wigwam, where hasty pregnancy was vigorously pursued and, once secured, recognized by both partners to mark the beginning of the end of the happy nuptials. While Powhatan kept a bevy of his favorites close at hand, others were dispatched to new lodgings elsewhere once they'd given birth. These young mothers took over the daily upbringing of the newest additions to the big man's growing brood, while he took up with his next devotee in his birch-bark woodlands love nest. Life was short. Life was hard. A chief needed to sustain his progeny.

Apart from populating *Tsenacomoco* with his offspring, Powhatan seems to have built his dominion through a sophisticated web of trading and security arrangements either negotiated with, or imposed upon, neighboring tribes. Like many a European monarch before him, Powhatan often helped knit together alliances by cooking up strategic marriages or assigning his own sons to the post of *werowance* in villages scattered throughout his domain.

As a military leader, Powhatan seems to have been at least as interested in caution as conquest. Combat losses were keenly felt in villages that commonly relied on as few as two or three dozen seasoned men for the constant hunting, fishing, and clearing of land required to keep the community viable. And in his own time, Powhatan witnessed the wiping out of his native village three separate times, probably from rivals' raids.

The massacre of an entire village was more extreme than common, however, in a place where the availability of land meant there was generally enough elbow room to keep arrows from flying most of the time.

Fighting among native Virginians, moreover, was very different from warfare in Europe, where for centuries military empires ruled by dictators and kings had been clashing in winner-take-all contests that could change the future of entire nations in a single campaign. There is no record of any such epic conflict in pre-English Virginia, where fighting could be grisly but seems to have been constrained by custom, resources, and comparatively low stakes.

As a general rule, one tribe would fight with another less to go to war than to assert itself; to test the other, reinforce territorial boundaries, or draw some other line in the sand; to mete out punishment for some perceived offense; or to send a warning designed to curtail some conduct or plan. War, for the Powhatan people, was more a way to demonstrate than dominate. "War was undertaken to right a wrong, to correct improper actions," wrote Gleach, the anthropologist. "It was a means of restoring justice and teaching proper behavior."

That may be dabbing a bit of anthropological gloss on a long trail of simple atrocity. The point, though, is that bloodshed was useless in Powhatan's world unless it communicated some purpose, unless it contained an element of what we might call diplomacy, yet another stream of power for Powhatan, who represented his people in negotiations with others in a way that often required patient and earnest statesmanship.

Powhatan led with what English observers noted was enormous, even majestic, presence, the ability to convey authority and to command influence through his very persona. That was important for a sixteenth-century chief, much as it is today, when leaders are valued for what we call charisma, the vital, if intangible, characteristic that helps get presidents elected.

By all accounts, Powhatan had the kind of charisma that makes for great television. Had CNN been around in his day, he might have become the Nelson Mandela of the seventeenth-century world, the Nobel Prize–winning embodiment of a proud, yet oppressed, people and their righteous cause, lionized on college campuses and by human rights activists around the world, a figure of unchallenged moral authority in whose reflected glory other world leaders might long to bask at state dinners and global summitry.

Add to that an engaging and articulate daughter with a bold demeanor and spit in her eye, and it's not hard to envision a celebrity martyr with near universal appeal, someone with the capacity to bring low the mighty. One can easily imagine the doleful sound of empire creaking with a few well-timed appearances before the United Nations, the Council on Foreign Relations, and the editorial board of the *New York Times*.

Powhatan, though, had no such magical conveyance upon which he might call to send his image, like smoke, through the sky and project his vision, like fire, upon a global screen. For all his powers—spiritual, political, military, and personal—Powhatan, like most leaders, was a man of his own place and time, dependent for his authority on the faith of his people, the resources he was able to garner from them, and his own ability to map out a course for their future that bent collective labors toward common goals.

All of that, and more, would soon be tested by a strange and foreign foe. It came out of the east on the wings of the wind, in the time the *cheawanta* sang, unforeseen by any shaman, unforetold but by the tides, gliding against the sunlit current, pressing ever further upstream, over the river's ancient and outstretched waters, the sacred arms of *yeokanta*.

3

LORDS OF NAVIGATION

CAPE HENRY—In October 1584, when the Powhatan people would have been relishing the autumn bounty of field and stream, a visionary geographer and Anglican priest named Richard Hakluyt hand-delivered to Queen Elizabeth in London a top-secret document that would change the world.

England, at that moment, was a second-rate power still struggling with the basics of nation building. The English language itself was only several centuries old, spoken by four million people at most. Many who deemed her authority illegitimate regarded Elizabeth as a pretender. She relied on warlords and often brutal repression to hold together a fractious kingdom taking in England, Wales, and a largely rebellious Ireland.

When Elizabeth was three, her mother was beheaded at the command of her father, Henry VIII, an early introduction into the bloodshed and internecine rivalries near the heart of the English throne. Much of Elizabeth's own court and its treasure were devoted to thwarting conspiracies and assassination plots. Population was surging far beyond England's ability to generate wages and jobs. Across much of the country, farmland had been exhausted, waters defiled, and forests all but denuded. Crime, inflation, and out-of-wedlock pregnancies were rampant, and parts of the economy were sliding toward depression.

Elizabeth, moreover, feared losing ground in what amounted to a cold war with Spain, the true European superpower of the day.

As the sixteenth century wound toward its close, Spain was a geographically blessed military and commercial giant straddling the two most important oceans in the Western world: the Atlantic and the Mediterranean. With a blue-water navy no rival could match, Spain possessed colonies, forts, and trade entrepots extending from the Netherlands and

Africa to the Americas, India, and the South China Sea. A century-old papal decree gave Spain exploration rights to all of the Americas and Asia; the better tables in Seville were graced with chocolate from Mexico, silver from Peru, tea from Ceylon, porcelain from China, and cinnamon, pepper, and cloves from the spice isles of the South Pacific.

Long before the English discovered what mercantilism and sea power could do for a modern state, the sun never set on the Spanish Empire.

Into that lopsided balance of power, Hakluyt ventured a radical idea: Elizabeth should build English colonies in America, undercut Spain's overseas source of wealth, ignore the ecclesiastical edicts of Rome, and, with New World riches at her command, set London on a course toward commercial and naval dominance that would eclipse the global reach of Spain and lead England to become the mightiest nation on earth. It must have seemed, to some, a novel form of madness.

Reverend Hakluyt, though, was no lunatic. An Oxford scholar who lectured on Aristotle and spoke at least seven languages, he was serving at the time in one of the queen's most sensitive diplomatic posts—as chaplain to her majesty's embassy in France.

When not leading vespers, Hakluyt was acting as, essentially, a spy, prowling the alleyways of Paris and warding off the chill winds of French seaports to pry information from fishermen, pirates, mapmakers, botanists, astronomers, shipwrights, merchants, compass designers, furriers, sea captains, and anyone else even remotely familiar with the Atlantic and the uncharted worlds beyond. He stayed up nights poring by candlelight over texts written in Latin, Greek, Spanish, Portuguese, Italian, and French—seafaring journals, nautical tables, celestial guides, and travelogues. And he dined with exiled Spanish courtiers and others who shared with him the secrets of the Castillians' global designs.

Nor was Hakluyt pursuing some vain hobby or personal pipe dream. He was acting on orders from Sir Francis Walsingham, the queen's secretary of state, and in concert with Walsingham's dashing court colleague, the mariner and soldier Walter Raleigh. Both hoped Hakluyt would mount a cogent and comprehensive argument for royal support of New World exploration. For different reasons, they had tired of watching England sit out the race to colonize the Americas. Walsingham thought England was missing out on a historic geopolitical play; Raleigh sought fortune and fame. It would not be the last time the English would debate the meaning and worth of America, but, for the time being at least, the differing interests coincided more than clashed.

Late in the summer of 1584, Hakluyt wrote a twenty-one-chapter treatise meant to serve the aims of both patrons, who urged Elizabeth to receive the godly geographer and his highly classified document, probably at Whitehall Palace, that fall.

Not even Hakluyt, who was thirty-two years old at the time, could have fully grasped the prophetic nature of his work—part grand strategy, part Jules Verne—even as he trudged up the palace steps, gripping his leather-bound masterpiece, the full twenty-six-word title of which has been shortened to its literary nickname, *A Discourse of Western Planting*.

BLUEPRINT FOR EMPIRE

A back-shelf classic of modern geopolitical thought, Hakluyt's *Discourse* lays out, with nearly symphonic precision of reason, a comprehensive vision that amounts to a military, economic, and political blueprint for British empire and a sweeping rationale for projecting English might around the world. In the process, it set a breathtakingly condescending tone for European dealings with America's native people and non-Christian people in general, even as it made a historic bid for social reform and the essential rights of man. In writing it, Hakluyt captured, with stunning clarity and candor, the contradictory values that shaped his era and would cast an enduring shadow across the face of the American experiment.

There was one rather large hole in Hakluyt's research. He'd never actually seen the New World, ventured forth across the rolling Atlantic aboard a leaking wooden boat, or, for that matter, traveled any farther from London than Paris. Inevitably, he got some things wrong.

"The passage in this voyage is easy and short. . . . It may be sailed in five or six weeks," he wrote, assuring the queen that, even for Elizabethan England, New World exploration was well within reach, a comparatively low-risk venture with the potential for boundless reward.

Others had dreamed New World visions as well, many of them equally naive. Some were inspired by Sir Thomas More, who lit the English imagination in 1516 with his *Utopia,* set on a fictional island loosely modeled on reports of Spanish exploits in South America. English priests joined their Spanish, Italian, and Portuguese counterparts in sermonizing on the virtues of conquest and colonization as a means of spreading the Gospel to the far reaches of the Americas. The works of William Shakespeare and other contemporary English playwrights and poets were infused with the adventurous spirit of possibility that New World exploration lent to the times. And Hakluyt himself had already published *Divers Voyages,* the first of three popular compilations of travels and discoveries, a body of work some scholars have called the prose epic of modern England.

Hakluyt's *Discourse*, though, was neither literature nor scripture: it was a national security brief. In it, he set forth the reasons England had to get into the New World colonization game, the ideological underpinnings for English explorations in America, and the specific benefits the queen could expect in return for her patronage. A man of the cloth with an ear for politics, Hakluyt also went to great lengths to identify a vast array of constituent groups whose interests would be well served by this grand enterprise.

One of the greatest strategic thinkers of his era, Hakluyt well understood the potential his *Discourse* created for peril—both for him personally and for the crown he served. He paid an anonymous scrivener to write out by hand just three known copies. Hakluyt kept one, another went to the queen, and the third seems to have gone to his court patron, Walsingham, who almost certainly shared its contents with Raleigh and select others. Beyond that, Hakluyt insisted the work be kept under wraps, lest it fall into a rival's hands, and "We should beat the bush and other men take the birds."

Hakluyt began his *Discourse* on the theological high road, as if he were opening a service at the Church of England, averring that "this western discovery will be greatly for the enlargement of the gospel of Christ"; it was as though he was proposing a kind of evangelical catch-up game with those pesky Spanish purveyors of global Catholicism.

Quickly reaching a bit closer to the Protestant heart of the queen, who had one eye on the growing strength of Catholic Spain's powerful armada, Hakluyt pointed out that the bid for America would accrue "greatly for the increase, maintenance and safety of our navy, and especially of great shipping, which is the strength of our realm."

The English navy, in fact, could surpass all others in time, Hakluyt surmised, if her majesty would make New World exploration a national priority. "It will breed more skillful, cunning and stout pilots and mariners," Hakluyt wrote. They, in turn, would develop the technology and skills needed to transform England's navy into a fleet that would offer the queen "a chief strength and surety in times of war, as well to offend as defend." He even conjured up the vision of a grand military-industrial complex that would spread to "cities, towns, villages, havens and creeks," bestowing rich rewards upon artisans of all stripes, "brewers, bouchers, smiths, ropers, shipwrights, tailors, shoemakers" among them.

There was no doubt, he reasoned, that America, with its "great navigable rivers," was home to the vast inland waterway that would provide the elusive northwest passage to China and Japan, the long-sought shortcut to Asian wealth and the navigational holy grail for sixteenth-century mariners.

And the queen could rest assured, Hakluyt informed her, that she was fully entitled to colonize America north of Florida—the northernmost reach of Spanish colonization—and south of the St. Lawrence River, claimed for France by Jacques Cartier in 1534. After all, legend had it, the Welsh Prince Madoc ap Owen Guyneth had explored North America in 1170—three centuries before Christopher Columbus first laid eyes on the New World, Hakluyt took pride in pointing out—and John Cabot had sailed for England when he visited the region—he called it "new found land"—in 1497.

In asserting England's claims, however, the inventive Hakluyt had to clear away the objections of two powerful interests: the Vatican, which had already decreed that Spain was entitled to that part of the world, and the Native Americans.

Though they preceded the *Discourse* by some fifteen thousand years, the natives, Hakluyt calculated, would be the easier of the two to deal with. They were, he wrote, "idolaters"—sinners, in other words, condemned by disbelief—who "worship the sun, the moon and the stars." Believing "not at all in God," he continued, these natives "are very easy to be persuaded . . . very desirous to become Christians." As no small bonus, he added, they would become "willing subjects" of the English crown—salvation and subjugation both thusly assured.

Beyond his own research, Hakluyt had been tutored in English attitudes toward the American Indians by his uncle and mentor, for whom he was named. If push between the two groups came to shove, Richard Hakluyt the elder reasoned, it was only right, if not preordained, that the English should prevail. After all, he wrote, "We are the lords of navigation, and they are not."

Having dispensed with the claims of the indigenous peoples, Hakluyt trained his rhetorical firepower on the Vatican in a theologically based critique of the papal bull that had excluded England from all New World discoveries. The Anglican Hakluyt dismissed the pope as a meddlesome faith-based potentate and called him "the great anti-Christ of Rome," an aspersion that must have brought a wry smile to the lips of Queen Elizabeth, who had been excommunicated by the Vatican fourteen years earlier. In Rome's judgment, she was the bastard child of an illegitimate marriage and had no lawful claim to the English throne, a condemnation that sanctified decades of Catholic conspiracies against her and her throne.

"Our Savior Christ confessed openly to Pilate that his kingdom was not of this world," Hakluyt testified. "Why then doth the Pope that would be Christ's servant take upon him the division of so many kingdoms of the world?"

Pivoting from indignation to justification, Hakluyt detailed the American colonies' potential to strengthen a growing nation. Exhibit A was Spain, a naturally "poor and barren" realm, he explained, that had been transformed by New World discoveries into a powerful state that took gold and silver from America and used it to fund a naval and merchant fleet second to none, hire mercenaries by the tens of thousands, and incorporate its military might and papal blessing to expand its empire and to menace every prince and province in Christendom.

Despite its wealth and might, Spain had become a vulnerable power, listing through the early stages of imperial overreach. The Spanish were spending heavily to fight a war of occupation far from their borders, in the Netherlands, and to fund military deployments around the world. Without the constant influx of wealth from its American holdings, Hakluyt predicted, "the Spanish Empire falls to the ground."

England could hasten that welcome collapse, he added, by using America as a platform from which to launch naval raids on Spanish ships returning from the New World loaded with treasure. "Two or three strong forts" along the coast, he advised, could harass Spain's King Philip II, "endanger his fleet . . . [and] in a few years, put him in hazard of losing some part of Nova Hispania," as much of the New World was known at the time.

Already, in fact, the ham-fisted ways of the conquistadors had fueled hatred of the Spanish among the indigenous peoples in much of what is now called Latin America. Spain, Hakluyt contended, had imposed a "great tyranny" on those people, enslaving, torturing, and murdering them. The groundwork was already laid, he said, for a revolution to overthrow Spanish rule. "The people kept in subjugation desire nothing more than freedom," he explained. "And, like as a little passage given to water it maketh its own way, so give but a small mean to such kept in tyranny, they will make their own way to liberty."

While he meant it as a slam against Spain, Hakluyt also gave vent to what he portrayed as man's natural aspirations toward self-rule, in a line that, in time, was to prove ironically prophetic. "When men are tied as slaves," he wrote, "all yell and cry with one voice liberty, liberty, liberty, as desirous of liberty and freedom."

The strategic argument for American colonies complete, Hakluyt built an equally compelling case for New World economic promise. In an era when idleness was regarded as a sin and often a crime, Hakluyt described England as a land where unemployment was so high that "multitudes of loiterers and idle vagabonds" bent their effort to "pilfering and thieving and other lewdness" with such devotion that "all the prisons of the land are daily pestered and stuffed full of them." In America, Hakluyt reasoned, "these petty thieves" could be put to work enriching the kingdom by mining the rich veins of silver and gold that undoubtedly awaited them; harvesting the primal forests for ship masts, pitch, tar, rosin, and soap ash; gathering hemp for cordage, honey for cakes, and beeswax for candles; dragging the broad coastal waters for pearls; cutting and shaping marble and other stone; tending silk worms; producing salt; killing whales for their oil and seals for their fur; catching salmon and herring; or raising cotton, oranges, lemons, and figs. Even those "valiant youths rusting" away for lack of jobs at home might yet find redemption in America, wrote Hakluyt, and, indeed, "may there be raised again, and do their country good service."

Not only could the jobless rabble of England be transformed into producers of wealth, he wrote, but also the "savages" inhabiting these New World lands would make splendid new customers for English goods. Those same Native Americans so eager to embrace the Gospel, Hakluyt assured the queen, would be "greatly delighted with any cape or garment made of coarse woolen cloth," providing a badly needed economic shot in the arm for countless "cappers, knitters, clothiers, woolmen, carders, spinners, weavers," and others.

With the simple addition of English enterprise, labor, and capital, in other words, America would become a splendid machine for producing the raw materials the mother country lacked, while consuming whatever England's workshops might kick out. In the process, this grand new venture would turn a handsome profit for those wise and well-off enough to invest, as well as for the royal sponsor of the colony.

The free trade bonanza would be a godsend, moreover, for down-on-their-luck English seaports and all who made their living from shipping, Hakluyt asserted, whether they were the farmers who provisioned the voyages from the hinterlands or those who built and manned the merchant fleet. Indeed, in a passage almost biblical in its reach, Hakluyt foresaw a full-scale economic turnabout, a recovery that would amount to a grand social renaissance, reviving the fortunes of "husbandmen, seamen, merchants, soldiers, captains, physicians, lawyers, divines, cosmographers, hydrographers, astronomers, historiographers, yea old folks, lame persons, women and young children by many means which hereby . . . shall be kept from idleness."

Lest the queen miss the implications of the societal restoration he envisioned, Hakluyt added a passage pointing out the stability to be gained from the economic adrenalin the New World would pump into England's sagging veins. "For when people know how to live, and how to maintain and feed their wives and children," he admonished, "they will not abstain from marriage as they now do," an argument that likely carried little weight with the famously unwed queen.

History is silent as to how she responded to Hakluyt's assessment. Elizabeth was undoubtedly a ruler more constrained than expansive. She didn't want to antagonize Spain, much less initiate the acts of war Hakluyt advocated. Her treasury lacked the funds for the grand gambit he outlined; such money as could be expended she was—wisely, it turned out—investing in a fleet that would defend England from the invasion force launched against her just four years later with the Spanish Armada. England's merchants, whose opinions she had to weigh carefully, were manifestly more interested in established commerce across Europe than in high-risk emerging markets overseas. And Elizabeth had only so much time to devote to grand schemes, pinned down as she was during so much of her reign by the need to stay alive in the face of ruthless foes.

It is clear, however, that within months the queen had knighted Sir Walter Raleigh and given him a royal mandate to set up England's first New World colony in the very lands Hakluyt described, a place the ever-calculating Raleigh named "Virginia" in honor of the virgin queen. Thus, the first English colony in America got its name from the crafty public relations ploy of an ambitious self-promoter who sought the queen's favor in his bid for immortality and wealth.

Raleigh's colony endured a year before it was abandoned. It was later resettled, then finally failed, in part because Elizabeth required every vessel that could float to wage England's 1588 fight for survival against the Spanish Armada. This prevented Raleigh from sending fresh supplies and settlers to the colony at a critical moment. The settlers who waited in vain for that relief vanished on Roanoke Island, in what is now North Carolina, and the fate of the so-called Lost Colony remains a mystery to this day.

By the time she died in 1603, Elizabeth had pursued no other such exploits beyond a few reconnaissance missions to the North American coast. It would be up to her successor, King James I, to pick up where she left off.

Hakluyt's *Discourse*, however, had clarified the case for colonization. It had gone a long way toward articulating English purpose in the world at the dawn of the seventeenth century. And it kept the dream of New World discovery alive in the royal court at Whitehall.

Hakluyt's ideas continued to circulate among London speculators, whom James granted, in April 1606, a royal charter to explore and settle Virginia. They set up a joint stock company—the corporate legacy of which can be traced in the shares traded on Wall Street today—called the Virginia Company of London to fund and direct the colony. Entire passages of its charter read as if they were shaped by Hakluyt, as, indeed, they probably were. As an initial shareholder in the firm, Hakluyt, who by then had been knighted, seems to have evolved from strategic adviser to corporate policymaker.

After stating as the company's purpose the establishment of a colony "into that part of America commonly called Virginia," the charter quickly stressed the colonists' role "in propagating of Christian religion to such people as yet live in darkness and miserable ignorance of the true knowledge and worship of God." In time, the mandate continued, the colonists "may bring the infidels and savages living in those parts to humane civility and to a settled and quiet government," a chilling passage, in retrospect, whose meaning would be revised and extended once the settlers hit the ground.

For their labors, "they shall have all the lands, woods, soil, grounds, havens, ports, rivers, mines, minerals, marshes, waters, fishings," and all other property and resources that might lie within fifty miles of their settlement along the coastline or one hundred miles inland of their colony, the charter asserted. Those tenets in place, the charter further ordered the colonists "to dig, mine and search for all manner of mines of gold, silver and copper," with 20 percent of whatever silver and gold they found to be paid to the shareholders, a formula modeled on the levies the Spanish crown assessed its own colonists.

Backed, as it was, by the full faith and force of the English throne, the royal charter granted the colonists and their stakeholders a monopoly on the Virginia trade and a seven-year holiday from English customs duties. The charter also imposed a strict prohibition against trade with any foreign power and granted the colonists the king's authority to use "all ways and means whatsoever" to defend themselves against anyone who might try to intrude upon their colony or impede its progress.

The Virginia Company was the royal stepchild of the joint stock firms first put together more than a century before in the Italian city states of Venice and Genoa, where merchants and shipmasters sought to spread the enormous risks and costs, in exchange for a share of the rewards, of overseas colonization and trade.

To that model King James added his own flourish. Wanting to retain political control over the colony, while others bore the financial risk, he structured something of a public-private hybrid. Investors could, indeed, profit from the enterprise and say much about how it was run. A council appointed by the king, however, would handle major decisions and have the authority to make laws the colonists must obey. Once on land, the colonists were to answer to a colonial council named by the company.

Through the charter, in short, King James put his appointees and London investors in control of the colony and those who would risk life and limb to establish it. The company penned what amounted to an order for the colonists to invade and occupy a foreign land, to repel and repress, by force if necessary, its native people, and to get quickly down to the business of generating a profit. Those decisions were to have profound consequences for the early settlers.

It's faintly painful to imagine how much of Hakluyt's expansive view of Virginia's possibilities got cut from the charter's final draft. Agriculture, fishing, lumbering, hunting, trapping, and the like were treated as sidelines, not meriting a mention. What was vital, in the end, was the quest for silver, copper, and gold, the chief focus of the Virginia Company investors' charge to the settlers.

At the same time, the charter contained no requirement either that the colonists build a coastal naval station from which to harry the Spanish main. Indeed, they would not be outfitted for such missions, and they were later instructed to build their colony far enough up a navigable river to offer protection from any Spanish coastal-raiding parties that might sally forth, placing them well out of position for privateering and raids.

IN THE LEE OF THE GOODWIN SANDS

It's nowhere on any manifest, but Hakluyt's vision was as much a part of the cargo as the salt pork, biscuits, and barrels of beer loaded aboard the three merchant ships that lay at anchor along the frigid Thames just downstream from central London on December 19, 1606, the last Friday night before Christmas. And it was certainly on the minds of the captains and crew of those wooden ships as they slipped out on the ebb tide, probably just past midnight, from the riverside steps near the taverns at Blackwall, bearing 144 men and boys bound for the very place Hakluyt had invested with such great hope.

If a marine architect were to design an early seventeenth-century fleet to ferry colonists to a distant, alien, and largely inhospitable new land, where they were expected to establish a permanent and self-sustaining outpost, it would not have looked much like the little flotilla of merchant vessels that drifted off into the darkness that night. It wouldn't be quite right to say the mission was funded on a shoestring, but it was no trophy operation either, particularly in light of the national aspirations it embodied. "The ships used for the early colonizing expeditions were not particularly suitable for the purpose," states the *Oxford History of the British Empire*, which goes on to describe them as "grossly overcrowded, even by contemporary standards, and unable to carry the victuals needed for a comfortable Atlantic crossing, let alone to sustain the colonists after their arrival."

The two-year-old flagship, the *Susan Constant*, was 116 feet long and just under 25 feet across at its widest point—not much longer than a college basketball court and half as wide. Seventy-one passengers and crew were crammed onto a craft with less than two thousand square feet of deck space—easily a third of which was taken up with masts, rigging, and other gear—and with about the same amount of room on the deck below, not counting the cargo and livestock hold. Its captain was a seasoned navigator and career pirate named Christopher Newport. He had gained fame but lost an arm stealing and sinking Spanish treasure ships, with the financial support of London investors and the tacit backing of the English crown, during more than a decade of criss-crossing the Atlantic and combing the Caribbean waters for profit and prey.

The second vessel, the *Godspeed,* was about half the size of the flagship. A small merchant craft that carried fifty-two men, its captain was Newport's lieutenant, Bartholomew Gosnold. Another able seaman and former privateer, Gosnold is credited with having discovered Cape Cod and Martha's Vineyard for the English four years earlier, without establishing any settlements there.

The smallest of the three was the *Discovery*. Just under fifty feet long— about a first down and a half on a football field—she carried twenty-one men. Her captain was John Ratcliffe, who had changed his name from Sicklemore in what some suspect was an effort to elevate his status. In keeping with the theory, Ratcliffe seems to have largely bought his way into the expedition with the purchase of four shares of stock in the Virginia Company. A share was valued at £12.5, nearly a year's wages for a laborer.

The travelers passed Christmas winding their way down the Thames, breaching its mouth sometime around New Year's Eve and sailing into angry North Sea waters. Rounding the Isle of Thanet, on the east coast of the county of Kent, they entered the swift and treacherous currents of the Strait of Dover and were beset by poor winds and rough seas. By January 5, after two weeks underway, the group had advanced less than a hundred miles. Winter gales forced them to drop anchor within site of shore, in waters known as the Downs, between the coastal town of Deal and the Goodwin Sands, a shifting bed of shoals that form a shipping graveyard perilous even today.

For some three weeks, they lay there, tiny vessels tossed by the waves, passengers and idle crew jammed together below decks, sleeping two or three to a berth and breathing air clotted with the earthy reminders of their seasick and unbathed shipmates and livestock—the locker room, to put it plainly, from hell. Those of lower station may well have drawn straws to determine who got to carry the communal chamber pot topside to chuck its contents over the side of the rolling, windswept deck without allowing any to slosh out on what would have been, for some, their only set of clothes.

To pass those gloomy hours, some longingly pondered the pebbled shoreline just off their bow, where sixteen centuries earlier Julius Caesar landed the invasion force that opened four hundred years of foreign occupation, bringing Roman governance, law, and Christianity to England. There was talk, no doubt, of the crucial battles in those very waters when, within living memory for most, their countrymen had prevailed against the Spanish Armada in a fight so desperate that farmers from the villages near Deal gathered plough chains to be hammered and melted into shot.

As they prayed by the hour for the weather to change, and as wasted days ground into weeks, conversation invariably lapsed. The jokes got old; tempers ran short; guys started to get on each other's nerves.

One passenger, in particular, seemed to be aggressively abrasive—a stocky, sawed-off stub of a man who seldom tired of highlighting for others his valiant past as a war fighter. He was an unconscionable braggart of modest means with a chip on his shoulder for the blue bloods among the group, a big mouth know-it-all with a sanctimonious air and little or no regard for decorum. His name was John Smith.

In his wide travels across the Mediterranean, Smith had learned what it was like to be thrown overboard. In short order, there were those aboard the *Susan Constant* who were ready to do just that.

The son of a tenant farmer, Smith fled a merchant's apprenticeship while still a teenager to follow his youthful dream of becoming a knight. He taught himself swordsmanship and various forms of hand-to-hand combat, training he augmented by reading English translations of Niccolò Machiavelli's *The Art of War* and the aptly entitled *Pirotechnia* by an Italian explosives pioneer named Vannoccio Biringuccio.

The home study soon came to be of use. Smith fought in wars in France and the Netherlands and widely across southeastern Europe to the edge of the Ottoman Empire, where he excelled in making devastating postmedieval cluster bombs out of pottery, gunpowder, and tar.

Hitching passage among traders along the Mediterranean, Smith was, in fact, tossed over the transom by Catholic travelers who regarded his queen as a heretic and Smith as disposable. He swam to safety on a nearby island, in what would be but one in a long series of narrow escapes.

While still in his early twenties, Smith plied his trade as an itinerant mercenary across the Balkans. While there, he decapitated three Turks in a series of tournaments on horseback, as chronicled by Smith in his modestly titled autobiography, *The True Travels, Adventures, and Observations of Captain John Smith, in Europe, Asia, Africa and America: beginning about the year 1593 and continued to this present 1629,* and detailed by his biographer, the late scholar and author Philip L. Barbour. Later, Smith was captured while fighting Crimean Tatars from present-day Ukraine, who took him to a Danube River market and sold him into slavery to an Ottoman captain.

Then, things got interesting.

The captain sent Smith four hundred miles away to Istanbul as a gift to a young girl named Charatza, who was apparently fascinated by this oddly exotic red-haired Englishman. Fearing her family would sell Smith if they learned of her interest in him, Charatza schemed to convert her young servant into a young Turk, perhaps even one suitable, some day, for marriage. She hatched a plan to farm him out to her brother, at a remote Black Sea military outpost, in the hope that, there, Smith would learn her language and ways to return a new man once she'd come of age.

Not one to tutor the infidel kindly, her brother instead stripped Smith bare, shaved his hair and beard, and had an iron ring riveted around his neck. "A dog could hardly have lived to endure" the treatment that followed, Smith later wrote, describing routine beatings and starvation rations.

While Smith was alone and tending a grain field one day, his master made the mistake of stopping by unescorted to dish out his customary abuse. Smith crushed his skull with a wooden threshing bat, stole his clothes, stuffed the naked corpse in a hay stack, and made off atop the dead Turk's horse, roaming the countryside for days until he stumbled upon a Silk Road byway.

He followed the ancient trade route to modern-day Poland and, eventually, made his way back to England, where he readied himself for his next grand adventure, now stalled in the churning lee of the Goodwin Sands.

Smith was not, in short, a man much given to self-doubt. Weeks shy of his twenty-seventh birthday, nearing middle age for the times, he was ready to put the lessons of hard experience to good use, and he had little regard for authority he considered inept or unearned. That went double, it seems, for those who lived off inherited status or married into wealth, descriptions that fit roughly a third of the passengers aboard the three ships.

In addition to a crew of about forty men all told, there were about one hundred men and a handful of boys headed for the new colony. Each had his own reasons for going, but the common thread was the hope that each would vastly improve his life, either by starting afresh in the New World or by helping to build an English foothold in America and returning to the mother country to enjoy elevated status and wealth back home.

More mixed litter than finely tuned team, the colonists were an unlikely collection of commoners and elites, assorted volunteers and recruits that would have never spent time together as a group in socially stratified England. They would, however, have had in common some link to the investors or royal appointees of the Virginia Company, either directly or through referrals. Gosnold, for instance, knew Hakluyt. Gosnold also knew Smith. And Smith apparently knew Hakluyt, possibly through Gosnold. It's not hard to imagine those two men endorsing Smith as the kind of battle-hardened self-starter that might be good to have along on the New World adventure. Smith was just a child when Hakluyt wrote his treatise to the queen. Yet, in describing the kind of settler needed to colonize Virginia Britannia, Hakluyt seems to have had in mind men strikingly like Smith when he called for "soldiers well trained in Flanders [the Netherlands] . . . men expert in the art of fortification . . . [and] captains of long and great experience."

About thirty-five of the colonists were regarded as "gentlemen," a label that implied status and wealth, usually inherited and attached to ownership of land. It also meant they were not the sort to be accustomed to manual labor or, for that matter, at ease around those who performed it.

At least a dozen men were listed as laborers, and another dozen were craftsmen skilled in carpentry, masonry, or bricklaying. There was a blacksmith, James Read, and a tailor, William Love. There were five or six boys and a preacher, Rev. Robert Hunt, a Hakluyt protégé.

In his writings, Smith expressed deep admiration for Hunt, portraying him as a faithful man of prayer who bore hardship without complaint. Smith even credited Hunt with coming to his aid in disputes—of which there were apparently many—that Smith, the commoner and soldier, had with several men of higher social rank.

A ship the size of the *Susan Constant* wasn't a place where people at cross-purposes could easily keep their distance, and Smith seems to have repeatedly run afoul of a member of the nobility named Edward Maria

Wingfield. The wealthy son of a former member of the British parliament, Wingfield was a Virginia Company shareholder who felt his voice should hold great sway in all matters. After some time hung up in the storms, Wingfield favored turning back to London. He was stunned to find the likes of Smith, the commoner, arguing against him. In Smith's account, debate became so acrimonious that Hunt's intervention was required to contain it.

Even before they left sight of England, the group had begun to square off, roughly split between those who favored merit-based leadership and those who believed some were destined by birthright to lead, ill-defined battle lines that would foreshadow even deeper divisions to come.

Adding to the sense of intrigue around the bilge pump, the Virginia Company had chosen the men who would make up the colonial council but put the list in a sealed box with orders that it not be opened until the travelers reached Virginia. Investors didn't want potential settlers deserting because they weren't picked to lead or had some personal beef with those who were. Whatever good it did, the tactic bred suspicion and rivalry among the colonists, at least half of whom had reason to believe they might well be destined to govern the rest.

It was the end of January before the weather finally turned. Already more than five weeks at sea, the weary adventurers only then began their journey in earnest, weighing anchor and setting off on a southeasterly course, running down the Atlantic seaboard of France and Spain. Favorable winds carried them twenty-one hundred miles in the next three weeks, before they landed for food, water, and several days of much-needed rest in the Canary Islands off the African coast.

Exactly what happened next isn't clear, but shortly after they left the Canaries in late February, patience with Smith ran out. He was accused of mutiny, apparently stemming from alleged insubordination, general irritation, or some combination of the two. Newport had him thrown in the brig, or whatever makeshift warren of restraint there was to be had. There, Smith remained for the duration of the fateful voyage, the former slave who murdered his master fervently grinding his figurative axe while he rolled with the swells and bided his time.

The specifics of the dispute aren't recorded. In later writings, though, Smith makes clear his contempt for those in charge of the voyage, blaming "our ignorant transporters" for lingering more than four months at sea on a journey that Smith asserts should have taken only two. As a result, Smith charged, the travelers ate food they'd hoped would get them through their first precarious months in the New World, even as they missed the chance to plant crops in early spring, a failing that was to have lethal consequences for dozens.

Historians speculate that Wingfield was the one who got fed up with Smith's second-guessing, pulled rank, and demanded that the impertinent commoner be put away. Years later, in his memoir, Smith would charge only that men of higher status and lesser mien had grown jealous of his judgment and contemptuous of his cocksure ways. Whatever the truth, Smith's detractors used his incarceration to buttress their case against him, interrogating his mates while the ships sped along the cusp of the westerly trade winds across the open Atlantic.

FRESH WATERS AND GOODLY TALL TREES

One month and thirty-one hundred miles later, they made landfall on the Caribbean island of Martinique. They lingered in the tropical waters for nearly three weeks of island hopping, taking on fresh provisions and planning an execution: Smith's. While muzzled in the brig, he had been tried by grumblings and convicted in absentia on evidence heavily weighted by the determined opposition of Wingfield, a disgruntled nobleman with corporate clout on his side.

During several days on the island of Nevis, carpenters went so far as to erect gallows—whether for Smith's actual hanging or as some final warning is not clear. By this point, though, some had wearied of Wingfield's vendetta and felt the persecution of Smith had gone too far. His life was spared, though Smith remained under restraint, as he would for several weeks to come.

Before his rigid discipline and able command would save the fledgling colony in Virginia from early demise, in other words, Smith became the first recorded inmate in English America—he was a self-made man of conviction jailed on his journey to the New World, in large part over frictions stemming from the Old World class divide; an impolitic outlaw, hated and spurned by the corporate elite, with decidedly more grit than tact; a don't-tread-on-me misfit, the original template for the archetypical American rebel.

Had Smith not slipped the noose in Nevis, probably with the aid of Gosnold and Hunt, the Virginia experiment would almost certainly have failed. What course events might have taken from there, historians can only guess.

None of this was clear as the three tiny ships set sail from the Caribbean on April 10, keeping the American coastline and its hazardous shoals many miles off their portside bow. Nearly three weeks later, after wandering the unpredictable crosscurrents off Cape Hatteras, the party lost its bearings. By the mariners' own reckoning, they'd overshot their projected landfall by three days. Some among the group, including the *Discovery*'s Captain Ratcliffe, were ready to chuck the expedition and head back to England without ever setting foot in North America, and they became all the more so when a tempest blew up and forced them to furl sail and drop anchor on the night of April 25.

The skies cleared after midnight and, in the milky first light of dawn, sailors spotted the low-lying coast of Virginia within sight of where they had ridden out the storm. Four months after leaving London, the colonists had arrived, miraculously having suffered but one recorded loss, the death of one man from apparent heatstroke in the Caribbean. Newport led the ships into the mouth of the Chesapeake Bay, where they anchored near a broad cape the colonists named for King James's eldest son, Henry.

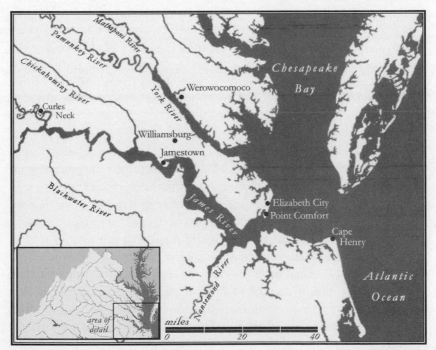

Landing at Cape Henry, the settlers of the first permanent English settlement in America soon journeyed up the James River, site of the first sustained contact between the British and Native Americans in what would become the United States. Map drawn by Rebecca Wrenn.

"There we landed," wrote George Percy. A noble with a long pedigree, he was one of about two dozen men Newport led ashore to explore a place Percy described as having "fair meadows and goodly tall trees, with such fresh waters running through the woods as I was almost ravished at the first sight thereof."

As the sun sank on the colonists' first day ashore, a handful of Native Americans armed with bows and arrows crept down the sand dunes in the shadow of dusk. They opened fire on the trespassers, wounding two, a harrowing, but tragically fitting, beginning to the difficult English-American relations ahead. Newport shot back with his pistol, and the natives melted into the darkness, perhaps unnerved by the blast or, more likely, out of arrows.

Back aboard ship, his heart still pounding from this initial contact with the locals, Newport ordered that the box containing the Virginia Company's directions and leadership roster be opened. The names of seven men were read out to make up the colonial council that would lead the rest.

Named were Newport, Gosnold, and Ratcliffe, already the first, second, and third in command. Wingfield, the high-minded nobleman, was on the list. So were John Martin, a sea captain who had picked up some of the colonists who had abandoned Roanoke Island two decades before, and George Kendall, who had been dispatched as the eyes and ears of Robert Cecil, secretary of state to King James and one of the largest investors in the Virginia Company, holding twenty-five shares of its stock.

There were undoubtedly snide smiles, oaths of despair, and gasps of general disbelief with the reading of the seventh and final council member's name: John Smith, the very rascal who sat, even then, imprisoned by his shipmates and perhaps even out of earshot of the announcement of his topside induction into the ruling class. In an early usurpation of power, the council refused to seat Smith, preferring to keep him confined.

The Virginia Company had provided additional instructions for the explorers, ordering them to set up their colony "in a fertile and wholesome place" at least a hundred miles upstream on a major river, "the farther up the better," lest they be exposed to attack by seafaring Spanish or French.

Should they happen upon more than one suitable river, the colonists were instructed to choose "that which bendeth most towards the northwest, for that way shall you soonest find the other sea," meaning the Pacific Ocean. Should the river flow from a large lake, the advice continued, it could well lead quickest to China, perhaps even India.

Before breaking ground, the colonists were to explore the river to the inland limits of its reach, or at least as far as it might be navigable by the tiny fleet. Once ensconced, the colonists were to be divided into three groups: one to build a fortified village, a second to plant crops and provide security, and a third to travel with Newport and Gosnold in search of silver and gold, "carrying half a dozen pickaxes" for exploratory mining.

There were general guidelines as well, including an explicit appeal for diplomacy and trade with the Native Americans. "In all your passages, you must have great care not to offend the naturals, if you can eschew it," the company instructed. The Indians, in fact, were a key to the survival of the colonists, who expected the native Virginians to provide them with food in exchange for copper and beads. "Trade with them for corn," the instructions continued, "to avoid the danger of famine."

There were other helpful tips as well. Hire locals as guides, but "take a compass" along when exploring new ground, just in case the natives decide to bolt. Don't let the Indians carry your weapons; they might run off with them and return later to kill you. Let only "your best marksmen" fire guns in front of the Indians, lest they figure out how hard it is to get the weapons to shoot straight.

The orders ended where the mission began—with an appeal to the colonists "to serve and fear God" in all they might do. "For every plantation which our Heavenly Father hath not planted shall be rooted out."

Thus admonished and so inspired, the party spent the next two days reconnoitering the wide mouth of the Chesapeake Bay, keeping one eye out for Spanish warships over the Atlantic horizon and the other peeled for native attacks from the brackish rivers, creeks, and coves. Convinced they'd found the New World gateway they'd been seeking, they returned to Cape Henry on April 29 to assert formal title to the land.

There, in what seems to have been a brief ceremony led by Newport and Hunt, the colonists erected a cross in the sand. There would have been prayers of thanksgiving from men eternally grateful to have been guided across the wide ocean, safeguarded from peril and delivered to a land of opportunity and hope. There were doubtless fervent appeals for holy intercession as they pondered their charge to convert the indigenous "idolaters" suddenly in their midst.

The planting of the Cape Henry cross, though, was much more than a seaside prayer service. In resurrecting the symbol of the crucifixion of Christ, they were staking their New World claim, formally seizing Virginia for England and its monarch, the high defender of the faith. Affirming

London's new place in the world, defying Rome and ignoring altogether the most powerful chief in Virginia, they put down their tracks in the sand. There would be, for the English, no turning back.

Over the next several days, Captain Newport led the tiny flotilla into the final leg of its voyage, up the broad and northwesterly winding waters the explorers had named for their king, the sure route to riches and the short cut to the Pacific that they called the James River.

4

VIRGINIA

JAMESTOWN—A long-elusive and seductive dream on the far side of the world, Virginia lay stretched out before them at last, its seemingly endless promise mirrored in the glassy face of fragrant waters.

Their arduous sea trial behind them, the English settlers sailed upstream on the balmy breath of spring, their faith rewarded with an answer to prayer: a vast riverside realm where they might build anew between verdant shores and towering clouds, so near to heaven and so far from home.

"The river which we have found is one of the famousest rivers that ever was found by any Christian," George Percy wrote in his diary, describing its deep and winding channel, broad tidal reaches, and natural harbors where oceangoing ships could tie right up to the trees looming over the muddy edge of its flow. "Wheresoever we landed upon this river we saw the goodliest woods as beech, oak, cedar, cypress, walnuts, sassafras and vines in great abundance," Percy gushed. "There are many branches of this river, which run flowing through the woods with great plenty of fish of all kinds."

Virginia in late April seemed a wonderland, a place where delicate dogwood blossoms and bright red cardinals lit the dense and primal forest like fairies flitting through the midday gloom, while raucous schools of silver-backed shad splashed and spawned in the sunlit shallows.

Ushering these wind-burned travelers into its fulsome bounty, the river bore their wooden ships weightless through an almost imaginary world where oysters as long as a man's foot lay scattered as thick as stones in the mud banks, there for the taking twice a day at low tide.

There were catfish the size of piglets, frogs as large as kittens, giant sturgeon with firm flesh and roe, and herring running so thick they could be netted until shoulders grew weary with the weight of them.

Bearded turkeys wandered wooded thickets in bevies of forty or more, their nests coddling large, fresh eggs to which the colonists helped themselves. Beavers by the thousands swam the river and its tributaries, building lodges and dams that created rice-studded marshes and woodland ponds, clear water havens for ducks, herons, geese, and cranes.

Where aged wetlands had filled into meadows, there were strawberries, wild grapes, and persimmons. Rabbits, deer, and squirrels roamed the forests and fields beneath skies that could be darkened for hours by impenetrable flocks of pigeons in Hitchcockian riots of flight.

"Heaven and earth never agreed better to frame a place for man's habitation," John Smith wrote, "were it fully manured and inhabited by industrious people," the English improving on paradise, as it were, by adding cow dung, pig droppings, and a little elbow grease. "Here are mountains, hills, plains, valleys, rivers and brooks, all running most pleasantly into a fair bay, compassed, but for the mouth, with fruitful and lightsome land."

DEVILISH GESTURES

Following the orders of their Virginia Company masters back in London, the travelers spent the next two weeks exploring upriver from Cape Henry, expectantly peering around each bend for signs that they were nearing the Pacific coast. Mindful of their charge "not to offend the naturals," they made stops along the way to introduce themselves to the first Virginians, taking note of their alien ways. "They hang through their ears fowls legs; they shave the right side of their heads with a shell, the left side they wear of an ell [a yard] long tied up with an artificial knot, with a many of fowls feathers sticking in it," Percy wrote in his diary. "They go altogether naked, but their privates are covered with beasts skins beset commonly with little bones or beasts teeth."

He wrote of a village chief donning a crown of deer skin, dyed red and adorned with two long feathers "like a pair of horns," and wearing copper-trimmed bird's claws in his ears. He described people who set out dried tobacco before they prayed to the sun, "making many devilish gestures with a hellish noise, foaming at the mouth, staring with their eyes, wagging their heads and hands in such a fashion and deformity as it was monstrous to behold." Upon arrival at one village, wrote Percy, they were met by Indians who "made a doleful noise, laying their faces to the ground, scratching the earth with their nails. We did think they had been at their idolatry."

First impressions Percy's writings may well be. He took them in, how-ever, through a lens ground by centuries of European history, religion, and culture that had nothing to do with the Native Americans' world—until, that is, the English arrived.

As they lay claim to land others had lived on for more than fifteen thousand years, the colonists viewed the indigenous people much as they were described by the English philosopher of the day, Thomas Hobbes, who wrote that "the savage people in many places of America" led uncivil and ungoverned lives that were, for the most part, "solitary, poor, nasty, brutish and short."

The settlers had arrived in Virginia from London at a time when Eng-lish language, culture, and religion had coalesced as a unifying force and were being bound for the ages in the written works of Shakespeare and the King James Bible, which was, at that very moment, being compiled by a royal committee of some fifty vicars and scholars.

In the minds of Percy and his fellow Englishmen, the lack of a writ-ten language placed the native Virginians somewhere beyond the outer lim-its of civilization. "Not only were they not like the English, they were not like the people of the Old World, who, for all their differences, were united from here [England] to China by this one thread: they all wrote and read," the British author Adam Nicolson wrote in *God's Secretaries*, an incisive look at how English social, political, and religious attitudes converged in the cre-ation of the King James Bible at the dawn of the seventeenth century.

And here were those very people, Percy's own voice makes clear, illit-erate and devilish monsters in skins of wild beasts and horns. They wailed, gyrated, and even foamed at the mouth, which is exactly how the Virginia Company had described the "infidels and savages" in this strange new land. What a blessing for these hapless natives, the settlers must have thought, that the company had sent noble Christians to lead them from the "darkness and miserable ignorance" of their brutish ways and into the "humane civility" and "quiet government" the English were so ready to share.

The native Virginians, moreover, had their own way of looking at these strange English newcomers, whether as wandering busybodies or threatening invaders, no one could quite be sure.

The colonists weren't the first Europeans to have passed this way. Span-ish had sailed into the Chesapeake Bay and up the James River for some distance nearly a century before, setting up a temporary camp in 1525 and another some fifty years later. Both settlements had been abandoned by the Spanish—where, for one thing, was the gold?—but their explorations alone brought deaths for both sides.

The people of *Tsenacomoco* knew of the English venture that had failed to the south, the so-called Lost Colony of Roanoke Island. And they would have heard stories that worked their way up the Atlantic seaboard of the Spanish conquests in Florida and the Caribbean, grim tales told around the campfire of enslavement of native people, bloody suppression, war, and disease.

Surely this, though, wasn't an invasion force, the Indians might well have thought, gazing upon the lightly armed and pasty-faced Englishmen, a third of whom arrived projecting nothing more hostile than a long pedigree, a superiority complex, and an overall bad attitude. Whoever this new crowd of trespassers might be, whatever their intent, they were strangers, *tassantassas* to the Indians, odd sorts with no discernible spiritual foundation, only curious superstitions and beliefs.

They bowed to a cross of silver or wood, somehow vesting great faith in it. There were several large ones on their big ships. The relied on the winds for power and drifted off in whatever direction the breeze seemed to blow, leaving their home most likely because their own country was so poor and arriving here in *Tsenacomoco* more or less by accident. If their own place was better, why had they come here?

They spoke no recognizable language, nothing remotely resembling Algonquin, Iroquois, or Souian, but prattled on in ornately inflected gibberish, then grinned like madmen. They wore clothing so ungainly they could hardly move in it, seldom if ever bathed, and smelled worse than wild animals. And where were their women and children? Had they come all this way to take the natives'?

The strangers at least had the good manners to offer precious beads and copper trinkets to their hosts. And they quickly learned to greet the native people with their favored salutation, *wingapo*, meaning something like "hello there, my good man." Still, their unexpected arrival triggered rigorous debate among tribal shamans and elders up and down the river as to whether the trespassers should be befriended or killed.

Hoping for the best, some tribes greeted the strangers with feasts of venison, turkey, and hot corn bread and a fraternal smoking of the pipe. Others regarded them with suspicion and dread. Some shadowed their flotilla in dugout canoes that seemed to appear out of nowhere, only to vanish into the blackness of outlying swamps and streams.

The colonists surveyed the river about sixty miles inland to a tributary they named for the Appamattuck Indians living there, roughly twenty miles downstream from the falls. They then drifted back with the current some twenty miles, eyeing the shoreline for an attractive parcel not too close to any Indian villages.

On May 14, 1607, they offloaded onto a low-lying neck of vacant land between the north bank of the river and a narrow, winding creek. They named the spot for their king, calling it James Fort and, later, Jamestown. With Smith still under some form of restraint, the rest of the council elected Edward Wingfield its president for a one-year term.

TRESPASSERS IN PARADISE

A week later, as the Virginia Company had ordered, Christopher Newport ventured off with Smith and twenty-two others in a wooden boat, called a shallop, which the group had brought along from England. They headed upstream in search of the river's headwaters, the shortcut to China, and whatever gold they might dig up with their pickaxes along the way, leaving the rest of the colonists behind to feather their new nest.

In locating their settlement, the colonists had largely followed orders, nestling into the elbow of a broad bend in the river opposite an island from which they could post sentries with a view far downstream, providing advance warning of any Spanish raiders who might venture their way. Shortly after unpacking their gear, Percy and a few others strolled out along a path through the forest, affirming that they had chosen well in landing at a place of "ground all flowing over with fair flowers of sundry colors and kinds as though it had been in any garden or orchard in England. . . . There be many strawberries, and other fruits unknown," wrote Percy. "We saw the woods full of cedar and cypress trees, with other trees, which issues out sweet gums like to balsam. We kept on our way in this paradise."

As they were later to discover to their woe, however, the natives considered the plot a wasteland for good reason. The creek bled into a marshy mosquito nursery, not the best neighborhood for hot nights spent sleeping in the tattered tents Smith described. They had no way of knowing it, but the English had arrived amid the worst drought to hit the region in nearly eight centuries, a dearth of rain that was to continue for several more years, during which time there was little fresh water to replenish the shallow wells they dug in the sandy clay. And the sweetly scented forests, tall grass, and scrub brush surrounding their lowlands hamlet would provide ideal cover for an attacking foe.

There were no such strikes for the first week or so, though in that time the settlers entertained large groups of Indians on two seemingly friendly visits that quickly turned tense. Smaller groups stopped by every couple of days, sometimes offering the colonists venison or corn.

The peace offerings, it turned out, were intelligence-gathering missions in disguise. The scouts reported back to their tribes on the vast store of supplies the English had brought with them and the clearing and building they had undertaken, clear signs the invaders intended to stay. Word that their great chief, Newport, and the others were out of pocket upstream apparently tipped the area councils in favor of attacking the uninvited guests, either to wipe them out or simply to demonstrate the superiority of Indian forces, in the hope that the English would pack up and leave.

On May 26, while lightly armed colonists tilled their fields and worked at constructing a timber fence, a war party of some two hundred Indians assaulted Jamestown with hatchets, clubs, and bows and arrows, catching the *tassantassas* off guard. With most of their weapons still packed in crates, the colonists fired back with what few guns they had. In peril of being overrun by warriors who outnumbered them two to one, the English were saved from possible slaughter only by firing cannons from their ships, raining lead down upon the Indians in a thunderous fusillade that severed tree limbs and put the native attackers to flight. Two colonists were killed, a dozen others were wounded, and several Indians died in the fight.

Newport and the others returned the next day and, in the wake of the melee, joined the rest of the colonists in redoubling their fortification efforts. By mid-June they had built a triangular-shaped fort enclosing an area roughly the size of a football field within a fence of wooden palisades about twelve feet high. That, for the next several years, was the extent of the British reach into the New World. That was England in America.

As the settlers pondered their precarious security position, Newport, Smith, and the others shared with their fellow colonists important and disturbing news. While on their journey upriver, they'd visited an Indian village high on a bluff just downstream from the falls. The name of the village was Powhatan, they'd learned, and it was the home of a mighty chief who ruled over all the river tribes below the falls. Above the falls, they'd been told, lived the regional foe, the Monacan Indians, who ranged as far west as *Quirank*, the Blue Ridge Mountains, beyond which, six or seven days by foot, lay a great body of salt water.

In truth, Powhatan village was the hometown of the big man. It was a dangerous place, though, so near to the fall line frontier, where skirmishes with Monacan warriors came as regularly each autumn as the fall of the leaf. Powhatan had moved from there long ago to an ancient and more readily defensible Indian site some twelve miles northeast of Jamestown, just downstream from where the Pamunkey and Mattaponi rivers flow together to form what is now known as the York River.

Unable to speak the Algonquin language or make themselves clearly understood in their own, Newport and Smith thought they'd met Powhatan on their journey upstream, when they were introduced to the local *werowance*. His name was actually Parahunt, and he was one of Powhatan's sons.

Mistaken identity, though, was only part of the problem. The colonists now had to wonder whether they'd come under attack by some local renegade or by the collective forces of a well-organized foe on the orders of their powerful chief, the very man they still believed had hosted them upriver just days before. As the colonists didn't know which chief ordered the attack, neither do historians today. The size of the assault force suggests coordination among several villages; most would individually support somewhere between thirty and fifty warriors. Local *werowances* would have had ample authority to conduct the raid on their own, though it's unlikely they would have done so without at least notifying Powhatan.

It's also not clear whether the Indians meant to destroy the settlers or merely to demonstrate native capability as a way to remind them whose land they were on and to assert territorial bounds. Had the big chief really wanted to wipe out the colonists, he could have mounted a war party many times larger than the one that first struck the encampment at Jamestown. He could have attacked, moreover, at night, and he had the capacity to send hundreds by land and an equal number by canoe on a stealth mission that could have easily overwhelmed the poorly protected colonists. It seems most likely that the attack took place without Powhatan's objections, but without his blessing or active involvement. The wily leader of *Tsenacomoco* seems to have calculated that the English were a nuisance he could afford to let the local *werowances* manage, at least for the time being.

This strategic ambiguity left the colonists to wonder how they were going to cooperate and trade with people who might feast them one day and attack them the next. With that vexing existential dilemma before them, the council released Smith from what had become by then largely symbolic restraint and seated him on the governing body.

Newport, as instructed by the Virginia Company, left Jamestown on June 22. He took the *Susan Constant* and the *Godspeed* and crew back to London with him, promising to return before winter with fresh colonists and supplies. He left behind about one hundred men, a third of whom had scarcely worked a day's labor in their lives, under Wingfield's uncertain command, in hostile territory, their pantry nearly bare. By the time he returned, two-thirds of them would be dead.

In the following weeks, the native Virginians learned that they could creep in twos and threes undetected to within bow range of the fort, let fly with arrows, then steal off largely unmolested back into the forest. Colonists ventured beyond the palisades of the fort at their own risk, with one being wounded or killed every several days while tending crops or gathering wood.

Local tribes alternated, though, between sniping at the trespassers and trading with them. Now and then, a party would appear bearing gifts—a deer, perhaps, or beaver meat, which the Indians considered a great delicacy and the English quickly learned to like—along with an invitation to make a truce as a prelude to commerce.

It was, at best, a "doubtful peace that we had with the Indians, which they would keep no longer than opportunity served to do us mischief," wrote Wingfield. "We had sometime peace and war twice in a day," echoed Smith, "the savages, being our enemies, whom we neither know nor understand."

Much as the English struggled to grasp the ways of the native people, so, too, did they grope with the unfamiliar challenges of the land they'd chanced upon.

None had ever experienced July in Tidewater Virginia, and they were poorly prepared for its trials. They soon learned what it was like to work in heavy clothing and armor of leather and cast iron beneath a blazing sun that sent temperatures soaring to nearly one hundred degrees in the humid lowlands. On steamy and breezeless nights, they lay sweltering and swatting at mosquitoes, wondering at each distant sound in the darkness when the next raiding party might strike, and praying for Newport's swift return.

The river, meanwhile, was suffering as well. With freshwater flows diminished by summer's heat and drought, the river wasn't being fully flushed. Rising volumes of brackish water pressed upstream. Salinity levels built up, as did impurities and waste, turning the river into a salty and disease-ridden soup. Once the shallow wells they dug went dry in the heat, "Our drink and cold water [were] taken out of the river," wrote Percy, "which was at a flood [tide] very salt and at low tide full of slime and filth, which was the destruction of many of our men." The poor water quality that meant salt poisoning and dysentery for the settlers was also affecting the once-plentiful fish, which sought refuge in the cooler depths of the river channel and out of reach of the colonists' nets.

Smith made several trading forays along the James River and up the Chickahominy, swapping copper and beads for such corn as the Indians were willing to spare. But the native Virginians, like the colonists, were finding food scarcer than normal because of the drought and were struggling to work out ways to cope. Selling off large stores of what food they had to the trespassers wasn't really part of the plan.

By mid-summer, the English were grinding through hard times. Their crops, such as they were, wilted in the heat-cracked earth, tended only in fits and starts by colonists who risked being maimed or killed by arrows whenever they set foot beyond the thin wooden palisade protecting their camp of tattered tents.

The colonists' store of wine and ale, which at least had the benefit of being free of disease, was gone. With food running low, Wingfield cut each man's daily ration to a pint of porridge made of barley or wheat, boiled in the same fetid waters they used for drinking. Much of the grain, moreover, had gone bad or become infested with worms and vermin through long months spent in the holds of their ships. "Our drink was water, our lodgings castles in the air," Smith wrote, capturing the mood of disappointment and despair.

BLOOD FOR CORN

It was amid this misery that the English began to confront, for the first time, but not the last, one of the chief threats that stalked New World explorers everywhere: famine. The Jamestown settlers were plenty familiar with grisly tales of Spanish and Portuguese colonists far to the south who had been driven by hunger to dire extremes: mutinies, eating snakes and rats, butchering their own horses for meat, even cutting the corpses of executed criminals from the gallows to consume their convicted flesh. Now the English colonists were beginning to feel the dark shadow of starvation closing in.

By August, they began to die in steady numbers: John Asbie, on the sixth, of dysentery; George Flowre, on the ninth, of heat stroke; the next day, William Bruster, shot by Indians; four days later, three more men gone. Seven others died over the course of the next week, including the able mariner Bartholomew Gosnold, who died after weeks of sickness of some sort; dysentery seems likely, although it's believed there were also may have been typhoid fever victims in the group. "Our men were destroyed with cruel diseases," wrote Percy, who chronicled the deaths in his diary. "But, for the most part, they died of mere famine."

Four months after relishing "this paradise," Percy had adopted an altogether different view of the New World, where nearly half of the settlers had perished. "There were never Englishmen left in a foreign country in such misery," he wrote, "as we were in this new discovered Virginia."

With September came welcomed rains and modest relief from the worst of the heat, though the colonists continued to perish at the rate of several each week. The English dragged their dead into the woods to be buried at night in hopes that the Indians wouldn't notice their quickly dwindling numbers and rightly calculate that the invaders had become too weak to defend themselves.

Having survived, if just barely, the summer's dismal toll, Smith and his fellow council members exercised their power to depose Wingfield on grounds of general ineptitude and charges that he had hoarded the colony's dwindling stores. He was jailed aboard the *Discovery,* becoming, in a sense, the first president to be impeached in English America.

He was replaced by the next in line for command, John Ratcliffe, a man Smith described as a "little beloved" leader "of weak judgment in dangers and less industry in peace." Though no more capable than Wingfield, the council's new president had the good luck to take up his new post in the fall. As autumn neared, there was more food to be had, though some villages would only part with their harvests at gunpoint, forced by the English to trade game and grain for copper, hatchets, and beads.

In the fall of 1607, Smith led a party of six or seven others to trade with the Kecoughtan tribe at their village near the mouth of the James. The Indians were cordial enough but offered only "a handful of corn" in exchange for Smith's offer of swords. Smith interpreted the offer, perhaps accurately, as a gesture of scorn meant to demonstrate how little the Kecoughtan thought of the settlers. In the Kecoughtan world, people who couldn't be troubled to feed themselves could, literally, drop dead.

The drought meant the Kecoughtan themselves were dealing with slim pickings. That was of no apparent concern to Smith, who ordered his men to rake the village with shot as the Kecoughtan fled. Some time later, the residents returned with a war party of about five dozen men, armed with clubs and arrows and led by a priest bearing an Okee effigy, "an idol," Smith wrote, "made of skins, stuffed with moss, all painted and hung with chains and copper."

The English fired on them, killing or wounding perhaps a dozen Indians until, once again, the Kecoughtan fell back into the forest. The Indians returned once more with a prayer for peace, along with whatever deer, turkey, ducks, and bread they could muster to spare their village and save their lives. In exchange they received such trinkets and wares as Smith deigned to bestow upon the terrified natives.

Word of Smith's style of gunboat diplomacy apparently traveled quickly upstream. In the weeks that followed, he built a reputation for bringing home the groceries at the Indians' expense. The barrel of a gun, he found, was a useful inducement to trade on his terms. By late November, the surviving colonists were gorging themselves on a bounty, some of which they harvested from the land, but much of it had been squeezed from the Indians by Smith and Company. "The rivers became so covered with swans, geese, ducks and cranes that we daily feasted with good bread, Virginia peas, pumpkins and persimmons, fish, fowl and diverse sorts of wild beasts," wrote Smith.

Still, by then, some of the colonists had had it with Virginia and were ready to abandon the enterprise and go back to England. Returning from a hunting, foraging, and trading expedition that autumn, Smith discovered the deposed Wingfield in the process of hijacking the *Discovery* with the help of several others. Among them was George Kendall, who had been removed from his council post the previous summer for what Percy recorded as "heinous matters" and Wingfield described as attempts "to sow discord" among the council members.

Smith ordered his men to open cannon and musket fire on the pinnance, ensuring the deserters that he would sooner sink the ship to the bottom of the James than see them sail off in it. Kendall, who was also accused of spying for the Spanish, was, within a fortnight, executed by firing squad near the riverside, becoming the first man on record in English America to get the death penalty for crimes against the state, such as it was.

A NEEDLE IN THE GLASS

The autumn cornucopia may have filled empty stomachs, but winter was coming, Newport had yet to return, and the colonists had not found either the gold they'd been ordered to mine for the Virginia Company investors or the shortcut to China they'd been instructed to seek. Ratcliffe and his peers parried any recriminations by blaming these shortfalls on Smith. They had put him in charge, after all, of explorations and Indian relations, which revolved mainly around securing food.

Hoping to stem the complaints and discover at last the source of new riches, Smith set out with nine others aboard the shallop on December 10 to seek out the headwaters of the Chickahominy River, a winding stream that wells up not in the far western mountains of Virginia but in the swampy lowlands that drain the broad and sandy plateau unfolding just north and east of the falls of the James. He had no way of knowing he'd launched an extraordinary journey that was to open one of the most compelling chapters in the American narrative.

Traveling up the Chickahominy, Smith passed through a series of familiar Indian villages, where he saw neatly tilled fields lying fallow in the frostbitten loam. With visions of the great salty waters playing in his mind, Smith pressed so deeply into the cypress-studded Chickahominy that finally the water became too shallow and narrow for passage.

With some of his comrades grumbling about the value of the extended tour, Smith took the barge back down river toward an Indian town, where he hired a pair of natives to ferry him and two of his fellow Englishmen—Jehu Robinson and Thomas Emry—deeper into the swamp by canoe. It seemed a good time to explore the Chickahominy, the happy absence of mosquitoes and water moccasins being enough trade-off for the biting cold.

The next day, Smith left the rest of his party—seven men—behind aboard the larger boat with orders not to go ashore. They disobeyed and went anyway, enticed by a bevy of flirtatious Chickahominy debutantes sent to lure them from their boat. Once on land, though, it was well-armed warriors, not women, who chased the Englishmen.

Running for their lives, they scrambled to the barge, looking back to find that one of their group—George Cassen, who had come to Jamestown as a laborer—had been left behind to a grisly fate, which the English learned of later from the Indians themselves.

The Chickahominy tied Cassen naked to a tree before a fire, cut off his fingers and toes one by one with mussel shells and sharp reeds, then tossed the bloody digits into the flames. They scraped the flesh from his head and face, burning it as well, split open his stomach, spilled his entrails into the fire, then burned what was left of their macabre woodlands altar, leaving body and tree to smolder as one.

Smith, oblivious to Cassen's fate, left Robinson and Emry behind with the canoe and one of the Indian guides by a fire they'd built at the edge of a muddy bog. Smith had scarcely left when he heard, through the still waters and barren trees, the whoops and hollers of a band of Indians, who jumped the men Smith left near his canoe and killed them.

Heading back to investigate, Smith was ambushed by a group he estimated at two hundred well-armed men, possibly a communal deer-hunting party diverted toward two-legged prey. Smith shot two Indians dead with his pistol and took an arrow in one thigh. As the Indians closed in, he stripped off a garter and used it to tie his native guide to his arm as a human shield. Fending off his attackers, he tried to escape.

Still tethered to his guide, Smith slipped into an icy quagmire and couldn't get out. Surrounded and sinking deeper, his legs going numb with the cold, Smith tossed aside his arms and surrendered, a captive once more, this time of Pamunkey Indians led by Powhatan's half-brother, Opechancanough. The Indians showed Smith his dead comrades, Robinson and Emry, but seemed to be under orders to treat Smith differently, holding him until Opechancanough arrived.

Minding the Virginia Company's instructions—or, more likely, simply being a good soldier—Smith had brought along his compass, which suddenly pointed to a novel way out of his predicament. Reverently taking out the round and jewellike instrument, its case carved from whale bone or an elephant's tusk, Smith ceremoniously presented the compass to Opechancanough, who regarded it as a wondrous treasure and appropriate tribute to his status as the high magistrate of upper *Tsenacomoco*.

The Indians had no reason ever to have seen glass before. They doubtless sensed a miracle in what Smith called "the playing of the fly and needle." As they pondered among themselves how the compass needle could spin inside what appeared to them to be a crystalline stone, Smith treated the group to an impromptu creek-side seminar.

Smith apparently had a good ear for language and had picked up a smattering of the local tongue on his trade outings. Still, it's hard to imagine that his captors understood much of what followed, when, by his own account, Smith held forth on "the roundness of the earth, and skies, the sphere of the sun, moon and stars and how the sun did chase the night round about the world continually, the greatness of the land and sea, the diversity of nations, variety of complexions," and anything else he could think of that might hold their interest while tempers cooled.

By Smith's telling, his audience was "amazed with fascination," never mind the language barrier. When his voice and imagination gave out, however, the adulation quickly waned. Smith was tied to a tree and surrounded by bowmen, their arrows notched for execution, when Opechancanough granted reprieve. Holding the compass high overhead, as if it marked Smith as some great shaman or high priest, the *werowance* ordered that Smith be cut loose and led to a Pamunkey hunting village, where he was treated to ceremonial dancing and fed more venison and bread than he could eat.

He was put up in a well-guarded lodge. Smith didn't describe it, but the Algonquin Indian tribes of eastern Virginia perfected a rectangular design with an evenly curved roof line that had a small hole in the top to allow smoke to escape from a fire that burned more or less constantly in the center of the dirt floor. The lodge was framed with smooth wooden poles made of several dozen saplings lashed together with a fine rope woven by the Indian girls and women from silk grass, which were then covered with wide slabs of bark cut from local trees when the sap rose in spring.

The next morning, three young women brought him a hardy breakfast of hot corn bread and venison. Personal effects seized when he was captured were returned. Smith was especially happy to get back his gunpowder pouch but curious to find it had been emptied. His captors were saving its contents, they explained, to be planted in the spring so that they, too, might harvest this magic seed of fury and smoke.

One day a Pamunkey showed up with plans to kill Smith. He was, apparently, the father of one of the Indians Smith had shot to death just before he was caught. Killing a man's son demanded revenge, a feature of the local judicial system that Smith duly noted.

A guard fended off his fellow tribesman, explaining that Smith's life was in the hands of a higher authority. The Indians, still beguiled by his apparently magical powers, took Smith to see the dead man in the belief he might be brought back to life. Playing on their hopes for a Pamunkey Lazarus, Smith assured them he could revive the young man if he could just get back to Jamestown to pick up a restorative potion he had waiting there. The Indians' faith in Smith's divinity didn't extend quite that far. Besides, they told him, they had a better idea. They prepared to attack Jamestown and urged Smith to betray his colony and advise the natives on the assault. If he would do that, Smith wrote, they promised to grant him "life, liberty, land and women," an early seventeenth-century Virginia variation of sorts on the pursuit-of-happiness theme.

Now, it was Smith's move. He had a trump card, it turned out, in the form of a notebook. He took out some paper, made strange marks on it, then told his captors, who had no experience with any written language of their own, to deliver it to Jamestown. If they did, he promised, the English would give them some specific goods—perhaps a hatchet, copper trinkets, and beads—which they could bring back to their chief. Smith actually wrote on the note a warning to the colonists that the natives were preparing another attack. He advised his fellow Englishmen to make a great show of their weaponry, so as to deter future strikes, and instructed them to give the Indians exactly the items he'd told them to expect.

After a three-day journey through snow and bitter cold, the Indians returned. They were astonished, Smith recalled, at how precisely he had divined their expedition, down to the last detail of what they would be given. In Smith's mind, at least, he had outfoxed the natives, saved the colony, ensured his survival, and further convinced the Indians of his magical powers, as they were made to believe that "the paper could speak."

THE CENTER OF THE WORLD

Over the next three weeks, Smith was led, under close protection and guard, across the coastal sweep of *Tsenacomoco*, a traveling winter road show starring the one and only barking paleface who could hold forth for hours in a foreign tongue, make paper talk, and cause a needle to spin inside a magic rock. They called on tribes up and down eastern Virginia as far north as the Rappahannock River, near present-day Washington. He was introduced to wives and cousins and children, conjurers, shamans and chiefs, and feasted and treated to tribal gaiety along the way. He whiled away long hours with Opechancanough, communicating through gestures, simple words, and drawings in the sand. Smith told the Pamunkey *werowance* he'd heard tales of a great salt ocean to the west, and Opechancanough assured him that, indeed, it was there, though no one seemed to understand anything about gold.

Afterwards, apparently upon his return to a hunting camp near the upper Chickahominy River, Smith was visited in his lodge by a Pamunkey holy man. His skin darkened with charcoal and oil, the priest was crowned with a tassel of snake skins and weasel pelts stuffed with moss and topped with a coronet of feathers. Joined by others similarly adorned, he led a three-day ritual meant to determine, through contact with the deities, whether Smith meant to bring good or evil to the people of *Tsenacomoco*.

Around a fire the priest sprinkled a circle of corn meal. Beyond that, he laid out a second ring of whole corn, then, farther still from the fire, a third circle of sticks. Amid ceremonial singing, orations, and incantations that Smith could not understand, the priest and his various conjurers somehow divined the truth about Smith. They explained to him only that the circles were a kind of map of the world—which, as everyone knew, was flat—with *Tsenacomoco* at its center, a New World Middle Kingdom, as it were. The corn meal symbolized the Powhatan people, cultivated and refined. The raw corn represented the sea, unfathomable and untamed, and the sticks were the place where Smith came from, a rough-hewn country somewhere along the outer edges of the known world. How and why the stick people had journeyed so far across the vast ocean to make contact with the civilized nation at the center of the world was a mystery, it appeared, which the high priests hoped to resolve.

Only after they'd reached their conclusion was Smith taken at last to an ancient and sacred village at the edge of a dense forest on a low bluff overlooking a broad river where three creeks gathered in a half-moon shaped bay. It was called *Werowocomoco*, or place of the great chiefs. Archaeologists have carbon-dated material from the site to the middle 1400s, meaning it was nearly two centuries old by the time Smith got there. A sparsely populated town, *Werowocomoco* was divided into two distinct districts that seemed to be separated into secular and spiritual wards.

Passing from the domestic and to the divine, Smith was led by a cordon of sturdy guards into a long, bark-covered lodge where a warm fire blazed in a smoky room smelling heavily of roasted venison and fresh corn bread. There, reclining before him on a rustic pedestal of wooden staves and flanked by two comely teenaged women, lay the most powerful chief in Virginia, the man the English called Powhatan.

Smith guessed his age as sixty, noting his lack of beard and the thickness of his brow. He wore a raccoon skin cloak and several necklaces of pearls and was surrounded by row upon row of senior aides and warriors, women and men, Smith wrote, recalling that the great chief projected "such a grave and majestical countenance as drew me into admiration to see such state in a naked savage."

Few relationships in American history have opened with more promise, only to end in more disappointment, than the one between Smith and Powhatan, two men thrown together from different worlds who had an astonishing amount in common. Both were determined if rough-cut leaders with less patience and polish than street smarts and gall; larger-than-life figures with extraordinary instincts and generally good judgment who relished the chance to trick or outwit a worthy opponent; men of their word who would readily make up lies from whole cloth if it better suited their purpose; men who could be trusted, in other words, except when they couldn't.

At his core, and in his heart of hearts, each man, too, was a natural-born killer, a field commander with the essential willingness to sacrifice those few, or many, required to defend the larger force, a ruthless captain capable of ordering atrocities against a foe if that was the best he could come up with at the time to protect his own.

Similarities aside, Smith and Powhatan came from different, and suddenly conflicting, worlds. Powhatan was the born-to-rule and self-assured chief for life of an expansive domain, a seasoned leader who had learned to play many levers of authority and influence at once in the course of expanding his realm fourfold. Smith was an up-by-his-bootstraps captain, a self-taught bomb maker who exercised power on far narrower terms: brute force, for the most part, augmented now and then by a mix of cunning deceit and economic bullying. Focused and stalwart, Smith had a poor track record for inspiring confidence among his compatriots and was even then struggling to earn respect from those settlers who largely despised him for having the temerity to reach beyond his appointed station in life.

The oddest of historical couples, Powhatan and Smith forged during their first meeting the beginnings of a great and terrible American rivalry. And while neither fully understood it at the time, each man, in that crowded and smoke-filled lodge, had more than met his match.

"He kindly welcomed me with good words, and great platters of sundry victuals," wrote Smith, the sole historical source for the encounter. To demonstrate his wealth and power, Powhatan put on a lavish spread replete with the great delicacies of his nation. Roasted venison, boiled turkey, and baked corn bread were on the menu, which likely also included pumpkin and squash, perhaps even fresh oysters and smoked fish, and almost certainly a kind of milk made with water and the crushed meat of nuts.

Further designating Smith as an honored guest, Powhatan ordered a large woman to bring Smith a bowl of fresh water to wash his hands. Smith recognized Powhatan's servant as the queen of the Appamattuck Indians, a woman who had hosted him with Newport's party the previous spring at her own village near the falls of the James. Having her serve at Powhatan's behest was a none-too-subtle gesture meant to underscore the long reach of his power. The great chief chatted amiably with his half-brother, Opechancanough, who seems to have borne more or less good tidings of his time spent with Smith. Whatever passed between them concerning the thinking of priests was lost on our historical narrator.

At long last, Smith later recalled, Powhatan got around to asking what he was doing in *Tsenacomoco*, at which point Smith composed a whopper. The English were simply minding their own business out on the open Atlantic, Smith began, when some Spanish ships opened fire on them, forcing the English to seek refuge in the Chesapeake Bay. The weather was terrible, he ad-libbed, so the English put to shore, where some local people shot at them. Most, though, had been very hospitable, Smith went on, and the English, for their part, had taken great care not to offend the naturals. Of course, the men needed fresh water, he explained, and some Indians told them they could find it upstream. Then, wouldn't you know it, one of the English boats sprang a leak, and that had to be fixed. And while the English repaired it, they heard tales of the great saltwater ocean lying to the west. Certainly, Smith added hopefully, Powhatan was familiar with that.

Smith continued with his tall tale, lying that Newport was his father. Newport was a great chief, Smith explained, and was very protective of his children. Newport was on the warpath even then, Smith said, because some

Monacans had killed one of his sons. In fact, the English could not stand those Monacans, Smith said, adding that they were even worse than the Spanish. Now the English were going to teach those Monacans a lesson. And that, Smith said, concluding his fabrication, was what the English were doing in *Tsenacomoco.*

Having received regular reports about the English doings along the James River since their arrival six months before, Powhatan would have found little in Smith's oration to believe, though he may well have been entertained by at least part of it. It took some courage, after all, for this helpless little worm of a *tassantassa* to assert so tall a tale in the face of an omnipotent chief who held the trespasser's fate in the palm of his hand.

Powhatan was intrigued by the prospect of attaining a menacing new ally against the Monacan scourge, as well as a second supplier of copper to relieve the Monacan monopoly on the rare and all-important metal. And that bit about Newport being Smith's father, well, that certainly seemed to make sense. That's how forces were structured in *Tsenacomoco,* after all.

Powhatan followed up with questions about England, asking Smith when the next ships might come, without letting on that he already knew a fleet was even then moving upriver from the bay. He said Smith would remain with him at *Werowocomoco* for four days, after which Powhatan's own scouts would guide him back to Paspahegh, the tribal territory where the settlers built Jamestown.

Powhatan then presided over what Smith described as "a long consultation," likely with the priests and elders among the group. What they actually said, Smith had little idea. "But the conclusion was, two great stones were brought before Powhatan," Smith later wrote in the style of his day, referring to himself in the third person while authoring what has become one of the most enduring legends in American history. "Then, as many as could laid hands on him, dragged him to them, and thereon laid his head," Smith wrote, describing being manhandled onto the stone slabs, where guards were "ready with their clubs to beat out his brains."

THE KING'S DEAREST DAUGHTER

As Smith lay pinned to the sacrificial altar, a striking American princess spoke up, Powhatan's favorite daughter, a child perhaps twelve years old. Her name was Matoaka, but Powhatan called her by her nickname, Pocahontas. Precocious, playful, and, like her father, strong willed, Pocahontas had taken an interest of sorts in this scruffy, red-bearded foreigner with the spunk to stand up and look the chief in the eye. Wait, she called out to her father, who waved the child away. Then, in Smith's words, "Pocahontas, the king's dearest daughter, when no entreaty could prevail, got his head in her arms and laid her own upon his to save him from death, whereat the emperor was contented he should live to make him hatchets and her bells, beads and copper, for they thought him as well of all occupations as themselves."

While many years later this episode would be enshrined in portraiture, embellished in literature, animated in cartoons, and engraved in stone, historians will debate forever the question of whether Pocahontas actually saved Smith's life. It's possible that she did, perhaps serving as the unwitting sign Powhatan and his priests were seeking to convey the will of the deities regarding Smith. Again, though, beyond Smith's own telling, there's no proof it ever happened at all.

Assuming it did take place, even if not exactly as Smith claimed, it's at least plausible that Pocahontas was playing a role in a carefully choreographed drama through which Powhatan intended for Smith to lose his life as an Englishman symbolically. That way, he might be born again as an Indian, much in the way Powhatan himself had left behind his own boyhood through the *huskanaw* on his journey toward becoming the chief. Such a stunt would have enabled Powhatan to retain face by demonstrating to his *werowances* and elders, the audience he most needed to impress, that he was fully able to do away with this English trespasser, even as he displayed both the confidence to spare Smith and the wisdom to court a potential ally who could provide imports of great value, especially copper and precious beads. It is clear that, having spared Smith's life for whatever reason, Powhatan felt the Englishman was forever in his debt. That, too, was only natural in Powhatan's world.

And so, two days later, Smith was taken to a great lodge where Powhatan appeared as if he himself had just undergone some sacred passage, blackened with the same sort of charcoal and oil paint the priests used to color themselves for special ceremonies and looking, wrote Smith, "more like a devil than a man." Powhatan declared that, from that day forward, he would regard Smith as his own son, according him a protected position of honor. He gave Smith the tribal name of Nantaquoud and even offered him land, just a short hike down the river from *Werowocomoco*. There, Powhatan could keep his eye on Smith as the English warrior contented himself with making toys and baubles for Princess Pocahontas and high-tech metal hatchets for her doting father.

That gesture of magnanimity, moreover, came with certain filial obligations. Smith would be expected to pay tribute to Powhatan, like any other vassal. For starters, Powhatan said, he could sure use a couple of those cannons he'd heard so much about. And a grindstone, come to think of it, would be so much better for making meal from corn than the old way of pounding the grain with a wooden pestle.

Then, just as Powhatan had promised, he sent Smith on his way back to Jamestown, accompanied by several warriors. They were led by the chief's most trusted scout, Rawhunt. A character Smith described as "exceeding in deformity of person, but of a subtle wit and crafty understanding," Rawhunt so lingered along the way that he inexplicably managed to drag out the twelve-mile trek into an overnight journey.

Rawhunt and his companions were to bring back to Powhatan the tribute he'd ordered. Once at Jamestown, Smith told them to help themselves, realizing they would not be able to haul the heavy cannon or millstone overland back to *Werowocomoco* as, indeed, they quickly concluded before heading home with the trinkets Smith gave them instead.

Having survived his ordeal, spared the colonists a drubbing, and been adopted as the great chief's new son, Smith doubtless anticipated that his return to Jamestown on the second day of 1608 would be a triumph. Instead, he found a frozen outpost reduced to three dozen beleaguered colonists, some of whom viewed him not as a returning hero but as a failed leader and a fugitive from the council's law.

Colonial justice was an oxymoron of sorts during Jamestown's early months. More *Lord of the Flies* than law of the land, the judicial code often seemed to be written at the tip of a pointed finger, with justice balanced on a scale that equated ill will and rank rumor with truth. A simple majority vote on the council, after all, was all that was required for a colonist to be sentenced to prison, public whipping, or, as George Kendall had already learned, even death. Those who didn't like it were invited to take their appeal to King James, with the modest proviso that they first find their way back to London to do so.

Ratcliffe, the troublesome incompetent formerly known as Sicklemore, interpreted his council president post as a license to beat other men with impunity. "Were this whipping, lawing, beating and hanging in Virginia known in England," Wingfield wrote, perhaps from his cramped prison cell aboard the *Discovery*, "it would drive many well-affected minds from this honorable action of Virginia."

Ratcliffe and his council blamed Smith for the deaths of Emry and Robinson. The Virginia Company instructions specified no punishment for failing to prevent death by Indian ambush, so Smith's accusers reached back a few thousand years for judicial guidance, at last finding the precedent they sought in the Old Testament canon of Leviticus, which preached the vengeful policies of "eye for eye, tooth for tooth . . . he that killeth a man, he shall be put to death." Thus counseled, they clapped Smith in the slammer and sentenced him to be hanged the next day. Where, Smith may well have wondered that night, was Pocahontas when he needed her?

Deliverance came this time by sea. Hours before Smith was to swing from the gallows, Newport sailed back into Jamestown with desperately needed supplies, a hundred new colonists and a swift demand that Smith and Wingfield be freed.

Skeptics who question whether Powhatan and Pocahontas deliberately spared Smith's life back at *Werowocomoco* must reckon as well with this question: did Powhatan save Smith from death yet again, this time at the hands of his rival colonists, by deliberately retaining him until his "father," Captain Newport, returned? Powhatan would have received daily briefings, after all, on Newport's progress upriver from the time his ship entered the Chesapeake Bay. His scouts may well have informed him, moreover, that Smith's enemies had the long knives out for him back in Jamestown, intelligence the Indians might well have picked up when they took meat or corn to the settlement for trade. Guessing when Newport might arrive, did Powhatan instruct Rawhunt to dilly-dally along the way and to overnight in a wintry woodlands hunting lodge rather than make straight for the land of the Paspahegh?

Whatever the truth, Powhatan had ample opportunity to do away with Smith and, for that matter, the entire attrited English colony at Jamestown before Newport's resupply mission could land. For some reason, the powerful chief decided against it. Indeed, just days after Newport's arrival, a fire swept through Jamestown, miraculously killing no one but pretty much wiping out the colony's scant structures in the dead of winter. In the weeks that followed, as Newport put his mariners to work alongside the settlers in helping to rebuild the town, Indians visited every couple of days, bringing beaver meat and venison from Powhatan, along with invitations for Newport and Smith to call on him at *Werowocomoco*. Princess Pocahontas often visited Jamestown as well, often chaperoned by Rawhunt, according to Smith. "Now, every once in four or five days, Pocahontas with her attendants brought him so much provision that saved many of their lives that else, for all this, had starved with hunger," he wrote.

There is no surviving evidence to suggest that Smith, then in his late twenties, ever shared a romantic relationship with Pocahontas. At the same time, there's no proof that he didn't. The colonists had no women of their own. Smith, for his part, never married. And Pocahontas, who was approaching marrying age for her culture—a half-sister, in fact, later married at eleven—would have been a prime candidate for a strategic wedding, if the ever-calculating Powhatan thought it might secure an alliance with the English and cement Smith in place as his "son."

Doubtless the old chief noticed that his daughter had impressed Smith, who wrote that Pocahontas "not only for feature, countenance and proportion, much exceedeth any of the rest of his people, but for wit and spirit, the only Nonpareil of his country." Hardly a Shakespearean love sonnet, that line nonetheless appears to be the most favorable personal reference to a female in the voluminous canon of Smith's autobiographical writings. Whatever Pocahontas was to Smith, she was far more than just a child.

By February, Smith and Newport decided to chance a visit to her home, leading a crew down the James by ship to the skirt of the bay and back up the York River to *Werowocomoco,* the Powhatan capital on a broad wooded plain. There, Smith introduced Newport to Powhatan, who had been anxious to meet the great sailing chief scarred in battle by the loss of an arm. For three days Powhatan hosted the English party, doubtless trying the patience of his people, who spent countless hours in freezing weather, preparing lavish feasts for their guests as a show of their own chief's greatness. Smith reciprocated by presenting Powhatan with three luxury gifts from England: a suit of red cloth, a hat—most likely of beaver skin, prized across Europe for its warmth and water resistance—and, what may have intrigued Powhatan most, a white greyhound.

Powhatan seems to have been pleased with the dog. But what, he wanted to know, about the cannons and the grindstone Smith had promised. Smith replied that he had insisted that Powhatan's men bring the guns and stone, but it seemed they were too heavy for them. The chief may well have chuckled at Smith's attempt to feign earnestness, but Smith's pranks were wearing thin. Let's take a little walk, Powhatan suggested, leading Smith to the river's edge. All of these waters I control, the chief said: the fishing, hunting and farming rights along its wooded shores, the villages east and west, and the dozens of canoes beached along its sandy bank. The canoes, Powhatan said, brought pelts, grain, and game from his many vassal tribes. They were also warships, he reminded Smith, that could carry hundreds of men, who upon his command could destroy any people who got in his way. At that point, Powhatan may have smiled, rested a heavy arm on Smith's shoulders, and perhaps even called him by the Algonquin name he'd given him, Nantaquoud. The stroll along the riverbank was a warning, though, and it's message to Smith was clear: don't underestimate old Powhatan; don't mess with the high chief of *Tsenacomoco.*

Once again, Powhatan, not the accouterments of his power or the tribute others brought, was the star attraction. "Powhatan carried himself so proudly, yet discretely, in his savage manner, as made us all admire his natural gifts," Smith wrote, "considering his education." Majestic, mighty, and prideful Powhatan may well have been, but, in Smith's eyes, he was still, and ever would be, a savage.

Powhatan and Newport soon set to casing each other out through corn and copper diplomacy. Understanding appears to have eluded them, however, partly because the two men saw commerce in entirely different ways. Newport's mercantilist world and privateering past had taught him, naturally enough, to wrangle the most grain he could for the least copper and fewest trinkets possible. Though in the end he offered far more generous terms than Smith thought prudent, Newport managed to offend Powhatan with his materialistic manner.

The chief quickly tired of the heave and hoe of haggling, which he considered beneath him. He found Newport's incessant bartering tedious. These *tassantassas* have been here now for ten months, he must have thought, and they still don't get it. Whose country do they think this is?

"Captain Newport," Powhatan finally sighed. "It is not agreeable to my greatness in this peddling manner to trade for trifles," Smith recalled from the conversation. For that matter, this was no way for Newport to behave, Powhatan lectured, noting that "I esteem you also a great *werowance*." Let's put aside this petty shop-talk, Powhatan suggested, and deal with each other like men. "Lay me down all your commodities together," Powhatan said. "What I like I will take, and, in recompense, give you what I think fitting their value."

Smith had seen the tactic used before, though likely more often in his early passage through the Ottoman bazaars than in the Virginia wilderness, and perhaps he had good reason to fear a hoodwinking. It's also possible, though, that Powhatan may have been honoring his guests and trying to bridge some mutual mistrust in a way neither Smith nor Newport could grasp. For while the English saw wealth and material gain as a mark of individual industry and success, and even a sign of God's favor, Powhatan viewed the entire concept differently, said Cornell University anthropologist Frederic Gleach. "That's the exact opposite of Powhatan society," he said, "where the greatest mark of wealth and of power was the ability to give things away." Put away your checkbook, Powhatan was saying. If you lay down what you have, and I take what I want, then give you what I might offer in return, there will be no winners or losers and no unseemly money grubbing. We both leave as great chiefs, having had the honor of being able to give away to the other something of great value. Trust me.

Beyond the transaction at hand, Powhatan seemed to be demonstrating that, on some level at least, he was willing to abide the settlers at Jamestown and even to share with them some part of his domain, if only they would start playing by the rules, beginning with that bit about understanding who's in charge. Instead, Smith warned Newport that the wily old chief meant to cheat him. Let me handle this, the cocksure Smith said, jumping in with a jug band snow job. Pulling out a handful of glass beads, Smith spun out yet another line of chicanery, telling Powhatan they were rare and highly prized by the great kings of Europe. Given that Powhatan was such a famous chief and trusted friend, Smith went on, they'd be willing to part with a sack of these precious beads in exchange for just a couple hundred bushels of corn.

Whether genuinely deceived or just fed up with the blue suede shoes and slap-on-the-back routine, Powhatan took the bait. He got the beads—near worthless bits of glass—and Newport and Smith returned to Jamestown with their ship loaded down with grain and beans, the original *Butch Cassidy and the Sundance Kid* act, a couple of corn-fed con men running a seventeenth-century scam on the Big Guy, sticking it to the Native American man and yucking it up all the way to the food bank.

John Smith was on top of the New World. The son of a yeoman had found a place at last where a man might survive, even thrive, on his courage and wits. No title, no patron, no ruffle-throated pretensions of nobility or high station were required here in Virginia. Its wide open spaces, peppered with a few illiterate savages here and there, provided the perfect setting for a man in his prime getting by on the Jacobean equivalent of a smile and a shoeshine—and a little gunpowder and shot.

Spring was coming and, with it, yet another supply ship bringing more fresh recruits to Jamestown. Newport left in March, taking with him Smith's council nemesis, the discredited Wingfield, as well as Gabriel Archer and John Martin. On his way out of town, Newport traded Powhatan swords for several canoe-loads of turkeys as a parting reminder of the growing benefits the Indians might derive from the transatlantic trade.

No sooner was Newport gone than Powhatan extended the same offer to Smith, who took the turkeys, then reneged on the swords. Over the next several weeks, the Indians responded by ambushing the English up and down the James, taking swords by force or theft. Smith laid down the iron fist, sending out search parties that shot, beat, imprisoned, and otherwise tormented the James River natives—and, in at least one case, burned their

Capt. John Smith several years after he left Virginia, as drawn by the Dutch engraver Simon Van de Passe. Courtesy of the Library of Virginia.

village and crops to the ground—in a campaign of terror meant to teach these insolent savages not to trifle with Capt. John Smith.

Back in *Werowocomoco*, reports of Smith's antics went down poorly with Powhatan, whose disappointment with his adopted English son was outweighed by his continuing belief that the intemperate red-headed runt might eventually come around. With the cold weather abating and local *werowances* complaining that half a dozen of their best men were being held prisoner in Jamestown, Powhatan turned to the most valuable strategic asset in his diplomatic corps: Pocahontas. Dispatched to Jamestown under Rawhunt's careful eye, she negotiated the release of the prisoners with Smith, who later wrote that he "delivered them [to] Pocahontas, for whose sake only he feigned to have saved their lives and gave them liberty."

The personal diplomacy crafted by Smith and Pocahontas established a basis for goodwill between the English and the Indians, setting the tone for at least some mutual accommodation in the months that followed. That summer, Pocahontas became a regular visitor to Jamestown, where she would frolic with the boys at the fort, her casual presence there a mark of the trust Powhatan vested in Smith and his small party of fellow settlers.

With Indian relations off the boil, Smith turned to the challenge from within: the Virginia Company's continued insistence, rooted in fantasy, that the colonists begin to send home gold, a preoccupation that distracted the council and misdirected precious labor that might have been better spent clearing land, raising crops, hewing timber, and improving on their Anglo-American relations. From council members, whom Smith derisively called "our guilded refiners with their golden promises," came orders for men to swing their picks into the sandy clays and organic loam of Virginia in a labor of abject futility. And, while Wingfield was gone, so was Gosnold, who, along with Rev. Robert Hunt, had been one of Smith's few champions on the journey. He was left with sundry company men convinced that they could find treasure where nature had left none, if Smith would only give gold digging the priority demanded by investors back home. "There was," wrote Smith, "no talk, no hope, no work but dig gold, wash gold, refine gold, load gold."

By June, Smith found relief from infighting, indolence, and wasted toil by mounting an expedition to the Chesapeake Bay, taking with him physician Walter Russell, two fishermen, five soldiers, and six others in a large open boat. Over the next seven weeks, they journeyed down the James to the bay, then struck north some two hundred miles along the length of the present-day eastern shore, exploring deep into the Susquehanna River channel, "searching every inlet and bay fit for harbors and habitations," Smith wrote.

They then traveled south along present-day Maryland, sailing up the Potomac River as far as the rocky falls and marshy lowlands where Washington, D.C., now stands, then back to the bay and southward toward the Rappahannock River, meeting with Indian tribes along the way and carefully noting distances, locations, water depths, and other features. In shallows where the Rappahannock pours into the bay, the group "spied many fishes lurking in the reeds," wrote Smith, who led his party in spearing with their swords what were probably flounder, taking "more in one hour than we could eat in a day."

There lives in that bay, however, one creature uniquely unsuited for gigging, as Smith quickly learned when he speared a large stingray. Striking back in self-defense with its whiplike tail, the ray spiked Smith on his wrist with a barbed and venomous stinger. Within hours he was in agony, his arm swollen like a sausage up to the shoulder. Smith was so certain he was near death that he ordered the party to a nearby island, where they conducted funeral services and began digging his grave in the gray mud and marl. Dr. Russell treated the wound with some sort of oil, however, and the swelling went down. By evening, Smith had recovered sufficiently to have the ray for his dinner. He called the spot Stingray Isle in honor of predator and prey, a name that to this day designates the marshy point at the southern lip of the Rappahannock River.

Returning to Jamestown in late July, Smith led a second Chesapeake expedition later that summer, filling in the blanks on an extraordinary map he put together of eastern Virginia that looks strikingly like versions produced using twenty-first-century cartographic techniques. In September, Smith was elected by the council to replace Ratcliffe as president. Nearly two years after being consigned to the brig by his disgruntled shipmates and nine months after being sentenced to hang, Smith had either outwitted or outlasted his rivals to become Virginia's chief executive, the military commander and political leader of British America. He was twenty-eight years old.

Suddenly, it was no longer just the Indians who had to deal with Smith, but also the Virginia Company, whose subscribers had staked great treasure on the belief that the New World would enrich England as it had Spain. Virginia, though, was not South America. Its climate could be harsh. It held no silver or gold. And, where Spanish conquests had resulted in either death or enslavement for untold thousands of indigenous people of the Caribbean, Mexico, and points south, the Indians of *Tsenacomoco* had skillfully played the English to a draw, trading with them one day, laying siege to them the next, in an inscrutable dance that made them a kind of essential foe, as necessary for the colonists' survival as they were threatening to it.

Smith had begun to absorb much of this, but the Virginia Company investors had not. Growing impatient with their mounting losses, they sent word of their disappointment on a return voyage led by Newport, who arrived in Jamestown that October with supplies and some seventy new settlers. Among them were the first two English women to arrive in Jamestown: one, a settler's wife known to history only as Mrs. Thomas Forrest, and the other, her maid, Anne Burras, who soon became the colony's first bride, marrying John Laydon, a carpenter.

One of Smith's first official acts as president was to deal bluntly with the carping of investors back in London, who had taken to second-guessing the colonists from the comfort of their cognac-scented English salons. Forgive me "if I offend you with my rude answer," Smith began a letter he wrote to the treasurer of the royal council in London, going on to point out that there were several issues he wished to straighten out. First, as to the company's complaints about infighting, get used to it, Smith advised, "unless you would have me run away and leave the country." Hewing an English foothold from this promising, but often forbidding, land is not for the faint of heart, Smith continued, noting that he couldn't do his job and keep everyone happy. As to the grumbling back in London that the settlers had yet to find the South China Sea, there was the small matter of the falls of the James, noted Smith, who enclosed for the executives' edification a detailed map. Newport had tried with 120 men to haul a ship around the rocks. Well, Smith explained, "If he had burnt her to ashes, one might have carried her in a bag; But as she is, five hundred cannot [get it] to a navigable place above the falls."

While those jesters floundered in the rapids upstream, Smith wrote, he had put the Jamestown settlers to work, chopping down trees for pitch, tar, and clapboard, samples of which he sent back to London, along with such soap-ash and glass as they could produce. Smith also advised the company that he had laid down the law to his fellow settlers: swing your axe or swing from a rope. Even so, he went on, he had to work with the crowd he had, a bunch of "ignorant, miserable souls" struggling to stay alive, what with hostile Indians and the wages of famine. Foolhardy missions like Newport's trip to the falls, Smith berated, hurt the settlers overall, with most of his men returning to Jamestown sick and half-starved. He was not sure, Smith wrote, how much more of that kind of help the colony could survive.

For that matter, Newport wasn't much of a leader himself, Smith went on, asserting that "Every master you have yet sent can find the way as well as he." And, wrote Smith, while it's great to have English sailors camped out in Virginia for weeks on end—getting drunk and raising Cain by night, and wolfing down what little food there was by day—maybe next time the company might invite them kindly to drop off their new colonists and supplies and quickly head back home for more of both, instead of lingering in Jamestown and bleeding its meager storehouse dry.

Returning to the matter of leadership, Smith offered his critique of the seven council members the company had picked. Wingfield had been kicked out and sent home. Kendall had been executed. Gosnold was a good man; unfortunately, he had died. As to that "poor counterfeited imposture" Ratcliffe, wrote Smith, "I have sent you him home, lest the company should cut his throat." If he ever expects to see England again, Smith directed, don't send him back here, an ominous warning of prophetic portent. In fact, Smith advised, don't send any more of the usual contingent of ruff-throated cronies; instead send some "carpenters, husbandmen, gardeners, fishermen, blacksmiths, masons and diggers-up of trees' roots." Thirty men like that, he wrote, would be better "than a thousand of such as we have."

Smith further directed the company to let him know next time what supplies he could expect to keep and not leave it "to the sailors' courtesy to leave us what they please." Otherwise, wrote Smith, the company could send anything it liked and the settlers wouldn't pay a farthing for it. He concluded with a sort of I-hope-we-understand-each-other-better-now sentiment, inviting any dissenters to feel free to join him in Jamestown, where their odds of surviving were about one in four. He warned the company not to go running off to the financial press predicting record Virginia Company earnings any time soon. In fact, wrote Smith, "as yet, you must not look for any profitable returns. So I humbly rest."

It's not hard to imagine how Smith's humble report went down back in London. And while Smith made a second career out of self-promotion and was often accused of exaggerating his successes and minimizing his shortcomings, no one could charge him with sugar-coating his assessment, either for his investors across the Atlantic or for his inconstant Jamestown cohorts, whom he assembled that fall for a reading of the proverbial riot act. "The greater part must be more industrious or starve," Smith admonished his fellow colonists. "There are now no more councils to protect you, nor curb my endeavors."

Fairly or not, Smith regarded most members of the colony as shiftless whiners unwilling to put in more than four hours a day of work. The rest of their time, he said, they squandered in idle amusement and "merry exercise." The free ride on the communal tab, he told them, was over, and this time it was his turn to draw on biblical inspiration for the conduct of his will. "He that will not work, shall not eat, except by sickness he be disabled," Smith decreed, paraphrasing from the apostle Paul's second epistle to the Thessalonians, then tossing in a newly coined homily of his own. "For the labors of 30 or 40 honest and industrious men shall not be consumed to maintain 150 idle varlets."

As Newport sailed back to England in early December, Smith led a party to accompany him downstream near the mouth of the river. On his way back to Jamestown, Smith detoured into the James River tributary of the Nansemond Indian tribe, a few miles upstream from the bay. In bitter cold, Smith's party journeyed up the Nansemond's river several miles to their tribal headquarters, not far from the city now known as Suffolk. Hoping to come away with four hundred bushels of grain, Smith was instead spurned by the Nansemond, who told him they had been "commanded by Powhatan," as Smith put it, not to trade with him.

The supreme chief may well have given such an order. By controlling trade with Smith, after all, he might have hoped to increase his leverage with the Jamestown trespassers or, at least, prevent inept Nansemond negotiating from driving down the price of corn. It's also possible the Nansemond simply made up Powhatan's supposed order to preserve precious supplies going into winter. Either way, Smith would not take no for an answer. He ordered his men to fire warning shots, putting the tribe to flight, then set fire to the first lodge he saw.

Fearing destruction of their village at the outset of what was to be one of the harshest winters of its era, tribal leaders acquiesced to Smith's demands, agreeing to hand over half the food they'd stored for the long winter and to plant extra portions for the English the following spring. "How they collected it I know not," Smith wrote, "but before night they loaded our three boats."

How they survived the winter with half their food stolen, Smith also knew not; nor did he much seem to care. In the unforgiving economy of the native Virginians, however, tribes provided for themselves or starved. That's likely what happened over the next several months to weaker members of the Nansemond—seniors, pregnant women, and infants among them—as the tribe made do with what Smith had left them during the cruelest season of the year.

It's also possible that the Nansemond were punished for trading with Smith if, indeed, Powhatan had forbidden it. There's no question that his patience with the English had worn thin, when, over the next several weeks, he invited Smith to *Werowocomoco* for a trading session, stressing his desire for English swords and guns.

In late December, Smith assembled a heavily armed party for the mission and led them down the James. Weather so cold that rivers froze half a mile out from shore drove the expeditionary force to spend Christmas near the bay with the Kecoughtan Indians, who seemed willing to put past conflict behind them and welcomed the English as honored guests. "We were never more merry," wrote Smith, "nor fed on more plenty of good oysters, fish, flesh, wild fowl and good bread, nor never had better fires in England, than in the dry, smoky houses of Kecoughtan."

The *Werowocomoco* welcome two weeks later was not quite as festive.

Captain Smith, you lying dog, what brings you to my capital, Powhatan wanted to know.

Your invitation, of course, Smith replied. Have you forgotten?

Ho, ho, Powhatan chortled. Now I remember. But I see you misplaced those weapons I asked you to bring.

Yes, good chief, Smith replied. I brought copper instead.

Well then, you may as well turn right around and head straight back home, Powhatan replied. No weapons, no trade. I can eat my corn, at least, but I can't eat your copper—and neither can you.

Beneath the barbed juke and jive were real tensions, reflecting the deepening personal strains between the two leaders and the widening chasm between their people. There were arguments over Smith's heavily armed entourage. Powhatan wanted them to lay down their pistols and muskets—"here they are needless," Smith recalled the chief telling him, "we being all friends, and forever Powhatans"—a gesture Smith, perhaps wisely, rejected.

Amid the atmosphere of rising suspicion, Powhatan and Smith voiced their mutual disappointment in each other and the distrustful turn their once promising relationship had taken. The grief must have seemed palpable for Powhatan, the old warhorse who, in the twilight of life, had staked his power and prestige on the notion that Smith might bring the *tassantassas* to heel, that they would come to understand the natural order of things here in *Tsenacomoco*, that the English and the Indians might learn to live together, even transform themselves from adversaries into allies. What followed was, if Smith's written account is accurate, an extraordinary oration that amounted to a farewell from Powhatan, in a tragic precursor to the enmity and bloodshed between Native Americans and Europeans that was to repeat itself again and again for hard centuries to come.

"I, having seen the death of all my people thrice, and not any one living of those three generations but myself, I know the difference of peace and war better than any in my country," Powhatan began. "But now I am old, and before long must die." It's true, he went on to tell Smith, you have frightened my people, so much that they're afraid to visit Jamestown. But what has it gotten you, and where will it lead? "What will it avail you to take that by force you may quickly have by love or to destroy them that provide you food? What can you get by war when we can hide our provisions and fly to the woods, whereby you must famish by wronging us, your friends? And why are you thus jealous of our loves, seeing us unarmed, and both do, and are willing still to, feed you, with that you cannot eat but by our labors?"

Some historians have regarded these words, recounted by Smith in later writings, as a ploy meant only to trick Smith into dropping his guard so that he might be captured and slain. True enough, Powhatan had gathered and placed on alert armed warriors sufficient to destroy Smith and his party. At the same time, Powhatan had good reason to be wary. And to dismiss even the possibility that he might have been reaching out yet again to the English seems a tone-deaf reading of history unsupported by events. Again, assuming the account is accurate—and that Smith had by then, after two years in Virginia, become functional, if not fluent, in Powhatan's tongue—it's hard to read the chief's speech as anything other than a well-rehearsed appeal for peace, an oral treatise laying out the terms of a mutually beneficial coexistence.

Ultimately, though, the speech descended into a sort of eulogy for the hopes he seems to have buried that day. "Think you I am so simple," he asked Smith, "not to know it is better to eat good meat, lie well and sleep quietly with my women and children, laugh and be merry with you, have copper, hatchets or what I want, being your friend, than be forced to fly from all to lie cold in the woods, feed upon acorns, roots and such trash, and be so hunted by you that I can neither rest, eat nor sleep, but my tired men must watch and, if a twig but break, every one cryeth 'There commeth Captain Smith!' Then I must fly, I know not where, and thus with miserable fear end my miserable life, leaving my pleasures to such youths as you, which, through your rash unadvisedness, may quickly as miserably end."

Powhatan concluded, "Let this therefore assure you of our loves, and every year our friendly trade shall furnish you with corn. And now, also, if you would, come in friendly manner to see us, and not thus with your guns and swords as to invade your foes."

If that was the proud chief's offer of a lasting *Pax Powhatania*, Smith rejected it out of hand. Perhaps he was too wary himself to pick up on its meaning or worth. Certainly he had his own reasons for skepticism. "The vow I made you of my love, both myself and my men have kept," Smith asserted, setting aside the small matter of village burnings and the commandeering of food at gunpoint. "As for your promise, I find it every day violated by some of your subjects." It's possible, too, that Smith perceived Powhatan to be losing ground, an aging warrior posturing from a position of weakness, a vulnerable rival ripe for defeat.

Whatever his calculations, Smith didn't regard Powhatan's oration as an olive branch. Hidebound by cultural bias and haunted by Hakluyt, he couldn't accept Powhatan as a leader who might be dealt with on equitable terms. Unable to imagine the shared future the old chief outlined or the rich possibilities such an arrangement might have offered the English as well as the Indians, Smith fell back instead on insults and threats. Since our weapons are superior to yours, he replied, "had we intended you any hurt, long before this we could have effected it." And, he falsely asserted, "as for the danger of our enemies, in such wars consist our chiefest pleasure." He went on to belittle Powhatan's vision of a stable relationship based on the trade of English goods in exchange for food, which Smith had already seen was the greatest source of wealth the old chief had, the centerpiece for tribal diplomacy and the leading means by which the Indian might honor a guest he held in high esteem. "For your riches we have no use," Smith sniffed. "We shall not so unadvisedly starve, as you conclude. Your friendly care in that behalf is needless." For the English, Smith baldly lied, have resources "beyond your knowledge."

Powhatan doubtless saw through the bluster as clearly as his scouts had seen the diseased and famished bodies dragged out of Jamestown one by one and buried in the forest beyond the palisades. Smith's bluff and bully tactics, though, were by then beside the point. The breakdown had become personal. Compromise was not possible with an adversary bent on insults and threats, in Powhatan's world, as in any other.

"Captain Smith, I never use any *werowance* so kindly as yourself, yet from you I receive the least kindness of any," Powhatan lamented. "No one doth deny to lie at my feet, or refuse to do what I desire, but only you, of whom I can have nothing but what you regard not. And yet you will have whatsoever you demand." Nor, Powhatan added, was this treatment any different from that Smith seemed to show his own leaders. "Captain Newport you call father, and so you call me," said Powhatan. "But I see for all us both you will do what you list, and we must both seek to content you."

Then, Smith, drawing on the same instincts that had led him to upbraid his fellow colonists and assail his London backers, decided to put the Virginia chief of chiefs in his place. "Powhatan, you must know," he began in a condescending retort, "as I have but one God, I honor but one king, and I live not here as your subject, but as your friend, to pleasure you with what I can." Smith continued, "I call you father indeed, and, as a father, you shall see I will love you. But the small care you have of such a child causes my men to persuade me to look to my self."

There, for all intents and purposes, ended the short, happy friendship of Capt. John Smith and Chief Powhatan. And with that friendship went the last best hope, for the near term at least, of genuine peace between their peoples. With his favored women and possessions, Powhatan left *Werowocomoco* and fled into the forest, en route to a new life as a leader in seclusion and decline, his immediate realm reduced to a remote village deep in the upper Chickahominy. Little is known of Powhatan's final days, but it's not hard to imagine a kind of Native American Captain Kurtz rattling about in the frozen marsh, his last days slipping through his fingers as his fevered mind wandered the murky swamp of remembrance, reexamining the heartbreak and the horror, and shuddering at the ghosts of what might have been.

Done at last with Smith, Powhatan ordered his men to kill the English captain that night in his camp outside *Werowocomoco*. Smith was spared only when Pocahontas put her own life at risk to venture alone into the forest on a wintry night and warn him of the planned attack. "Pocahontas, his dearest jewel and daughter, in that dark night came through the irksome woods," Smith wrote, warning that "Powhatan and all the power he could make would after come kill us all. . . . If we would live, she wished us presently to be gone."

Her own life imperiled, her dreams dashed, in no small measure, by the parting of the two men who loomed largest in her life, and certainly sensing, and likely fearing, what their split might portend for her people, Pocahontas was distraught. Smith tried to console her with trinkets, a sadly fitting token of how poorly he grasped her predicament. "Such things as she delighted in he would have given her," Smith later wrote of himself. "But, with the tears running down her cheeks, she said she durst not be seen to have any, for, if Powhatan should know it, she were but dead. And so she ran away by herself as she came."

5

DEMOCRACY IN AMERICA

JAMESTOWN—John Smith's self-described rude, if humble, missive to the leaders of the Virginia Company was a wake-up call to the London investors and the royal masters they served. After two years of heavy losses, they could not ignore his call for change, even if they were in no mood to be lectured by this haughty upstart from a shabby colonial outpost that had yet to return the first shilling on their investment. A cunning woodsman and scrappy fighter this homespun son of a country commoner might be, but what he knew of able governance, the board of directors concluded, might well fit on the tip of a bodkin and still leave room for a broadsheet. If this were the best that might come of council rule in Virginia, some investors concluded, it might be better to stifle democracy in America than to help instill it.

England itself, for that matter, was deep in the throes of a long contest between parliamentary governance and monarchial rule. Rooted in thirteenth-century councils of advisers to the throne, the English parliament had evolved into a representative body that gave voice to popular grievances and hopes. While even King James's enemies largely distrusted democracy as a potentially chaotic course of governance, the parliament was useful in helping the king build the consensus he needed to raise taxes and negotiate tricky political shoals. In those ways at least, Parliament was essential to James, though the power sharing those functions required compromised, and in some ways challenged, his authority as king.

Crown and Parliament, moreover, weren't the only struts in the rickety scaffolding of representative governance being tacked together in London in early 1609. Once a clubby group of devoted adventurers, the Virginia Company had grown by then to include nearly seven hundred individual shareholders, an early conglomerate taking in nearly sixty different companies, representing an array of groups ranging from cabinetmakers to fishmongers bound by the quest for profit. Working out the best way to achieve that, though, was a corporate concern, which had somehow to accommodate different interests and views through discussion, debate, and voting.

All of those tensions—royal, parliamentary, and corporate—were far from Smith's mind that spring, a time he spent instituting his work-or-starve doctrine in ways that busied colonists with the mundane, but vital, tasks of clearing land, planting crops, and seeking some form of industry that might enable the colony at last to pay its way. The great debates in London, however, would soon reverberate through Jamestown.

In the months Smith spent trying to whip the settlement into shape, the Virginia Company convened a commission to figure out what was wrong with Jamestown and recommend corrective measures. Twenty-five years after laying out his blueprint for New World settlement, the Rev. Richard Hakluyt was among those impaneled for consultation. The result was a plan to restructure the failing colony.

The company shredded its old charter and penned a new compact, signed May 23. The new charter diluted the king's sway, formally placing the colony under the direct control of the Virginia Company. It also did away with the colonial presidency, reduced the local council to an advisory board that had no real authority, and combined the powers of both into the new post of governor, who was to be named by the company.

Having peeved much of the company's leadership, the prickly Smith was passed over for the job. It was granted instead to Sir Thomas Gates, a company man who had fought in the Netherlands. Gates had been to the New World before. He helped rescue some of the settlers at the colony Raleigh had founded in 1585 at Roanoke Island, off the coast of what is now North Carolina, before other inhabitants there vanished without a trace several years later.

With Gates in charge, Smith was to serve in the number-two post on the advisory council weakened under the new Virginia charter of 1609. Smith was assigned the defense portfolio. As it happened, he never assumed the position.

In early June, Gates and Newport left England for Jamestown aboard a fleet of nine ships bearing about five hundred settlers, fresh supplies, and the new charter. En route to Virginia, the fleet languished in the blazing tropics long enough for some three dozen travelers to die of heatstroke or dehydration. It was hurricane season in the south Atlantic, and in late July the group was broken up by a furious storm later immortalized by the greatest writer in the history of the English language. Before Shakespeare got his hands on the story, though, the actual account of the soon-famous tempest was written by someone who was actually there, the playwright's friend William Strachey.

"It could not be said to rain; the water like whole rivers did flood the air . . . [and] beat all light from heaven, which, like a hell of darkness, turned black upon us," wrote Strachey, a scholar and former diplomat who was aboard the flagship, the *Sea Venture*, with Gates during the storm. For days the wooden vessel was pounded and tossed on angry seas that washed over its deck and threatened to swamp the tiny craft, its creaking timbers moaning as if they might split into pieces at any moment. Men held candles over their heads and waded into the ship's rolling belly in shoulder-high water that lapped over their faces, groping with their free hands for leaks they plugged with sides of beef. "Our clamor drowned in the winds and thunder," wrote Strachey. "The sea welled above the clouds."

After four days and nights of terror, the *Sea Venture* ran aground off the coast of Bermuda, where the ship's one hundred fifty men, women, and children miraculously made it safely ashore. There they spent the next eleven months as castaways, building two ships, which they appropriately named the *Patience* and the *Deliverance*, from native cedar and materials salvaged from the wrecked *Sea Venture* before making their way to Jamestown the next year.

The tale of their extended journey, or much of it at least, is still told today on stage. Strachey had once aspired to become a playwright, an ambition he nurtured as a shareholder in the Blackfriar's Theatre. A London playhouse on the Thames River, Blackfriar's was home to the King's Men, a theater troupe associated with a writer named William Shakespeare. Strachey conveyed his account of the storm and the shipwrecked party's Bermuda experience in a letter he addressed "to a certain lady" back in London. The mysterious recipient has never been identified. Strachey's letter, however, seems to have found its way into the hands of the Bard, who incorporated its rich imagery in his romantic New World comedy *The Tempest*, a 1611 production thought by some Shakespeare scholars to be among his greatest works.

A political storm center, meanwhile, was gathering over the banks of the James. With Gates and his party presumed lost at sea, the rest of the storm-ravaged fleet limped into Jamestown in mid-August, bringing some three hundred men, women, and children, along with John Ratcliffe, John Martin, Gabriel Archer, and other of Smith's former rivals. They informed the colonists of the new charter, which they assumed had gone down with the *Sea Venture*, and told Smith his days as Jamestown's leader were over. Unable to produce the written charter, however, or to convince Smith to step down on their word alone, his rivals were reduced to plotting and scheming against the grizzled captain, who, in any event, had only a month left in his yearlong term.

Perhaps hoping to split his opposition, Smith ordered Martin, George Percy, and sixty others on a mission down the James. There, they were to collect a down payment on the food the Nansemond Indians had promised the previous winter in lieu of having their village burned to cinder. The Nansemond, though, did not have fond memories of the arrangement or of the lean winter they had spent scraping by on half-rations. When Martin's party sent a pair of messengers to inform the Nansemond that it was time to fork over their harvest once more, the Nansemond instead scalped the bearers of bad fortune and scraped out their brains with mussel shells. Martin exacted swift and brutal revenge, ordering his men to attack a Nansemond outpost and to sack an island village that was sacred ground to the native people. Their mosque, their synagogue, their church, the island was the place where the Nansemond had reverently enshrined the bones of generations of their chiefs on the last stop of their spiritual journey toward the western heavens. "We beat the savages out of their land, burned their houses, ransacked their temples, took down the corpses of their dead kings from their tombs and carried away their pearls, copper and bracelets, wherewith they do decorate their kings' funerals," wrote Percy, perhaps recalling the biblical lilt to the original charter's admonition: "For every plantation which our Heavenly Father hath not planted shall be rooted out."

In the decidedly unheavenly scrum that followed, the son of the Nansemond chief was captured, tied to a tree, and—accidentally, Percy claimed—shot in the chest. Some time after that incident, not far from there, an English trading party was killed. Their bodies were found with their mouths stuffed with corn bread, a gesture of the contempt the Indians had developed for people who couldn't, or wouldn't, feed themselves and would sooner lay waste to entire villages, destroy centuries-old sacred places, and terrorize women and children than trouble themselves to raise crops of their own.

With English-Indian relations listing toward all-out war, Smith, the pyrotechnics expert, suffered a near-lethal burn from a gunpowder explosion while aboard a boat upstream from Jamestown near the falls. In his account, Smith was sleeping when his powder bag exploded and "tore the flesh from his body and thighs, nine or ten inches square in a most pitiful manner." The blast nearly killed Smith on the spot. "To quench the tormenting fire, frying him in his clothes, he leaped overboard into the deep river," Smith wrote, "where, before they could recover him, he was near drowned."

What triggered the explosion isn't recorded, but the fuse for a political blowup had been lit long before. Determined to the point of obsession, unquestioning of his ways and views, quick to act, loath to listen to others, and believing, without doubt, that he was on a mission from God, Smith had become a man at war with his own world. He had come to an unfamiliar and generally unwelcoming land with a poorly equipped, disparate, and hastily thrown-together band of misfits who, by and large, lacked the training, disposition, and cultural intelligence to succeed in Virginia. Most had died there. Smith saved the rest from collapse and, through his uneasy ties with Powhatan and Pocahontas, probably kept Jamestown from being destroyed by the Indians.

Still, it had been a bitter business of brutality and bloodshed, with more of both yet to come. In its conduct, Smith had alienated the very people he depended upon in London, Jamestown, and *Werowocomoco.* The stage was set for his eclipse.

Smith returned to Jamestown and, while struggling with the rudiments of colonial medical care for his painful burn, got word that Ratcliffe and Archer had conspired to kill him. He was soon visited in his recovery tent by one of their confederates, armed with a pistol. Seeing Smith, the would-be assassin either lost his nerve or got religion, refused to fire, and left. In Percy's account, Smith, "an ambitious, unworthy and vainglorious fellow," sought to strip Ratcliffe, Archer, and Martin of any leadership role and to establish himself as the "sovereign" of Virginia, though it's hard, given his crippling wound, to imagine how. Whatever the truth, contention triumphed. Within days of the September 10 end of his yearlong term as president, Smith, under siege by his rivals and suffering from an injury that still threatened his life, threw in the towel. He boarded a ship bound for England. The greatest adventure of his life was over. Settlers sent false word to Powhatan that Smith was dead as, for the old chief, he might as well have been. Smith never laid eyes on Virginia again.

Of all the English colonists, Smith stood out for his willingness to delve into Powhatan's world, trying to understand the values, habits, and interests of the Indians, if only because doing so was necessary for trade and avoiding all-out war. For all his flaws, he was the best ambassador to the

Powhatan the English had. And he was the only one, in Jamestown's early years at least, with the ability to impose order and direction upon the motley and intently quarrelsome crowd that clawed out the English foothold in America. "He was the right man for the job," said Powhatan expert Helen Rountree. "Without him, that colony would have failed in a matter of months."

And yet, for all that, Smith ultimately lacked the cultural insights, political dexterity, and diplomatic skills required to recognize and seize the possibility of enduring peace with the Indians, whom he would later demean as "an idle, improvident, scattered people." The faction-rent stew pot known as the local council was a better instrument for fomenting dissent, it turned out, than for resolving the unforeseen conflicts and embracing the opportunities the colonists confronted in this strange and hostile land. Even as Smith sought, through decisive and stern leadership, to overcome those shortcomings, he lacked the authority to override the Virginia Company's incessant press for exploration, driven by the misguided belief that the James River could lead the colonists to gold, silver, and a shortcut to China. Rather than settle in, get along, and adapt to the rhythms of the Powhatan world, said Rountree, "The colonists were ordered to do exactly the kind of things that angered the Indians."

Even as the lines of Smith's vessel were cast from the trunks of the riverside trees, Ratcliffe, Archer, and Percy were haggling over who would replace him as leader. They settled on Percy. In fact, though, with Gates presumed dead, the council abolished, and no written charter to guide the colonists, the leadership was in disarray. Smith left behind a well-fortified and reasonably well-supplied colony of some five hundred men, women, and children, the strongest Jamestown had ever been. By the time he arrived in England two months later, the settlement was drifting without a rudder into the most disastrous season of its history.

November brought waterfowl in great numbers, just weeks after the autumn harvest was complete. The poorly managed colony, though, was running out of food, its granary all but empty, its fishing nets in tatters, lying useless in the fertile river waters. Percy sent Ratcliffe on a trading mission to Powhatan's new seat in an upper Chickahominy village, but things went terribly wrong. There were arguments over terms, and disagreements about supposed hostages. Ratcliffe's men were killed, and he was stripped naked, tied to a tree, his flesh and fingers shaved off by women, and his body burned at the stake. After that turn of events, Jamestown would receive no further bailout from the locals, who instead lay siege to the settlement, lying in wait along its forested fringes and winging arrows at any who might sally forth from its gates.

As winter set in, Percy ordered the execution of settlers caught stealing from the dwindling storehouse shelves. By Christmas, starvation began to stalk the rest. "Now all of us at Jamestown [were] beginning to feel that sharp prick of hunger," wrote Percy. "A world of miseries ensued." The horses were the first to go, killed and butchered for their meat, followed by the town's dogs, cats, rats, and mice, probably in that order. When the pack animals, pets, and vermin were gone, the colonists boiled their boots and chewed the leather. Some ventured beyond the palisades, risking death by Indian snipers, to forage for nuts and dig for roots. "And now, famine beginning to look ghastly and pale in every face, nothing was spared to maintain life and to do those things which seem incredible," wrote Percy.

How hungry does a man have to be to feed on the flesh of a rotting corpse? With grim echoes of the Spanish survival tales buried deep in their conscience, the colonists found out, digging up bodies from shallow graves with whispered prayers for their daily bread. Some didn't wait for a burial, wrote Percy, but rather "licked up the blood which hath fallen from their weak fellows."

When once a pregnant woman went missing, suspicion fell upon her husband. Percy weighted the man's feet and strung him up by his thumbs until the suspect confessed. He had "murdered his wife, ripped the child out of her womb and [thrown] it into the river, and after [that] chopped the mother in pieces and salted her for his food," wrote Percy, who had the man executed.

"To eat, many of our men this starving time did run away unto the savages," Percy wrote, "whom we never heard of after." Others turned in at night to be found dead in their beds the next morning—men and women as well as children. With firewood running short and the forests too dangerous to cut fresh timber, the colonists sought warmth by burning furniture and even homes left behind by the dead.

As famine and disease took their daily toll, a settler named Hughe Pryse ran into the town center cursing heaven and vowing that no God would create creatures he meant to starve. "But it appeared the same day that the Almighty was displeased with him," wrote Percy, because Pryse ventured madly into the woods for prey, was shot by Indians, and left for dead, his body "rent in pieces" by wolves.

Receiving word of the settlers' misery, Powhatan doubtless spent much of the winter mulling over Smith's parting scorn. "For your riches we have no use. We shall not so unadvisedly starve."

A THING ONCE SO FULL

Between the intelligence he gleaned from his snipers and reports of starvation and cannibalism from deserters so desperate as to take their chances among the Indians rather than remain in Jamestown and starve, Powhatan must have believed his troubles with the English had finally reached a bleak end. Without Smith, the settlers had lost their moorings. Even when spring came, they continued to starve, too weak or otherwise unable, it seems, to harvest the shad and herring that swam upstream in great schools to spawn.

What finally made its way upriver to save what was left of the settlers was not some natural migratory force but rather an eerie specter long ago presumed lost: the Bermuda castaways, tacking up the windswept James aboard the *Patience* and *Deliverance*. Expecting a cheerful welcome upon their long-delayed arrival at Jamestown, they tied up instead to a tumbled-down ghost town. As Gates got his first good look at the charred and ramshackle colony he'd been dispatched to govern, ordering the ringing of the church bell to summons any settler still at large, he was received by the skin-and-bones remnants of the one colonist in nine who had survived. "We are starved, we are starved," some stammered as they emerged from their homes to stagger out into the light.

Of the five hundred settlers Smith had left behind eight months before, all but sixty had died on Percy's watch. Jamestown was a shambles. "Viewing the fort, we found the palisades torn down, the ports open, the gates from off the hinges, and the empty houses rent up and burnt," wrote Strachey, who arrived with Newport and Gates. "Virginia was a thing once so full of expectance as the air seemed not to have more lights than that holy cause. . . . Now how the back face, Janus like, with the repining eye, is now turned upon it."

Over the next two weeks, a dispirited Gates tried to pick up the pieces of Jamestown. Having received the appointment of a lifetime, it had taken him a year to get there. He'd survived one of the worst hurricanes ever recorded by men at sea in wooden ships, led efforts to build a temporary settlement from scratch in Bermuda, watched men craft new vessels from virgin timbers, and prayed as the makeshift boats sailed across the Atlantic and up the Chesapeake Bay, only to find his hopes for at last governing Virginia reduced to sand.

By early June, he'd had enough. Three years after it was settled, Jamestown had failed. The settlers would all pack up and leave for good the scene of the most fearsome tragedy in the short history of English exploration of the New World, a disaster that had cost even the survivors their fortunes, their health, and, for some, their families. For days the colonists scrambled, as best as their worn bodies could. Rejuvenated by thoughts of returning to England, they made pitch and tar to caulk the *Deliverance*, *Patience*, *Discovery*, and *Virginia* and baked bread for the long voyage home.

Embittered settlers wanted to burn what was left of Virginia Britannia on their way out, seeking what relief might be found in cremating the lifeless remains of their broken dreams. Instead, they buried their cannon in the muddy clay by the river's edge and set sail for England, watching their brief and disastrous American experiment fade from view as they sullenly drifted downstream.

While Jamestown had been sinking to its knees, the Virginia Company had dispatched a new governor assigned to replace Gates, whose fate remained unknown to his London backers. Even before he was shipwrecked, Gates knew his assignment was to serve only until the arrival of Thomas West, also known as Lord De La Warr, who would take over as governor of Virginia. Neither man could have foreseen just how timely the transfer of power might be.

A half-day's journey down the James, Gates' woebegone fleet pulled up alongside Hog Island, on the right bank of the James, where the ships lay at anchor that night. The next morning, to their astonishment, a boat came upstream bringing them a message that would, quite literally, turn the tide of American history. English ships had arrived at the mouth of the James, bearing fresh supplies, food, and some three hundred new settlers. One of them was West.

A more dreary directive would be hard to imagine than the one Gates and his exodus party received from West, who had gotten word somehow that the group had abandoned Jamestown. Survivors one minute, deserters the next, they stared through dazed and hollow eyes as Gates gave them the bad news. In his first order of business as Virginia's new governor, West directed the entire group to turn back, on pain of prosecution for breaking their settlement contract with the Virginia Company. Twenty-four hours after confronting abject defeat and symbolically laying the moribund colony to rest, the survivors were forced to make a new beginning, on the very snakebit ground they'd just left behind, and to make their peace with the memories it held.

The first governor of Virginia to have absolute power, West was granted unchallenged authority over an expanding domain. The 1609 charter had increased Virginia to include all lands two hundred miles north of Point Comfort, two hundred miles to the south, and northeast from there as far as the Pacific Ocean. Virginia, at least as the English defined it, took in most of today's United States, with the exceptions of New England, Florida, and the Southwest.

Equally expansive was the Virginia Company's vision of executive authority. West had the power to impose martial law, which he did, stipulating in writing a wide array of offenses punishable by death, including much of the behavior Smith identified in the unvarnished critique he'd written to the company two years before. Under West, and the military leader who replaced him a year later, Thomas Dale, a strict code of conduct evolved. Mindful of the infighting that had nearly paralyzed the settlement, the new laws made clear who was in control. Anyone who would stage a mutiny, flee the colony, or even "dare to" speak ill of its governor or his masters back in London could be hanged or shot to death.

Separation of church and state was no more a concern than freedom of speech. Morning and evening prayers were required, as was regular attendance at church. No-shows were whipped in the public square. Blasphemy was strictly forbidden, and no one was to "speak impiously or maliciously against the holy and blessed Trinity, or any of the three persons, that is to say, against God the Father, God the Son and God the Holy Ghost, or against the known articles of the Christian faith, upon pain of death."

Security remained of paramount concern, and it was death to any soldier who would not fight, who would surrender to the Indians or even talk to them, lose his weapons on the battlefield, compromise a covert mission with excessive noise, or fake illness to get out of combat. Domestically, it was a capital offense for a settler to refuse to work, to steal from the common store, to run away from the colony, or to trade with the Indians without permission.

The strict code addressed health issues as well. Anyone who would "dare to do the necessities of nature" within a quarter-mile's walk of the palisades would be publicly whipped, "since by these unmanly, slothful, and loathsome immodesties the whole fort may be choked and poisoned with ill airs." Equally loathsome under the new regime were the crimes of sodomy or adultery, each of which was punishable by death. There were even war-crimes provisions aimed at preventing atrocities that might provoke the Indians' revenge. Any settler could be sentenced to death who set fire "willfully or negligently" to an Indian dwelling, temple, or corn field or to anyone who pillaged an Indian village or mistreated a native—unless ordered to do so by the military commanders.

In that summer of 1610, the native Virginians would understand the true intent of that caveat and of the protections afforded them by the settlers' war-crimes prohibitions. In July, Gates attacked the Kecoughtan near Point Comfort and ran them off of their lands. Ostensibly, the attacks were sparked by the death of an Englishman at Kecoughtan hands, though Gates quickly ordered two forts built on the strategic stretch of riverfront land, which was later named Elizabeth City, in honor of the daughter of King James.

In August, Percy, bearing the weight of a man who'd seen most of colony perish under his command, led an assault team of seventy English soldiers on a night raid to a nearby village of the Paspagheh tribe. Under pretense of seeking prisoners and stolen arms, and with the memory of Ratcliffe's torture still smoldering in his mind, Percy's men surrounded the village as the Indians lay asleep. At the signal of a pistol shot, the English attacked, putting fifteen or so Indian men to the sword as the rest of the village fled.

As Percy assembled his men in the deserted Paspagheh town, an aide brought in the village queen, accompanied by her children and an Indian man. Percy upbraided his underling for taking the prisoners alive and immediately had the male prisoner beheaded. He commanded his men to torch the village, destroy neighboring crops, and throw the children in the river, where his men took turns, Percy later recounted, "shooting out their brains in the water."

Percy led his men a few miles downstream to another village, which was similarly sacked and burned, houses, temples and corn fields alike. By day's end, one of Percy's captains took the queen into the forest and ran her through with his sword, by Percy's account, though he pointedly does not say who ordered her death.

As a military commander, Percy was not held liable under Virginia's new war-crimes provision. The muddled details of responsibility for the crimes would have mattered little to Powhatan and his people. Ruthless they could be, in fighting against the English as amongst themselves. The wanton murder of women and children, however, signaled a new set of rules in Anglo-Powhatan relations. If Smith had been a soldier whose tough tactics Powhatan might respect, Percy had shown himself to be a very different kind of man. The Powhatan had a word for it: savage.

A year later, West returned to England after a long bout of illness, leaving behind Gates as governor, soon replaced by Dale. A former soldier, Dale set about hardening the code of martial law, which he enforced with terrifying zeal. Colonists caught violating his strictures were stretched on a wooden rack until their joints were pulled apart, or they were hanged, shot to death, burned at the stake, or chained to a tree and allowed to starve to death, treatment defended by at least one of his peers. Decrying colonists who would plot and scheme and "would rather starve in idleness than feast in labor," Ralph Hamor, who served as secretary of the colony under Dale, deemed the harsh treatment essential to the colony's survival. "If the law should not have restrained by execution, I see not how the utter subversion and ruin of a colony should have been prevented," wrote Hamor. Even torture was justified, he added, because some miscreants were so incorrigible that "the fear of a cruel, painful and unusual death more restrains them than death itself."

When he wasn't inflicting draconian oppression on his own people, Dale expanded the colony to new riverside settlements below and above Jamestown. In September 1611, Dale and a couple hundred men journeyed a day and a half upstream to a high bluff at a broad river bend now known as Dutch Gap. There they built a new settlement and named it Henricus, in honor of the king's son, Prince Henry, who died of typhoid fever the following year. By then, Henricus had grown into a second English village, a palisaded fort with four corner watchtowers, storehouses, and a brick church in a community many preferred to Jamestown. Henricus was built on the south bank of the river, a few miles downstream from the falls, on land that was occupied by Arrohateck Indians before the English ran off the native people, much as they did the Appamattuck Indians when the settlers built their third town, Bermuda City, some fourteen miles downstream from Henricus.

Upon his return to London, the ailing West would have debriefed the Virginia Company on the colony's continuing travails, further detailing, no doubt, the already grim picture investors had deduced from their mounting losses. Virtually unable to attract new capital to the foundering enterprise, the company seized the next year on a novel approach to raising money to fund the embryonic British Empire: a lottery.

With the reluctant approval of King James and the Church of England, the Virginia Company sold lottery tickets to the public, discovering no shortage of gamers willing to hazard hard coinage for the chance to win the £1,000 grand prize, a fortune at a time when the typical working-class family scraped by on little more than a pound a month. Having begun as a corporation, Virginia had evolved into a gamblers' stake with a lively populist following back in England.

Not that the colonists weren't struggling to make an honest go of it. Contemporary descriptions have led some historians to portray the Jamestown colonists as lazy and inept imbeciles who had journeyed from the lap of British luxury to the harsh Virginia outback and were too fearful of soiling their starched, ruffled collars to trouble themselves with plough or hoe. Recent archaeological finds, though, have cast doubt on that picture. "What we're finding is, that's not the case," at least as the colony began to mature and spread out, said Jamestown archaeologist Jamie May. Pretty quickly after realizing there was little gold or silver in Virginia, the settlers diversified, she said. "They were trying all kinds of industries, things you have to finesse the record to find."

Painstakingly digging through layer after stratified layer of sand, clay, and organic debris, May and her colleagues with the Association for the Preservation of Virginia Antiquities continue to coax long-held secrets from Jamestown, many of which are little more than hinted at in the writings the colonists left behind. Rusted bits of early seventeenth-century slag, for instance, tell May the colonists were making small amounts of iron from the thin veins of ore they found in the creek-side marsh. They made the first American glass from the local sand; from the riverside clay, they formed and baked the first crude, but functional, bricks. They smoked sturgeon meat and packed roe in salt. From deep forests of tall pines, they harvested resin and turpentine, the bonding agent and solvent of their day. They milled oak and other hardwoods for wainscoting and furniture, and from cedar they cut shakes for roofing and trim.

Jamestown had become the first manufacturing center in English America, with much of its production exported to the mother country. Even as the colonists and their London backers were struggling to develop a workable system of governance for the English beachhead in America on the James, the settlers were searching for some local product—anything, in fact—that might at last generate the profits the flagging outpost needed to survive.

A MATTER OF NO SMALL MOMENT

The seeds of the colony's success, though, ultimately derived not from a gambler's stakes or a miller's staves but rather from the Caribbean. After experiments growing *apooke*, the bitter tobacco the Virginia Indians smoked, a settler named John Rolfe, one of the Bermuda castaways, somehow secured seeds from the far milder tobacco grown in the West Indies and planted it in his fields near Henricus. In 1612, Rolfe sent some of the new leaf back to London, setting off the modest beginnings of what was to become the first profitable export from English America, a cash crop that would, in time, secure the fortunes of Virginia for some of its stakeholders.

Rolfe's tobacco also laid the foundations for the riverside plantation culture that would bring fabulous riches to a select few, while fueling a near-insatiable demand for ever more labor, and ever more land, ultimately drawing legions of Africans to America in chains and pitting the English settlers in increasing conflict with the Native Americans.

One, in particular, was quickly drawn into the fray. The colonists had heard little from Pocahontas in the three years plus since Smith's return to England. In the spring of 1613, however, a settler-soldier named Samuel Argall got word that she was on an extended visit with Patawomeck Indians, near present-day Washington, D.C. In a curious show of thanks for her efforts to prevent Jamestown's demise in her youth, Argall hatched a plan to kidnap Pocahontas, then around eighteen years old, by swapping her Patawomeck hosts a copper pot for their tricking her into boarding his ship.

Argall sent word to Powhatan that he could retrieve his daughter only by handing over a group of captured Englishmen, as well as weapons and tools the Indians were accused of stealing and a shipload of corn. Powhatan delivered an urgent message to Argall, pleading for his daughter's safekeeping and promising that all demands would be met if Argall would simply return Pocahontas for the ransom at a village along the Pamunkey River, near its confluence with the Mattaponi, where the two form the river now known as the York.

Instead, Argall stiffed Powhatan, sailed down the Chesapeake Bay, hastening past the mouth of the York and up the James River to show off his captive. More concerned with rescuing his daughter than with saving face, the aging Powhatan took the initiative, sending the English prisoners back to Jamestown, along with a boatload of corn and such tools and weapons as he could scavenge, informing the settlers that the rest of the wares had been broken, lost, or stolen. The English took a hard line: meet all our demands in full, or we keep the girl.

Pocahontas was thought to have been married at the time "to a private captain called Koçoum," wrote Strachey. Matrimony, though, could be a transitory state for the women of *Tsenacomoco*, as Pocahontas had witnessed firsthand in her father's lodge. It's possible that Kocoum had put her out, which might explain her prolonged visit with the Patawomeck, perhaps because the spirited princess and her husband simply didn't much get along. It's also possible that Kocoum considered the marriage terminated once Argall made her the captive of a rival group, not an altogether uncommon outcome for the captive bride of a brave.

In any event, neither Powhatan nor Kocoum made any further gesture to secure her release. Pocahontas, for her part, was sent upstream to Henricus, where she became a fast student of English and Christianity under the enthusiastic tutelage of the Rev. Alexander Whitaker, minister of the local church. Summer passed, as did fall, then winter. The following spring, nearly a year after Pocahontas was captured, an English party escorted her to a town on the Pamunkey River where they hoped to find Powhatan.

The big chief wasn't there. As other Indians, some of them related to her, came out to greet and to gawk at Pocahontas, she spurned them. If they really thought so much of her, she demanded, why had they allowed her to languish in captivity? The go-chase-yourself moment was no act. Pocahontas wasn't going home. She returned, instead, to Henricus and her adopted way of life. Either the child once fascinated by John Smith had matured into a young woman who preferred at least some of the English ways to the woodlands culture she'd known before, or her pride prevented her from going back to the people who'd done so little to secure her return.

Her acculturation had been enhanced, it turns out, by the attentions of a man whose fortunes had been rising as tobacco exports grew: John Rolfe, it appears, had fallen hopelessly and helplessly in love with the beguiling Algonquin princess. Having lost his infant daughter to death in Bermuda, and his wife after that in Jamestown, Rolfe was a prosperous widower battling an attraction to Pocahontas he deemed alternately sinful and sublime. In what may be the most peculiar betrothal request in American history, Rolfe wrote a letter to Gov. Thomas Dale, first apologizing for his feelings for Pocahontas, then asking for permission to marry her. "It is a matter of no small moment," the smitten Rolfe began, quickly confessing that, during frequent visits with Pocahontas under the watchful eye of Reverend Whitaker, he had developed "within the secret bosom of my breast . . . [a] settled and long continued affection" for this child of the savage chief. Rolfe then made clear that this was no fleeting burst of spring fever, no "unbridled desire of carnal affection." Well, maybe that was part of it, he conceded on second thought, but he had chastened his lusty thoughts "so far forth as man's weakness may permit."

After assuring the hard-line Dale that he well knew he was courting the very kind of displeasure God had cast upon those Old Testament characters guilty of "marrying strange wives," Rolfe penned a line better suited to *The Taming of the Shrew* than to *Romeo and Juliet,* apologizing for finding himself uncontrollably "in love with one whose education hath been rude, her manners barbarous, her generation accursed."

Yet, for all his fault-finding, Rolfe was a man consumed, his life taken over by what he detailed as "the many passions and sufferings which I have daily, hourly, yea and in my sleep."

Rolfe is a wreck, Dale doubtless concluded. He may never produce another pipeful of tobacco, the governor might well have chuckled, if he persists in this lovesick state.

"What should I do," Rolfe pleaded at last, finally vowing to bring this poor, ignorant Indian girl to the foot of the cross if Dale would but consent to the wedding.

And consent he did—"another knot to bind the peace the stronger," Dale reasoned.

Baptized and given the Christian name Rebecca, Pocahontas married Rolfe the next month, April 1614, presumably at the main church in Jamestown. No one seems to have recorded the minister's name, but the service was likely presided over by either the parish reverend Richard Bucke or by Whitaker, the minister who had been the couple's chaperone during their yearlong covert courtship at Henricus.

THE PEACE OF POCAHONTAS

Pocahontas had long believed Smith to be dead, though her father had his doubts. Still, Powhatan blessed her marriage to Rolfe. In keeping with his lifelong refusal to visit the *tassantassas*, though, Powhatan did not attend his daughter's wedding. Instead, he sent two of her half-brothers and her uncle, Opechancanough, who represented her family and walked Pocahontas down the aisle, as her former husband, Kocoum, slipped quietly from the pages of history.

The first recorded marriage of an English man to a Native American woman held more than passing symbolic meaning to both of their people, raising hopes on both sides for improved relations and ushering in years of relative peace. Rather than warring with one another, the two groups forged a new beginning and even a new economy. Beyond the corn-for-copper trade, an intricate web developed that generated jobs and income for the Indians, who would hunt for the English, providing them with pelts, fish, and game, in exchange for pots, pans, hoes, and other farm implements, knives, swords, and even guns. Indians became regular and welcomed guests at Jamestown, Henricus, and other English settlements. Some even lived among the English, learning their language, laboring in their fields, and getting trained in the use of English weaponry that they might better bring down geese, turkey, rabbits, and deer to fill the settlers' pots.

Little was written of the impact all of this had on the life of Powhatan's people. It's not hard to imagine, though, that jagged social fault

MATOAKA ALS REBECCA FILIA POTENTISS : PRINC : POWHATANI IMP:VIRGINIAE ❧

Ætatis suæ 22. Aᵒ.
1616.

Matoaks als Rebecka daughter to the mighty Prince
Powhatan Emperour of Attanoughskomouck als virginia
converted and baptized in the Christian faith, and
wife to the worᵗʰ Mʳ Joh Rolff.

Pocahontas, the favorite daughter of Chief Powhatan, as she appeared to Dutch engraver Simon Van de Passe during the visit the Virginia princess paid to London as a
young woman. In the only known portrait of Pocahontas made during her lifetime,
the illustrator referred to her by her given name, Matoaka, and her Christian name,
Rebecca. Courtesy of the Library of Virginia.

lines opened as young Indians moved from their traditional ways to explore the new opportunities and challenges the English presented. People who had no concept of land ownership, investment, or a cash-based economy suddenly found themselves vested in the rudiments of capitalism. Some developed a taste, though often not a tolerance, for the wine, beer, and whiskey the English brought with them from London or began to brew from native berries, barley, and corn.

The English urged the native Virginians to turn away from their "idolatry" and embrace Christianity. And while there's no evidence that their evangelism reeled in many converts—other than the fully indoctrinated Pocahontas—some were willing to add the Father, Son, and the Holy Ghost to the native deities already tucked into their spiritual quivers.

Historians can only speculate as to what all of this may have meant for native tribes. How did parents deal with young sons who broke with generations of tradition to go to work for individual wages rather than take part in communal labor for the good of the tribe? What did the worship of strange new divinities mean for the once all-powerful priests, werowances, and shamans, the spiritual leaders and authority figures that had held family, village, and tribal life together since ancient times? And how many young Indian women and girls heard the story of Pocahontas, who soon gave birth to a son, only to begin questioning their own lives, the options before them, and the choices they made?

If history is silent on such questions, it is clear enough about the impact the changes had on the colonists. With the locals helping to feed them, the settlers focused on raising the new cash crop. In 1616, they produced twenty thousand pounds of dried tobacco leaf. Most was packed into wooden hogsheads and rolled onto cargo ships bound for London, where Virginia tobacco and its addictive influence quickly became a mainstay of tavern and parlor life. Rolfe's exotic leaf fetched three shillings a pound at a time when that was roughly equal to two days' wages for a common laborer.

YOUR COUNTRYMEN WILL LIE MUCH

Not everyone in England was enamored of tobacco. King James was so obsessed with the new craze that he published a diatribe against what he called "this filthy novelty," warning in his *Counterblaste to Tobacco* that smokers were "sinning against God" while partaking of "a custom loathsome to the eye, hateful to the nose, harmful to the brain [and] dangerous to the lungs." As a medical warning, the king's *Counterblaste* was about three and a half centuries ahead of its time. The English largely ignored it. As their demand for Virginia tobacco grew, so did the settlers' quest for fertile acreage. Within nine years of Rolfe's initial planting, the English carved out another three dozen settlements they called "plantations" along the banks of the James, from the falls at what is now Richmond to the river's mouth at the Chesapeake Bay. In the process, the *tassantassas* took over thousands of acres of prime farmland along the essential transport corridor the river had provided indigenous people for thousands of years, pressing the Virginia Indians ever further from the water and ever deeper into the forests and fields, putting new pressures on the peace of Pocahontas.

While tobacco had begun to generate revenues for the colony, its investors at the Virginia Company remained deeply in debt and in more or less constant pursuit of new capital to keep their endeavor afloat. An average of two ships per year made the journey from England to Virginia, down from an average of five per year in the colony's first half-decade. "In 1616, a decade following the initial landing and after an investment of well over 50,000 pounds sterling and the migration of more than 17,000 settlers, Virginia counted only 351 European inhabitants," wrote John McCusker and Russell Menard in *The Economy of British America, 1607–1789.* "Its survival as an English colony in the Americas was far from certain."

In a flash of promotional fervor, the colony's investors seized upon a new marketing scheme. They would bring the Virginia princess to London, escorted by her English husband, the tobacco prince, and let all of England come to know through her what an exotic and prosperous future awaited those who would invest their money—or, better yet, their lives—in the New World.

Powhatan, too, saw merit to the mission. He sent along with Pocahontas a council elder named Uttamatomakkin, who was instructed to count all the people in England and report back on the state of their nation. Upon their arrival in the English port of Plymouth, Uttamatomakkin dutifully began cutting a notch in a long stick for each person he saw until the numbers quickly overwhelmed his hand-hewn census report.

Of all England's people, certainly none was more interested in the visit than the man who had once regarded Virginia as his destiny and all of the American continent as his realm, the still influential but greatly diminished and rapidly aging John Smith. During the seven years since his medical evacuation from Jamestown, Smith had lobbied in vain for someone in the Virginia Company to back him for a return voyage. As his frustration mounted, Smith had doubtless passed many a long winter's night pondering those dry, smoky houses of Virginia, where he had dined on fresh oysters that fine Christmas Eve amid such gaiety, promise, and hope. When he learned that Pocahontas was coming to his country, it must have seemed a miracle to Smith.

He wrote a letter to King James's wife, Queen Anne, urging her to receive Pocahontas in a manner befitting her status as Algonquin royalty. In that letter, Smith set down in writing for the first time his account of how "Lady Pocahontas," as he referred to her, had twice saved his life. "Next under God," he wrote, the Native Virginian princess had been "the instrument to preserve this colony from death, famine and utter confusion."

As Pocahontas was crossing the Atlantic, Smith was preparing for an exploratory mission to New England, which he did later visit. Amid those preparations, and, perhaps, his own trepidation, Smith let uncomfortable weeks pass before calling on Pocahontas, who was staying in a house outside London. When at last he showed up, it was anything but a tender scene. Pocahontas, for openers, refused to speak to him. "She turned about, obscured her face, as not seeming well contented," is how Smith delicately put it. More to the point, Pocahontas, who had been shocked upon her arrival in Plymouth to learn that Smith was still alive, was livid. "In that humor," wrote Smith, "her husband, with divers others, we all left her two or three hours." Things were still frosty when Smith returned to the room. Affairs quickly heated up, though, when Pocahontas gave Smith an unforgiving piece of her strong-willed mind, chastising him for betraying her father and for staying gone lo those years with no word.

Returning cruelty for neglect, she taunted Smith, calling him her "father" and saying she was his "child," a line of justifiable insolence Smith tried to cut off by reminding her that she hailed from royalty while he was, after all, the son of a mere yeoman.

Oh really, Pocahontas shot back with what Smith termed "a well set countenance." Smith was not afraid "to come into [her] father's country, and cause fear in him and all his people," she said. "And fear you here I should call you father! I tell you then, I will, and you shall call me child."

Then she got to the heart of the matter.

"They did tell us always you were dead, and I knew no other until I came to Plymouth," she said. "Yet, Powhatan did command Uttamatomakkin to seek you, and know the truth, because your countrymen will lie much."

Whatever else lay behind the exchange, devoid of passion it most certainly was not, one indication of the importance Pocahontas had once placed on their friendship.

Weeks later, aboard a ship drifting down the Thames bound back to Virginia, Pocahontas died at around the age of twenty-one, perhaps of some sort of lung infection contracted from breathing London's vile air. The ship went ashore at the riverside town of Gravesend, where Rolfe had her buried in the chancel of St. George's Church. It was March 1617, ten years after the English first arrived at Jamestown.

A year later and a world away, her father, Chief Powhatan, died, having lorded over his chiefdom for some fifty years and overseen the first sustained relationship between native people and the English settlers in North America. Somewhere deep in the forests of Tidewater Virginia, his body was raised on a scaffold of wooden poles until all but his bones had moldered away. Many months later, his remains were ceremoniously wrapped by high priests and tucked away at his people's holiest shrine, a sacred place near the confluence of two rivers, far from the probing menace of the encroaching strangers. The old chief's soul, though, was long gone, his people believed. It had drifted beyond the high mountains far to the west, to the land of the setting sun, there to join with the great spirit of Okee and to watch over the people of *Tsenacomoco* forever.

A LAUDABLE FORM OF GOVERNMENT

To the Virginia Company investors, the loss of Pocahontas, the alluring and fertile New World matriarch, must have seemed harrowingly emblematic. Death knells were being sounded for the Virginia colony itself, which was, at that point, on the seventeenth-century economic equivalent of life support. Even the name of the far-off venture had entered the London lexicon as a barbed synonym for a perilous and foolhardy enterprise doomed to fail.

Edwin Sandys, though, was not a man accustomed to failure. A leader in the English House of Commons, a critic of monarchy, and a constant thorn in the side of King James, Sandys was the treasurer of the Virginia Company and an ardent student of the colony's travails, many of which were freshly revisited when investors ordered an audit of the company's books. Spooling the audit results together with a decade's worth of written and oral reports from settlers on the ground, Sandys authored an overview calling for another revamping of the colony, this one more comprehensive and forward leaning than the first.

One problem Sandys cited was the collective nature of the colonists' labors, bent, as they were, on producing food for the communal store and not for the immediate benefit of the person who did the work. A related concern was that the land the settlers worked was owned by investors in London, not the people who plowed the earth and tilled the soil. The military basis of the harsh legal code was yet another disincentive for settlement, concluded Sandys, who also felt the colony was ill served by the practice in which Virginia Company executives, who never laid eyes on America, were naming advisers to assist the governor in Jamestown.

Adopted in 1618 as the basis for the company's third charter, Sandys' plan established private ownership of land. Settlers who paid their way to Virginia were entitled to fifty acres and another fifty acres for every additional passenger they financed; those who had lived there for three years or more received one hundred acres. The new charter also provided for small gardens for those settlers who were paying off their passage through indentured service—usually seven years—to the company. Settlers were still expected to produce corn for the communal store, though it took the form of a tax, in essence, while the bulk of settlers' output was for their private consumption or sale. Martial law was largely replaced by statutes reflecting the English legal system.

Apart from those important and practical changes, the Sandys charter contained a provision that would, in time, prove monumental. The Great Charter of Privileges, Orders and Laws empowered the Virginia governor to call for the election of two representatives from each of the colony's major settlements. He was then to convene a general assembly, made up of himself, a company-appointed council of state, and the delegates chosen by the settlers themselves. Sandys' charter had created the first representative legislature in the Western Hemisphere, the distant forerunner of democratic governance in America.

It was a modest beginning, to say the least, little more than a way for the Virginia Company to give landowners a limited voice in managing the colony. And it was a far cry from government by the people, as we know it today. Little is known as to exactly who was able to vote for these representatives—certainly not women, servants, or slaves—and it's a fair bet that the larger a person's landholdings the greater his political sway. Still, it was a start. "The assembly is clearly not an outcome of some sort of proto-revolutionary group of colonists trying to spread democracy. That would be ridiculous," said James Horn, director of research at the Colonial Williamsburg Foundation. "But it was a recognition that if you were investing in the colony you should have a say in the way the Virginia Company, and the colony, was run."

It was one thing for the Virginia Company to dictate terms to the hundred-odd settlers who first landed at Jamestown. Even then, central control from London was a poor substitute for the collective judgment of men on the ground. By 1619, though, as the colony spread out, new instruments of government were clearly required. "From 1617 onwards, to revive its ailing finances, the Virginia Company encouraged private investors to develop tobacco plantations along the James River. One fundamentally important outcome of that was the need for a governing institution that would represent them and protect their interests," Horn wrote in *A Land as God Made It,* an authoritative account of the Jamestown experience.

And while there may be no unbroken ancestral line reaching from the Jamestown assembly to the U.S. Congress, the gathering of those first elected burgesses did mark the rough beginnings of democracy in America. "The establishment of the assembly was important in that it recognized that people who ventured themselves and their purses should have a say in how their government is run," Horn said in an interview. "That was the promise of America for Europeans—that they had an opportunity to become landholders, maybe get rich, and have a say in running their affairs—and, to some extent, it still is."

Calling for "the settling there of a laudable form of government," the charter compared the Virginia General Assembly to the Virginia Company's own quarterly meetings, called courts, overseen by the company president, appointed council members, and representatives of the shareholders. The charter declared as the assembly's goal "the happy guiding and governing of the people there inhabiting, like as we have already done for the well ordering of our courts here." Formally, at least, the general assembly's decisions were subject to the company's consent. In practice, the assembly's core functions—writing laws, setting taxes, and serving as the colony's high court—were precisely the sorts of duties better managed in Virginia than in London, and the company tended to let most of the assembly's decisions stand.

Historians have long debated whether Sandys meant to establish Virginia as a democratic outpost or whether democracy was an accidental outgrowth of his desire to maintain corporate control over the settlement at the expense of King James. The Oxford-educated English parliamentarian had declared publicly that the people were sovereign, a radical—and potentially treasonous—position in a country ruled by a monarch. In his influential role within the Virginia Company, Sandys had advocated for replacing the raised-hand vote with the secret ballot box in the polling of shareholders, a reform that benefited smaller investors who feared pressure from wealthy subscribers. "Sandys was a consistent champion of popular rights and representative government," author and historian Matthew Andrews wrote in his 1944 book, *The Soul of a Nation,* a history of the Virginia colony. Andrews dedicated the book to the memory of Sandys, calling him the "founder-in-chief of representative government in America."

Other scholars contend that pragmatism, not democratic impulses or lofty ideals, drove Sandys, who was simply looking for a way to invest the colony with competent decision makers who knew the territory, actually lived there, and had the confidence of their fellow settlers. "Sandys cut his pattern for the Virginia assembly to fit the design of the company's corporate structure, not to resemble Parliament," wrote University of New Orleans history professor Warren Billings in *A Little Parliament,* a richly drawn portrait of the early Jamestown experiment in democracy. "He had no wish, contrary to myth, to see representative government transplanted to America," wrote Billings. "Instead, his rationale sprang from his twin desires to improve the management of a distant plantation and to avoid the missteps of the past."

THE ARTS AND MYSTERIES OF RULING OTHERS

Whatever his intentions, Sandys set in motion, by accident or by design, the imperfect stirrings of democracy in America, a long-running and ever-evolving drama that opened on a Friday, July 30, 1619, in Jamestown. There, on what was likely a sweltering and humid day, two representatives, called burgesses, from each of eleven settlements, then called boroughs, gathered with Gov. George Yeardley and his six-member State Council. "The most convenient place we could find to sit in was the choir of the church," wrote John Pory, a council member Yeardley named speaker of the assembly. It was just as well that the first representative legislature in the country met in a sanctuary, Pory noted, "as men's affairs do little prosper where God's service is neglected."

With that in mind, the Rev. Richard Bucke, a former Bermuda castaway, opened the session with a prayer "that it would please God to guide us and sanctify all our proceedings to his own glory, and the good of this plantation," Pory recorded. Thus blessed and so admonished, the assembly got down to the business of membership, at which point the legitimacy of four of the twenty-two burgesses was immediately thrown up for grabs.

Pory, as speaker, raised questions about the two delegates from Capt. John Warde's plantation: Warde himself and his lieutenant, a man named Gibbes. Warde had come to the colony and settled upstream from Jamestown near Henricus without first securing a land patent, a deed with conditions attached, from the Virginia Company. He somehow acquired property through his own means instead, and thus his claim to legal residence was deemed specious.

The second issue involved a plantation named Brandon, which belonged to Capt. John Martin, the son of a knighted London alderman and master of the mint. The well-connected Martin had received special consideration by the Virginia Company. It had inserted in his land patent a clause excusing him from having to obey the colony's laws, except those requiring him to contribute to the common defense of the settlement. If the people of Brandon would not be bound by the law, Yeardley asked, why should they have any say in writing it?

The delegates voiced support for Warde. Patented or not, he was well regarded by his peers and had been, in their view, the very kind of effective settler the colony needed to survive. Besides, it was pointed out, nothing in the charter specifically excluded anyone from the assembly simply because their property rights had not been ordained by the company. Point taken: Warde and his lieutenant were duly sworn in and seated. Martin, though, was a different matter. After discussion, the burgesses ordered that the Brandon delegates, Thomas Davis and Robert Stacy, would not be part of the assembly unless Martin agreed to abide by colonial law. "Otherwise, they were utterly to be excluded," wrote Pory.

In the opening minutes of representative government in America, the Virginia General Assembly had debated questions centered on tensions between the English authority and the colonists' ability to elect their own leaders and govern themselves. In the case of Warde, the colonists rejected the idea that the Virginia Company might dictate who was qualified to be elected as a burgess, striking an early blow for self-determination. Regarding Martin, the assembly recoiled just as strongly against the notion that special treatment bestowed in London might be translated into privilege in Virginia. In different ways, both decisions bore the distinct stamp of an independent-minded people resentful of rule from a faraway land, in a prophetic prelude to larger issues to come.

Their ranks thus reduced to twenty, the elected burgesses got on with their first matter of business with the state council and governor. Fittingly, perhaps, it dealt with Indian relations and, ironically, also involved Martin, who had led the sacking of the Nansemond tribe in the summer after the starving time. Nine years later, his reputation for harsh dealings with the natives had only widened.

After hearing that Martin's men had stolen at gunpoint corn from an Indian canoe on a James River tributary, the assembly acted as a court of law, approving a warrant that summoned Martin to report to Jamestown "with all convenient speed" to answer for actions the assembly feared "might breed danger and loss of life to others of the colony."

Pory then, in the sole record of the historic assembly, admitted to feeling "extreme sickly, and therefore not able to pass through long harangues," such as even the most benign of legislative sessions might produce. Pory knew that far better than most. Of the assembly's twenty-seven members, he was the only one who had actual parliamentary experience, having sat in the English House of Commons for six years before coming to Jamestown.

While Pory guided the assembly proceedings along lines very loosely tracing parliamentary practice, the members were neither schooled in law nor trained in the drafting and debate of legislation. "The General Assembly and colonial statutes were the creatures of novices," wrote Billings. "In a sense, the General Assembly merely happened. Hewing to no grand design, a succession of governors, councillors and burgesses schooled themselves in the arts and mysteries of ruling others." As lesson one, Pory led the student lawmakers on the legislative equivalent of a forced march, laboriously reading aloud, as would have been done in Parliament, a two-volume set of codes the Virginia Company expected the assembly to rubber-stamp. Instead of allowing them to do so, however, Pory set up a pair of assembly committees. After a dutiful second reading, he assigned each panel to review the codes, not, he insisted, "to correct or control" the company's writ, "but only in case we should find ought not perfectly squaring with the state of the colony, or any law which did bind or press too hard, that we might by way of humble petition seek to have it redressed." Between Smith and Pory, the London investors were beginning to get an idea of precisely what it meant to be humble in Virginia. The queasy speaker further instructed the assembly to consider such laws as its own members might wish to introduce, as well as any petitions the group might vote to send back to the company in London. So charged, the assembly took a dinner break, returning at dusk to continue its work, fortified by the fruits of field and stream and determined, as Pory wrote, "to establish one equal and uniform kind of government over all Virginia."

As the summer light faded and the enormity of the mission they'd undertaken set in, the weary assembly voted to suspend its proceedings until the next day. And so, twenty-seven in all, the pioneers of the rough-edged and almost accidental beginnings of democracy in America streamed out of the church and into the steamy darkness, piling into makeshift bunks in borrowed quarters scattered about the dusty town at the far edge of the known world, with little or no idea of the historic voyage they'd launched.

OF EQUAL FAVOR AND LIKE LIBERTIES

Through the mind-simmering heat of the next several days, the Virginia assembly labored to craft the petitions, debate the policies, and pass the laws that would begin to bind the riverside settlements into a single community, setting limits on collective behavior and personal conduct and lending guidance and direction to the efforts of a struggling colony of some seven hundred fifty people.

The assembly gave top priority to Indian relations, strained by mutual distrust and the growing English appetite for land. The first English law ever enacted by a representative legislature in America, in fact, forbade any settler from injuring or oppressing the native people of Virginia, in recognition that the colonists' own survival depended on peaceful relations with them. "By this present General Assembly," the statute reads, "be it enacted that no injury or oppression be wrought by the English against the Indians whereby the present peace might be disturbed and ancient quarrels might be revived." Settlers were instructed to be wary of either encouraging or rejecting native guests and to watch them closely and to limit visitors to five or six at a time. "For generally (though some amongst many may prove good) they are a most treacherous people."

At the same time, the assembly urged each settlement to take in native children and steep them in Christian values and English ways. The assembly petitioned the Virginia Company for funds to build a college to educate those who showed promise, an idea the company embraced. The assembly went on to deal with matters concerning commerce, planting, and daily life, drafting provisions that comported more closely with English codes than with the martial laws that had sprung up pall mall until then. They passed laws, naturally, against vice. Laziness was outlawed, with the leader of each settlement authorized to assign "idlers" to specific tasks until they demonstrated a willingness to change their ways. Card playing and gambling were likewise ruled out of bounds, with offenders to be fined and the winnings confiscated. Authorities were to pay out the first ten shillings of the take as a reward to whomever reported the infraction, with the rest to be donated for "charitable and pious uses." Public drunkenness was addressed. Revelers got a discrete word of prayer with the parish minister for the first offense, a public upbraiding for the second, and a fine and twelve hours in a crude stockade for the third. Following the company's own instructions, the assembly urged landowners to avoid planting excessive amounts of tobacco and to diversify the local economy by planting mulberry trees, hemp, vineyards, and flax.

Martin appeared as summoned and stood before the assembly. Refusing to bow to its authority, he was denied representation by the body. For his treatment of the Indians, he was ordered to put up a cash bond any time his men journeyed toward the bay as insurance against future abuse. And the burgesses sent word of his defiance back to the Virginia Company, along with an appeal for the company to make clear that Martin, and all colonists, would be equally bound by the assembly's will. In Virginia, the burgesses asserted, the colonists expected to receive "equal favor and grants of like liberties and immunities," wrote Pory, stressing the necessity of "uniformity and equality of laws."

On the fourth of August 1619, the first representative body of government in America adjourned, with a decision to reconvene on March 1 of the next year. It would be decades before the Virginia General Assembly would evolve into a fully functioning democratic legislature. Another century would pass beyond that before the body played its role in lending voice to a new nation bridling at the yoke of the British Empire. And yet, as they left the small church at the edge of the river that day to return to their homes and their farms, those part-time legislators had already taken the first steps in that long and perilous journey. As it happened, a passage of comparable hazard and historical moment had also begun that very summer, was underway even as the assembly adjourned, and was about to converge with the beginnings of English America, just downstream from where they met.

6

WADE IN THE WATER

POINT COMFORT—Far to the south, in the clear, warm waters of the Gulf of Mexico, the Portuguese slave vessel *Sao Joao Bautista* was sailing toward Vera Cruz in the summer of 1619, when it was set upon by the *White Lion,* a Dutch warship, and a British corsair, the *Treasurer.* Piloted by Capt. Manuel Mendes de Acunha, the *Bautista* had left the port of Luanda, in Portugal's West African colony of Angola, several weeks before, its cargo hold packed with three hundred fifty enslaved Africans. How many had survived the grueling transatlantic voyage isn't known. As many as one-third may have already perished, as was common aboard slave ships of that time, because of malnutrition, seasickness, and disease that ripped through the bodies of people squeezed together for weeks at a time in dank and fetid quarters.

Partners in piracy on the high seas, the Dutch and British forced the *Bautista* to hand over an unknown number of slaves, leaving behind 147 aboard with Acunha, who later sold them in the slave markets of Vera Cruz. Over the next several weeks, the *White Lion* and the *Treasurer* worked their way through the Caribbean, likely selling off some slaves at ports of call along the way. The privateers split up at some point and, separately, sailed northward along the American coast.

At the end of August, the *White Lion* sailed into the Chesapeake Bay and landed at the mouth of the James River, on a fingertip of land the English had named Point Comfort. Either there or as far upstream as Jamestown—the precise location isn't recorded—Gov. George Yeardley and the English cape merchant Abraham Piersey gave the *White Lion*'s crew corn and other provisions in exchange for twenty or so Africans. They are the first Africans known to have come to an English colony in what is now the United States, arriving more than a year before the Pilgrims landed at Plymouth Rock.

In the single month of August 1619, the seeds of democracy and slavery had been sown side by side along the banks of the James, the twisted paradox of American beginnings rooted in a contradiction that would confound and conflict the nation for centuries to come. Slavery was not to be some alien practice awkwardly grafted onto the trunk of American liberty. It was an integral and essential part of the nation's inception, without which the very means of American independence might never have been secured. Its origins passed with barely a historical whisper. "About the latter end of August a Dutch man of war of the burden of 160 tons arrived at Point Comfort," the tobacco entrepreneur John Rolfe reported several months later to Virginia Company treasurer Edwin Sandys. The ship, Rolfe wrote, "brought not anything but 20 and odd Negroes, which the governor and cape merchant bought for victual (whereof he was in great need as he pretended) at the best and easiest rate they could." In a separate letter later published in John Smith's *General History of Virginia*, Rolfe stated simply, "About the last of August came in a Dutch man of war that sold us twenty Negars."

Those brief lines, from the father of the industry that, on the strength of slave labor, was to transform Virginia from a money-losing outpost to a dazzling jewel in the crown of the British Empire, comprise the fullest surviving account of the arrival of the first Africans in English America. They arrived without passports, possessions, or anything else that might have documented their past. No one knows where they came from for certain. It's likely, though, that they came from the Portuguese colony of Angola, then a narrow sliver of territory poking inland from the Atlantic Ocean and wandering eastward along the great Kwanza River. They may well have been urban dwellers back home in Angola, sophisticated, upper-middle-class people not so different in social rank or economic standing from the leaders of colonial Virginia.

As the *White Lion* sailed into Point Comfort, the Portuguese viceroy in Angola was in the midst of a bloody campaign of conquest meant to expand the colony. He allied his meager forces with a far more potent army of African mercenaries, called the Imbangala, who were feared for their ruthless ways. Their arrangement was simple and straightforward. The Imbangala would move through the countryside, sacking and pillaging villages and towns at will, enslaving those they didn't kill, treating women and children however they chose, then selling their captives to the Portuguese. The blood bargain the allies struck was as efficient as it was brutal. In just three years, these mercenaries and their colonial patrons enslaved an estimated fifty thousand Africans. Most were shipped out of the colonial capital of Luanda and across the Atlantic to the Portuguese colony of Brazil or to Spanish holdings in Mexico and South America, according to research done by John Thornton and Linda Heywood. Both are professors of history and African American studies at Boston University who have spent years poring over Portuguese colonial records, ships' logs, receipts from slave sales, and other original source material to compile their findings.

In the months before the *White Lion* delivered its pirated human cargo to Virginia, the Portuguese conquest centered on a cool plateau about one hundred fifty miles east of Luanda, a region called Ndongo. Its heart was the royal capital of Kabasa, a town of as many as thirty thousand people between the present-day Angolan towns of Masangano and N'Dalatando. Most, if not all, of the slaves the *White Lion* took to Virginia were likely captured during Imbangala raids to those parts. "The historical evidence points to their being probably from the area around the capital of Ndongo," Thornton said in an interview. "This was the biggest net of slaves and the timing is exactly right for this ship."

The people of Ndongo were an urbane and highly developed group. They spoke a common language, Kimbundu. On the outskirts of Kabasa, they grew sorghum and millet, tended large herds of cattle, and raised chickens and goats. They wore clothing made of cotton and a kind of cloth made from bark. They built local and regional markets where they could purchase luxury items, like iron and salt, imported from the far corners of the African continent. And while they are thought to have been the first Africans to come to the English colonies in North America, they were not the first on the continent.

THE BLOOD AND BONES OF MEN

With roots in classical Greece and Rome, Western slavery predated the English settlement of America by at least two thousand years. It had been a feature of Middle Eastern and African life for even longer than that. Centuries before the transatlantic slave trade began, hundreds of thousands, if not millions, of enslaved Africans had been transported along well-established routes across the Red Sea, Sahara Desert, Indian Ocean, and Persian Gulf.

The first African slave known to have come to the Western Hemisphere arrived in Hispaniola in 1501, just nine years after Christopher Columbus stumbled into the Caribbean, thinking he'd landed off the coast of China. In 1519, a full century before the first Africans sailed into the mouth of the James, a slave ship arrived in what we know today as Puerto Rico. Africans were also brought to Spanish colonies as far north as what is now Georgia as early as 1526. By the time the first Africans arrived in Virginia, in fact, slave traders from Spain and Portugal had already shipped some 275,000 enslaved Africans to colonies across South America and the Caribbean. Their labors carved out vast and richly prosperous plantations across lands where local labor was scarce because disease and Spanish conquest had wiped out entire groups of indigenous peoples in the decades after Columbus arrived. Well before the first Africans journeyed up the James, slavery had become central to European settlement in the Western Hemisphere. "To establish slavery in Virginia it was not necessary to enslave anyone," wrote Yale University historian Edmund Morgan in his classic study *American Slavery, American Freedom*. "Virginians had only to buy men who were already enslaved."

Over the next three and a half centuries, some 12.4 million enslaved Africans—about as many people as today live in the African nation of Zimbabwe—were jammed into slave ships and sent across the Atlantic. It was the largest forced migration in human history, what the nineteenth-century abolitionist Martin Delany termed "the shameful traffic in the blood and bones of men, the destiny and chastity of women." Some 1.4 million of those died en route, including an estimated 100,000 who perished during the slave revolts that broke out on about one slave voyage in every ten. While there is no record of it, at least another million enslaved people are thought to have died in captivity on the ground in Africa, while being force-marched overland to coastal slave depots or held in crowded pens for weeks at a time awaiting their departure before ever boarding a slave vessel. Of the 10 million who survived African captivity and the open-sea voyage, somewhere between 500,000 and 600,000—about 5 or 6 percent—arrived in what would become known as the United States. The rest wound up across the Caribbean and South America. An estimated 3.2 million went to Brazil, 1.6 million to Cuba, 1.1 million to Jamaica, and 526,000 to Barbados, according to Emory University historian David Eltis.

Virginia, though, was not Latin America, and in 1619 at least, it had no tradition of slavery. Settlers had only begun to assemble the sprawling tracts of land that would later evolve into wealthy riverside plantations. The first Africans appear to have arrived in a world of ambiguous labor relations where they were sold into service somewhere at the murky confluence of slavery and indentured servitude. "Slavery was just one of many forms of labor. There was indentured servitude and debt servitude and a variety of other forms of coercion. Plus, there was wage labor and tenant farming," explained University of Maryland historian Ira Berlin, one of the country's leading scholars of American slavery. "Prior to the advent of the plantation system, they seem to have had a very, very open, porous kind of servitude. Lots of people of African descent were able to wriggle out of bondage," Berlin said in an interview. "These were very nebulous kinds of arrangements, which allowed people of African descent to integrate themselves into the society in a way that they were not going to be able to do [again] for another century or more." Initially, at least, Africans along the James typically found themselves toiling in the fields and lodging alongside English tenant farmers and servants.

Passage to Virginia cost a full year's pay for working Englishmen, few of whom had the means to save that kind of money. As many as two-thirds of all the English who came to Virginia during the 1600s agreed to serve as tenants or indentured servants, generally for a period of four to seven years or until they reached some specific age, in order to pay their way to the new colony or to acquire land there. "In a time of primitive capital markets, servitude was a primary means of financing migration for people unable to purchase passage," historians John McCusker and Russell Menard wrote in *The Economy of British America: 1607–1789.*

These English servants had rights under English and colonial law, though they hardly enjoyed the legal protections the wealthy landowners were accorded. Indentured servants could be sold, inherited, or passed along as part of an estate. Corporal punishment was the norm, administered arbitrarily with little if any public oversight. Servants shown to have committed a crime commonly had their period of servitude extended, a policy that placed some in a state of almost perpetual obligation one step removed from enslavement. Some, indeed, were forced to migrate even if they didn't want to, as was the case with one hundred orphans as young as twelve whom the Virginia Company essentially impounded in London and shipped off to the James River settlements to be farmed out as apprentice labor. "In Virginia under severe masters they may be brought to goodness," Sandys wrote in a 1620 letter to the mayor of London. In a reference to "one hundred children out of their superfluous multitude," Sandys asked permission "to transport these persons against their wills" to Virginia, knowing that, statistically, at least half would die within a year of their arrival.

A PETTICOAT AND LAMBSKIN GLOVES

Women, too, were needed, not only to do the work of gardening, dressing out game, cooking, and making and mending clothes, but also to help build English families. And in Virginia, English women were in short supply. In 1621, the Virginia Company struggled to find just twelve who would risk their lives and cast their fates to the capricious winds of marriage to the first settler willing to pay 120 pounds of tobacco for the privilege of taking a bride. "We send you in this ship one widow and eleven maids for wives for the people in Virginia," the company notified the colonists in a 1621 letter. "There are near fifty more which are shortly to come," the curious bridal notice continued, recognizing that the colony "can never flourish till families be planted and the respect of wives and children fix the people on the soil." Sometimes the wrong people fall in love, and "though we are desirous that marriage be free according to the law of nature," the company allowed, "yet would we not have these maids deceived and married to servants, but only to freemen or tenants as have means to maintain them." As a final proviso, the notice made clear that the so-called head-rights system, under which a settler got fifty acres of property for each servant whose passage he paid, did not apply to taking on a wife, who was expected to provide offspring in lieu of land.

As with the colony itself, the bid to ship women to Virginia to find husbands—a mission uncharitably referred to as the "fishing fleet" by some—was a corporate venture. Before they could become brides, the women were the subject of a joint stock offering. The Virginia Company was all but broke. To raise money to send women across the Atlantic, the company sold stock in what amounted to a colonial wife auction. A prospectus was issued, with the goal of delivering a hundred "young, handsome and honestly educated maids" to the English settlements along the James. The initial public offering was undersubscribed: it raised only enough to send about seventy women. Not altogether young Cupids at heart, forty-four investors staked a play on the bridal futures market. They could earn profits of 50 percent or more on the sale of the wives—though they had to up the price to one hundred fifty pounds of tobacco to do so— according to an article by David Ransome in the *William & Mary Quarterly*, a journal of colonial scholarship. The venture shipped out fifty-seven women to Virginia aboard three separate vessels. The youngest of the group, Jane Dyer, fifteen, tucked away a few personal treasures in a small wooden chest, along with the goods the company provided each prospective young bride: a new petticoat, lambskin gloves, two pairs each of stockings and shoes, a hat, two smocks, and an apron, as well as sheets and rugs.

Among the women who journeyed to Virginia were some who had fallen on hard times, often meaning they'd lost the husband or father they depended on to provide for them. Marie Daucks and Anne Richards, both twenty-five, were London widows. About one-sixth of the women were orphans, including Ellen Borne and Elizabeth Pearson, both nineteen. Some, like twenty-three-year-old Catherine Finche, whose brother was a London crossbow maker, had family support they could draw on but either chose not to or were compelled to strike out on their own. These women came from London, Suffolk, Essex, and Wales and places like Hampshire, Gloucestershire, Yorkshire, and Derby. They were daughters of farmers, shoemakers, and clothiers, and some, like twenty-one-year-old Sara Crosse, whose father was a baker, carried with them skills they'd learned through the family trade. Others, like Cicily Bray, twenty-five, had ties to the landed gentry. They were, in other words, a cross-section of middle-class England. Many came with written testimonials penned by well-to-do clergy or kin, attesting to the women's integrity, sobriety, and worth. By and large, they offered the men awaiting them in Virginia a chance to marry above their station. "Alongside criminals and waifs from the streets of London were women from a noticeably different level of society, daughters of the gentry or of artisans and tradesmen, who were recommended by the prosperous and well placed for their virtues and skills," Ransome wrote in his 1991 article.

With what heady mix of adventure, anticipation, and dread they sailed that year, and with what heroics they summoned the courage of spirit to prevail, we can only guess today. Few kept diaries; many couldn't read or write. Whatever their expectations, the women found grave hardship in Virginia. Within two years, most were dead, taken by Indian attack or disease. "For the maids," concluded Ransome, "it may have been better to travel hopefully than to arrive." Hopes sometimes brightened only to dim, at times upon confronting a would-be mate for life. Some of the women couldn't make up their minds, it seems, for love nor money. "To the great contempt of the majesty of God, and ill example to others, certain women within this colony have of late, contrary to the laws ecclesiastical of the realm of England, contracted themselves to two several men at one time," the general assembly pointed out, "whereby much trouble doth grow between parties."

In a 1624 statute, the assembly ordered that ministers advise their parishioners that any man or woman vowing marriage to more than one person at a time would be subject to a public whipping or some other punishment, "according to the quality of the person so offending." It was hardly an infallible formula for marital bliss, as Elizabeth Williams learned the hard way. An indentured servant to Stephen Gill, she fell under the spell of one William Chittwood, who proposed to her and gallantly bought her freedom as a sort of prenuptial gift. Once she became part of his household, however, the groom got cold feet, preferring, it seems, to keep her as a servant rather than take her as his wife. A woman wronged, Elizabeth took the caddish Chittwood before the general assembly. Acting in its capacity as Virginia's high court, the body found Chittwood in breach of his betrothal vows. "Chittwood hath dishonestly gone about to forsake the said maid," the court adjudged, giving him ten days to "consummate matrimony with the said Elizabeth Williams" or let her walk away unencumbered and unclaimed.

Yet, even in a community where white servants were bound to their overseers for years, indigent children were swept from the streets of London and forced to make their way in Virginia, and women could be had as wives for roughly their weight in tobacco, Africans quickly found themselves near the bottom rung on the social ladder. The lowliest English servant, for one thing, could at least speak the settlers' language. As the colonists couldn't speak Kimbundu, however, the Africans had to learn English. That meant they were regarded in the colony as functional illiterates, initially at least, struggling to make sense of their new predicament and to make themselves understood. Their past, however meritorious, held little meaning to those they worked for, who quickly dismissed their African heritage and even their names. Planters simply made up names for their African servants, when they used any name at all.

And, while white servants arrived with contracts and had come, for the most part, voluntarily, the Africans had no such agreements and no say in their fate. They would never have been in Virginia, after all, if they hadn't already been stolen twice: once from their homes in Africa by marauding raiders and colonial slave traders, then again by pirates on the high seas. "The black men and women brought to Virginia from 1619 to 1629 held from the outset a singularly debased status in the eyes of white Virginians," Columbia University historian Alden Vaughan wrote in the *William & Mary Quarterly*. "If not subjected to permanent and inheritable bondage, black Virginians were at least on their way to such a condition." The way was soon hastened by events beyond their control.

THINGS DIRTY AND EVIL

A thick-stemmed weed that grows as tall as a man, the tobacco plant has a voracious appetite for nitrogen, potash, and other nutrients. In five or six crop seasons, it depleted the soil, consuming the minerals the river left across the tidewater's broad alluvial plains and the organic compost of the ancient forests. Feeding the leafy beast set Virginia planters on an incessant quest for virgin ground to satisfy burgeoning British demand. The result was that they occupied and cleared more and more of the native Virginians' traditional hunting, foraging, and farming lands, even as they assumed control of irreplaceable frontage along the river, the spiritual waters the Powhatan people had relied on for millennia for food, transportation, and communications.

By the spring of 1622, the English had built some fifty large farms and dozens of smaller settlements along the banks of the James River, clearing and asserting control of a widening band of prime land reaching from the Chesapeake Bay to the falls near present-day Richmond. The Indians found themselves driven further from the river and deeper into the forests, fields, and outlying lands. Following Powhatan's death four years before, his people were led by Opechancanough, who watched the peace of Pocahontas disintegrate with the growing marginalization of the native tribes.

For the colonists' part, the official policy was accommodation, though on terms harshly prejudicial to Indian interests. The Virginia Company allotted ten thousand acres near the Henricus settlement for a college where the colonists hoped to indoctrinate native people in English customs and ways. George Thorpe, a former member of the British parliament, was assigned to oversee a hundred tenants tasked with clearing the land, building the school, and providing for students and staff.

Trade between the colonists and the Indians was lively, and many English seemed to believe they could live peaceably among the native people. "The houses generally sat open to the savages, who were always friendly entertained at the tables of the English and commonly lodged in their bed chambers," wrote Edward Waterhouse, a settler and Virginia Company shareholder.

Not all the colonists, however, believed they could live in harmony with the native people. As settlers replaced woods and meadows with tobacco fields, moreover, the colonists became dispersed and increasingly vulnerable, even as the native people saw the territory their distant ancestors had occupied for centuries taken over by the *tassantassas*.

In early March 1622, an Indian known for his courage and strength, and thought by his own people to be immortal, was believed to have murdered an Englishman who worked a medium-sized plot of land. In response, settlers killed the Indian, Nemattanow, affectionately called Jack of the Feather for his affinity for festive wilderness adornment. The death of the popular warrior was the final insult for Opechancanough, who concluded that peace with the greedy invaders was not possible. The trespassers occupied practically all of the great river, along banks north and south, and were incessantly pressing for more and more land. Meeting with his high priests, military advisers, and local *werowances*, Opechancanough hatched a plan meant to run the insatiable squatters out of *Tsenacomoco* for good.

Two weeks later, on the morning of March 22, 1622, the Christian Good Friday holiday, settlers up and down the river were visited by Indians, who bore gifts of game, conversed casually, and, in some cases, joined their English hosts at table. Suddenly, in a unified and convulsive strike, the Indians pounced. Grabbing table knives, English daggers, picks, and hoes, whatever they could get their hands on, they stabbed, bludgeoned, and otherwise slaughtered every white man, woman, and child they could overtake in a series of well-coordinated attacks. "They came unarmed into our houses, without bows or arrows, or other weapons, with deer, turkeys, fish, furs and other provisions to sell and truck with us for glass, beads and other trifles," wrote Waterhouse. "Yea, in some places, [they] sat down at breakfast with our people at their tables, whom immediately with their own tools and weapons either laid down or, standing in their houses, they basely and barbarously murdered, not sparing either age or sex, man, woman or child; so sudden in their cruel execution that few or none discerned the weapon or blow that brought them to destruction."

Jamestown itself was spared by a warning from an Indian servant. The attacks were devastating, however, at about one-third of the other plantations up and down the river. Within hours, the Indians had killed at least 347 settlers, more than one-fourth of all the colonists, in what the English quickly dubbed a massacre. Among the dead were several of the women who'd journeyed to Virginia just months before, including the teenage Jane Dyer and the widow Marie Daucks. Thorpe was killed and his body mutilated in a blood-curdling rebuke of his notions of an English college for the native people of *Tsenacomoco* and his vision of peaceful cohabitation on English terms.

With the voices of accommodation stilled by the slaughter, the English recalibrated, placing themselves on a war footing aimed at destroying or banishing the first Virginians from their native lands. "Our first work is expulsion of the savages," Virginia governor Francis Wyatt wrote in a letter to an unknown recipient. "Extirpating of the savages," he predicted, would take seven years. It would be time well spent, Wyatt asserted, "for it is infinitely better to have no heathen among us, who at best were but as thorns in our sides, than to be at peace and league with them." Guided by that policy, the colonists set about a series of missions, razing Indian villages, killing indigenous people, and destroying their crops, deliberately targeting the chief source of food for thousands of people utterly dependent upon the land for their survival.

A year after Opechancanough's attacks, the Indians extended a purported olive branch, sending word to Wyatt that they would hand over a few English prisoners and ink a peace accord if the governor would send an envoy to meet the great chief. Wyatt tapped as his ambassador a settler who had been made a captain, presumably because of his record in fighting the natives, a man named William Tucker. He was a general assembly burgess from the settlement on land the English had taken from the Kecoughtan near the mouth of the James. Along with a dozen other settlers, Tucker journeyed by boat downstream, around Point Comfort and up the York River, to one of its two mother streams, the Pamunkey, where the party was greeted at a large village by Opechancanough and others. After speeches and a probable smoking of pipes, Tucker proposed a proper English toast to commemorate the peace, ordering his men to roll out stocks of wine, while he tippled from a separate bottle. The spirits served to the Indians, though, had been laced with poison back in Jamestown. Opechancanough's people quickly fell ill or became drunk on what must have seemed to them to be, quite literally, firewater. It's not clear whether any were killed by the toxic wine, though there were reports at the time that two hundred died. As he left the village, Tucker ordered his men to open fire on the incapacitated natives, killing dozens and taking a number of scalps. Beyond defense or even retribution, English intimidation evolved into a strategy for acquiring ever more property for settlement and for the planting of more and more tobacco. Opechancanough had hoped his coordinated attacks would force the settlers to leave Virginia. Instead, they brought on war and policies that were increasingly oppressive to the native people and indulgent of the colonists who abused them.

Back in London, with word of Opechancanough's attack, the death knell was sounded for the beleaguered Virginia Company. Aging and near death, King James decided the work of building an empire was too important to be left to the shareholders. In standing by the colony through its darkest hours, they laid the cornerstone for English settlement in America, though few if any understood that at the time. In the king's mind, though, the colony's survival had come at too dear a cost. On June 26, 1624, the company was dissolved. James declared Virginia a royal colony, changing it from a private corporation sanctioned by the crown to a political appendage of England. After seventeen years of lost treasure and lives, the Virginia Company was pronounced a failure. Jamestown had become a quagmire. "The disaster had been more than the failure of a private venture," Lewis and Clark College historian Irene Hecht wrote in the *William & Mary Quarterly*. "It represented a national debacle as well, since the colonization of Virginia had drawn upon the energy, enthusiasm, money and people of all segments of English society."

Uncertain about the path ahead and unable, in the waning months of his life, to further advance the struggling colony's fate, James took stock of the situation. He ordered the settlers to conduct a head count, which they compiled in January and February of 1625 as the *Musters of the Inhabitants in Virginia*. The list, a sort of census, is published in *Adventurers of Purse and Person*, a genealogical reference on Virginia's oldest families.

Between 1607 and 1624, somewhere around seventy-two hundred people went from England to Virginia. By 1625, just one in six remained. A few had returned to England; most had died in Virginia. The muster named some 1,220 people among the living, of which 90 percent had been born in England or elsewhere in Europe. Most of the rest were born in the fledgling colony. There were two Native Americans living among the settlers, even after Opechancanough's uprising. Ages were recorded for just over half of the colonists. Based on that sampling, about 60 percent were under the age of twenty-five, though few were children. The census also listed twenty-three blacks, though surely others had come and either died or otherwise not been accounted for in the listing. In addition to the "20 and odd" that had arrived aboard the *White Lion* five years before, ten more had arrived later aboard the *Treasurer*. Almost certainly others had come, as Dutch and English vessels preyed upon Spanish and Portuguese slave ships for the better part of forty years following the piracy of 1619. English and Dutch maritime records suggest that some four thousand slaves were stolen on the high seas in that way. As many as six hundred of them may have been taken to Virginia over the four-decade period, by Thornton's rough estimate.

Compiled by the settlers themselves, the information included in the 1625 muster varied from one plantation to the next. Consistently, however, white settlers—servants and landowners alike—were listed with full names and ages. In most cases, the muster also included the specifics of when they had arrived and even the name of the ship that brought them from England to Virginia. With two exceptions—Africans whose names were listed as John Pedro and John Phillips—the blacks were noted either by first name only or by no name at all. In the muster, Abraham Piersey counted thirty-six servants, white and black, on his riverside settlement, one of the richest in the colony at that time. Full names, dates of arrival to the colony, the ship they traveled on, and, in most cases, ages were recorded for all twenty-nine of Piersey's white servants. The seven blacks, though, were listed without names, ages, or any description other than man, woman, or child. Writing his will in 1627, Gov. George Yeardley gave further indication of just how soon the settlers began to differentiate Virginians along lines of race, designating that to his heirs he would leave "good debts, chattles, servants, negars, cattle or any other thing."

The absence of names in the muster, the reference to blacks as "negars" by leaders like Yeardley and Rolfe, and the mention of them alongside livestock were not accidental slights, historians contend, but clear signs of the comparatively low regard the English planters had for blacks from the moment the first Africans arrived in Virginia. "Census takers had already marked off blacks as different twenty years before the courts in the 1640s recognized them as enslaved," Wake Forest University historian Anthony Parent wrote in his 2003 book, *Foul Means: The Formation of a Slave Society in Virginia, 1660–1740*. Dates of arrival and ages, moreover, were crucial bits of information for white servants bound for some period of years or until they reached a certain age. The lack of such information for black servants was an ominous sign. "At the most, the sequence of Yeardley's listing, in which Negroes come between servants and cattle, implies a status lower than servants, perhaps relegated to servitude for life, a crucial step on the path toward a system of permanent and inheritable slavery based primarily on color," wrote Vaughan. "Blacks, from the outset, suffered from a prejudice that relegated them to the lowest rank in the colony's society." At a time when the English were waging war against the Indians, the lumping of black people into a kind of subservant category suggests to some historians the origins of a rough-grained caste system, with people of color beginning to emerge as American untouchables. "In seizing Indian land and enslaving blacks, the great planters began to accentuate the racial differences between themselves and darker people," wrote Parent. "The English had a cultural predisposition to view blackness as symbolic of things dirty and evil. . . . They began associating light-skinned people with civilization and dark-skinned people with savageness."

Those sensibilities didn't originate in Virginia. English and other Europeans had long regarded Africans much the way they saw Native Americans:

as inferior beings, childlike yet dangerous and even devilish people beyond the reach and protection of Western law and Christian teachings. "They were accused of cannibalism, of having sex with animals and being more like apes than men and women," University of Cambridge historian Betty Wood wrote in *Slavery in Colonial America: 1619–1776*. "Since the English commonly associated the color black with sin, it was all too easy to arrive at the conclusion that God had decreed perpetual bondage as part of the Africans' punishment."

ANTONEY AND ISABELL

In Virginia, those attitudes toward race did not translate immediately into slavery. In time, though, such thinking helped to form the ideological foundation and moral justification for enslaving blacks. It didn't happen overnight; nor were all Africans who arrived in the colony treated the same. While most were bound in some capacity to the landowners who bought them, some may have worked as tenants, farming property in return for a share of the stakes. Others earned or bought their freedom after some period of labor, much as white indentured servants did, and some were married and started families.

The first such couple on record showed up on the 1625 muster at the plantation of none other than Capt. William Tucker, the Kecoughtan assemblyman and Pamunkey poisoner, who by then had built a substantial estate by the mouth of the James near Point Comfort. On his muster, Tucker listed himself and twenty other family members and servants as inhabiting a spread that included three houses and a log palisade for defense against any repeat of the 1622 attacks. It is the bottom line of Tucker's muster, though, that commands attention: "Antoney Negro: Isabell Negro: and William their Child Baptised." Those few words—the only surviving documentation of the first African American family on record in the English colonies that were to become the United States—hold keys to a complex world.

Anthony either adopted or was given his name, likely as the result of contact with Portuguese slavers or colonists. Not only did the Portuguese try to convert the people of present-day Angola into Christians, but they had biblical texts translated into Kimbundu and preached regularly to enslaved people before they boarded the slave ships to South America. Some were even baptized before the harsh Atlantic passage to inoculate their souls against the threat of eternal damnation.

If Anthony came from the royal capital of Kabasa, as Thornton suggests, he might well have been a man of high station and education, perhaps even privilege. His selection of Isabella as his bride suggests the same might well have been true of her. They appear to have seen merit in adopting Portuguese names, and they clearly understood that the English, like the Portuguese, like all people with the light skin of a candlestick, had a way of dividing the world into Christian and non-Christian folk. By seeing to it that their son was baptized, they may have been protecting him, not only from the eternal condemnation of the damned but from the more timely, if temporal, vagaries and vicissitudes of the Virginia labor system. "Most of the English believed you couldn't hold a Christian in lifetime servitude," said Thornton. Anthony and Isabella appear to have understood that.

So, perhaps, did an African couple residing at nearby Wariscoyack Plantation, owned by a London merchant and shipowner named Edward Bennett. The Wariscoyack muster listed "Antonio a Negro," who arrived in 1621, and "Mary a Negro Woman," who arrived the following year. Antonio went by the name of Anthony. He married the only African woman on the property, Mary, and, over some period of years, the couple earned or bought their freedom from Bennett. There's no record of how that happened, but a closer look at Bennett and his dealings with other servants gives some hints.

Bennett stood out early on by listing in his muster the dates that Anthony and Mary arrived in Virginia, even including the names of the ships they arrived aboard. A man of education and status, Bennett had served as deputy governor of English merchants in the Netherlands and also as an elder in a Pilgrim church in Amsterdam before becoming involved in the Virginia settlement. His experience there began with disaster. Before coming to Virginia himself, Bennett arranged passage for 120 immigrants, who arrived at his property a month before Opechancanough's uprising. The attacks killed fifty of Bennett's company, which comprised one-seventh of all the fatalities from the strikes.

Among the handful of Bennett's servants who survived were Anthony and a white man named Wassell Webling. Both arrived in Virginia aboard a ship named the *James*. The son of a London brewer, Webling was contracted to serve Bennett for three years, general assembly records show. Webling agreed to provide "true and faithful service in all such labors and business as the said Edward Bennett or his assignees shall employ me in" in exchange for passage to Virginia and room and board. At the end of his service, Webling was to receive fifty acres from Bennett and to pay fifty shillings and two days of work per year in rent, a sign that Bennett valued loyalty enough to ensure that he and his former servants remained in close touch. While no similar contract between Bennett and Anthony has surfaced, it's possible Bennett took a similar approach with his black servants, perhaps even feeling a special sense of duty to those who had lived through the 1622 attacks. That's the most plausible explanation, at least, for how Anthony and Mary acquired land at a new settlement on Virginia's eastern shore, across the Chesapeake Bay from Wariscoyack.

There, they took on the English surname Johnson and just as quickly adopted what was becoming the accepted route to financial security in seventeenth-century Virginia. In 1651, Johnson bought five servants of his own—some, perhaps all, were Africans—receiving two hundred fifty acres in head rights for them. The following year, Anthony Johnson successfully appealed to the local court for tax relief after fire destroyed much of his property, demonstrating that, at that time at least, free blacks had access to the legal system. At least two of his sons became landowners as well, part of at least thirteen free African households known to have existed on Virginia's Eastern Shore, the first such African American community in English North America. Within a few years of arriving in America as a servant, Anthony Johnson made himself into the wealthiest black man anywhere in mid-seventeenth-century Virginia and one of the most prosperous landowners, black or white, anywhere on the eastern shore. He also went down in history as the first African, though by no means the last, known to have become a slaveholder in what would become the United States.

Even so, Anthony Johnson was an exception to the broader rule for Africans in colonial Virginia, where an aristocracy was beginning to emerge of first-generation English immigrants, who began to game the fledgling economic, political, and legal system in British America to their advantage. Early on, that process began to draw distinctions between black people and everyone else, the first steps toward putting in place a set of laws and court rulings that gradually sanctioned, and ultimately codified, the lifelong enslavement of Africans and their descendants. In 1639, the Virginia General Assembly ordered that "all persons except negroes" were to keep arms and ammunition for the defense of the colony or face a fine. The distinction was important. By excluding blacks from militia service, the burgesses were, in effect, denying them the right to bear arms. A full ban would eventually follow. The ability to impose order at the barrel of a gun, in other words, would belong to "all persons except negroes." The provision did more than simply grant white settlers a monopoly on firepower, as important as that was to become. It also reduced blacks to second-class status in a society where defense was essential. It denoted them as inferiors who were not expected, were not entitled, were seen as somehow not able, to help defend the colony. Excluding blacks from military service, a fundamental duty prerequisite to full citizenship, was an early step toward the complete disenfranchisement of blacks that would echo for centuries to come.

The next year, a black servant named John Punch ran away from his master with two white servants, a Scotchman named James Gregory and another man named Victor, who was Dutch. Learning that the three had taken up in Maryland, their owner, Hugh Gwyn, asked the general assembly, sitting in its capacity as Virginia's high court, for permission to sell all three in the neighboring colony and be done with it. The court, though, saw in that proposition a dangerous precedent and ordered the three returned instead. When they got back to Jamestown, all three men were given thirty lashes for running away. The white servants were further punished by the addition of time to their period of indentured servitude. Punch, though, was sentenced to service for life. As early as 1640, in other words, a Virginia court sanctioned lifetime servitude for a black man, when it declined to do so for white servants in identical straits.

Four months later, not coincidentally, the general assembly took note of the "diverse servants that run away from their masters," causing "much loss and prejudice" against the landowners. Burgesses voted to empower local sheriffs to "hire boats and hands to pursue said runaways," with the costs to be borne by county taxpayers. Capturing fugitive slaves and returning them to their private owners became with that act a public obligation. The following year, Massachusetts became the first English colony in America to recognize formally the enslavement of blacks in its laws. It would take time, though, before Virginia's black population reached a level warranting comparable attention from its general assembly, which continued to be preoccupied largely by commerce and Indian relations.

In 1644, Opechancanough, then approaching one hundred years of age, staged a last stand along the banks of the James, essentially launching a repeat of the uprising he'd ordered twenty-two years before. This time, the Indians killed almost five hundred settlers. While catastrophic, the fatalities didn't threaten the colony's survival. After two decades, in which about one thousand new English settlers had arrived along the banks of the James each year, the population of British Virginia had grown to nearly ten thousand. Virginia's native people had been overwhelmed by English invaders.

Two years later, the English captured Opechancanough and jailed him at Jamestown. There, a settler mortally wounded the defenseless captive, killing the last great chief of *Tsenacomoco*. His people had little means to retaliate, and his successor, Necotowance, sought peace. The general assembly set aside land near the falls of the James as a prelude to the first formal Indian reservations. The Indians, who had called the region home for centuries, found themselves marginalized. They were reduced to trading and negotiating from an increasingly weak hand with the English. And they were coping with imported ills they were not accustomed to—alcohol, for instance, and alien disease—while they struggled to adapt to the settlers' economy and laws without losing forever their ancient culture, traditions, and way of life.

Some writers have laid the blame for the decline on Opechancanough, citing his failure to find a middle ground with the colonists. Others credit him with doing the best anyone in his position could have done to seek compromise and preserve the Powhatan chiefdom in the face of a relentless onslaught from a foreign invader that pressed intensive farming on large plantations to try to make the colonial experiment in Virginia succeed. "They could not have coexisted," said the Powhatan scholar Helen Rountree. "Both sides used the land entirely differently and were not able to cooperate for space." She paused, then abridged her conclusion. "If the Europeans had stayed home they could have coexisted. But the Europeans would not budge, and they also had too big a population to go back to a time when they were gentler on the land."

IF ANY SHOULD CHANCE TO DIE

By 1650, there were some fifteen thousand English settlers in Virginia, where they outnumbered the native people, though it isn't clear by how much. There were perhaps three hundred Africans in Virginia, a number that tripled over the next ten years. In England, birthrates were slowing, wages were rising, and an economy increasingly linked to global trade had begun to surge. Improving prospects back home made it harder for Virginia landowners to find people willing to sign on for indentured servitude so far from the motherland. And, in Virginia, opportunities for upward mobility meant that former indentured servants were becoming landowners who needed servants themselves, at the very time English merchants were dramatically expanding their presence in the transatlantic slave trade.

Until the middle of the seventeenth century, the business of buying stolen people along the west coast of Africa and transporting them for sale in America was dominated by the Portuguese. Between 1600 and 1650, they shipped an estimated 444,000 enslaved people out of Africa, according to Eltis, the Emory University historian. Eyeing markups of 1,000 percent and more on the sale of each enslaved African, first the Dutch and then the English began to challenge Portuguese control of the commerce in coerced labor. Between 1650 and 1700, the British ascended to dominance, shipping 360,000 Africans to English colonies in the Caribbean, with comparatively few winding up along the North American coast, from present-day Savannah to New England.

Against the shifting mosaic of the transatlantic slave trade, the Virginia General Assembly began to grapple in earnest with the legal and moral dilemmas posed when Christian people became slave owners in a colony that promised democracy and a shot at prosperity for some, while imposing oppression and enslavement upon others. In 1661, Virginia became the third English colony—following Massachusetts in 1641 and Connecticut in 1650—to establish slavery as a legal institution. Over the next decade, the Virginia General Assembly—the same body that spawned democracy in America with its calls in 1619 for "equal favor . . . like liberties . . . and uniformity and equality of laws"—began to tighten the statutory noose around black people, inch by legislative inch.

In 1662, in a departure from legal tradition, the assembly declared that children inherited their mother's status, not their father's as English law decreed. "Whereas some doubts have arisen whether children got by any Englishman upon a negro woman should be slave or free, be it therefore enacted and declared by this present grand assembly that all children born in this country shall be held bond or free only according to the condition of the mother," the assembly decided. That meant a white man could then have sex, consensual or otherwise, with a black slave without fear of having to support any offspring, which could, instead, be put to work or sold.

Still, interracial intimacy was frowned upon, at least in theory. "If any Christian shall commit fornication with a negro man or woman," the statute continued, "he or she so offending shall pay double the fines imposed by the former act." That provision fell hardest on blacks, who took the brunt of the punishment for such relationships when they became known. In October 1640, the court in Jamestown found that a white settler named Robert Sweat "hath begotten with child a negro woman servant." His punishment was to "do public penance" during church services the next day in Jamestown, customarily a matter of donning a white robe, standing before the congregation, and publicly confessing a sin. "The said negro woman," the court ordered, "shall be whipped at the whipping post."

That decision contrasted sharply with one made by the same court just a few months earlier, when William Beard's white servant, Thomas Bates, was found by the court to "have used the company of the said Beard's wife in the night scandalously and unlawfully," though evidently not against her will. "Bates shall at two of the clock in the afternoon, at the most public place in James City [Jamestown] receive 30 stripes at the whipping post," the court ordered; the lashing was to take place that very day. Not blaming Bates alone, Beard charged his wife with leading a "lewd and idle life." Beard's spouse, however, was spared punishment, the court "having intelligence that his wife is great with child and therefore not without danger to receive corporal punishment." The same "intelligence" was deemed no cause for mercy for Sweat's black paramour. Nor was it a whipping offense for a white man to have illicit sex with a black servant, as it was for a white man who did so with a woman of his own race, however "lewd and idle" that woman might be.

In 1667, the general assembly was presented with another thorny question. White planters wanted to be able to preach the Gospel to their slaves without having to worry that their conversion to Christianity might lead to freedom. The lawmakers willingly obliged, agreeing that "the conferring of baptism doth not alter the condition of the person as to his bondage or freedom." Christian converts could then be held as slaves, the assembly decreed, so long as they were black, a provision that cleared the way for plantation evangelism leading to "the propagation of Christianity by permitting children, though slaves, or those of greater growth, if capable, to be admitted to that sacrament." White Virginians, in other words, might copulate with black slaves one day and convert them the next, while enjoying at least some statutory protections from the potentially unwelcome consequences of either pursuit.

The next year, the burgesses went further still, making it lawful for slave owners to beat their servants for trying to run away. For decades, a servant who tried to escape had been punished by having the letter "R," for runaway, burned into his or her cheek with a scalding iron. And since planters could further chasten runaways by prolonging their period of indentured servitude, the assembly reasoned that "moderate corporate punishment" was perfectly acceptable as well.

Some constituents, however, were clearly not satisfied. And so, in 1669, the assembly passed a law that explicitly allowed a slave owner to beat a slave to death. "The obstinacy of many of them," the assembly wrote, meant the slaves couldn't be "suppressed by other than violent means." And so, "if by the extremity of the correction" a slave "should chance to die," the slave owner would automatically "be acquitted from molestation." Surely no planter would deliberately kill a slave, the legislators agreed, because to do so would be "to destroy his own estate."

The following year, the burgesses made it illegal for blacks who came to Virginia as Christians to be held in lifetime slavery. Struggling to reconcile the widening gap between their religious beliefs and the race-based slave society they were building, the burgesses drew a distinction between blacks who arrived as true believers and those who might embrace Christianity on Virginia soil simply as a way to escape a lifetime under the planter's lash.

As slavery became institutionalized, its victims chafed at the yoke of the law. Fears of revolt began to stalk the landowners who had come to dominate the general assembly and the growing number of administrative posts the legislators controlled. In 1670, with some two thousand blacks making up 5 percent of the colony's population of some forty thousand, the general assembly prohibited blacks from owning firearms or other weapons. At the same time, concerned that the rapid strides in coercive labor might somehow backfire, the assembly passed laws prohibiting blacks from owning white servants. By 1670, the flexibility of indentured servitude for blacks had begun to give way to the harsh rigidity of slavery in Virginia.

A similar evolution was taking place elsewhere across the British colonies, in North America as well as in the Caribbean. Merchants in the port cities of London, Liverpool, and Bristol took note. In 1672, the Royal Africa Company was founded to trade in African gold and ivory and to supply slaves to British colonies in America and the Caribbean. Over the next fifty years, British slavers shipped some 620,000 Africans across the Atlantic, part of the 3 million slaves British vessels would transport before the transatlantic slave trade ended two centuries later, according to Eltis, the Emory University slavery expert. Along with his colleagues, Eltis has compiled his findings from actual maritime records for nearly thirty-five thousand slave voyages. He estimates those records represent 82 percent of all the transatlantic slave voyages undertaken between 1501 and 1867. His findings are to be published in a forthcoming book by the Cambridge University Press.

A LITTLE COLONY IN ITSELF

Virginia's transformation into a slave society was both feeding, and being fed by, the rise of a group of political and economic elites, forerunners of the wealthy planters who would amass enormous riverside spreads built and supported by legions of enslaved blacks who, by 1670, were raising enough tobacco to fill eighty ships a year. Early Virginia colonists had arrived from England with a wide variety of backgrounds. Some were well connected but not poised for greatness back home, as was often the case for second or third children in families where wealth was customarily passed down to the first-born son. Others brought a skill or trade, perhaps carpentry, blacksmithing, or animal husbandry. Still others came from poor or middling stations that promised little hope for success. All of them could thrive in Virginia if they could endure the hardships and survive the perils awaiting them in its riverside lands. It was a place, at least for a time, where a settler's past might be readily overcome, where talents and skills could be quickly leveraged. A servant like Anthony Johnson could acquire land of his own. A merchant like Abraham Piersey could become a king, lording over a vast settlement with dozens of servants at his command. And some could be elected by their peers as burgesses to the general assembly, where they could cement their status and extend their influence through political patronage and the crafting of laws. Opportunity seemed to swell without limit, absent the Old World barriers the settlers had left behind. "Those were the halcyon days of democracy in Virginia," historian Daniel Boorstin wrote in *The Americans: The Colonial Experience.* "But they did not last long."

By the mid-1670s, a new aristocracy was taking hold in Virginia, especially along the coveted James River waterfront reaches that wedded fertile farmland to a ready stream of ship-laden commerce and communications linking the Old World to the new. Over the next decade alone, a dozen well-placed planters secured royal patents to tracts ranging in size from ten thousand to fifty thousand acres. The rich got richer, moreover, often through insider schemes that manipulated, or outright defrauded, the systems of head rights, taxation, customs duties, and land use in the young English foothold in America. Large landowners were increasingly named to the Council of State or elected as burgesses, positions they used to place themselves and their peers in jobs such as justice of the peace, tax assessor, official surveyor, clerk of the court, or customs collector. Most general assembly members also sat as justices on local courts. They then used their ties to these posts to further their holdings. "The emerging elite secured hundreds of thousands of acres by using their official posts to bend the rules," wrote Parent, the Wake Forest historian. "False claims and malfeasance combined to form an enormity of abuse. Boundaries were exaggerated; false certificates were submitted; office clerks were bribed."

By turning the institutions of legislation and administration to their exclusive advantage, the dominant landowners made it harder and harder for the poor to emerge from indentured servitude and gain a grubstake for themselves. Increasingly, affordable plots they could get their hands on were deeper in the wilderness and in areas prone to isolated Indian attacks. For a growing number of those who had risked all they had to seek opportunity and hope in the new colony, the rise of an overbearing cadre of wealthy landowners made Virginia look disappointingly like the rigid, class-based society they'd left behind in England. "If the plantation was a little colony in itself . . . the colony of Virginia was in turn ruled like a large plantation," wrote Boorstin, noting that the general assembly itself had been reduced to "hardly more than the political workshop of a ruling aristocracy."

Boorstin, it turns out, wasn't the first to notice the rapacious nature of the early plantation owners and the corrosive influence they had on democracy in Virginia. The first whiff of trouble came in September 1663, when authorities were warned that nine servants along the York River, not far from Powhatan's old headquarters at *Werowocomoco*, were plotting an armed overthrow of the government in Jamestown. Though the planned insurrection was headed off, several instigators were hanged, and a servant named Birkenhead was awarded with his freedom and several hundred British pounds sterling, a veritable fortune in colonial Virginia, for revealing the plot. Decades later, Virginians still commemorated Birkenhead Day. It was designated a colonial holiday by the general assembly, recalling the "mutinous villains" who were poised to bring "inevitable ruin" to the colony "had not God in his infinite mercy prevented it." Little is recorded of the would-be insurgents. Seven years later, though, the general assembly in Virginia said the plot was the work of the most "dangerous and scandalous" among them: English convicts released from prison and sent to Virginia.

TO VIRGINIA OR BE HANGED

While most of the convicts sent to America arrived in the eighteenth century, the practice began on a small scale in 1615, when King James judged that some felons might better be sent to America than to the gallows. That way, he explained in a January 24 decree, they "may live and yield a profitable service" to the fledgling British Empire. Death was a common and frequent sentence in seventeenth-century England, where some three hundred separate felonies were punishable by hanging. At a time when the crown was struggling to find settlers willing to risk life and limb in the unknown wilds of Virginia and the Caribbean, it seemed a waste, said the king, to condemn to the noose those "who for strength of body or other ability shall be thought fit to be employed in foreign discoveries or other services beyond the seas." So, he authorized judges to mete out clemency, of a sort, to criminals convicted of anything short of "willful murder, rape, witchcraft or burglary." Two days later, on January 26, seventeen convicts were released for transportation to America. Most, if not all, are thought to have come to Virginia, the first of several dozen over the ensuing decades to be told, in effect, go to Virginia or be hanged.

While no complete records have been found of the early shipments of criminals, the practice had caused political outrage in Virginia by 1670. Meeting that April, the general assembly warned that the colony was "too much hazarded and endangered by the great number of felons" who escaped the public hangings each Monday at London's infamous Newgate prison by boarding ships bound for Virginia instead. The assembly passed a law meant to stop it. Beginning the following January, the statute ordered, "It shall not be permitted to any person trading hither to bring in and land any jail bird or such others who, for notorious offenses, have deserved to die in England."

Virginia's landowners were facing trouble enough with their own riffraff, it seems, without being burdened by the rabble of London. None was to become more troublesome than Nathaniel Bacon, who left behind his own frothy wake when he journeyed from England to come to Virginia. Son of the English gentry, Bacon disgraced his family by trying to cheat a neighbor out of his inheritance. Bacon's father-in-law despised him, writing his daughter Elizabeth Duke out of the family will as her punishment for marrying Bacon. Thus discredited, his future prospects bleak, Bacon journeyed to Virginia. There he used his father's contacts and money to buy a large spread covering a neck of land at a sharp river loop named the Curles, just downstream from present-day Richmond. There, Bacon quickly became the archnemesis of the most powerful man in Virginia, the haughty and sometimes arrogant Gov. William Berkeley.

The fifth of seven children, Berkeley was born in 1605 to a wealthy English landowner who served in Parliament and was a shareholder in the Virginia Company. After graduating from Oxford and studying law, Berkeley used his family's close connections to King Charles to secure a string of diplomatic postings and other perks of high station, including a royal monopoly on the sale of ice. A skilled writer with a cutting wit, Berkeley penned a number of plays, the most famous of which, *The Lost Lady*, was performed for the king's court. After he helped Charles fight Scottish Presbyterians in the so-called Bishops Wars, a grateful king dubbed Berkeley a knight. In 1641, Berkeley received the appointment of a lifetime; King Charles named him governor and captain general of Virginia, where he arrived the next year.

One of the most pivotal figures in the history of colonial America, Berkeley served for twenty-seven years, over two separate terms, as Virginia's governor, longer than any other chief executive in the state's history. Three and a half centuries after his death, his legacy remains occluded by a fog of controversy. Some historians have cast Berkeley as an indispensable statesman who nurtured the growth of democracy in America through perilous times, strategically employing his familiarity with the English crown to defend the fledgling colony against the authoritarian instincts of King Charles. His meticulous biographer, Warren Billings, credits Berkeley with bringing the first bicameral legislature to America. It was at Berkeley's urging that elected burgesses began sitting in their own house in the general assembly in 1643. In the new House of Burgesses, the people's delegates could speak as a separate body, independently of the royal governor and his appointed Council of State, maintaining a relationship to those men of power much like the British parliament's to the English king. "Division also enabled the members to acquire more of the habits of a representative legislature," Billings wrote in *A Little Parliament*.

Others contend that Berkeley broke the great promise of New World colonization by presiding over aristocratic and royalist rule that made a mockery of individual enterprise and class equity along the monarchy's American frontier. On balance, he seems to have walked a middle line that drifted from one interpretation to the other, reflecting, perhaps precisely, the opposing forces at the heart of the seventeenth-century Virginian enterprise.

Whatever history's verdict, Bacon and many others in Virginia considered Berkeley a royal pain. The feeling was more than mutual. Apart from a hundred "good families," the colony was made up chiefly of "those of the meanest quality and corruptest lives," Berkeley wrote to the king's court in *A Discourse and View of Virginia* in 1662. Berkeley was drawing on his experience over twenty years as Virginia's governor when he concluded that "never any community of people had good done to them but against their wills."

However distant he found himself from the common will, Berkeley was a political survivor. He arrived in Virginia amid promising, but difficult, times. The Indian attacks that killed five hundred settlers took place two years after he assumed office as governor. He got past that disaster, in part, by building close alliances with the emerging planter class, the one hundred families he held in esteem, and becoming a staunch advocate for them in communiques with the royal court. Others in the colony, though, never forgot the hundreds more killed by Indians on Berkeley's watch. Lingering suspicions that he was inept at defending the colony would dog him for the rest of his career.

Adroit at personality politics and doubtless familiar with the anti-smoking rant drafted by Charles' father, Berkeley displayed his gift for diplomacy in his treatment of that subject. "The vicious, ruinous plant of tobacco I would not name," he wrote in his *Discourse*, "but that it brings more money to the crown than all the islands in America besides." Berkeley rightly perceived that Virginia's near total reliance on tobacco production consigned the colony to the status of a developing nation, unable to produce much of anything it needed and completely at the mercy of a market controlled by England. On his own James River plantation, Green Spring, he experimented with an array of products that would have done Richard Hakluyt proud, raising corn, hemp, and flax and producing glass, bricks, and pottery. Over crystal glasses of his Virginia wine, Berkeley would urge his fellow planters to diversify as well, a message most found less appealing to their ear than were his spirits to their palate.

Berkeley was also a strategic thinker of extraordinary vision, as when he held forth in his *Discourse* on the potential Virginia and the other American colonies presented for the growth of a British Empire. "Our numbers there are now at least two hundred thousand English," Berkeley wrote, "and if (as in human probability they will), our numbers double but every 20 years, in one age more how great will our power, strength and reputation be in this new Western World?"

For all his gifts, Berkeley could be difficult, even prickly. He once admonished the colonial clergy to "pray more and preach less." And while his general assembly backers vouched that he "always had an ear open to the complaint of the meanest or poorest man or woman," that may have been a cynical word play on his failing hearing. In truth, Berkeley was more closely attuned to the interests of the several dozen large landowners who dominated Virginia's political and economic life than to the tens of thousands of small farmers, trappers, tenants, artisans, servants, and slaves who did the essential work of building the colony. Over time, he lost their faith. And, whatever else might be debated, Berkeley was no democrat, at least not in the way future Virginia leaders would define the term. "I thank God there are no free schools nor printing" in Virginia, Berkeley reported to a royal commission in 1670, explaining that educated people were hard to control and a free press exposed government to critics. "God keep us from both!"

Authoritarian accents, though, couldn't keep Berkeley's Virginia clear of global and colonial events that wrought turmoil on Virginians during his long tenure. Beginning the year Berkeley arrived in Virginia, England underwent a decade of civil war. King Charles, who had dissolved Parliament in 1629, was forced eleven years later to recall the body. He needed Parliament's help to restore his damaged legitimacy and, among other things, persuade his subjects to pay their taxes. It was not, though, a happy partnership. By 1642, armed conflict broke out between the king and parliamentary rebels led by Oliver Cromwell and his English Puritans. With his forces outmaneuvered, Charles was sent before a parliamentary court and sentenced to death. He was beheaded at Whitehall Palace in 1649, his son, Charles II, was sent into exile in Europe, and Berkeley was left bereft of his patron back in London.

Cromwell's Commonwealth government in England passed the so-called Navigation Acts, requiring Virginians to trade only with England. The prohibition was meant to thwart Dutch traders, but it also hurt Virginians, making them reliant on a closed market for both the export of their tobacco, driving down prices for their leading cash crop, and the purchase of textiles, spirits, farm implements, and other manufactured goods. "We cannot but resent that forty thousand people should be impoverished to enrich little more than 40 merchants who, being the only buyers of our tobacco, give us what they please for it," Berkeley protested. "Indeed," he went on, those merchants "have forty thousand servants in us, and at cheaper rates than any other men have slaves."

Loyal to the memory of Charles and hoping for his son's eventual return from exile, Berkeley and the general assembly he led rejected Cromwell's Commonwealth and its peculiar—to royalists like Berkeley—suggestion that sovereignty resided with the people, who were, under God, the source of legitimate power. Virginia became a remote holdout from Cromwell's new world order, the fourth dominion of the exiled crown, which continued to claim title to England, Scotland, Ireland, and Virginia. Hoping to put a stop to this resistance, Cromwell's forces sailed up the James in 1652, demanding that Berkeley surrender the colony and his governorship. It was the first time British troops imposed London's will on the rebellious American colony; it wouldn't be the last. Berkeley made a show of arms but relented in the face of superior force. He later explained that he had the firepower to wage battles sufficient to destroy Virginia but not to save it. He surrendered to Cromwell's forces and stepped down after negotiating the retention of his riverside plantation, Green Spring, five miles upstream from Jamestown, where he went into retirement.

After Cromwell died in 1658, his son Richard briefly assumed his post as lord protector but was unable to preserve power. Under pressure from loyal monarchists, he abdicated the next year. When Charles II was restored to the throne in 1660, Berkeley was reinstated as Virginia's governor.

Elected to the position by the general assembly and later recommissioned as governor and captain general by Charles II, Berkeley came out of England's civil war with his hand strengthened, able to claim the support of both the king in London and the burgesses in Virginia. He would soon need all the help he could get.

Dutch traders had established their own American colony in 1624, in a place they called New Amsterdam, known today as Manhattan. The Dutch had maintained close links to Virginia as well, trading in tobacco, slaves, and furs. Berkeley complained, in fact, that by 1662 the Dutch were buying two hundred thousand beaver skins a year from Virginia Indians. In exchange, railed Berkeley, the Dutch "supply our enemies with ammunition and guns in greater proportion than we have them ourselves." The Navigation Acts, designed largely to cut off such trade, did not wear well in the Netherlands. Between 1652 and 1674, the English fought three wars against the Dutch, seizing New Amsterdam by force in 1664 and changing the colony's name to New York.

Worried that Anglo-Dutch hostilities would hit home, Berkeley appealed to London for arms and ammunition to defend the colony from Dutch raiders, but he received little more than an aging British frigate. It arrived at the mouth of the James without so much as a mast. The castoff British vessel did little to deter a fleet of Dutch fighters that sailed up the river in 1667, found the poorly defended colonial tobacco fleet lying at anchor, and burned twenty ships to the waterline. Six years later, nine Dutch warships sailed into the bay expecting to reprise that victory. With only two British warships to harry the Dutch, Berkeley ordered merchant vessels armed and posted troops aboard tobacco ships. The Dutch still managed to destroy six tobacco ships, and four other English ships were lost in battle. Given the extent to which the English were outgunned, those losses might have been seen as a win of sorts for the Virginians. Berkeley nevertheless drew sharp criticism for failing to defend the colony from attack. Eventually, however, neither Cromwell's army nor Dutch warships presented a mortal threat to Berkeley's government. That would come from an opponent even closer to home.

BY CONSENT OF THE PEOPLE

Bacon arrived in Virginia well positioned to take his place among the landed gentry. His checkered past in London meant little in the colonial wilderness. He was Cambridge educated and a graduate of the prestigious law school at Gray's Inn. He had a cousin who was a member of the Council of State. Bacon was even, for that matter, a cousin, by marriage, to Berkeley.

In 1675, the year after Bacon purchased a working farm at a sharply winding bend in the river called the Curles—later named Curles Neck—Berkeley welcomed his distant kin by naming him to the council. The move assured Bacon's status as a young leader on the rise in a colony whose governor was more than seventy years old. At twenty-eight, Bacon would have looked to any observer at the time like the promising protégé of Virginia's grand old man, a political heir-apparent touched by good fortune and waiting in the wings for his powerful mentor's inevitable decline.

That same year, one of the worst Anglo-Indian wars on record broke out in Massachusetts between English colonists and the Wampanoag Indians. Their chief was a man named Metacom; the English called him King Philip. As the foreign settlers pressed further inland and deeper into his people's territory, the chief struck back in the hope of stemming the foreign invasion. Like the Virginia Indians, the Wampanoag had built up substantial arsenals through decades of heavy trade in beaver and otter pelts. In a year of fighting that ended in the summer of 1676, some twenty-five hundred colonists and five thousand Indians were killed in what came to be known as King Philip's War.

The New England bloodshed was mirrored in violence further south. On the frontiers of the Virginia settlement, English plantations, hamlets, and small farms came under hit-and-run attacks by Indians, some of whom weren't native to Virginia but had drifted down from the north. Men, women, and children were killed. Some were hauled off and tortured to death. Colonists across Virginia were terrified. By the spring of 1676, the attacks had killed an estimated five hundred colonists in Virginia, as many as died in the massacre of 1644. Among them was one of Bacon's overseers. Amid mounting frustration with the aristocracy and a lack of confidence in Berkeley as commander in chief, the new generation of Indian conflict ignited social unrest among the disillusioned working class in Virginia.

Berkeley cobbled together a militia but did little to confront the Indians. Critics charged that he was treading lightly to preserve the interests he and his cronies had in the domestic fur trade. Perhaps this was so. After three decades in Virginia, though, Berkeley also understood the complex and precarious web of relationships that had developed between English settlers and native people in the decades since Opechancanough's last stand. Many of the Indians cooperated with the colonists and were regarded as essential allies. Not only were mass undifferentiated assaults immoral, Berkeley felt, but they could be counterproductive, turning friends into foes and risking all-out war. Berkeley preferred to handle matters in a more nuanced way.

Whether careful diplomacy could have kept the peace will never be known. In May 1676, defying Berkeley's calls for moderation, Bacon led a group of volunteer vigilantes on a series of raids against far-flung Indian villages. Scores of native people were killed. Bacon, who'd been in Virginia just two years, didn't trouble to distinguish between those Indians who had actually carried out the winter attacks and those who had had nothing to do with them. While the attacks may have seemed like justice to Bacon and his men, they looked to others, Indians and many English as well, like an undisciplined rampage that had more than a whiff of naked aggression meant to run indigenous people out of their homes for the benefit of Bacon's land-starved followers.

Berkeley was outraged that Bacon would blatantly disobey his orders and take leadership of an independent militia. That was dangerous, Berkeley understood, and it was treason. Berkeley pronounced Bacon a rebel, suspended him from the Council of State, dissolved the House of Burgesses, and called for new elections, the first in fifteen years.

Berkeley's critics frequently raise the long gap between elections as evidence of his disdain for democracy. For ten years of that period, though, Berkeley was out of office and had no authority to call elections. Berkeley seems to have been perfectly comfortable with collective decision making, in fact, so long as he was comfortable with the collection of decision makers. The outcome of the spring elections of 1676, though, would give him little comfort. There was no political party system in place at the time, but the election results amounted to an opposition victory.

Among the winners was Bacon, who was elected as a burgess from Henrico County. It was a stunning repudiation of royal authority and a humiliating public rebuke of Berkeley, who had stripped Bacon of his council post and branded him a traitor just weeks before. Being elected to Berkeley's little parliament was one thing: taking a seat on it was another. When Bacon showed up for the general assembly meeting in Jamestown in early June, Berkeley had him arrested on charges of mutiny, a hanging offense.

After a few days spent contemplating his fate within the musty confines of the Jamestown jail, Bacon wrote out a confession, promising never again to challenge the royal governor's authority. He appeared before the assembly on bended knee begging for clemency. Hoping to end the matter without overplaying his weakened hand, Berkeley pardoned Bacon and restored him to the assembly, where the recovering rebel was able to make common cause with a handful of other freshman delegates either aligned with him or sympathetic to his concerns. Among the raft of laws Bacon helped push through the assembly that month were two that raise troubling questions about his reasons for waging war on the Indians. One empowered the settlers to hold Indians captured in war as slaves for life. The other allowed colonists to lay claim to land vacated by the Indians, even if the natives had been run off of it.

Beyond promoting the enslavement of the Indians and forced dispossession of their lands, Bacon tapped into a rich vein of discontent among Virginia's struggling class. After the assembly adjourned toward the end of June, hundreds of small stakeholders, indebted sharecroppers, former servants, and black slaves rallied around Bacon, calling for armed insurrection. Casting aside his jailhouse conversion and casting his lot with the armed masses, Bacon agreed to lead them in what amounted to all-out revolt. That decision locked him in a blood duel with Berkeley over control of the colony. It plunged Virginia into a civil war that raged for six months.

Over a blistering summer, the two groups skirmished across the Virginia tidelands. At one point Berkeley fled Jamestown and took refuge across the Chesapeake Bay on the eastern shore. Bacon's men all but annihilated the Occaneechee Indians, who had been close allies and fur-trading partners of Berkeley. Bacon's men attacked the Occaneechee's Southside Virginia villages along the Roanoke River, near what is today the town of Clarksville. Bacon drove Pamunkey Indians into the wilds of Dragon Swamp, a steamy netherworld of water moccasins, mosquitoes, and bald cypress trees seeping into the York River tributary of the Mattaponi. There, Indian men, women, and children felled huge timbers and hid. Bacon's men found them, slaughtered some, and took dozens prisoner; the lands they had fled were suddenly available to settlers availing themselves of the new legal powers contained in what became known as Bacon's Laws.

In a prelude to an attack on Jamestown, Bacon raided a number of plantations, kidnapped the wives of several of Berkeley's supporters, then displayed them alongside captive Indians before trenches outside the Virginia capital. Overtaking the city's defenders, Bacon's men put Jamestown to the torch.

In the best of revolutionary traditions, Bacon composed a manifesto of sorts, assailing Berkeley for having failed, over the long course of his rule, to subdue "the barbarous heathen" and for instead "having protected, favored and emboldened the Indians." He added a litany of populist grievances, decrying high taxes, cronyism, and the packing of local courts with Berkeley's "scandalous and ignorant favorites." For good measure, Bacon criticized Berkeley's regulation of the trade in beaver pelts, an especially sore point for Bacon's neighbor and friend, William Byrd, who inherited his uncle's riverbank business swapping English cloth and crockery to Indians for deerskins and furs. In his "Declaration of the People," Bacon went on to indict Berkeley and twenty of his "confederates"—council members, aides, and large landowners—as "traitors to the king and country." He demanded that all of them surrender or face attack and warned that anyone caught harboring them would face reprisals. He signed the document, "Nathaniel Bacon, general, by consent of the people."

INDEBTED, DISCONTENTED, AND ARMED

Bacon's true motives and intentions may never be known. He left behind little that he had written. His wartime record—pillaging plantations, including Berkeley's cherished Green Spring, massacring Indians and taking their land, using colonists' wives as human shields—terminally undercut whatever case might have been made for Bacon as heroic patriot. Headstrong and petulant, his bridges burned back home in England, he doubtless was seduced by the homegrown support of hundreds of men in arms. His brash manner and strategic misjudgments sparked a regional civil war that brought new death and destruction to the struggling English beachhead in America. And his unchastened attacks on Indians helped to galvanize race-based hatred at a time when blacks, Europeans, and Native Americans were all struggling to find their way in the new world evolving along the banks of the James.

At the same time, political and economic conditions in Virginia had become deplorable for the majority of the population. Many saw Bacon as a leader who, however flawed, could pilot the struggling colony toward brighter days. If he was cruel to the Pamunkey and Occaneechee, moreover, Bacon also led a fully integrated militia, a force with as many as four hundred blacks playing a vital role in what they saw as a freedom fight. This was nothing short of revolutionary in a state that had long before outlawed blacks' possession of arms and their participation in the militia. Some historians, in fact, credit Bacon with striking the first blow for American independence from an oppressive British crown—and drawing a line dividing rebellious patriots from subjects loyal to the king—one hundred years before the Revolutionary War.

By accident or design, Berkeley had presided over the rise of a landed aristocracy that was squeezing out opportunity for the lifeblood of the colony: the tens of thousands who crossed the Atlantic possessing little but the will to build a better life. Many of those who managed to work out their time as indentured servants found their hard-earned freedom little more than a passport to poverty. If Bacon believed he was leading a people's revolt, his own followers provided ample evidence to support his claim. Even planters close to Berkeley had warned in the months leading up to the troubles that conditions were so grim for the majority of Virginians that it was a wonder they hadn't risen up already. In writing of the history of the rebellion, Berkeley's backers in the general assembly blamed the uprising on "the distempered humor predominant in the common people." Not for these lawmakers were the people sovereign. Indeed, the high assembly opined, Bacon and his fellow rabble-rousers were "ill affected" people possessed of "an itching desire in them to pry into the secrets of the grand assembly of the country, and to take upon them to calumniate and censure the same." After nearly three decades as Virginia's chief executive, Berkeley himself despaired of ever being able to manage the place. "How miserable that man is that governs a people where six parts of seven, at least, are poor, indebted, discontented and armed," he wrote that summer, words that would reverberate in cannon and musket fire a century later.

In the fall of 1676, with much of Virginia under his control and the rest hanging in the balance, Bacon died of dysentery near the town of Gloucester. His compatriots were said to have put stones in his coffin, perhaps to weigh it down along the edge of the York River so that Berkeley's men couldn't dig it up and hang the corpse from the gallows. Bacon's remains were never found, but two dozen of his followers did wind up with their necks in the noose. By the following January, Berkeley had put down the last remnants of insurrection and set about executing participants in Bacon's Rebellion, some with evident and disturbing glee. When William Drummond was captured and brought to the governor, an almost giddy Berkeley bowed low in feigned deference meant to mock a man who had irritated him for more than a decade.

A wealthy planter with more than six thousand acres of prime riverside land, Drummond was appointed by Berkeley as governor of coastal Carolina in 1664. He repaid Berkeley by sniping at him behind his back. Berkeley had to intervene to stop Drummond and his cronies from running Carolina Indians off their land, and he later charged Drummond with failure to perform on a contract to shore up fortifications at Point Comfort as defense against Dutch raiders. Backing Bacon was the final straw. "Mr. Drummond, you are very welcome! I am more glad to see you than any man in Virginia," Berkeley crowed when his longtime antagonist was delivered in January 1677. "Mr. Drummond, you shall be hanged in half an hour!" A military tribunal headed by Berkeley found Drummond guilty of treason and rebellion, and he was hanged, indeed, a week after his capture.

Berkeley was unrelenting in punishing other insurgents. James Crews, a House of Burgesses member and Bacon cohort who owned a six-hundred-acre plantation at Turkey Island across the river from the Curles, was sentenced "to be hanged by the neck until he be dead." The same punishment was ordered for Giles Bland, Richard Farmer, Robert Stoaks, and nearly two dozen others in Bacon's band. When the wife of one condemned man, Thomas Cheeseman, fell to her knees to beg Berkeley to spare her husband and take her life instead, Berkeley scoffed and called her a "whore."

When news of Berkeley's zeal for retribution reached London, Charles II reportedly exclaimed, "That old fool has hanged more men in that naked country than I did for the murder of my father." The king sent a royal commission to find out what went wrong in Virginia and how best to correct it—along with a thousand British troops to quell rebel holdouts and reassert the crown's control. Arriving in a squadron headed by the *Bristol*, the redcoat vanguard dropped anchor in the frigid waters of the James at the end of January. The rest of the regiment arrived two weeks later. The *Bristol's* captain, John Berry, bore a blunt royal order for Berkeley: return to London at once. King Charles sent Col. Herbert Jeffreys to replace him as governor. In early May, in failing health and nearly deaf, Berkeley left Virginia for the last time. He sailed down the James into the bay and across the Atlantic to England, where he died that July, far from the land where he had invested three and a half decades of his life. "He was a gifted, clever man with a quicksilver turn of mind and a vaulting ambition," Billings wrote in his authoritative biography, *Sir William Berkeley and the Forging of Colonial Virginia*. "He uniquely marked Virginia. That imprint was both his accomplishment and his failure."

IT SHALL BE LAWFUL TO KILL

If you throw a spear at the king, the adage goes, make sure not to miss. For better or worse, Bacon's Rebellion came up short. Its failure marked a turning point, opening a new era of suppression meant to strengthen the royal governor's grip on colonial Virginia and the security of the landed aristocracy that controlled its economic and political core. The first step was the imposition of what amounted to martial law, with Virginians ordered to provide housing and food for the British troops. The forced quartering of the king's soldiers began as punishment for people like William Hatcher, "an aged man," court records show, who apparently didn't take up arms during Bacon's Rebellion but merely spoke ill of the crown. In the spring following the uprising, a court led by Governor Jeffreys found Hatcher guilty of "uttering diverse mutinous words tending to the disquiet of this, his majesty's country." The old Virginian was ordered to deliver "with all expedition, eight thousand pounds of dressed pork" to British troops deployed in Henrico County.

Col. Henry Gooch was similarly fined six thousand pounds of pork, to be delivered to the British troops, after being convicted of "treason and rebellion against his most sacred majesty." William Tiballs and Henry Gee were found guilty of "uttering diverse scandalous and mutinous words." Each was likewise ordered to provide one thousand pounds of pork to the redcoats, as were Thomas Maples and Thomas Baker. On those six convictions alone, the British regiment had been allotted the equivalent of eighteen pounds of pork per man, likely better rations than they'd received back in England. By summer, however, either the courts had emptied themselves of defendants or Virginia's farmers were running out of hogs because Governor Jeffreys began ordering area justices to commandeer provisions and billeting space from residents. They were directed to provide room and board to the troops for the pittance of two shillings a week per soldier.

Beyond burdening a struggling underclass with the billeting of troops, the Virginia General Assembly took on the task of securing wealthy planters against the prospect of future revolt. Especially unnerving to these legislators and their landed constituents was the way white servants and freedmen had fought side by side with black slaves during Bacon's Rebellion. With the slave population growing, planters wouldn't risk that kind of alliance again. Their solution was to use the law to divide and conquer, deepening and more clearly defining slavery as a function of race. By drawing a statutory line between blacks and whites and enforcing those distinctions with whips and chains, Virginia stepped up its transformation from a cradle of freedom into a crucible of coercive labor.

A law entitled "An act for preventing negroes' insurrections" forbade blacks from bearing arms, from gathering together in groups, from leaving their homes, or from even burying their dead without written permission from their owners. "Whereas the frequent meeting of considerable numbers of negro slaves under pretense of feasts and burials is judged of dangerous consequence," the 1680 statute began, slaves were forbidden to leave their owners' property without written permission. Violators were to be taken to the nearest constable, who was then "required to give the said negro twenty lashes on his bare back well laid on, and so sent home to his said master, mistress or overseer." The act made it an especially egregious offense for a black person to confront a Christian—by which the assembly meant chiefly a white person. The statute's reference to "any negro or other slave" began what would become a more deliberate effort to link blacks with Indians and people of mixed race—mulattos—as a group to be segregated from whites. The act set white people apart as a separate and specific class enjoying special protections and benefits under the law and was a step toward making people of color their subjects. "If any negro or other slave shall presume to lift up his hand in opposition against any Christian," the law stated, the slave would receive "thirty lashes on his bare back well laid on" for each offense. Conviction required only the testimony of a white person.

Half a century after Anthony Johnson built his estate on the eastern shore, Virginia's ruling aristocracy decided that was one success story too many for the colony's blacks. "Great inconveniences may happen to this country by the setting of negroes and mulattos free," the general assembly decreed, voting that "no negro or mulatto, after the end of this present session of assembly, [could be] set free by any person or persons whatsoever," unless the former slave was sent out of Virginia for good. The planters who dominated the Virginia General Assembly could not reconcile themselves with the idea of freedom for black people and would not tolerate it in their midst. They depended utterly on slaves to produce more than ten million pounds a year of tobacco bound for Britain, producing vast wealth, much of which was then used to combat black workers' will to be free. Forty years before, the assembly had empowered local sheriffs to raise posses to hunt down slaves who fled their owners' land. The 1680 statute gave slave hunters broad authority to treat runaway slaves as prey. "It shall be lawful," the assembly ruled, "for such person or persons to' kill the said negro or slave so lying out and resisting." Building on decades of Virginia law sanctioning the enslavement of blacks, the 1680 provisions empowered whites to deal with slaves as inferiors. In the process of granting whites license to beat slaves, even to kill them, with impunity, the colony's elected burgesses chipped away at the notions of community that had briefly linked laborers, both black and white. The sense of social kinship once shared by workers was cleaved by a wall of racist division, with a disenfranchised subclass of black people on one side and a legally superior group of white workers and servants on the other. Called by Secretary of State Condoleezza Rice "our national birth defect," that division ripped American community at the seams.

"That's a big turning point," University of Maryland slavery scholar Ira Berlin said of the legal aftermath of Bacon's Rebellion. In addition to disenfranchising blacks, the laws joined whites of all stations in a new community based less on economic and social status than on skin color. It forged the beginnings of a poor white class whose race-based ideology could be manipulated and wedded to the agenda of wealthy whites. Even when the economic interests of the two groups diverged—as it generally did—the belief they shared in their racial superiority, a delusion enshrined in law, became a powerful and unifying bond. At last, said Berlin, "The former white indentured servants begin to get some status in this society."

It would be hard to find a place anywhere in the world where the frictions of history had rubbed hotter over nine decades than in seventeenth-century Jamestown. As the century drew to a close, the old settlement and scene of so much famine and discovery, trauma, and birth had aged far beyond its years. As Jamestown tired, the colony grew weary of it. But Virginia had no other town of note. The riverside plantations with their deepwater wharves were communities unto themselves, places where passengers arrived from Europe, the Caribbean, or the American colonies to the north and south, as did a wide range of imported goods. There was the shoddy little village leaching out from William Byrd's fur and tobacco trade upstream at the falls, but, apart from that, there was little in the way of urban development anywhere in the colony of some sixty-four thousand people, 10 percent of whom were slaves.

Midway between the James and York rivers, however, a new community was rising some six miles inland, near the Indian trails that once linked the seat of Powhatan to the precarious English village on the James. Inhabitants of Middle Plantation, as the inland community was called, had begun lobbying to become the new capital of Virginia after Bacon burned Jamestown to the ground. Once scoffed at, the idea gained currency after 1693, when James Blair, the highest ranking Anglican priest in Virginia, persuaded London to charter a new college at Middle Plantation, a place that already had a fine brick church and a growing collection of taverns and shops. In a deferential nod to royal patronage, Blair named the college for its sponsors at court, the diminutive and asthmatic reformer, King William III, and his striking cousin, who was fifteen when she married him, Queen Mary II.

In 1698, the statehouse in Jamestown burned. A member of the State Council, Blair seized the opportunity to spike the old capital for good, appealing to the general assembly the next year to abandon Jamestown for the new community a short horse ride away. To make his case, Blair assigned five students from the new College of William and Mary to address the assembly. The youthful orators perfectly symbolized the fresh start a new capital could provide. And, in 1699, the legislators voted to leave Jamestown behind, this time for good, and build a new seat of government at the Middle Plantation town, which the assembly renamed for its king, Williamsburg.

AT THE DOOR OF EVERY CHURCH

By 1705, Virginia had completed its grinding shift from a community of mixed, if unequal, races to a full-fledged slave society. In October of that year, the general assembly passed a series of acts that together comprised a comprehensive slave code. It relegated black people, from conception, to the status of property, human chits to be bought and sold, even gambled away, at the will or whim of their owner. A study in racial debasement and a disturbing glimpse into the shadows of the human soul, the 1705 code stripped enslaved Africans and African Americans of their citizenship and basic rights. It indemnified white people against the consequences of even the most violent treatment of slaves. And it made savage dealings with blacks an accepted, routine, and even mandatory pillar of colonial life, part of an intentional policy designed to hold black people in a perpetual state of terror.

Three centuries after the slave code was written, its words ring with the power of a society to imbed its values, however misguided, in its laws. It articulates the authority that elected legislators willfully and deliberatively vested in a legal edifice built on a foundation of bigotry. It stands as a hoary monument to one group's ability to legitimize, and then wage, a kind of undeclared war on an entire race of people, backed by all the majesty and malignancy of the state, without fear of retribution or loss. It documents, as vividly as can be expressed by words that carry the force of law, an essential part of our national beginnings. It reminds us of where we have come from as a people, and it holds us to account for who we are.

"Be it enacted, by the governor, council and burgesses of this present general assembly, and it is hereby enacted by the authority of the same," the act begins, "that from and after the passing of this act, all negro, mulatto and Indian slaves, in all courts of judicature, and other places, within this dominion, shall be held, taken and adjudged to be real estate [and not chattels] and shall descend unto the heirs and widows of persons departing this life, according to the manner and custom of land of inheritance, held in fee simple."

Under the 1705 statutes, no "negro, mulatto or Indian" could hold office, "ecclesiastical, civil or military, or be in any place of public trust or power." And in the interest of providing for "a speedy prosecution of slaves for capital crimes," the statutes required that blacks stand trial "without the solemnity of a jury." A slave could be convicted and executed on the oath of two witnesses, "or of one with pregnant circumstances." The witnesses, however, could not be slaves. They were forbidden from testifying in court, having been adjudged by the general assembly to be "persons incapable in law."

As in the 1680 statutes, slaves caught hiding in the woods or swamps or trying to escape to freedom were singled out for especially harsh consideration under a provision that allowed them to be hunted like game. "It shall be lawful for any person or persons whatsoever to kill and destroy such slaves by such ways and means as he, she or they shall think fit," the statute read. Runaways taken alive often fared no better, under a provision that entitled local courts to mete out whatever "punishment to the said slave, either by dismembering, or any other way, not touching his life, as they in their discretion shall think fit, for the reclaiming [of] any such incorrigible slave, and terrifying others from the like practices." Better to leave a disobedient slave maimed, the code made clear, than unrepentant.

The code also anticipated an economic dilemma, namely, that punishing a slave could be costly to its owner, particularly when the punishment involved dismembering or hanging a laborer in his or her prime. And so the law provided that the court would attach a monetary value to any slave killed or maimed by the criminal justice system. That amount would then be taken from the public treasury and paid out to the convicted slave's owner as recompense for his loss. In that way, even the majority of Virginians who didn't own slaves were required to participate in the slave society by contributing tax money to subsidize the execution and dismembering of those who risked their lives to be free.

The assembly, though, was just getting started. Under the 1705 code, a white person convicted of stealing a hog could pay a fine of £10 to avoid twenty-five stripes on the back. The same offense carried a mandatory thirty-nine lashes for a black, Indian, or mulatto and a penalty of four hundred pounds of tobacco—about one-third of a year's output for a full-time laborer. An overseer of four or more slaves was exempted from militia service, his role in controlling blacks being deemed an essential security function.

Another statute made it illegal for anyone to do business with a slave without the owner's permission. Meant to discourage slaves from stealing, that provision was also a tool of control over slaves who might, through personal industry, devise ways to earn money that might one day be used to purchase freedom for themselves or a family member.

Mixed couples remained a legislative concern, and a law was passed requiring that a white woman who gave birth to the child of a black or mixed-race father would have to pay £15 to her local church or be sold into five years of indentured servitude herself. Either way, the child would be bound as a slave until the age of thirty-one. A white person who married a black was subject to six months in prison and a £10 fine. Ministers who presided over such a wedding could be fined ten thousand pounds of tobacco.

As a final blanket amnesty for slave owners, the 1705 statutes affirmed that it was legal to punish a slave by beating, as provided for under the 1669 law, and if that slave "shall happen to be killed in such correction, it shall not be accounted felony." Instead, the act stipulated, the offending party shall be acquitted and the case forgotten, "as if such incident had never happened."

There was little point in passing a slave code if no one read it. So, to help spread the word and to ensure that no one might profess a "pretense of ignorance" of its terms, the general assembly ordered that copies be made and posted by each county sheriff. Not everyone might make it past the courthouse, though, so the assembly looked to the one institution that touched each Christian life, ordering that twice each year, after prayers and sermons, the slave code be tacked up "at the door of every church and chapel" everywhere in Virginia. That way, each September and March, worshippers could appeal for salvation in the sanctuary, then bone up on the fine points of human bondage on their way out the door. "This generation," University of Missouri historian John Rainbolt wrote in the *William & Mary Quarterly*, "laid the basic foundation for Virginia's slave codes that would serve until the Civil War."

Over the next fifty years, tens of thousands of enslaved people were brought from Africa to Virginia's tobacco coast, where their unrequited labors, and the work of the generations they bore, carved plantations of unfathomable wealth out of the land. Small worlds unto themselves that took the place of towns, plantations with names like Shirley, Westover, Berkeley, Kingsmill, and Brandon took shape, little cities of several hundred that grew their own corn and fruit and wheat, raised cattle and chickens and hogs, tanned leather, brewed whiskey, and built ships and grand homes, all on the backs of people imprisoned by a system of lifetime work without pay.

As slavery sank its roots along the banks of the James, black people struggled to build their own families and homes, even some semblance of community, against the long odds enslavement imposed, an essential part of one of the most compelling sagas of survival in the annals of human history. They struggled, as well, to maintain their own spiritual center, drawing on the beliefs of their African forebears, adopting bits and pieces of Christian teachings, and reviewing for posterity the wisdom and hope to be found in the telling of stories, the cooking of food, and the singing of songs handed down from one generation to the next.

Out of the forced ferment of that rich exchange grew the African American spiritual hymns that formed the taproot of gospel music and, later, the blues. One of the most enduring hymns of the genre is the rolling spiritual "Wade in the Water," a haunting fusion of ancient African traditions, Christian teachings, and the longing of slaves to be free. Through simple lyrics—"Wade in the water; wade in the water, children; wade in the water; God's gonna trouble the water"—the hymn conveyed meaning on at least three different levels: it could be sung in reverence to African ancestors, as a baptismal hymn, or as a coded "map song" advising runaway slaves to use rivers and streams to cover their tracks from bloodhounds and bounty hunters. "It was kind of a reminder to people," said University of Denver professor Arthur Jones, founder of the Spirituals Project, dedicated to the preservation and study of African American spirituals. "If you are escaping, and there's a stream, go through the stream and walk along the stream," explained Jones, "because not only will people lose your footprints, but they'll also lose your scent, because you're in the water, you're wading in the water."

It isn't known where or when this spiritual originated, though some believe it evolved in the coastal plantations of Virginia or the Carolinas sometime in the early 1700s. Some of the Africans who arrived in this country in chains brought with them an ancient rite of ceremonially laying a cross of wood over the surface of a river or stream. That symbolized the connection between the living, above the surface, and the spirits of the ancestors, which were believed, in many African cultures, to reside beneath the surface of the water. One theory holds that slaves sang this hymn as a way to practice those ancient traditions without invoking the wrath of their white overseers because the cross had obvious meaning to Christians, who saw in the water the new beginnings of baptism.

In the New Testament, the disciple John tells of a place in Jerusalem where the sick and lame gathered beside a pool named Bethesda. "At a certain season," John tells his followers, an angel of the Lord came down and "troubled the water." The first one into the troubled water would be cured—divine intercession would heal the lame and set believers free of a life of illness and woe.

Generations of American blacks drew inspiration from the Old Testament story of Moses, who led the Israelites out of slavery in Egypt, bidding them to have the faith to wade into the Red Sea before God troubled those waters, parting them to create a passage for the Israelites' escape, then closing the sea upon Pharaoh's drowning army.

Whatever the origins of the hymn, it was sung by slaves across the American South and is still sung in churches there as a powerful reminder of the faith that fed generations of black Americans on their long journey toward freedom. It's a symbol also of the spiritual link between the James River slaves and the waters that bore their African ancestors into America, clinging to the belief that surely, some day, God would trouble those ancient waters as well.

Her name is lost to history, but in the decades when the slave code was beginning to stamp its imprint on human lives, a child of Africa and Virginia may well have hummed that very hymn as she wandered the fields and the forests alongside a wide place in the James. She lived with the other slaves in a dirt-floored, clapboard cabin on a tobacco plantation called Utopia, just downstream from Jamestown, but only for a few fleeting years. When she died, someone made her a coffin: pine slats, a few handfuls of nails. She wore a simple string of amethyst beads the day they laid her small body down, beneath the oak and sycamore trees looking out over the river from atop a high waterside bluff.

When he found her three centuries later, Garrett Fesler noticed she was facing east, like the two dozen others in the burial grounds near the old slave quarters at Utopia. A senior archaeologist with the James River Institute for Archaeology, a private firm in Williamsburg, Fesler excavated the site a decade ago, before developers built a golf course and a community of million-dollar homes there. Standing on the once-sacred ground beneath cloudless skies in early spring, Fesler gazed down the river and toward the sea. It was no accident, he said, that the slaves buried their dead by the riverside, facing Africa for all eternity. "The symbolism of having them on the top of the bluff and overlooking the water is a powerful testament," said Fesler. "The connection with the water, what transported them into enslavement, must have had a tremendous impact on their thinking." A soft breeze blew in off the river. "It became the highway, the connection of the body of water that brought them here and their desire at death to be carried back to where they came from, that journey to the other side, to the other world."

7

LIBERTY OR DEATH

MANAKIN—In the spring of 1736, a promising young surveyor named Peter Jefferson agreed to provide a cask of rum-spiked punch from Williamsburg's Raleigh Tavern to his wealthy friend and neighbor, William Randolph. A member of one of the most influential families in British America, Randolph lived at Tuckahoe, his tobacco plantation overlooking a placid stretch of the James River, about fifteen miles west of the falls. In exchange for the arrack elixir, Randolph signed over to Jefferson two hundred acres of wilderness land on a tributary far upstream, in what was then the Virginia frontier.

There was more that bound the two men, it turned out, than property and punch. Jefferson took a shine to his friend's first cousin, Jane Randolph. Three years later, they were married, and the two men's friendship turned to kinship. And so, when Randolph died a widower in 1745, his last request was that Jefferson and his wife leave their frontier farm in the Blue Ridge foothills and move to Tuckahoe to look after the three orphaned children Randolph left behind.

By then the Jeffersons had children of their own, including a son, two years old, who traveled the sixty-five miles to his new home astride the neck of a horse, with a pillow as his saddle and an African American slave riding along behind to keep the toddler from tumbling off. The boy's name was Thomas Jefferson. He stayed at Tuckahoe nearly seven years, roaming its oak and elm woodlands by day, huddling with siblings and cousins in the upstairs bedrooms of the red-brick and white-clapboard manor house by night, and gazing out upon the river through the large south-facing window of the one-room schoolhouse where the future author of the Declaration of Independence learned to read and write.

The story of Jefferson's childhood at Tuckahoe is part of the larger tale of how the James River plantation culture lent political voice to a group of disparate and largely disconnected colonies struggling to coalesce around the idea of representative government and to gain their independence from the mightiest military empire the world had ever known. Tuckahoe was but one of several dozen large tobacco plantations along the James that together formed a cradle for administrative leadership and political thought in eighteenth-century Virginia. The entire plantation civilization depended on slaves, without whose forced and stolen labor the riverside world of wealth and privilege could not have been built, or even imagined. Even as a nursery for white leadership, moreover, the system was as inefficient as it was inequitable, bequeathing official roles based on birthright while sidelining or overlooking entirely potential talent not graced with land and wealth. And yet, out of the moral inversion of this fatally flawed system grew much of the vision that would shape a new country born of the guiding ideal of the American Revolution, that all men are created equal. It was not inevitable that it would turn out that way; it was a miracle that it did.

"Wealth and power were riveted to one another during the 18th Century. In order just to sit at the table, just for openers, you had to have a plantation and slaves," said Roger Wilkins, professor of history and American culture at George Mason University, in Fairfax, Virginia. "They were elitists. These guys were not, in that sense, egalitarians. But they did believe in these enlightenment principles and they believed in them very profoundly." Some historians have suggested, in fact, that it was the daily exposure to slavery that made those early colonial leaders hold freedom so dear. "All of them understood how important freedom was, because they saw its absence always," explained University of Texas historian James Sidbury. "And all of them came to believe that all of those who had freedom shared a certain kind of equality."

Historians search largely in vain for a self-made man who rose to political stature in eighteenth-century Virginia without family ties and money gained from land and the slaves that made it productive. Leadership positions were the exclusive domain of an insular ruling class whose names were inextricably tied to their holdings: the Harrisons of Berkeley Plantation and Brandon, the Hills and Carters of Shirley, the Eppes of Appomattox Manor, the Tylers of Sherwood Forest, the Burwells of Kingsmill, and the Randolphs of Wilton, Turkey Island, and Tuckahoe, named for the tuberous staple of the riverside Indians' diet. Built by legions of African slaves, these large plantations became the respective seats of family dynasties. The arrangement looked to many then, as it does today, like an attempt to remake in America the system through which English dukes and landed lords oversaw grand fiefdoms within a class-based political and legal order fashioned to protect and advance their interests.

No family was better served by Virginia's landed oligarchy than the Byrds of Westover. Born in London in 1652, William Byrd was the son of a goldsmith. As a young man, Byrd came to Virginia to assist his uncle, Thomas Stegge, who brokered deerskins and beaver pelts with Monacan and Powhatan people from his trading post at the falls of the James. While mastering the business of skin and fur, Byrd became a militia captain and member of the Henrico County Court. Like many other well-off Virginia settlers, Byrd married a wealthy widow, enhancing the estate he inherited upon the death of his uncle Tom. One of Nathaniel Bacon's neighbors and drinking partners, Byrd shrewdly, if not altogether heroically, skirted Bacon's Rebellion in 1676, averting the risk of execution in the wake of its failure. He was elected to the House of Burgesses the following year. Two years after that, he was made a colonel and given command of colonial defenses at the falls. He later was named to the State Council and served for a time as the colony's auditor general in charge of overseeing tax assessments and collections, receiving 5 percent of the take as his handsome commission.

Over the next three decades, Byrd used his positions of power to further expand his wealth, mostly by engrossing enormous parcels of land and acquiring slaves to work them. He saved a large fortune by keeping thousands of acres of his holdings off the tax books for years on end. His fellow council members happily went along with the scam, and by the time of his death in 1704, the enterprising Byrd had amassed riverside tracts totaling some thirty thousand acres, mostly at his plantation at Westover and at the trading depot he built upstream at the falls. His son, William Byrd II, won a charter from King George II to set up a town there, which Byrd named Richmond, apparently after the English palace in Surrey County that his royal majesty used as a lodge.

William Byrd II used his inherited wealth to build what remains to this day one of the nation's finest homes: Westover, a three-story Georgian mansion overlooking a long, broad sweep of the lower James. Educated by private tutors and later in London, the younger Byrd had a literary mind and could read Latin, Greek, French, and Hebrew. Returning to Virginia from the mother country, Byrd became the most ostentatious of the James River grandees. He built an entire wing to house more than thirty-five hundred books on subjects ranging from philosophy and science to gardening and art, the largest private library in America at that time. Visitors who came by river disembarked at Byrd's private wharf and sauntered through a tulip poplar ellipse on their way to the red-brick manor house. Those who journeyed by horse or carriage along the three-mile drive leading from Westover to the muddy road that linked the plantations to Williamsburg were greeted by an ornate brick-and-wrought-iron gate capped with stone and a matched pair of enormous gilded lead eagles, deliberately regal and fittingly predatory symbols of the family's affluence and reach.

In a colony with no single commercial center or public exchange—no Philadelphia, Boston, New York, or even Charleston—a plantation like Westover was a self-contained universe that functioned like a small town, both producing and consuming goods in the global market. Engines of wealth for the burgeoning British Empire, plantations along the lower James—as well as Virginia's other Chesapeake rivers, the Potomac, the Rappahannock, and the York—were commercial nodes in a worldwide web of trade, transportation, and communications. Letters, newspapers, and dry goods arrived by ship from England and British colonies, along with slaves brought directly from Africa or by way of the British West Indies.

Some plantation owners operated their own stores, buying wine, coffee, sugar, rum, paper, cloth, and other British products right off the ships, then selling them to locals at a handsome profit. Tall-masted vessels would leave for the return trip loaded down with hundreds of hogsheads—large barrels built to be rolled along the colony's rutted and rocky roads—each stuffed with twelve hundred pounds of dried tobacco. Large plantations operated their own grist mills and shipped out wheat flour and corn meal. Cattle were raised; beef and tongue were salted and exported to Europe and the Caribbean colonies by the barrel load, as were cured ham, lumber, and staves. Travelers embarked from the plantation wharves as well, where they booked passage for Europe, the Caribbean, or other of the British colonies along the eastern seaboard.

While the plantations were communities unto themselves, they were anything but independent. They relied, absolutely, on the labor of slaves and the favor of markets that were controlled in England. To survive a James River plantation required no particular management genius or affinity for fine books so much as the combination of good prices for its tobacco exports and the strengths and abilities of African workers who, by law, were unpaid.

Similar to other trade and transit centers throughout history, the James River plantations became cultural collection points of sorts, places where politics and commerce merged. They were also centers of a social life that tied American opportunity to the families, customs, and minds of Europe.

A plantation like Berkeley, where native timber was used to build oceangoing vessels in its riverside shipyard, often served as an inn for a select clientele of family, friends, and acquaintances. Some would make themselves at home in the so-called bachelors' quarters, a separate, four-bedroom guest lodge built near the brick manor house. "People would come and stay for a week," said Malcolm Jamieson, the third generation of his family to own Berkeley, built on land settled in 1619 by English colonists who held the first Thanksgiving there, a year before the *Mayflower* arrived at Plymouth. "They would stop off at these plantations, play cards and talk politics, and talk about concepts and talk about grievances." Listening to Jamieson on a brick patio opening onto one of Berkeley's five terraced lawns, it was not hard to imagine the world he described, a place where a ship might bring in new books and news that could spark weeks of conversation and debate. "It was almost like what we think of as a university atmosphere," he said. "It was a great melting pot of ideas. The river had a lot to do with it, the same way that Boston Harbor had a lot to do with that hotbed of trade and wealth."

Much as it was a crossroads of human experience and thought, the James River was no academic retreat. The grand estates along its shores were profit-driven corporate ventures hand-carved out of the primal forest by slaves wielding axes and picks. The plantations existed to make money for their owners, most of whom regarded public service as a natural appendage of personal fortune, an opportunity to expand the dynastic reach so exquisitely expressed by the talons of gold at the gates of Westover. In young Jefferson's Virginia, wealthy planters like the Byrds were not scornful of government; they were wedded to it. Tobacco barons who gave themselves the title of gentlemen, members of the aristocracy eagerly embraced the roles later played by political parties, caucuses, conventions, and primaries, taking it upon themselves to produce and manage a shallow and self-perpetuating pool of governing elites bound by clan and culture, courtship and kin. "The roster of eighteenth-century gentlemen served almost like a permanent list of nominees for political office," Duke University historian Charles Sydnor wrote in his 1952 classic on eighteenth-century Virginia politics, *American Revolutionaries in the Making*. "Birth into one of the ruling families was almost essential to the making of a political career."

Virginia's political system was hardly unique. Family connections and wealth lay near the center of power in colonies ranging from Georgia to the so-called River Gods of the Connecticut River Valley and extending to the trade and shipping magnates of the Massachusetts Bay Colony, making colonial politics "essentially a contest among prominent families for the control of state authority," Brown University historian Gordon Wood wrote in *The Radicalism of the American Revolution*. "Few if any of the common people regarded government as a means by which economic and social power might be redistributed or the problems of their lives resolved," Wood wrote. "Politics remained essentially a preserve of the dominant gentlemanly elite."

One step removed from hereditary governance, the system was plagued by obvious inequity and rampant dysfunction. "Since everyone in the ruling class was kin to somebody else in it, the Virginia government was something like a large family," author Clifford Dowdey wrote in *The Great Plantation*, a history of Berkeley, "with all of a family's spites and jealousies, as well as the binding intimacies between some individuals." The electorate was in little position to negotiate. Only white men who owned land and were twenty-one or older could vote. Indians and black people, slave or free, were disenfranchised, as were women of every hue and stripe. There was no secret ballot. Voters cast their choice orally and in the presence of others, including the county sheriff, who oversaw elections. More often than not, the candidates themselves would be present; for citizens who dared vote against an incumbent, speaking truth to power was no mere turn of phrase.

The cushioned life of a wealthy landowner shaped the personality of privilege for the planter elites, imbuing many with a sense of entitlement that doubtless crippled more character than it ever produced. The squandering of inherited fortune was no less a feature of the James River culture than anywhere else. "In Virginia," explained Jamieson, "this web of kinship would frequently go from shirtsleeves to shirtsleeves in three generations."

Still, for the most part, even haughty and self-indulgent youths were expected to grow into managers of some competence; the survival of their plantations depended upon it. If Virginia's landed aristocracy maintained a wholly inequitable and nearly unbreakable lock on public office, their plantations were also proving grounds of sorts for would-be public servants. Sons of the gentry had tutors to prepare them for university life, whether at the nearby College of William and Mary or back in England, still considered home by much of Virginia's elite. They learned through experience how to administer a plantation, a complex operation that combined farming, production, commerce, and high finance. And they were called upon to manage challenges and opportunities for their families, hired help, and slaves in a public setting where neither failure nor success could long be concealed from the varying constituents they served. As a breeding ground

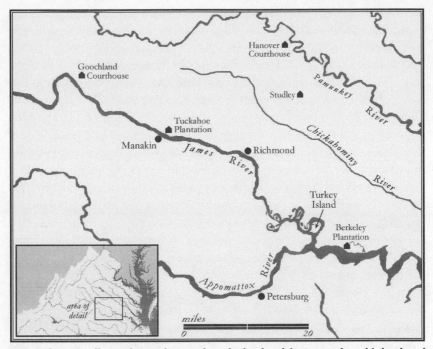

Young Thomas Jefferson learned to read on the banks of the James, from his boyhood home at Tuckahoe, and Patrick Henry gave his famous "Liberty or Death" speech in a Richmond church near his birthplace at Studley. Map drawn by Rebecca Wrenn.

for public servants, the true test of the system, according to Sydnor, was less a matter of equity than of the quality of leadership it produced. "Democracy must do two things and do them well. It must develop men who are fit to govern," wrote Sydnor (a forward-leaning analyst for his time who certainly would include women were he writing today), "and it must select for office these men rather than their less worthy contemporaries."

Tuckahoe would appear to have played its part.

PENCIL-POINT SKETCHES AND POKEBERRY INK

In an agricultural economy based on slaves and the aggregation of large parcels of land from the ever-widening frontier, surveyors like Jefferson's father worked hand in hand with the ruling elites, transforming fields and forests into personal property with a tripod, compass, and measuring chain. Part of an educated and empowered upper middle class, he made a good living plotting tracts for large landowners, sometimes acquiring prime real estate for himself as his fee, and selling maps to hunters, trappers, and land speculators.

Raised on an outback farm near where Fine Creek trickles into the south bank of the James, a few miles west of Tuckahoe, Peter Jefferson had little formal education. He never studied law but mastered the codes and complexities of property claims and deeds through work that wedded lawyerly precision with an expeditionary soul. Surveyors, in his day, were also civil servants, politically well connected professionals whose vocation took them near the center of government and economic affairs. Peter Jefferson was named county surveyor, a prominent political appointment. He was also a militia officer and a justice of the peace, a key role in colonial America as the justices made up the county court.

It all must have made for scintillating conversation around the dinner table at Tuckahoe, where young Thomas Jefferson lived until he was nine, raking the first rasping notes over the cat-gut strings of his violin, wandering the swampy lowlands along the riverside, exploring the broad fields of tobacco and corn, and skipping barefoot down the sandy drive leading out to the old river road. He was five when he began joining his older cousin, Thomas Mann Randolph, in the one-room schoolhouse—sixteen feet square—where a local parson taught reading, writing, and arithmetic to the boy who would one day help lay the ideological foundations for the United States.

In those unmeasured days of boyhood, though, it wasn't the rule of law or the rights of man that sparked Jefferson's interest so much as the fireflies he chased across the darkened lawn on August nights or the heat lightning that flared in a distant fury behind the tree line along the river's opposite shore. In autumn, he savored hot apple cider and gingerbread from the kitchen in the brick cottage a quick dash from the house. And many a winter's evening slipped past in the upstairs bedroom where he and the other children swapped ghost stories while candlelight shadows crept along the high, molded ceiling and walls, pressed wind-burned faces against frosty windows at the sound of approaching hoof beats in snow, and breathed in cool dawn air laden with smoke and ash as the fire in the bedside hearth burned low.

In the short autobiography he wrote seven decades later, Jefferson touched little on his days at Tuckahoe, but much about the way he spent his time there would have been determined by the place itself. Resembling a large farm as much as a grand estate, Tuckahoe testifies to young Jefferson's life spent with a foot in two worlds—as a slave-owning planter at the unploughed edge of the American frontier. Like other riverside plantations,

Tuckahoe was a community unto itself, a place with several dozen slaves, whom Jefferson would have watched practice the carpentry, blacksmithing, butchering, cooking, planting, tilling the fields, and countless other skilled and laborious tasks at the heart of plantation operations. It may well have been one of those slaves who first sharpened a goose quill for the young Jefferson and taught him to make crimson ink from a mash of plump wild pokeberries. A strong swimmer later in life, Jefferson may well have first dog-paddled in summer shallows and pools in the James. It's hard to imagine that he wouldn't have spent at least some time trying to coax catfish from its muddy bottom with chicken liver or a fat night crawler hooked on the end of a line. And he told his grandchildren of being given a gun by his father and sent into the forest for game, whereupon he took a turkey from a pen, roped the hapless foul to a tree, and shot it, the only known boyhood hunting tale in the lengthy canon on the man who would later draft the American revolutionary call to arms.

One of a handful of plantations built along the river upstream from the falls and rapids at Richmond, Tuckahoe was a place of folk history and lore, of blue heron and black crows on the wing. Jefferson and his family could have rowed across the river and hiked to the Dover coal mines, dating to 1730 and thought to be the oldest coaling operations in America. He also could have boated to the nearby village of some two hundred French Huguenots, protestant refugees fleeing the religious intolerance of King Louis XIV. They called their town Manakin, a European adulteration of "Monacan," the name of the indigenous people who had roamed the area free and unfettered since antiquity, before the Randolphs and the Jeffersons and the Huguenots came.

Young Jefferson undoubtedly traveled to Richmond to attend the fairs held on the second Thursday and Friday of each May and November. On those spring and fall weekends, the fledgling riverside trade mart became a colorful, brew-scented emporium, a wondrously egalitarian place where everyone from the highbrow to the commoner could bid on cattle, cakes, and crockery, feast on fruited jams and pies, and be entertained by fiddlers, storytellers, dancers, and games.

Unlike the Tidewater plantations downstream from the falls, Tuckahoe could not be reached by oceangoing ships. Only smaller boats, like canoes and minibarges the Huguenots called bateaus, could navigate the riffles and rapids, the shallows and shoals, of the river's western reaches. Yet, if Tuckahoe was remote, it was not removed. It was connected by the river to the larger world beyond and to the issues of the day by Peter Jefferson's surveying practice and his equally wide-ranging mind.

Thomas Jefferson was still small enough to sit on his father's knee when some of the most influential surveyors in the colony gathered in the black walnut-paneled parlor at Tuckahoe. With the smoke of Virginia tobacco clouding the air and with toasts to King George II, they resolved a dispute that divided the government in Williamsburg over vast holdings in the so-called Northern Neck of Virginia between the Potomac and Rappahannock rivers. It's not hard to imagine the young boy thrilling to the tales the old surveyors told of their backwoods adventures and capital talks. In later years, Jefferson recalled with near reverence his father's affinity for the opening land, the instruments he used to take its measure, his notes on the fields and streams, and the pencil-point sketches of a boundless new world aflame with promise and hope.

While still at Tuckahoe, Peter Jefferson produced the first modern map of Virginia with his close friend Joshua Fry, the English-born surveyor of Albemarle County, justice of the peace, member of the House of Burgesses, and mathematics professor at William and Mary. The Fry-Jefferson map was an extraordinary achievement for 1751. At a time when local cartography more typically depended on the memory of hunters and Indian guides, Jefferson and Fry incorporated the precise surveys that every landowner was required to place on file at county courthouses and at William and Mary. The map richly detailed the inlets and waterways of the Chesapeake Bay, the meandering course of the James, and the parallel chains of mountains buckling southwest-to-northeast through Virginia's western reaches like the exposed spine of a fallen dinosaur. More than a sketch of topography, the map literally plotted the future of mid-Atlantic westward expansion from modern-day Pennsylvania to North Carolina, doubtless stirring in young Thomas Jefferson the beginnings of a lifelong fascination with the vast possibilities of the inland frontier.

I DO NOT THINK MYSELF OBLIGED TO OBEY

The Fry-Jefferson map also pointed the way toward riches for Virginia's new royal lieutenant governor, a surveyor and customs administrator named Robert Dinwiddie. Born near the town of Glasgow in Scotland, Dinwiddie was a stockholder in the Ohio Company of Virginia. The company was founded by Thomas Lee, who owned Stratford, a large tobacco plantation on the Potomac River, and served in the House of Burgesses. The British crown granted the company a charter in 1747 to develop territories west of the Allegheny Mountains, with the caveat that the partners quickly establish their claim to the land, lest French adventurers beat them to it.

With precisely that goal in mind, Dinwiddie dispatched a diplomatic mission from Williamsburg across the Allegheny Mountains in October 1753 to the region near present-day Pittsburgh, where French trappers and explorers had become increasingly active. For his envoy, Dinwiddie needed a sturdy and reliable man who was good with maps, someone who could lead a small party of militiamen through the Virginia and Pennsylvania wilderness. He tapped a twenty-one-year-old surveyor from the Northern Neck named George Washington.

Through his incessant land speculation, Dinwiddie would have been aware of Washington, who had spent four years making a name for himself with his precise surveys of northern Virginia tracts. Better known to Dinwiddie, though, was Washington's older half-brother, Lawrence Washington, a justice and adjutant general of the Virginia militia. Lawrence Washington had served on the failed British naval strike against the Spanish port of Cartagena, in present-day Colombia. The mission was commanded by Vice Admiral Edward Vernon, in whose honor the Washington family's Potomac River plantation, Mount Vernon, was named. After Lawrence died of illness in 1753, Dinwiddie decided the younger Washington would have to do for the Ohio River embassy post.

More than simply Dinwiddie's profit was at stake. The British government was concerned that rival France would settle into the frontier heartland and develop a land bridge linking its Canadian holdings along the St. Lawrence Seaway with French Louisiana in the south, essentially boxing in British America along the eastern seaboard. It was Washington's job to talk the French out of it. Traveling on horseback nearly five hundred miles from Williamsburg to Pennsylvania's far west, Washington presented French captain Jacques Legarduer de Saint Pierre with a summons, informing the French officer that Virginia's royal magistrate and his fellow Ohio Company shareholders had decided to "require your peaceable departure." The French captain, comfortably ensconced in a fort his men had built on the Allegheny River, peaceably dismissed the future president instead with a uniquely francophone reply to the summons: "I do not think myself obliged to obey it."

Unequipped to compel compliance, Washington returned to Williamsburg that January, leading his party through ice and snow, to report to Dinwiddie that French forces had, indeed, established a military beachhead in the region and that they seemed to have acquired extensive alliances with Native Americans enriched by the French fur trade. It was a diplomatic failure for which Washington was hardly to blame. Dinwiddie, indeed, was impressed, not only with the young Washington's mission but with the threat to British settlement the astute young strategist had identified. Dinwiddie had Washington's report of the journey published in

Virginia with copies sent back to London, where it was read with great interest by King George II.

That spring, Dinwiddie sent Washington back to the western territories, this time as the second in command of some three hundred militiamen. Leading the mission was Peter Jefferson's old friend, Joshua Fry, whom Dinwiddie had named commander of the Virginia militia. Fry fell from his horse en route and died of his injuries at the end of May. Washington was promoted to colonel and placed in charge of the Virginia regiment, his first military command. He was twenty-two years old.

Nearing the forks of the Ohio River, Washington's party met a small group of French fighters and killed ten of them. Though Washington had no idea of it at the time, he had just led what turned out to be the first of a series of skirmishes that would billow into the Seven Years' War, also called the French and Indian War, pitting British and colonial American troops against French fighters and their Native American allies. Over the coming decade, the conflict would establish the British as the dominant rulers of colonial North America, while setting the stage for the Revolutionary War.

On that summer day, though, Washington and his men had stumbled into just the vanguard of a force of French soldiers, frontiersmen, and Indians that outnumbered Washington's men five to one. In the counterattack, Washington's forces were surrounded, fighting back against withering musket fire until a deluge soaked their flintlocks and powder, leaving only a bayonet charge into vastly superior numbers as the alternative to surrender. With one-third of his men already dead or wounded, Washington decided to capitulate rather than sacrifice what was left of his regiment. He surrendered on July 3, 1754, a date that haunted the American commander to his grave.

A year later, Washington was back in the forests and river valleys of Pennsylvania, this time serving as aide-de-camp to British general Edward Braddock, commander in chief of British forces in America. A strict disciplinarian, Braddock had a spit-and-polish style that was as uneasy a match for Washington's motley militia as the regimented and red-flannelled British troops were for the buckskin-and-broadcloth Virginia frontiersmen accompanying them. Historians can only imagine what the two groups found to talk about. When some of the Virginia woodsmen tippled the corn liquor in their canteens, Braddock had them whipped, winning more contempt for the crown than colonial allegiance to it.

On July 9, 1755, the lead units of the Anglo-American force of some fourteen hundred troops surprised a contingent of French and Indians on the Monongahela River, near present-day Pittsburgh. Under the leadership of British officer Thomas Gage, the Anglo-American vanguard collapsed before a withering counterattack, enabling the French and Indians to out-flank the British, their bright red coats brilliant targets in the summer for-est. In the ensuing fight, Washington had three horses shot from beneath him. A musket ball tore his hat and several others ripped through his clothes. While Washington, miraculously, escaped unhurt, Braddock was mortally wounded. As he lay dying, the British commander in chief be-queathed to Washington a pair of pistols and what may have been his most treasured possession, a blood-red military sash twelve feet long that had be-longed to Braddock's father. The gift was an unmistakable mark of the es-teem in which the hard-bitten English high commander had come to re-gard the young American colonel.

Once again, though, Washington witnessed abject defeat. Some nine hundred British and American troops, two-thirds of the total force, were killed or wounded in a rout that shocked Americans and British alike. Four years of similar setbacks would bedevil the Anglo-American forces until British general James Wolfe's decisive victory against the French at Quebec turned the tide of the war. It ended formally in 1763 with the Treaty of Paris, in which France surrendered its claims to Canada and all American lands east of the Mississippi River. It was the brief high-water mark for the British Empire in America, a moment when colonists felt like winners soar-ing the gusting thermals of London's global ascent. For the first time in his-tory, the English had stepped from the shadow of continental European su-periority—geostrategically, at any rate—and in America the growing colonies thrived beneath the political and security umbrella of the king and all his might.

If it didn't quite rule the waves, Britain's royal navy certainly dominated the Atlantic, a major factor in its defeat of the French. British frigates pa-trolled American coastal waters, shielding the colonial trade from pirates, much as British law protected the rights of colonists. With roots that reached back to the Magna Carta and spread to the Enlightenment, the bicameral par-liament—comprising the House of Commons and House of Lords—and the English courts had laid down a body of law and judicial precedent that to-gether amounted to a British constitution. Based on individual rights and lib-erties, the British constitution, on paper at least, protected freedom of speech, provided for trial by jury, prohibited arbitrary arrest, enshrined the principle that the people were the true sovereigns, and made clear that executing their will was the solemn duty of governments and kings. "Englishmen and colo-nials, who considered themselves Englishmen, believed that the British system of government was the best in the world," Carol Sue Humphrey wrote in *The Greenwood Library of American War Reporting*. "Through its balanced system that divided power between king, lords and commons, it gave representation to all sections of society." To be a British subject anywhere in the thirteen American colonies was to enjoy the protections and benefits of the most enlightened government of its age. Colonists walked a bit taller than they had just a few years before and began to see the world, and the American place in it, with newfound optimism and pride.

So it certainly must have appeared to Thomas Jefferson, twenty years old and in his second year of law school at William and Mary when the Treaty of Paris was signed. In the decade Washington had spent battling the French alongside British commanders and troops, Jefferson studied Latin and French, drank deeply from the streams of classical thought, learned architecture, and played his violin three hours a day. Shortly after his family left Tuckahoe and its one-room schoolhouse on the James, Jefferson came under the tutelage of the Irish-born minister James Maury. A rigorous instructor and intellectual man for all seasons, Maury had emigrated from his native Dublin as a child, settling near Shadwell, the Rivanna River plantation Peter Jefferson built on land he acquired in part with the cask of Raleigh Tavern punch. A chaplain to Virginia troops fighting in the Seven Years' War, Maury set up a school for boys near the town now known as Charlottesville, an hour or so from Shadwell by horse. There, he schooled Jefferson and two other future presidents, James Madison and James Monroe, in mathematics, literature, history, geography, and good manners from a log cabin in the Blue Ridge foothills.

At the height of the Seven Years' War, Jefferson left Shadwell and Maury to enter the College of William and Mary and the lofty intellectual milieu of Williamsburg. There, from the time he was seventeen, Jefferson was mentored by some of the best-cultivated minds of the age, beginning with his Scottish professor of science and math, the courtly William Small. "He made me his daily companion," Jefferson wrote in his autobiography, "and from his conversation I got my first views of the expansion of science and of the system of things in which we are placed."

Small and Jefferson frequently dined with the royal governor, Francis Fauquier, a London native. Like Dinwiddie, Fauquier's formal title was lieutenant governor. In practice, though, both functioned as the colony's chief executive because the royal governors they served elected to remain in England, an act of arrogance Virginians viewed with contempt. Called by Jefferson the best Virginia governor of the colonial era, Fauquier was considered a renaissance man, as fond of theater, classical music, and gambling as of the equally subtle art of governance. Rounding out the group of eminent elders was Jefferson's lifetime friend and legal compass point, his law professor George Wythe.

Born on his family's Elizabeth City tobacco plantation on the former Kecoughtan territory near the mouth of the James, young Wythe watched his family fortunes begin to fade after his father's death. Wythe's mother, Margaret Walker Wythe, tutored him in the classics and endowed her intellectually thirsty son with a lifelong love of learning and books. He struggled to pay tuition at William and Mary, finally leaving to move to the fledgling trade depot of Petersburg on the James River tributary named for the Appomattox Indians, where he read law under an uncle. Wythe was admitted to the bar in 1746, returned to Elizabeth City to practice, later served in the House of Burgesses, and became, at his Williamsburg alma mater, the first law professor in America.

Jefferson, Fauquier, Wythe, and Small might have made a devastating law firm. Instead, they became an intimate and mutually stimulating quartet, regularly dining together at Williamsburg's ornate Governor's Palace. A short walk from the college, the grand brick mansion was approved by the same general assembly that wrote the comprehensive slave code of 1705. It took sixteen years to complete the palace, a proud and square-jawed edifice meant to project royal authority from the center of sixty-three acres of ornamental boxwood, winding canals, and lawns that required two dozen slaves and full-time servants to maintain. After an evening of conversation, music, and wine, Jefferson could have wandered upstairs to the mansion's candlelit cupola, watched moonlight flicker from the waters of the James River four miles away, and dared to dream that he might one day inhabit the governor's palace himself, perhaps just as quickly banishing the thought as an idle schoolboy fantasy.

The idea would have seemed even more preposterous, though, to the rough-cut twenty-four-year-old farmer, failed storekeeper, and father of three who rode thirty miles on horseback to the Goochland County Courthouse a few miles upriver from Tuckahoe on an April day in 1760 and applied for a seat at the bar, having never attended the first law class. It smacked of the kind of brazen disregard for convention better suited to a barkeep—he had been that too—than to a man who expected to practice law. Patrick Henry, though, wasn't a man to be silenced by convention.

BUCKSKINNED BARRISTER

Neither a general's boot nor a scholar's staff had inflicted discipline on Henry, who grew up on the banks of the Pamunkey River, nearer to the ancient realms of Powhatan and Opechancanough than the contemporary seats of the Randolphs and Byrds. More prone to follow native instincts than elitist notions, Henry was a natural-born troublemaker, an establishment outsider who seemed better suited to bucking the system than profiting from it. At a time when the sons of plantation owners went to London or to William and Mary to study law, Henry was forced to take a bootstraps approach: thumbing through law books on his own by firelight and pumping lawyers for information at the backcountry tavern where he served ale across the dusty road from the courthouse in the new county of Hanover. Whether his self-styled immersion study lasted six months or only six weeks remains a point of historical intrigue. Either way, by April 1, 1760, he'd grasped the general gist of English law, the basis for the study of American jurisprudence at the time, perhaps with a special focus on the Bill of Rights passed by the British parliament a century before.

It took Henry two days to ride the fifty miles from Hanover to Williamsburg, where he went to William and Mary to take the oral exams prerequisite to hanging out his shingle. There, Henry stood for inquiry before four distinguished scholars. All four of them were burgesses, led by none other than Wythe, who would one day sign the Declaration of Independence that Henry's fierce oratory would do so much to advance. On this day, sixteen years before that, however, Henry was a man without credentials before a court of no appeal. He may well have been wondering whether he had taken a wrong turn on the muddy road from Hanover. He almost certainly was praying that he might somehow summon the rhetorical skills to paper over the veneer of his haphazard hearthside legal study and hoodwink these legal eminences into letting him skate through his first and final legal exam.

From Peyton Randolph and his brother John, another of Henry's inquisitors, there were doubtless probing questions on the origins of English law. Both had studied in London at the Inner Temple, one of four exclusive law schools that made up the Inns of Court, an almost religious order of legal education rooted in fourteenth-century precepts and mores. Thinking back on his own self-study in the hayseed river town of Petersburg, Wythe may have lent a more sympathetic ear as Henry sweated and silver-tongued his way through the inquiry, though none was impressed with his command of text. Somehow, though, Henry showed promise enough to convince the group that he wasn't a complete charlatan. They signed off on his license to practice law—with a special emphasis, to be sure, on practice—comforted by the expectation that the budding barrister would return to the rustic jurisdictions of Hanover, there to quietly bury his career in a swamp of probate judgments and petty claims. Two weeks later, Henry was admitted to the bar at Goochland, where he promptly filed a breach-of-contract suit on behalf of a domestic client, won a judgment of thirty pounds sterling, pocketed fifteen shillings for his services, saddled up, and rode back home.

No land-grant riverside aristocrat, Henry was a buckskin-breeches, speak-your-mind product of what his biographer, Henry Mayer, called "the second Virginia." The near hinterlands beyond the wealthy plantation culture, Henry's world was a place where a growing middle class reached for the next rung on the social and economic ladder. His father, John Henry, was born in Scotland, where he attended Kings College for four years. He left without a degree and journeyed to Virginia to join his older brother, an Anglican priest with a parish near the marshy lowlands along the winding Pamunkey. Like Peter Jefferson, Patrick Henry's father was a surveyor. He took title to twelve hundred acres of rich Pamunkey loam, then married his neighbor, a well-to-do widow named Sarah Winston Syme. A woman of quick wit and forceful personality, the widow Syme had inherited a sizable inland plantation of her own, as well as various tracts that swung west of the falls and stretched to the piedmont banks of the James. Melding his education and landholdings with the good name of the Winston family, John Henry soon became a county justice of the peace, militia colonel, and vestryman at his brother's church. The family's fortunes, though, never quite took flight. John Henry fared poorly at plantation management. And when his wife's son from her first marriage came of age, he inherited his share of the estate, so John Henry moved his family further upland.

In its own way, though, the home young Patrick Henry grew up in was as intellectually challenging as the parlor Peter Jefferson kept at Tuckahoe. Schooled in the classics, John Henry was a stimulating conversationalist who devoted some time to tutoring young Patrick. John Henry also seems to have had his hands full trying to keep up with his wife's independent spirit. Religiously, it was a house divided.

HOLY THUNDER

Henry's father and uncle, an Anglican priest, both hewed to the conservative outlook of the Church of England, calling on the hierarchical text of the King James Bible for a voice that could summon the sanctity of monarchs in the same breath as it might reference the glory of God. The two most important men in Henry's life, his father and uncle believed strongly in the authority vested in a royally licensed clergy.

Many colonists, though, had begun searching for spiritual direction beyond what they were getting from dark-robed elders droning through tired homilies. What some were calling the Great Awakening had begun to stir yearnings for religious freedom, diversity, and tolerance.

Like all Anglican clergy in Virginia, Henry's uncle, who was also named Patrick, was ordained by the bishop of London and had sworn allegiance to the crown. And, like most other official ministers in Virginia, the Reverend Henry leaned on Virginia's House of Burgesses to outlaw the unlicensed freelance preachers who had begun roaming the colony, spouting off unsanctioned from pillar to post about the innate godliness to be found in each human heart.

Most of these itinerant iconoclasts drifted down from the northern colonies. They appealed, though, to a growing number of working-class Virginians, and even slaves, who were seeking a more intimate and less authoritative form of worship than they found in the stricture-bound Anglican Church. One devotee of the new order was Patrick Henry's iron-willed mother, Sarah. Undaunted by the antagonistic views of her husband and brother-in-law, she often took her teenage son with her to hear the blazing sermons of Samuel Davies, an evangelical Presbyterian. A tall, gaunt, and charismatic orator, Davies held informal, but energetic, services at self-styled meeting houses, riversides, and barns across Hanover County, preaching that faith should be decoupled from the authority of the state and allowed to shine from within the soul of the faithful, regardless of their rank or station in life. At the foot of his willow-bank pulpit, Davies' growing flock began to read their Bible as more than just a terse moral code wrapped around a plea for patriarchal order. They found affirmation in stories and inspiration in scriptures they could apply to their daily lives.

"The Awakeners created a mass movement," University of California historian Gary Nash wrote in *The Unknown American Revolution*. "They challenged upper-class assumptions about social order and the deference due to established figures." It was a message tailor-made for young Patrick Henry, who entertained his mother on long wagon rides home by quoting extended passages of Davies' animated sermons. "He drew from evangelicalism an appreciation of fiery and theatrical presentation," wrote Nash, "and the needs of the humble."

Dipping deeply into both of those wells as a young lawyer, Patrick Henry built a reputation as a fiercely effective advocate. He more than made up for his threadbare legal training with knifepoint wit and soaring oratory few courtroom adversaries could withstand. The clergy itself fell prey to his prowess in 1763, when Henry successfully argued against ordained ministers like his uncle in a dispute over their official pay. It wasn't the preachers, in the end, who lost the most in the case but King George III, whose colonial authority was challenged in a way that presaged greater conflict to come.

For decades, Virginia preachers had been paid in tobacco, the closest thing Virginia had to a domestic currency. Faced with an economic slump, the Virginia General Assembly had passed a law allowing the clergy to be paid in cash for one year, the effect of which was a temporary pay cut for men of the cloth. Under pressure from the Anglican clergy, the king's privy council in London ordered Governor Fauquier to overturn the statute. He did so, but in a way that prevented ministers from recovering back pay.

This was an imperfect solution in the eyes of ordained priests like Jefferson's old schoolmaster, the Rev. James Maury. He filed a lawsuit in Hanover County against the parish tax collector, Thomas Johnson, hoping to recover lost wages. The case was heard in November 1763, at the Hanover Courthouse. Maury had good reason to expect a favorable result: The judge was John Henry, the Anglican parson's brother, sitting in his capacity as justice of the peace. Sure enough, a local jury readily went along with Maury's complaint; damages were to be decided the next day.

Having lost the case on its merits, Johnson's lawyer handed off responsibility for the damages phase of the trial to a junior attorney, his young friend Patrick Henry. The judge was more than a little conflicted: his brother stood to gain from the damage precedent; his son was arguing against such rewards. Patrick Henry grasped, however, that the so-called Parsons Cause was more than a mere wage dispute. The working man's Demosthenes who cut his rhetorical teeth on the explosive sermons of Davies, Henry cut to the quick of the question: who makes the laws for Virginians, an elected House of Burgesses in Williamsburg or a king accountable to no one and an ocean away? Henry understood, too, the clerics' instinct to dig in their heels over that very issue and to side with the monarch and protector of the faith against those insolent infidels gathering by the river for worship when they ought to be filling the straight-back pews of the Church of England instead. Awakening, indeed.

Rather than quibble about pennies, Henry reached for the stars, taking the spellbound Hanover Courthouse crowd on an hour-long tour de horizon of democratic thought and Enlightenment ideals. Men were born, he said, with inalienable rights. The king drew his authority from the people, he thundered, the only true sovereigns of any state. No one had the right to make law for free Virginians without the consent of Virginians themselves. And who were these unelected parsons anyway, these rapacious, ecclesiastical harpies who placed their own pocketbooks so high above the sacred will of the people "that they would snatch the last hoe cake from the widow and the orphan?" Reward them not, Henry concluded, they deserve instead to be punished!

Applause erupted in the courtroom, as Henry's father gaveled for order in vain. The jury retired and quickly returned, awarding Maury the bare minimum available under the verdict handed down the day before. He was entitled, jurors ruled, to a single penny and not one cent more, a stunning rebuke of the previous day's verdict. Henry was hoisted as a hero onto the shoulders of the capacity crowd and catapulted to the front lines of the political showdown brewing between the colony and the crown. Two years later and newly elected to the House of Burgesses, Patrick Henry would reprise his roar.

FROM THEIR OWN CONSENT

England had won the Seven Years' War against its bitter rival, France, but at tremendous cost. Waging the transatlantic conflict had left Britain deeply in debt, even as it struggled to administer the huge expanse of American land it had gained in the Treaty of Paris. Was it not reasonable, King George III and Parliament agreed, that London set some ground rules about future settlement and require the thriving colonies to pony up for their own defense? With that thinking in mind, the British took two key steps that immediately began to grate on the American colonists' nerves. First, in the Proclamation of 1763, the British government forbade the settling of lands west of the Appalachian Mountains and ordered colonists already there to leave and move back east. Farmers, fur trappers, and land speculators were annoyed. They regarded the expulsion of the French from those parts as a green light for westward expansion. Next, Britain authorized the deployment of up to ten thousand redcoats, mostly in the west, to enforce the new settlement boundaries and to be a sort of buffer between settlers and Indians. While far fewer than that number were actually sent, many colonists viewed the decision as a step toward establishing an imperialist occupation force. London, though, regarded the troops as essential security the colonists should gratefully support through their taxes.

In 1764, the British government imposed the American Revenue Act, prohibiting the import of foreign rum and levying taxes on molasses, wine, silk, and coffee. The soak-the-rich scheme riled mostly merchants and upper-class plantation owners, those who could afford fine luxury goods. London, though, would soon cast a wider net. The 1689 English Bill of Rights prohibited standing armies during times of peace without parliamentary consent. Generations of parliamentarians had gotten around that noble-sounding, but largely impractical, constraint by passing annual "mutiny acts," authorizing the use of military force to put down this mob uprising or that civil dissent. In 1765, Parliament invoked the same reasoning to justify the quartering of British troops in America, by force if necessary, "in inns, livery stables, ale houses," and such. If none were to be found, the act authorized British soldiers to use "houses, outhouses, barns or other buildings," so long as they were "uninhabited," the definition of which was left to the armed soldier. The act further required that colonists provide British troops deployed in the American colonies with food, bedding, firewood, candles, salt, and even their fill of beer or rum. Again, though, the act's impact was not particularly widespread. The vast majority of British troops at the time entered the colony at New York, whose people bore the brunt of the Quartering Act and staged noisy protests against it.

In March, though, Parliament overreached. It passed the infamous Stamp Act of 1765, requiring that all printed matter in the colonies—from newspapers and pamphlets to receipts and playing cards—be published on paper taxed and stamped by the crown. Tone deaf to the gathering colonial grievances, King George and the parliament had touched the third rail of colonial discontent, electrifying sentiments of self-rule in America and galvanizing the growing resentments of colonists across class lines. In taxing printed matter, the Stamp Act unwisely punished the two dozen or so newspaper publishers spread out across the colonies. That unleashed a torrent of editorial opposition that helped to solidify public opinion against the new tariff. It also helped establish support for a free press with the right to take British authority to task. And it seems to have particularly incensed a certain Hanover County lawyer who happened to be trying to scratch out a living for his family of five through a business built around contracts and warrants, notes and bonds, surveys and wills, all of which suddenly required the advance cash payment of the new stamp tax.

For weeks that spring, the colonies sputtered and balked. It wasn't until mid-May that the colonists at last found their voice, not surprisingly to some, in the same young lawyer who had riveted the packed Hanover County courtroom in autumn two years before. Buoyed to public prominence by his role in the Parsons Cause, Patrick Henry was elected that spring to the House of Burgesses from Louisa County. He rode immediately to Williamsburg, presented his election papers to the general assembly clerk, was sworn in, and took his seat at the statehouse, surrounded by the aristocratic plantation society stalwarts that made up the House of Burgesses. "Henry had entered a tobacco planters club," Mayer wrote in *A Son of Thunder*, his biography of Henry. "The wealthiest members—the great Tidewater magnates and their sons—wore elegant silks and satins and gloried in the whirling mix of politics, commerce and merriment," wrote Mayer. "For the past forty years, at least half the men of political consequence in the House had come from fewer than a dozen families, themselves intertwined beyond measure, so that claims of blood and public interest could scarcely be disentangled."

A crusty and conservative lot with much to lose from annoying the crown, the Virginia House of Burgesses—like assemblies in the American colonies elsewhere—had initially responded to the Stamp Act with more resignation than resolve. By late May, in fact, the whirling mix had just about lost its spin: most House members had already packed up and gone home. Presiding over what was left of the body was the most unlikely of revolutionaries: the quintessential establishment figure of British Empire in America, Peyton Randolph. Within a decade, Randolph would be hailed by Williamsburg militiamen as "the father of your country," blacklisted by the British, and sought for hanging. On this day, though, Randolph was the embodiment of caution, reflecting with great clarity the overall composition of the House. It was not a body looking for trouble, least of all with the British government.

"One interest dominated the House, indeed dominated Virginia's government and politics: tobacco planters—landed, slave-owning, hard-driving producers of a staple sold in England and on the European continent," University of California historian Robert Middlekauff wrote in *The Glorious Cause*, a survey of the American Revolution. "Other interests existed in the colony—religious dissenters in the West, Baptists, Presbyterians and Methodists—but these radicals of the spirit had not yet forced their way into the government of the colony."

Few would have mistaken Peyton Randolph for a radical spirit of any denomination. On the day in 1721 when Randolph was born in Williamsburg, the defining contours of his life were already in place. His father, born at the family's Turkey Island plantation near Curles Neck just below the falls of the James, was a wealthy attorney who represented the British king, then served as speaker of the House of Burgesses. As a young boy, Peyton Randolph grew up at the family's one-hundred-acre estate, Tazewell, in the heart of the Virginia capital—his capital. As a teenager, Randolph walked to classes at the College of William and Mary. After graduating, he traveled to London to study law at the Inner Temple. He returned to Williamsburg with the twin blessings of education and privilege and quickly began to assume the successively influential positions he'd been groomed for since birth: vestryman at Bruton Parish Church, member of the House of Burgesses, justice of the peace, and, like his father before him, attorney general to the English king.

By 1765, Randolph was a senior burgess with a deeply vested interest in preserving the status quo. That's precisely why the politically calcified speaker of the House, John Robinson, assigned Randolph to preside over what Robinson hoped would be a reliably tepid reply to the Stamp Act. The assembly session had dragged on all spring; what few members remained were mostly congratulating each other on their way out the door, extending regards to the family and invitations for social visits to the bachelors' quarters of their riverside spreads.

Into that convivial and retiring frat-house atmosphere, freshman Henry tossed a political stink bomb. With just 39 of the 116 House members still there, Henry rose to protest the Stamp Act in terms few of the remaining burgesses were in a mood to entertain. Virginians had not cast aside their English right to representative government when they came to America to build on new shores, he began, and they enjoyed that right no less in the colony than they would in England. For that matter, he railed, only the Virginia General Assembly had the right and the authority to tax the people of the colony, and those who would challenge that right were a threat to freedom on both sides of the Atlantic. That included, he suggested, King George III, who was a tyrant deserving of judgment. "Caesar had his Brutus, Charles the First had his Cromwell and George the Third. . . . "

There is no transcript of Henry's remarks, though a number of observers later recalled that memorable line. Some also recalled Robinson's interrupting Henry at that point with accusations of treason, upon which Henry, having made his point, either concluded with the words "may profit by their example," as some remembered, or simply let the line drift off uncompleted. In the collegial confines of the conservative House, he had already said, and done, enough. "The echoing of his bugling voice hung in the chamber like the reverberation of a bomb, and the well mannered family affair was never to be the same," wrote Dowdey. "A radical element had entered." Henry crow-barred his way into the well-mannered family with the force of his oratory. That much is known from at least one reliable, if unofficial, witness, who called Henry the greatest orator he ever heard. "I was yet a student of law in Williamsburg," Thomas Jefferson wrote in the autobiography he penned late in life. "I attended the debate, however, at the door of the lobby of the House of Burgesses, and heard the splendid display of Mr. Henry's talents as a popular orator. They were great indeed; such as I have never heard from any other man. He appeared to me to speak as Homer wrote."

The next day, by a single vote, the divided House approved a set of four resolutions enshrining the substance of Henry's appeal. In its "Four Resolves," the House stated that Virginia colonists were entitled to "all the liberties, privileges, franchises and immunities" British people everywhere enjoyed. Only elected representatives, the House added, offered assurance against "burdensome" taxes. And it was this very notion of representative government—democracy, in other words—that was "the distinguishing characteristic of British freedom, without which the ancient constitution cannot exist." The heart of the matter, the House concluded, was that Virginians had an absolute right to be governed by laws and policies "as are derived from their own consent."

Randolph and other champions of the status quo opposed Henry's resolutions—some challenged his election papers, hoping to have him unseated—and were livid that they passed. "By God, I would have given 500 guineas for a single vote," Peyton Randolph fumed on his way out the chamber door, within earshot of his young cousin, Thomas Jefferson, back to watch the thrilling denouement of the political drama Henry had set in motion the day before.

A fifth resolution was passed as well, though the House voted to annul it the next day as one of the session's final acts of business. Colonial newspaper accounts published it along with the others, though, lending it the weight of public favor, if not the force of law. "Resolved, therefore, that the General Assembly of this Colony have the only and exclusive right and power to lay taxes and impositions upon the inhabitants of this colony," it stated, "and that every attempt to vest such power in any person or persons whatsoever, other than the General Assembly aforesaid, has a manifest tendency to destroy British as well as American freedom."

Henry had fired the first shot across the bow of the British Empire in America. In memorable and passionate prose, he articulated the overarching offense of taxation without representation and its ugly stepchild, government without consent of the governed, principles upon which more forceful dissent would soon be waged. The clarity of his thought and the power of his persuasion, moreover, had moved Virginia's reluctant House of Burgesses to transform his complaint into official policy. His voice, amplified in newspaper reports and mimicked in taverns, meeting houses, and assembly halls up and down the eastern seaboard, helped to unite the colonies in common cause. And his logic clarified the legitimate grievances behind riots and other mob actions against the hated tax from Boston to Georgia, helping to solidify the revolutionary impulses gathering in the American soul.

LETTERS FROM A FARMER

Over the next four months, similar resolutions were approved by the assemblies of Rhode Island, Pennsylvania, and Maryland, as Stamp Act opposition coalesced across the colonies. There were public demonstrations against it. Royal commissioners charged with collecting the taxes were threatened and intimidated into stepping down from their posts. Dissidents ran riot in Boston, destroying the house of Massachusetts lieutenant governor Thomas Hutchinson.

In October, delegates from nine colonies convened a Stamp Act Congress in New York, where they issued "A Declaration of Rights and Petition to the King." Essentially a power-sharing proposal, the declaration called for self-rule within the orbit of the British Empire. It stopped short of calling for American independence from English rule and even acknowledged allegiance to the crown and Parliament. In a direct challenge, though, the congress stated that only colonial legislatures had the power to tax the colonists. No Virginia delegates were in New York. An increasingly agitated Governor Fauquier had refused to reconvene the House of Burgesses to name delegates to the congress. Henry's voice could be heard, though, echoing in the declaration, which condemned the Stamp Act for its "manifest tendency to subvert the rights and liberties of the colonists."

The British parliament backtracked, then quickly regrouped. It abolished the Stamp Act the next year, while passing the Declaratory Act, affirming Parliament's authority to tax the American colonists. As if to remove any doubt about that, Parliament passed the equally provocative Townshend Acts in the summer of 1767, imposing customs duties on the colonies for imported paint, glass, paper, lead, coffee, chocolate, and tea. The acts more irritated Virginians than enraged them, but they further fueled colonial discontent with British high-handedness, especially as the acts dissolved the New York legislature as punishment for the state's failure to provide sufficient lodging to British troops.

Philadelphia lawyer John Dickinson may have best captured colonial sentiment in the fall of that year, when he wrote an influential series of essays published in newspapers across the American colonies as *Letters from a Farmer in Pennsylvania*. Criticized by royal governors as dangerous and seditious, Dickinson's *Letters* lent a homespun credence to the ideas being espoused by people such as Henry and his Boston counterpart, the populist agitator and polemicist Samuel Adams. The son of a Maryland tobacco planter, Dickinson was another American graduate of London's Inner Temple. His message was that Britain and the English-speaking American colonies were tethered by culture, family, history, and trade, but the mother country had no right to tax colonists, who had no one in Parliament to speak for them. Britain may be strong militarily, he argued, but its economy had grown dependent upon the transatlantic trade. If Americans refused to buy the goods Britain insisted on taxing, Dickinson reasoned, perhaps that would sober up King George III and his policymakers to the merits of reason and the rights of man.

Though a wealthy city lawyer with a magnificent country estate, Dickinson hit upon a public-relations triumph in casting his treatise as the musings of a simple husbandman. His ideas took wing, and he came to be seen as both sage statesman and folk hero, a character that was to resurface again and again on the stage of American politics.

One person following Dickinson's performance with great interest was Massachusetts legislator Samuel Adams, a Boston malt maker's son and graduate of Harvard College. A bit like Henry, Adams was raised by a father who held public office, serving as justice of the peace, and did well in business until his fortunes flagged. Adams himself won election as Boston's tax collector but botched the books so badly the town treasurer took him to court. Unlike Henry, though, Adams' constituents were the very merchants and artisans who relied on the British paints, glass, and paper that were hit with customs duties under the Townshend Acts.

The month after Dickinson's essays were published, Adams presented Massachusetts legislators with his *Circular Letter*, assailing the practice of government without the consent of the governed and urging colonial resistance to the Townshend Acts. The Massachusetts House of Representatives adopted the *Letter* as a resolution, then sent copies to the legislatures of every British colony in America, asking that they embrace it as well.

London countered by ordering British governors in the colonies to dissolve any assembly that endorsed the *Circular Letter*. The British government also alerted Gen. Thomas Gage, the same who had struggled alongside Washington against the French, to ready his forces in New York for a possible deployment to Boston. Within months, dozens of towns had voted to boycott British imports affected by the duties, in line with Dickinson's suggestions, while several colonial assemblies struggled for ways to defy the Townshend Acts and align themselves with Massachusetts.

In an effort to keep the peace in Williamsburg, Fauquier had simply refused to recall the House of Burgesses. When he died in March 1768, the president of the State Council, John Blair, called the House to order. Not only did the Virginians endorse Adams' *Circular Letter*, but they also called for protests and tacked on a petition to London asserting that the Virginia assembly was every bit the equal of the British parliament as a legitimate legislative body.

In August, the Massachusetts legislators agreed not to import British goods taxed by the Townshend duties until the offensive acts were rescinded. The group made exceptions for the salt, fish hooks, and lines the local codfish industry depended upon and the lead shot needed to hunt ducks and geese. Over the next year, similar boycotts were put in place by almost every port city in British America as far south as Charleston. The nation's largest slave depot, Charleston retained similar exceptions for essential hunting and fishing gear but added that it would "not import, buy or sell any Negroes" coming in through the Royal African Company so long as the Townshend Acts remained in force.

It was in this atmosphere of growing colonial unity and mounting dissent against the crown that Jefferson began his political career. At twenty-five, he had come of age, begun his law practice, inherited Shadwell's 2,750 acres and some two dozen slaves, and set them to work on the grand manor house he designed and named Monticello. Jefferson was visiting Williamsburg in October 1768, when the capital was focused on the arrival of Fauquier's replacement, Norborne Berkeley. A descendent of the former Virginia governor William Berkeley, who had clashed swords with Nathaniel Bacon a century before, Norborne Berkeley was more formally known as Lord Botetourt. While Jefferson doubtless bore remorse over the death seven months earlier of his close friend, Governor Fauquier, he took some comfort in knowing that Botetourt had served in the English House of Commons, where he may have at least acquired a decent respect for individual rights and democratic ideals.

True to expectations, Botetourt promptly dissolved the general assembly and issued a call for elections to seat new burgesses for a new government. Jefferson decided to run. In mid-December, he was elected to the House of Burgesses by voters gathered in the Albemarle County Courthouse in Charlottesville. The town had been founded five years before and named for Queen Charlotte, the German princess who became the wife of King George III and mother of their fifteen children. That May, when Botetourt convened the general assembly, Jefferson was sworn in as a freshman member of the House of Burgesses. Just four years earlier, he'd stood in the doorway to hear Henry rally the body to action over the hated Stamp Act. Now Jefferson was one of them himself, a young legislator poised to make his mark.

One of Jefferson's first legislative initiatives of note failed. Taking aim at the Virginia slave code, Jefferson tried to eliminate the prohibition on freeing slaves. His proposal would not have freed them, but it would have allowed slave owners to do so if they chose. It was summarily shot down by the conservative legislature as "indeed, during the regal government, nothing liberal could expect success," Jefferson later explained. "Our minds were circumscribed within narrow limits, by an habitual belief that it was our duty to be subordinate to the mother country in all matters of government, to direct all our labor in subservience to her interests and even to observe a bigoted intolerance for all religions but hers."

Subservience to the mother country, though, was fast losing favor. Jefferson's legislative career was merely days old when the House of Burgesses prepared to take up its own nonimportation agreement to protest the Townshend Acts. Upon learning of the agenda, Governor Botetourt summoned the speaker of the House, Peyton Randolph, and declared the assembly dissolved. Not to be dissuaded by formalities, the burgesses walked down Duke of Gloucester Street and repaired to the Apollo Room of the nearby Raleigh Tavern. There, perhaps refreshed by that establishment's famous rum punch, the legislators unanimously elected Randolph to preside over their rump convention, which quickly approved Virginia's own nonimportation agreement. It built on the others in place elsewhere and added that Virginians would not kill, "or suffer to be killed," any local lambs, an effort to build up the breeding stock of domestic sheep and discourage imports of British wool.

Among the burgesses who voted to approve the measure was George Washington. "At a time when our lordly Masters in Great Britain will be satisfied with nothing less than the deprivation of American freedom," Washington wrote in a letter to his Potomac River plantation neighbor and fellow House member George Mason, "it seems highly necessary that something should be done to avert the stroke and maintain the liberty which we have derived from our ancestors."

The nonimportation accords demonstrated, once again, that the colonies could coordinate a potent, if civil, response to unpopular parliamentary moves. Unhappy British merchants pressed London lawmakers to repeal the Townshend Acts, and Parliament did so, leaving in place only levies applicable to shipments of tea. The colonial victory, however, went down poorly with King George. He sent warships to Boston harbor in the spring of 1768 to protect customs officials threatened by mobs. Riots broke out after British officials seized the merchant sloop *Liberty,* owned by the wealthy Massachusetts trader and consummate politician John Hancock, under suspicion that it was being used to smuggle wine. The royal governor ordered the Massachusetts legislature to rescind its nonimportation accord, dissolving the body when it refused. In October, British troops were sent to Boston.

Rather than cooling tempers as London had hoped, the troop presence inflamed Bostonians. Under the strain of mounting tensions, redcoats opened fire on a jeering, but unarmed, crowd on March 5, 1770, killing five. The first colonist to fall was a runaway slave named Crispus Attucks, who was shot twice in the chest at close range. Thought to have descended from African and American Indian ancestors, Attucks has gone down in history as the first casualty of the American Revolution, though all-out war was still five years away.

Ever alert to an opportunity to demonize the British, Samuel Adams quickly labeled the shootings "The Boston Massacre." While Britain responded by withdrawing its troops, Adams' characterization stuck. Many Americans saw the incident as proof the English crown meant to crush colonial hopes for self-rule. The stage was set for the next showdown. It was nearly four years in coming and it came, not surprisingly, in Boston.

By 1773, Britain's East India Company was nearly bankrupt after years of economic warfare across the Atlantic. In response, Parliament granted the merchant fleet special status to ship tea directly from India to the colonies at cut rates meant to reduce the pain of the tea tariff. When three tea-freighted ships—*Dartmouth, Beaver,* and *Eleanor*—arrived in Boston harbor, Adams and fellow instigators arranged for about fifty activists to dress as Mohawk Indians and slip aboard the ships on the night of December 16, 1773. Over the next several hours, they broke open some 340 chests of tea and dumped them into the harbor.

Critics have charged over the years that the crafty Adams and his merchant constituents staged a mercantilist stunt to protect their commercial interests, then gussied it up as a blow for liberty. The Boston Tea Party, though, has endured as the single most memorable act of colonial defiance in the lead-up to the Revolutionary War. King George III, of course, was not amused. He ordered Boston harbor closed, throwing hundreds of merchants, dockhands, and others out of work, and sent redcoats back into town, this time as a near occupying force, lighting the fuse that led to Lexington and Concord.

A SUMMARY VIEW

For many leaders in the American colonies, the occupation of Boston was the last straw. Just that year, on a recommendation Jefferson authored, the colonies had forged a political bond through the use of so-called committees of correspondence. The committees provided official communications and policy coordination among the colonial legislatures in a first step toward national governance. To formalize their ideological alliance and speak to London with a single voice, they scheduled a joint meeting of delegates representing the legislatures of every colony. With nearly thirty thousand people, Philadelphia was the largest city in the colonies, and it was reasonably central besides. The group decided to meet there in September 1774 and called itself the Continental Congress.

In Virginia, burgesses scheduled a summer convention to elect delegates to send to Philadelphia. They weren't able to convene as the House of Burgesses because the body had been suspended by the royal governor who succeeded Botetourt. His name was John Murray, a Scottish noble better known as Lord Dunmore. In the days Jefferson roamed the grounds of Tuckahoe as a boy, Dunmore saw his own rebellious father imprisoned in the Tower of London. At twenty, Dunmore cleared the family name, joining the British Army. He spent nine years in the House of Lords and was tapped to become governor of New York until Botetourt's 1770 death. Shortly after Dunmore arrived in Williamsburg the next year, his wife, Charlotte, gave birth to their eighth child, a girl the couple named Virginia.

En route to the capital for the August convention, Jefferson fell ill with dysentery and had to turn back home. He sent to Peyton Randolph and Patrick Henry one copy each of a document he'd written that summer at Monticello. An uncertain speaker who could only envy Henry's oratorical gifts, Jefferson expressed himself best on paper. That became clear that summer when his colleagues in Williamsburg received from him what amounted to a final appeal for self-rule for American colonies within the British Empire. Jefferson didn't sign the untitled document, perhaps realizing the criticism of King George it contained could become grounds for treason in the wrong hands. Randolph read it aloud to fellow burgesses. It was published by a Williamsburg printer, without Jefferson's knowledge, under the title *A Summary View of the Rights of British America*. Its author was listed simply as a native Virginian. Copies were circulated around the American colonies and reprinted in Philadelphia and London.

Jefferson began his *Summary* by laying out "the united complaints of his majesty's subjects in America" in words that, two and a half centuries later, fairly burst from the page with the power of eloquent expression—or, as Jefferson himself put it, "with that freedom of language and sentiment which becomes a free people claiming their rights." Those rights flowed from no less a font of freedom than Britain itself, Jefferson averred, drawing on ideals set forth by classical philosophers, decades of parliamentary precedent, and the Enlightenment figure, John Locke. A seventeenth-century English philosopher, Locke wrote that government drew its legitimacy from the consent of the governed and that leaders were obliged to employ the natural laws of tolerance and reason to protect their citizens' life, liberty, and property.

In his *Summary,* Jefferson went on to reject the claim that the colonists should pay taxes to offset the cost of the Seven Years' War. That conflict was waged, he wrote, to protect the British Empire against France, not as a favor to the American colonists. They built the colonies on their own dime, he wrote, and "not a shilling" of those resources that king and Parliament controlled. "America was conquered, and her settlements made, and firmly established, at the expense of individuals, and not of the British public," Jefferson wrote, in lines that echoed the early struggles of Capt. John Smith and others to secure from London resources that were desperately needed by starving settlers along the James. "Their own blood was spilt in acquiring lands for their settlement, their own fortunes [were] expended in making that settlement effectual; for themselves they fought, for themselves they conquered and for themselves alone they have right to hold." The money British investors had staked in the colonies was amply repaid by the colonial trade, Jefferson continued, vowing that Americans would not be taxed or regulated "by any power on earth but our own." He defended the Boston Tea Party as the act of "an exasperated people" and went on to lambaste the British government for closing the port in response. "The whole of that ancient and wealthy town," he wrote, "is in a moment reduced from opulence to beggary."

On and on went Jefferson, railing against parliamentary oversight of colonial governance and warning that Americans would not consent to be ruled by legislators an ocean away, where they were "removed from the reach of fear, the only restraining motive which may hold the hand of a tyrant." How, for that matter, Jefferson asked, could a country the size of

Britain ever expect to hold sway over a continent the size of America? The proposition defied not only "the common feelings of human nature," he wrote, but also "the principles of common sense."

Turning his quill to the British royalty, Jefferson served notice that he and his colonial kinsmen would never tremble before a monarch nor pay sycophantic homage to a crown. "Let those flatter who fear," wrote Jefferson. "It is not an American art." Nor, he made clear, was allegiance to kings an American trait. "Kings are the servants, not the proprietors of the people," he wrote in a line that surely set teeth to gnashing in the court of King George, even among the most devoted readers of Locke's *Two Treatises on Government.* Jefferson then charged the king with abusing his authority to veto laws passed by colonial legislatures. The sole example Jefferson provided of the king's "wanton exercise of this power" had to do, astonishingly, with slavery. Jefferson contended that the colonies wanted to do away with it, but the king, bowing to the interests of British slave merchants, wouldn't let them. "The abolition of domestic slavery," wrote Jefferson, "is the great object of desire" in the American colonies, "where it was unhappily introduced in their infant state." Before slavery could be abolished, though, the British government would have to put an end to its transatlantic slave trade, Jefferson maintained. King George would not do so, Jefferson further charged, "thus preferring the immediate advantages of a few African corsairs to the lasting interest of the American states, and to the rights of human nature, deeply wounded by this infamous practice."

Slavery, as Jefferson saw it, had been planted in British America at its roots. It was sustained, he believed, less by the demands of the colonists than by the vast profits the slave trade generated for the British Empire. As he had already learned from the House rebuff of his antislavery proposal, Jefferson was by no means speaking for all Americans, especially not for the large plantation owners who depended on slaves for their wealth as much as the Royal African Company's investors in the slaving depots of Bristol and Liverpool did. Still, even in his early writing, Jefferson made clear his personal passion on the issue and his belief that antislavery sentiments were widely held.

"White Virginians were conscious of their self-perceived role as leaders in the battle for liberty in the world, and certainly the existence of slavery bothered them, it bothered some of them," said Sidbury, the University of Texas historian. "It's a very complicated story." Part of the complexity bordered on delusion, said George Mason University's Wilkins, author of *Jefferson's Pillow,* a look at the conflicting instincts of the founding fathers, most of whom owned slaves. "They were going to do mental gymnastics, speak with forked tongue, whatever it took for them to be for freedom and slavery at the same time," said Wilkins. "A guy who didn't want to get up and look himself in the mirror and say, 'I'm an ogre, and I'm running a penal colony,' could say, instead, 'I'm for freedom and liberty and justice, and if the black people had the capacity to be self-governing like we are, they would be.'"

Whatever Jefferson may have thought to himself while shaving, he closed his *Summary View* with a vivid appeal, not for independence from Britain but for an equitable partnership within the British Empire. Indeed, a break from the mother country "is neither our wish, nor our interest," he wrote in the summer of 1774, adding that a perpetual union of British subjects on both sides of the Atlantic, bound by "fraternal love and harmony through the whole empire . . . is the fervent prayer of all British America!" Those bonds, though, could not come to chain a free people. "The God who gave us life gave us liberty at the same time," wrote Jefferson. "The hand of force may destroy, but cannot disjoin them."

Too radical and risky to be adopted by the House of Burgesses, Jefferson's *Summary View* was widely read in Philadelphia that September. Much as Patrick Henry had done with his Stamp Act resolves a decade before, Jefferson had clarified the sentiments of a growing number of American colonists and advanced a new way of looking at the transatlantic conflict. Though he wasn't in Philadelphia that September, his writing set the tone, if not the agenda, for the Continental Congress, where fifty-six delegates gathered representing every colony except Georgia.

The Virginia delegation to the Congress was headed by Peyton Randolph, who was elected president of the Congress, the first chief executive of what would become the United States. He was accompanied by Patrick Henry, George Washington, and several other Virginians. They joined the Boston agitator, Samuel Adams, his Massachusetts compatriot, the Harvard-trained lawyer John Adams, and John Dickinson, the popular Pennsylvania pamphleteer, among others.

Over the next five weeks, the delegates agreed to a set of resolutions assailing the closing of Boston Harbor, the long train of tariffs, the habitual suspension of colonial legislatures, and a litany of other "grievous acts and measures." They agreed that by virtue of "the immutable laws of nature [and] the principles of the English constitution," the American colonists had the right to "life, liberty and property." They asserted that the colonial legislatures had "exclusive power" to levy taxes and make laws in the American colonies. And they agreed to a continental boycott of British goods until their complaints were addressed and their rights and assertions recognized. The First Continental Congress and the resolutions it produced in

October 1774 were seen by many in America as a last chance for the colonies and their British overlords to settle their differences without a clash of arms. If such a possibility indeed existed, it was an opportunity missed.

THE SWORD IS DRAWN

In the spring of 1775, the Virginia burgesses scheduled yet another unauthorized meeting, their House sessions held in more or less perpetual suspension by the royal governor, Lord Dunmore. A new dimension had emerged, though, in the old cat-and-mouse game of burgesses meeting in the Apollo Room under Dunmore's nose. The mounting tensions between colonists and the crown had stirred fears that the governor might at last take action against those who spoke out and published direct attacks against the king. With British warships plying the waters of the lower James, the better part of valor, the burgesses agreed, might be to meet in a venue other than one that happened to be among Dunmore's favorite dining haunts.

So, late March found Virginia's 120 political representatives converging not on the grand, gay capital at Williamsburg but on the muddy little collection of pine plank homes, slouching taverns, and tobacco hovels that had grown up around William Byrd's pelt-and-hide post at Richmond. It was a town of about six hundred people occupying houses and shops seated squarely on plots Byrd had laid out in parallel lines stepping back from the river's north bank or wandering up the steep slopes rising from its rock-strewn edge. Along the south bank, near the town of Manchester, slaves and white laborers quarried coal that was loaded into oaken bateaus and shuttled to the iron foundry at the deepwater port of Warwick downstream. Overlooking it all from a hilltop perch was the Henrico Parish Church, founded in 1611 on the river's opposite shore by the Rev. Alexander Whitaker, the parson who brought Pocahontas to Christianity and may have presided over her wedding to John Rolfe.

On March 20, 1775, the Henrico Parish Church, later named St. John's, was the only building in Richmond large enough to hold the burgesses. Its rector, the Rev. Miles Selden, was a friend to what was quickly taking form as the revolutionary movement, and he opened his sanctuary to the cause. And so, after hours, in some cases even days, of hard riding over rough roads, the legislators tied up their lathered horses in the churchyard, exchanged greetings, and sauntered into the two-story white clapboard building with the small bell tower squatting atop the front peak of the roof.

Two future American presidents rode in that Monday morning—
Washington from his Potomac River plantation, Mount Vernon, and Jefferson from Monticello. There were five who would sign Jefferson's Declaration of Independence the next year—Carter Braxton, Benjamin Harrison,
Richard Henry Lee, Thomas Nelson, and Francis Lightfoot Lee. Peyton
Randolph rode in from Williamsburg and was elected to preside over the
convention. Jefferson's first classmate, his cousin Thomas Mann Randolph,
had come up the old river road from Tuckahoe. And in from his thriving
Hanover County estate of Scotchtown came Patrick Henry. Seldom the
most jovial of burgesses, the ever-combustible Henry was in an unusually
dark mood. Sarah, his wife of two decades and mother of their eleven children, had died just weeks before after what sounds today like a long struggle with depression. At thirty-nine, a grieving Henry said he had become
"a distraught old man."

With opening prayers from Parson Selden and sympathetic nods to the
grieving Henry, the Virginia convention got underway. Not even Selden
could have divined on that cool day in spring that in the crowded sanctuary where Jefferson, Henry, and Washington sat were what historians would
one day call the pen, the tongue, and the sword of the American Revolution. For three days, the convention members discussed and debated the
way ahead in rhetoric that pushed, then pulled, across both sides of the line
between war and peace. Tensions were eased by tavern breaks and conversation in the hilltop churchyard, where stiff-kneed burgesses could stretch
their legs in a chilly breeze, look out over the river, and contemplate the
roar of the rapids below.

On Thursday, March 23, the session came to a boil, when Henry rose
in the crowded sanctuary to make the case for war—or at least to put Virginians in a position to defend themselves should war come. The British
parliament had prohibited colonists from importing ammunition and arms.
Redcoats were enforcing the edict across New England. Colonists'
weapons were being seized. It was time, Henry said, for Virginians to arm.
"A well-regulated militia is the natural strength and only security of a free
government," Henry said, drawing practically verbatim from language used
months before in a Maryland congressional resolution. "Resolved, therefore, that this colony be immediately put into a state of defense, and that
a committee be named by the convention to prepare a plan for embody-
ing, arming and disciplining such a number of men as may be sufficient for
that purpose."

Richard Henry Lee from Westmoreland County rose to second
Henry's motion, which was immediately opposed by Benjamin Harrison of

Berkeley and several other Tidewater planters. Fearing the damage war could mean for their tobacco production and shipments, these conservatives argued for a conciliatory approach to Britain. Edmund Pendleton from Caroline County urged delay, asking where Virginia would get the troops, the arms, the military "sinews," as he called them, required to do battle with the royal British Navy and infantry.

Braced for opposition and girded for debate, Henry launched into one of the most important speeches in American history, climaxing in a battle cry that has crystallized with time into a part of the national credo. "It is natural for man to indulge in the illusions of hope," he began. "We are apt to shut our eyes against a painful truth." After a decade of mounting repression from the British government, however, Henry could see nothing to warrant optimism. "I have but one lamp by which my feet are guided, and that is the lamp of experience," he explained. And now, even as the burgesses skulked away from their statehouse to meet in a church, he warned, British forces were making "warlike preparations, which cover our waters and darken our land."

The cautious Peyton Randolph, who opposed Henry's heated Stamp Act resolves a decade before, glared down from the canopied pulpit where he presided over the day's proceedings, a kind of shotgun wedding of church and state.

"Suffer not yourselves to be betrayed with a kiss," Henry preached, warning against a sitting monarch with an "insidious" smile and teeth of steel. "Are fleets and armies necessary to a work of love and reconciliation," he wondered out loud before riveting members to their seats with his response. "These are the implements of war and subjugation, the last arguments to which kings resort!" With lawyerly polish and Protestant grace, Henry enthralled the room. His voice rose to a crescendo that seemed to rattle the thin, leaded window panes, then plunged to a whisper that brought emotions to a hush. "They tell us, sir, that we are weak," he shrugged. "But when shall we be stronger . . . when we are totally disarmed and when a British guard shall be stationed in every house?" The strength for rebellion, Henry vowed, would come from the righteousness of the fight. "Three millions of people, armed in the holy cause of liberty, and in such a country as that which we possess, are invincible by any force which our enemy can send against us."

Having earlier dismissed as vain any hope of reconciliation, Henry then played on the even thinner belief, at that moment anyway, that France, Spain, and the Netherlands might come to the colonists' aid. "There is a just God who presides over the destinies of nations and who will raise up friends to fight our battles for us," Henry assured his fellow burgesses in lines resonant of Shakespeare and Davies. And there was more to waging war, he pressed ahead, than simple sinew and steel. "The battle, sir, is not to the strong alone, it is to the vigilant, the active, the brave." Besides, said Henry, Britain had left Virginians no choice, as their Bay Colony brethren already had learned. "There is no retreat, but in submission and slavery! Our chains are forged! Their clanking may be heard on the plains of Boston! The war is inevitable—and let it come! I repeat it, sir, let it come!"

With a plea for independence and a call to arms, Henry delivered the thunderous close, casting the choice before the burgesses not as a question of war or peace, but of life or liberty. "Gentlemen may cry peace, peace—but there is no peace," Henry intoned, rising to the great orator's finest moment. "What is it that gentlemen wish," he asked, outstretched arms searching for the heavens. "Is life so dear or peace so sweet as to be purchased at the price of chains and slavery? Forbid it Almighty God! I know not what course others may take," said Henry, fists clenched and eyes ablaze, "but as for me, give me liberty, or give me death!"

As with Henry's speech opposing the Stamp Act, there was no written copy of his Richmond speech; none was ever found among his papers. The version handed down through history comes mostly from notes scribbled down by George Tucker—or, as his parents named him, St. George—a young lawyer who had studied under Wythe at William and Mary and was apparently part of the crowd pressed around the church window to hear one of the great moments in American rhetoric. Three decades later, Tucker, by then a U.S. district judge in Richmond, shared his recollections of the speech in writing with his friend William Wirt, an attorney in nearby Petersburg. Wirt consulted several aging Virginians, including Jefferson, who had witnessed the speech before publishing it in his 1817 biography, *Sketches of the Life and Character of Patrick Henry*. The man Jefferson called the greatest orator of his age could not be consulted: Henry had died eighteen years before, at sixty-three.

There's no way to know verbatim what Henry said that day, but Tucker's notes and Wirt's research seem to have produced a faithful facsimile of his unforgettable lines. Tucker may have burnished the prose a bit here and there, but other witnesses concurred with his rendering, while none was known to dissent. It is known beyond doubt that the speech was persuasive in a sharply divided body with more than its share of fence-sitters. Backed by Jefferson, Washington, Lee, and others, Henry's motion to create a Virginia militia, an act of war against the crown, passed the 120-member body by a margin of five votes. Henry was named chairman of a committee to set up county militias across Virginia, many members of which emblazoned their hunting shirts with the battle cry he had coined: "Liberty or Death."

Sooner than Henry himself might have imagined, the words themselves bore the mantle of truth. On April 19, 1775, just weeks after his stirring speech, British infantry clashed with colonial minutemen and militia units in the towns of Lexington and Concord outside Boston. Both sides accused each other of firing the first shots in the Revolutionary War. By day's end, though, the rebels had stood down the redcoats and driven them back to Boston, with the loss of 273 British dead or wounded and 95 casualties on the colonial American side. Henry's dark warning that "the next gale that sweeps from the north will bring to our ears the clash of resounding arms" had proven tragically prophetic. "The sword is now drawn," declared the *Virginia Gazette* in Williamsburg, "and God knows when it will be sheathed."

THE EMANCIPATOR

With Henry's war cry and the *Gazette*'s burning question before him, Governor Dunmore ordered British marines to seize fifteen small barrels of colonial gunpowder from the Williamsburg magazine and store it aboard a British schooner in the nearby James. Henry rallied a Hanover militia and led it toward Williamsburg, where Dunmore sent little Virginia and the rest of his family to less opulent, but more secure, quarters aboard the HMS *Fowey*, a British man-of-war anchored in the York River a few miles away. Dunmore then readied two hundred redcoats to defend the Governor's Palace and warned that he would order the *Fowey* to shell the neighboring community of Yorktown to rubble if Henry entered the capital. The standoff was eased by middlemen, who paid the colonial legislature for the stolen powder. Henry called off the militia and was branded an outlaw by Dunmore, who soon fled Williamsburg. The last royal appointee to inhabit the Governor's Palace, Dunmore joined his family aboard the *Fowey*.

The next month, Henry joined Washington, Jefferson, and others in Philadelphia for the Second Continental Congress. As they met, New England colonists lay siege to British forces in Boston, which countered in mid-June with artillery fire and infantry attacks at the battle of Bunker Hill. Colonists were forced to retreat, with 140 killed and 271 wounded. British casualties, though, were far higher, with 226 killed and 828 wounded.

With fighting engaged in Boston, the Congress in Philadelphia authorized the creation of a continental army of 20,400 troops—the first to come from Virginia, Pennsylvania, and Maryland—to back up the scattered militias and minutemen in Massachusetts. The next day, June 15, 1775, the Congress named Washington as commander in chief, largely because of his experience fighting alongside the British in the Seven Years' War, the political and administrative skills he exhibited in the Congress, and his background as a native of Virginia, the oldest and most populous colony. As General Washington rode off for Boston, having refused to accept any pay for the post, the Congress dispatched envoys for covert diplomacy aimed at winning support in their challenge to the British from the Spanish, the Dutch, and the French.

While girding for war, the Congress was still geared for peace. In July, it adopted a *Declaration of the Causes and Necessity for Taking Up Arms.* Drafted by Jefferson, it outlined colonial grievances with the British government, stressing that the Congress desired neither independence nor war but was being forced by British military action to make a choice between submitting to tyranny or resisting it. The Congress made clear its preference for peace, so long as the colonies could govern themselves as part of the British Empire.

Backed by Parliament, though, King George determined to put a stop to such talk. He declared the colonies to be in rebellion and publicly condemned colonial rabble-rousers as the product of "a very criminal nature." He vowed to combat any effort to challenge his "supreme authority" and sent twenty-five thousand fresh troops to the continent, raising the total deployed there to forty thousand. That autumn he announced plans to hire foreign mercenaries to fight the colonial troops. Though the use of mercenaries had long been common across Europe, few steps imaginable could have done more to cement King George's image as a tyrant than his decision to pay thirty thousand Hessian soldiers from the German states to cross the Atlantic to kill British subjects in America.

There was one measure, however, that could further enrage the landed gentry. Lord Dunmore knew that group well enough to understand exactly what it was. Dunmore had spent much of the fall of 1775 threatening the thinly defended port city of Norfolk, at the mouth of the James, from his new headquarters aboard the HMS *William*. Chased from the Virginia capital by Patrick Henry, this son of a Scottish rebel was running a government-in-exile aboard a British warship afloat in the very waters that bore John Smith to Jamestown. There, within sight of the Point Comfort landing where the first Africans in English America had arrived in chains a century and a half before, the last royal governor of Virginia promised freedom for any slave willing to stand with British troops and take up arms against the sons of American liberty. Let the likes of Henry, Washington, and Jefferson, slaveholders every one, talk about freedom, Dunmore reasoned, while he delivered on that promise to Americans of African descent.

It was a scene no playwright could have imagined. Dunmore's proclamation, though, was no script; it was a strategic masterstroke. It filled colonial whites with dread, weakening the political hand of the militants. It provided hundreds of recruits for the British crown. It forced colonial militias to expend precious resources on slave patrols. And it pinned down hundreds of potential colonial fighters too afraid to abandon their plantations and farms to fight for fear their slaves would leave to join the enemy. That was no idle threat on a continent of 2.5 million people where one in every five was a slave. It certainly wasn't taken lightly in Virginia, home to nearly two hundred thousand slaves, 40 percent of the colonial American total. To many of these blacks, Dunmore's proclamation was a clarion call. Some answered by fleeing Jefferson's Monticello; others ran away from the Williamsburg home of Peyton Randolph, who died of a stroke in Philadelphia that fall.

By December, several hundred Virginia slaves had escaped their plantations and homes to enlist in what Dunmore dubbed his "Ethiopian Regiment." Bearing sashes with the ingenious slogan Liberty to Slaves, the black recruits joined British regulars in a fierce battle against local and Carolina militiamen at Great Bridge on the Elizabeth River, where the southern reaches of Norfolk melted away into the edges of the Great Dismal Swamp. The colonial troops pushed back against what some derisively termed Dunmore's "speckled regiment," forcing the mixed-race army to retreat. Dunmore, who had briefly set up his headquarters in Norfolk, pulled out and took to the British flotilla anchored just offshore.

Even then, slaves continued to come, making their way down the James in stolen boats to clamber aboard British vessels and enlist in the cause of black liberty. The flood of runaways Dunmore's proclamation unleashed eventually amounted to mass revolt. Over the next several years, an estimated ten thousand slaves in Virginia fled their plantations and homes to join forces with the redcoats. British generals repeated Dunmore's offer everywhere, setting off what historian Gary Nash called "the greatest slave rebellion in American history." Elsewhere across the southern colonies, thousands more slaves would join the fray, acting as spies and guides for British forces, building forts, preparing food, digging trenches, and fighting in the pursuit of freedom in America. "For blacks, the news that the British Were Coming was a reason for hope, celebration and action," historian Simon Schama wrote in *Rough Crossings*, an analysis of the role of slaves in the American Revolution. "Without exactly seeking the part," wrote Schama, Dunmore had become "the patriarch of a great black exodus."

Jefferson was so incensed by Dunmore's policy that he railed against it the next year in his draft of the Declaration of Independence. In a section his fellow delegates at the Continental Congress in Philadelphia later abridged, Jefferson assailed the British for conducting an "assemblage of horrors" in transporting enslaved Africans to America. He then wrote that, through Dunmore's decree, King George III was "exciting those very people to rise in arms among us." It was as if, Jefferson wrote, the British were using the promise of freedom for "paying off former crimes committed against the liberties of one people, with crimes which he urges them to commit against the lives of another." Although the Continental Congress muted the reference, traces of Jefferson's furor over the matter remain enshrined in the most sacred secular document in the land, in the lines of the Declaration of Independence in which the Congress asserts that the British monarch "has excited domestic insurrections amongst us."

Dunmore's promise, though, was largely betrayed. In his camp alone, outbreaks of smallpox and typhoid killed blacks by the score. The corpses of some were deliberately spread about along James River plantations by British troops bent on sparking an epidemic among the colonists, an early experiment in biological warfare. Over the course of the war, some slaves did finally make it to freedom. Some were shipped to British Nova Scotia, far to the north, while others were sent to colonies in Africa. Hundreds more, though, were simply shipped by the British to the Caribbean and resold into slavery there to the sweltering sugarcane fields of Barbados, thought by many historians to be among the harshest slavery posts of the age. It would not be the last time the slave card was played in the fight for American independence. That battle, though, had just begun.

WE HAVE IT IN OUR POWER

As 1776 opened and the fighting spread, an English-born Quaker named Thomas Paine published a forty-seven-page pamphlet in Philadelphia that picked up on one of Jefferson's themes and extended it into an argument for American independence. In *Common Sense,* Paine amplified the argument that an island nation could no more govern a continent half a world away than the American colonists could resign themselves to rule by a British king and an aristocratic parliament. With armies facing off across much of the eastern seaboard, the colonies remained deeply divided over the question of independence. Powerful planter and merchant interests were still advocating some sort of power-sharing arrangement within the British realm, while many poor and middle-class colonists were wondering why they should fight and die to support the moneyed elite. With the force of reason and a straightforward style he'd honed penning essays for Philadelphia newspapers, Paine argued against the British Empire in America and helped popularize independence as a common goal. "Reconciliation is now a fallacious dream," Paine wrote. Starting from scratch and empowered to create a government driven and constrained by the public will, Americans united could "form the noblest, purest constitution on the face of the earth" he wrote. "We have it in our power to begin the world over again."

The most influential American pamphlet of its age, Paine's essay ignited colonial aspirations for a new nation. Paine, who had failed at teaching, tax collecting, and corset making in England before sailing to Philadelphia just sixteen months before, even proposed a name for this bold new land: the Free and Independent States of America. A publishing phenomena at a time when books were printed page by page and bound by hand, Paine's pamphlet and proud call for the new country had sold more than one hundred thousand copies by May, when burgesses convened in Williamsburg as the Virginia Convention. Within weeks, members of the Virginia Convention of 1776 completed four breathtaking achievements. They declared the royal government of Virginia dissolved. They directed the Virginia delegation to the Continental Congress meeting in Philadelphia that summer to propose independence from Britain. They adopted a resolution of rights that became a model for the Declaration of Independence and the U.S. Bill of Rights. And they wrote a plan for a new state government that would serve as a foundation for the U.S. Constitution.

Few political gatherings anywhere have achieved as much. The intellectual center of gravity that pulled it all together came mostly from two men. One was Thomas Jefferson, who submitted three successive drafts of the plan for government, or Virginia Constitution, to the convention by courier from Philadelphia, where he was attending the Continental Congress. The other was a legal giant who never went to college and struggled much of his life to summon the motivation to walk out his front door, the wealthy Potomac River tobacco planter George Mason. In his book *The Faiths of Our Fathers*, Alf Mapp summed up the paradox of Mason, a man "who labored for decades in the service of a community that widened from county to colony to nation to world, fought a lifetime battle against lethargy . . . [and] who so dreaded speaking in public that he almost fainted when he did." Ten years old when his father drowned off a sinking ferry near the family estate, Mason buried much of his youth between the pages of classical literature and legal texts he ploughed through in his uncle's fifteen-hundred-volume library. Inheriting Gunston Hall, a fifty-five-hundred-acre estate just downstream from Mount Vernon, Mason led a life that bordered on reclusive, preferring the quiet and paper-strewn study in his palatial manor home to the social gaiety and political whirlwind of Williamsburg.

Mason had not even arrived in Williamsburg by the middle of May, when his fellow conventioneers voted not only to endorse independence but to propose it the next month in Philadelphia. As the key member of the committee the convention put together to draw up the Virginia Declaration of Rights, however, Mason drafted one of the most important documents in American history, a political masterpiece in whose passages can be heard preludes to the Declaration of Independence, the U.S. Constitution, and the federal Bill of Rights. "All men are by nature equally free and independent, and have certain inherent rights," Mason's Virginia Declaration of Rights begins, "namely, the enjoyment of life and liberty, with the means of acquiring and possessing property, and pursuing and obtaining happiness and safety." The purpose of government, the declaration makes clear, is to help secure and advance those rights. "All power is vested in, and consequently derived from, the people," the declaration continues, going on to state that "the legislative and executive powers of the state should be separate and distinct from the judicative."

Having laid the cornerstones of life, liberty, and the pursuit of happiness as the goal and purpose of government by the people, Mason had also framed up the three separate branches of government. He then established the principle of civilian control of the military. "In all cases," his declaration stated, "the military should be under strict subordination to, and be governed by, the civil power." The declaration then articulated fundamental rights that would be guaranteed to all Americans fifteen years later, protecting citizens against warrantless search and seizures and staking out the right to "a speedy trial by an impartial jury." It protected freedom of religion, stating that "all men are equally entitled to the free exercise of religion, according to the dictates of conscience." And it provided explicit protections for newspapers and publishers. "Freedom of the press is one of the greatest bulwarks of liberty," the Virginia Declaration of Rights decreed, "and can never be restrained but by despotic governments."

Endorsed by the convention in mid-June, the Virginia declaration set the tone for two weeks of work on the state constitution, three drafts of which were penned by Jefferson. So closely does his blueprint for Virginia government track the ideas contained in Mason's declaration that the two documents read as though they might have sprung from the same mind. Due to acts of "misrule," the constitution began, the British government in Virginia, after 169 years, "is totally dissolved." That was the end of the House of Burgesses, established a century before by Gov. William Berkeley, and marked a transition for the general assembly, which first met that hot summer in 1619 at Jamestown a few miles away. The new general assembly, the constitution provided, would consist of a House of Delegates and a Senate, both made up of popularly elected representatives. Those two houses, in turn, would elect a governor and an eight-member Council of State. After years of being bullied by a succession of royal governors, the Virginians intentionally made the executive post weak. Governors would serve for a term of one year, they could not block or overturn laws the general assembly passed, and they could not dissolve the assembly, which was to meet at least once a year. The constitution further provided for the separate executive, legislative, and judicial branches called for in the earlier Declaration of Rights.

On June 29, 1776, after adopting the constitution, members of the convention elected the first American governor of the original English colony, an old friend and veteran of the billowing revolution, Patrick Henry. Enfeebled by malaria he'd picked up from some summer ride through the swampy reaches of his native Hanover County, Henry raised a shaking right hand and took the oath of office. He swore to defend the new Commonwealth of Virginia and to uphold the constitution that would serve as its guide. He promised to blend law, justice, and mercy into his judgments as chief executive. And he vowed to do all of this in recognition of the rights, and in accordance with the will, of the free people of Virginia, "so help me God."

WE HOLD THESE TRUTHS

Three weeks after the Virginia Convention voted to break colonial ties with Britain, Richard Henry Lee rose before the Continental Congress in Philadelphia to propose "that these United colonies are, and of right ought to be, free and independent states; that they are absolved from all allegiance to the British crown; and that all political connection between them and the state of Great Britain is, and ought to be, totally dissolved." It was June 7, 1776. The congress had been inching in the direction of independence for months, rejecting parliamentary authority the previous December and agreeing in May that even George III held no sovereignty over the American colonies. Over those very points, war had raged for months, with the Patriots suffering one setback after the next in fighting concentrated in New York and Canada.

Still, some colonies had yet to sign off on independence, hoping upon diminishing hope that disputes with the mother country might yet be patched up. Some delegates feared the impact declaring independence might have on the struggling effort to spool together an American military that could match British might. Others insisted independence was pointless without a government in place to unite the colonies, raise money to fight the war, and put in place the alliances the young country would need to prevail.

After four days of such talk and continued discouraging news from the northeast, the Congress decided to put Lee's resolution on hold while a committee prepared a statement laying out the reasons for independence, so that it could then be put to a vote. The congress impaneled five men to prepare the document: John Adams of Boston, Benjamin Franklin of Philadelphia, Roger Sherman of Connecticut, Robert Livingston of New York, and Thomas Jefferson, who was assigned to draft the Declaration of Independence.

He did so in the parlor of a two-room, second-floor apartment he rented in a three-story brick home at the corner of Market and Seventh streets in Philadelphia. There, seated in a Windsor chair and bearing down on a folding writing box of his own design, Jefferson composed the symphony of conscience and reason that distilled American purpose and defined American democracy not just for the revolutionary moment, but for the ages. "We hold these truths to be self-evident," he wrote, "that all men are created equal, that they are endowed by their Creator with certain inalienable rights, that among these are life, liberty and the pursuit of happiness; that to secure these rights, governments are instituted among men, deriving their just powers from the consent of the governed."

In penning what may be the best-known lines in American history, Jefferson later explained that he wasn't striving for something novel or sentimental. He was trying instead to draw on the collective wisdom of all humankind and to state the case for American independence and government by the people in a simple yet persuasive way. "It was intended," Jefferson later wrote, "to be an expression of the American mind." Nearly two and a half centuries later, few if any have succeeded more fully at that. "This is the seminal statement of the American Creed, the closest approximation to political poetry ever produced in American culture," Jefferson biographer Joseph Ellis wrote in *American Sphinx*. Abraham Lincoln, no stranger to political eloquence, felt much the same. In the rare fullness of Jefferson's clarity, Lincoln later wrote, the Virginian had managed to capture "an abstract truth, and so to embalm it there, that today, and in all coming days, it shall be a rebuke and a stumbling block to the very harbingers of reappearing tyranny and oppression."

It isn't clear how long Jefferson, who was thirty-three years old at the time, spent drafting the Declaration of Independence. He was tasked with writing it on June 11. Adams, Franklin, and the rest of the drafting committee signed off on it, with minor revisions, on June 28. Congress adopted Richard Henry Lee's independence resolution on July 2. After two days of debate, Congress approved the Declaration of Independence shortly before noon on the Fourth of July, as church bells pealed through Philadelphia to herald the birth of the nation and the dawn of an age.

During at least part of the time he was writing it, Jefferson was also editing drafts of the Virginia constitution. Its preamble included a long list of grievances against King George III, echoing the litany of complaint that forms the main body of the Declaration of Independence. Jefferson seems to have taken the essence of some of the language Mason used in the Virginia Declaration of Rights and abridged it slightly for his congressional draft. He had read Paine's *Common Sense* and may have had his copy with him by his writer's box in Philadelphia. And Jefferson unquestionably drew, as well, from the *Declaration of the Causes and Necessities of Taking Up Arms*, which he had written for the Congress the year before, as well as *A Summary View of the Rights of British America,* his first attempt to synthesize Enlightenment thought and classical ideals with the eighteenth-century American condition. His genius for doing precisely that, in a way that illuminated the course of the American Revolution, shines through in the Declaration of Independence.

Even Jefferson, however, felt the blade of the editor's knife. He was particularly annoyed that a critique of the English slave trade was cut out on the insistence of several delegates—not only from southern slave states like South Carolina and Georgia, but also "our northern brethren," Jefferson wrote, alluding to the slave traders that operated out of several northeastern ports. Jefferson had not issued a clear cut cry for abolition or for liberating a single slave. Instead, he had railed out against King George, accusing him of waging "cruel war against human nature itself, violating its most sacred rights of life and liberty in the persons of a distant people who never offended him, captivating and carrying them into slavery in another hemisphere or to incur miserable death in their transportation hither." The broadside was originally part of the long list of American grievances against British rule, not part of any call for action. To the extent his critique implied action, it targeted the importation of additional slaves, not the practice of slavery itself. "Jefferson knew from his experience in the House of Burgesses that many established slaveowners in the Tidewater region favored an end of imports," wrote Ellis. "Their own plantations were already well stocked and new arrivals only reduced the value of their own slave populations." In retrospect, historians see in Jefferson's careful phrasing the contradiction—some say hypocrisy—of a man who became the architect of American liberty but could not free the nation's slaves and would not free his own—except, that is, for the children he is thought to have sired by his slave and mistress, Sally Hemings.

As a final edit, members of Congress inserted into Jefferson's text the independence resolution as Richard Henry Lee had first proposed it, on the directions of the Virginia Convention. "These united colonies are, and of right ought to be, free and independent states," the declaration stated, going on to make clear "that they are absolved from all allegiance to the British crown, and that all political connection between them and the state of Great Britain is, and ought to be, totally dissolved." And to that end, in Jefferson's original words, "we mutually pledge to each other our lives, our fortunes and our sacred honor."

After a formal copy was engrossed in ink on parchment in a scrivener's careful hand, John Hancock became the first of fifty-six American patriots to affix their names to that pledge. In doing so, they were committing treason against the king, no small consideration given that British general Thomas Gage carried with him royal warrants left blank for the names of any American he judged deserving of the noose.

The signers were a composite of a wealthy and educated ruling class. Georgia delegate Button Gwinnett and seven other signers had come to the colonies from British homes; the rest were American born. The youngest, Edward Rutledge from South Carolina, was twenty-six. Franklin, at seventy, was the oldest. All but five had children; Virginia's Carter Braxton had eighteen. More than half owned slaves, and one, William Whipple of New Hampshire, was a sea captain thought to have traded in them. Half were lawyers, but there were merchants as well. Four were doctors and one, New Jersey's John Witherspoon, was a man of the cloth.

By the time they signed the Declaration of Independence, its contents were widely known. John Dunlap's print shop turned out copies on the night of July 4. Horse-mounted express couriers set off the next morning delivering copies of the document to Continental Army officers and colonial capitals, where newspapers quickly published reprints. For all the promise they conferred upon Americans at the time, and all the majesty they convey today, Jefferson's words were mere intentions on July 4, 1776. Between the drafting of his bold design and the beginnings of the nation he envisioned lay five years of destruction and bloodshed.

LIKE THE DAY OF JUDGMENT WAS COME

As Philadelphia echoed that summer with the sounds of celebratory church bells and the clattering hooves of couriers' steeds, the single largest military invasion force ever launched against the United States was streaming into New York harbor. King George had decided to abandon Boston, occupy New York, and deploy forces along a line extending north along the Hudson River to Canada. The idea was to cut off the ferocious New England fighters and then pacify the soft mid-Atlantic colonies of New York, New Jersey, Pennsylvania, and Delaware, where his intelligence sources told him support for American independence was thin. It wasn't an altogether unsound approach. Somewhere around 20 percent of American Tories are thought to have remained loyal to the crown throughout the war. An even larger percentage remained on the fence well into the opening months of war, when many viewed the American rebellion as a doomed and desperate cause.

King George had his troubles as well. Indebted still from the long war against the French, he faced the challenge of enlisting an army for a dirty job: crossing the Atlantic to suppress a populist uprising of English kinfolk struggling to build a new colony an ocean away. At the same time, the king had to maintain sufficient soldiers to maintain an expanding global empire ranging from the Caribbean to India. To carry out the king's American war strategy, Britain emptied its jails, poorhouses, and slums to round out the regiments bound for America. Between July 3, 1776, and early August, an armada of more than three hundred transport and supply vessels, backed by six dozen warships and twelve hundred cannons, entered New York, disgorging thirty-two thousand English, Irish, Scottish, and Hessian troops on Staten Island. There they linked up with another sixty-five hundred troops Gage had evacuated from Boston.

Anticipating the British would descend upon New York—then a city of some twenty-five thousand artisans, merchants, laborers, and others—Washington had marched his army of some nineteen thousand troops south from Boston. In a strategic blunder that nearly ended the war before it began, Washington deployed his men in New York, splitting his force between Long Island and Manhattan, hoping to bottle up the British there. Washington, though, underestimated the strength of the British forces, who trapped half his army in Brooklyn Heights. They narrowly avoided annihilation, escaping to the southern tip of Manhattan on the night of August 29 in rowboats screened from British view by a dense fog and manned by colonists from the Massachusetts fishing communities of Marblehead. Two weeks later, Washington's forces temporarily checked the British at Harlem Heights. By November, that battle, too, was lost. Washington's army escaped to the north by leaving behind a rear guard some three thousand strong. Most were captured, gutting the Continental Army of one-sixth of its force and leaving New York occupied by the British for the remainder of the war. The city became a refuge for Tories and deserters and a hellhole for American prisoners of war, hundreds of whom died of malnourishment and disease aboard leaky British prison ships.

Washington spent the next six weeks engaged in a strategic retreat, leading British pursuers northward, up the Hudson River valley and toward White Plains, before crossing the river and moving south along its western banks and into New Jersey. As the momentous year wound toward a close, neither the British nor the Americans had secured the knockout blow each assumed would assure their side a quick victory. Troops began settling into winter quarters for the long wait until spring.

The Continental Army was backed all the way into Pennsylvania, just north of the capital at Philadelphia. Washington was also backed up against a deadline. Banking on a short war, the Congress had attracted recruits based on enlistments that ended December 31 of that year. With days on the contract running down, Washington hatched a bold, if desperate, scheme. On a cold and windy Christmas night, he led twenty-four hundred of his best troops across the ice-choked waters of the Delaware River, expertly navigated by the Brooklyn Heights heroes, the boatmen of Marblehead. After a seven-mile overnight march, Washington's men surprised fourteen hundred Hessians at Trenton on the morning of December 26, 1776, killing thirty and taking most of the rest prisoner. Four Americans were killed and several were wounded, including a future U.S. president, James Monroe of Virginia.

Over the coming year, the British seized Philadelphia but suffered a stunning defeat at Saratoga, New York, where American forces commanded by Horatio Gates and Benedict Arnold forced the surrender of fifty-seven hundred British troops. That winter, Washington camped his army of about twelve thousand men at Valley Forge, eighteen miles northwest of Philadelphia. There they huddled against the freezing cold, poorly fed and thinly clothed, in an epic struggle for survival that became the symbol of the sacrifice and endurance at the heart of the American Revolution. With spring came news that the victory at Saratoga the previous fall had helped lead France to grant diplomatic recognition to the United States, bringing immediate aid and, eventually, French soldiers and arms against the British. The Spanish declared war against the British the following year, and the Dutch the year after that.

Over the next two years, as British and American forces battled mostly across New Jersey, Pennsylvania, and New York, the Continental Army struggled for recruits. Fine words and erudite speeches lent form to the American Revolution; winning it would take flesh and blood. And while it was one thing for representatives from the various colonies to debate political views, battling alongside a South Carolinian or taking orders from a Georgian didn't always come naturally for a minuteman from Rhode Island. Bleeding and dying for ground settled within memory by family members, moreover, wasn't quite the same thing as marching for weeks and months on end to fight on someone else's farm six hundred miles away. Men who signed on to fight for American independence got a crash course in what it meant to serve in a continental army.

As the sacrifice needed to sustain the war ground on, class divisions began to surface, especially in the South, where society was divided along clear and largely impregnable lines tracing the contours of race and status, poverty and wealth. Yeomen grew weary of taking casualties, while wealthy planters paid bounties to hire surrogates, then stayed home to look after their holdings. Farmers forced to abandon their fields to take up arms couldn't help but resent overseers who dodged militia duty to boss slaves around. Wives, too, grew tired of having their husbands and sons come home crippled by war, if they returned at all, leaving no one to bring home the bacon or work the farm.

"Though few explicitly stated it, most people believed that only the poor and the marginal would or should join the Continental army," University of Sydney historian Michael McDonnell wrote in the *William & Mary Quarterly*. "Would-be recruits forced patriots to raise bounty money, bargained with their neighbors for their services as substitutes in the militia and resisted and evaded the draft when forced into service. In some places they violently resisted any and all attempts to conscript soldiers. In other places, once drafted, they simply deserted and found refuge, usually with friends and family." As volunteers grew scarce, sheriffs and justices of the peace were empowered to impress into service what the Virginia General Assembly termed "rogues and vagabonds," which soon came to include men who could wield a gun but had fallen into arrears on their taxes.

In south-central Virginia, McDonnell reported, several hundred poor farmers with families complained to their local leaders. Extended militia service, these men charged in a joint petition, worked such inequitable hardships on them that if they survived the war to return, they "would find our wives and children dispersed up and down the country a'begging or at home a'starving," while, along the great riverside plantations, "overseers are a'living in ease and affluence."

In 1779, the Virginia General Assembly elected Jefferson as governor. It was hardly a plum post. The local currency was falling like a rock; the treasury had been drained; county militias could barely front a force; ammunition, horses, and wagons were scarce and growing scarcer. Shortly after moving into the grand Governor's Palace where he had dined long before as a student with the royal magistrate, Jefferson ordered Virginia militia units to the Ohio River valley. They mutinied and refused to leave Virginia. What was Jefferson going to do about it—call out the militia?

Virginia had sent thousands of recruits to the Continental Army, but enlistment fell far short of the targets Congress had set. Meanwhile, the numbers of casualties, prisoners of war, and missing in action steadily rose. By 1780, Washington's Continental Army was a battle-weary and equipment-starved force that struggled to muster six thousand troops.

Threadbare morale was further depressed that year by the desertion of Benedict Arnold, who turned coat to lead British troops against Americans, just when the redcoats began pressing the southern colonies in earnest. In May of that year, British forces captured Charleston, opening the door to a campaign targeting the wealthy rice and indigo plantations of coastal South Carolina. Looking south and fearing the same, Jefferson moved the Virginia capital from Williamsburg, easy prey for British marines based on warships on the James, to Richmond, further upstream at the falls.

Richmond's wartime population had doubled since the old House of Burgesses met there fifteen years before. The city had become a rustic trade and manufacturing community, with wharves, tobacco warehouses, a few brick homes, and a rope yard for ships rigging. Assembly members met in Billy Wiley's large, barnlike wooden house, sharing space with his saddle shop and nibbling on hot bread and ginger cakes from his wife's bakery—or so one of Jefferson's slaves, Isaac, recalled.

In August 1780, the Americans suffered a major defeat in the South Carolina town of Camden. Hundreds of Virginian militiamen were captured in the fight. That autumn, Jefferson began ordering county militias to send troops to help defend Richmond from attack. "Let every man bring his own blanket," Jefferson wrote, a candid assessment of the accommodations they might expect in Richmond. "Lose not a moment's time."

Hoping to address the inequities the fighting had imposed upon the poor, Virginia passed a law assessing what was essentially a war tax based upon property holdings. Under the law, wealthy plantation holders would pony up the lion's share of the money the state paid out to attract new recruits. Officially, recruits willing to sign on for the duration of the war were being offered $300 apiece, though many bargained for twice as much. And while officially the Continental Army resisted the use of slaves, historians estimate that perhaps five thousand blacks—both free and slave—fought on the American side. And why not? Wasn't this a war about freedom? Surely, these free blacks believed, the colonists who were fighting for their own liberty meant to free the slaves once the war was done.

The handful of vessels that made up Virginia's defensive fleet were manned, in part, by slaves, many of whom had long prewar experience as watermen hauling oysters, fish, and crabs from the Chesapeake Bay. One, named Caesar, piloted a schooner named the *Patriot* with sufficient distinction that the Virginia General Assembly bought his freedom, though not until 1789. After his death, Caesar's daughter, Nancy, received 2,667 acres of Ohio land as belated reward for his service in the American Revolution, the late historian Virginius Dabney wrote in his 1971 book *Virginia: The New Dominion*. A slave named James slipped fluidly in and out of the ports of Norfolk and Hampton, providing key intelligence to the colonists' ally, French major general the Marquis de Lafayette

By November, with the dearth of militiamen leaving the mouth of the James vulnerable to imminent British naval attack, the general assembly added two incentives to attract recruits. The first was land. A man who enlisted would receive, at war's end, three hundred acres, enough for a grubstake and sufficient to entitle the owner to vote. As an added inducement, the assembly made an offer that crystallized the deepest and most enduring irony of the American Revolution. As payment to fight for American liberty, new recruits were promised a slave. "A bounty of a negro not younger than ten or older than 40 . . . will, I believe, produce the men for the war," Joseph Jones wrote from the general assembly on November 10, 1780. Four years after Jefferson laid the cornerstone of American independence on the foundation that "all men are created equal," a militiaman fighting for that very principle could march into battle with the words "liberty or death" emblazoned across his chest and expect Jefferson's own government to give him in return cash, land, and the lifetime service of another human being, who could be beaten, worked to death, or sold like a dog. A colony impregnated at its birth with slavery, Virginia had reduced itself to offering slaves as an incentive for white Americans battling for freedom, even as their British foes dangled the promise of liberty in front of blacks willing to fight on behalf of the crown that had chartered the company that had enslaved them for profit. Both sides called it democracy, and slaves were caught in the middle, agonizing over how best to find advantage in the war.

As 1781 opened, the river that first tied the American colonies to London once again ushered in British ships, led this time by newly minted Brigadier General Benedict Arnold. Coursing up the James in a flotilla of twenty-seven ships bearing twelve hundred infantry troops and one hundred horses, Arnold found the river scarcely defended all the way upstream to Westover, home to the powerful Byrd family, reliable Tories from whom Arnold could expect no trouble. There he disembarked his troops on January 4 and marched them to Berkeley two miles upstream, the home of Benjamin Harrison. Reluctant revolutionary that he was, Harrison had, in the end, broken trust with the crown and signed the Declaration of Independence. That made him a traitor in Arnold's well-trained eye.

"If they had of caught him here, they probably would have hanged him," said Berkeley historian Jim Curtis. Harrison, though, had fled, along with his family. Arnold ordered his forces to stack the manor-house furnishings out in the yard, then strip the family portraits from the walls and toss them on top. He set the pile on fire and watched as a century of cherished Harrison possessions drifted over the James in a dark stream of smoke. Arnold's men shot the cattle, made off with about forty slaves, and marched an additional twenty miles or so along the river road leading into Richmond, where they met no greater resistance than that offered by the mud that sucked at their boots. To announce their arrival, Arnold's men fired three cannon rounds into the city from a pine-shaded plot at the east edge of town, clipping the peak of a butcher's house, setting the city's two hundred militiamen to flight, and inciting general pandemonium. "In ten minutes not a white man was to be seen in Richmond," Isaac Jefferson recalled years later. "They ran as hard as they could." In memoirs he dictated to a prominent Petersburg scholar named Charles Campbell, Jefferson's longtime servant remembered the sight of the British in their red coats marching down the valley toward Shockoe Creek along the rutted road that would eventually become Main Street. "It was an awful site," Isaac said. "Seemed like the Day of Judgment was come."

Not one to idly await his own great reckoning, Jefferson saddled up his fabled horse Caractacus and raced west along the river road toward Westham, leaving Isaac, Jupiter and his wife, Sukey, Mary the seamstress, and six other slaves behind in the governor's rented quarters. Arnold's men searched the house for Jefferson, instead finding a cellar full of fine wine and Antigua rum. They unloaded the corn crib and fed their horses, rationed out beef and ham from the meat house, and assured the terrified slaves that all they were after was the scoundrel who had drafted the Declaration of Independence. As proof of their benign intent, they showed off the pair of silver handcuffs they'd brought along to bind Jefferson's wrists.

Arnold sent horsemen after Jefferson, while infantry units remained behind, billeted against the winter cold in the very room where Patrick Henry had first uttered the American battle cry, the sanctuary of St. John's Church. By then, Jefferson was supervising salvage and destruction operations at the foundry and powder magazine at Westham, an undertaking cut short by Arnold's approaching cavalry. When the British arrived, the place was deserted. They threw the Americans' weapons into the river and a nearby canal, blew up the powder magazine, and bedded down for the night.

Jefferson had headed west to join his family at Tuckahoe. When Arnold's men showed up there the next morning, the Jeffersons were gone. Staying one step ahead of their pursuers, they had crossed the frigid river waters near the Huguenot village at Manakin Town, then made their way further upriver to the old family place on Fine Creek. Arnold's men tarried briefly at Tuckahoe, helping themselves to its stores and taking away a number of slaves but leaving the frame manor house intact. Arnold's mission was to capture Jefferson and any other rebellion leaders he might find and to destroy such military materiel as might be had. With Virginia on the verge of collapse, however, Arnold had every reason to think he and his compatriots would soon inherit control of the newly suppressed colony. Destroying its valuable manor homes simply made no sense.

Wheeling back to Richmond, Arnold's men set fire to some riverside tobacco warehouses on their way out of town to deny Jefferson currency he might use to recruit and arm fresh troops. The flames spilled over, and a handful of nearby buildings caught fire. After two days of terror, the British troops abandoned the city, returned to their ships, and floated on the current downstream to the mouth of the James. Aided by the capture of Isaac and perhaps one hundred other slaves, Arnold's forces occupied Portsmouth and settled in for the winter. With the April thaw, Arnold set his fleet to menacing business once more, journeying upriver to within sight of Richmond to burn the port town of Warwick, a manufacturing center that had provided clothing, shoes, flour, and meal to revolutionary Virginia.

Arnold's days of harrying Virginians with impunity, however, were fast coming to an close as the war moved toward its endgame along the banks of the James. That spring, while Washington's forces were camped outside New York to keep British forces there pinned down, the French major general the Marquis de Lafayette led some twelve hundred men into Virginia. Over the coming weeks, the force grew in strength with the addition of local militia and American fighters to nearly forty-five hundred. Up from North Carolina marched British general Charles Cornwallis, linking up with Arnold and taking command of Portsmouth and operations along the James, with a combined British force of about seventy-two hundred troops at his command.

In early June, an increasingly desperate Jefferson gathered his general assembly compatriots for an emergency legislative session in Charlottesville, while Cornwallis and Lafayette skirmished up and down the former Indian grounds between the York and James rivers. Learning that Jefferson, Patrick Henry, William Harrison, and a dozen other key revolutionary figures were holed up in the Blue Ridge foothills, Cornwallis ordered British general Banastre Tarleton to strike out on the night of June 3, stage a lightning cavalry raid on Monticello, and capture Jefferson and those in league with him.

Tarleton's path took him past a tavern at the sleepy backwoods crossroads of Cuckoo, where a strapping American militia officer named Jack Jouett had hoped to pass a quiet evening. Watching Tarleton's cavalry thunder past at the head of several dozen British troops, Jouett had little doubt as to their mission. Determined to beat them to Monticello, Jouett spurred what was reputedly the fastest horse in Louisa County over a forty-mile sprint through a moonlit web of little-traveled bridle paths, hunting trails, and wagon roads. Jouett arrived at Monticello, his face and hands slashed from thorny brush and low-hanging limbs that left him scarred for life, just as Jefferson and his guests were sitting down to breakfast. Jefferson rode out down one side of his mountain while Tarleton's bone-tired dragoons rode up the opposite slope, the Virginia governor's fourth hair's breath escape in as many months. Tarleton's forces helped themselves to Jefferson's cattle, sheep, and hogs, burned his barns, destroyed tobacco, corn, and fences, stole the horses they could use, slit the throats of the ponies too small to ride, and made off with thirty slaves.

Weary of fruitless hare-and-hound games with Lafayette's forces across Hanover County, Cornwallis repaired briefly to Williamsburg. In early July, he moved to Jamestown, hoping to cross the river there and return to Portsmouth. Lafayette's forces chased him, though, approaching Cornwallis from the rear. They fought a pitched battle at Green Spring, the plantation William Berkeley had built a century before, until both forces disengaged. The next day, July 7, Cornwallis led his troops across the James aboard long-boats, then marched them down the south bank of the river and across the waters of the ancient Nansemond tribe at Sleepy Hole Ferry and into Portsmouth. There, Cornwallis stewed in his headquarters, searching for some way to bring the long war to an end. Late that summer, it came to him. Looking across the gaping mouth of the James and into the Chesapeake Bay, the battle-worn commander saw it all spread out before him like bone and ivory pieces on a rosewood chessboard: the unsurpassed sea power of the royal navy, protecting the strategic center of Virginia, resupplying and reinforcing his command at will, while he used the fertile rivers as military highways to bring ruin and collapse to the American cause. He may have chortled to his top commanders and poured them a brandy or two before toasting the tedious General Henry Clinton, his troops buttoned down in New York, while Cornwallis readied his troops to strike the summer death blow to Virginia. God save the king!

All that was left was to pick out the best spot from which to conduct the raids. Rolling out the finest maps and nautical charts the royal engineers could produce, Cornwallis looked at the rivers reaching into Virginia like tidewater fingers on an outstretched hand. And suddenly, there it was, a quiet river harbor just around the tip of the narrow southern peninsula, an inviting and centrally located little place called Yorktown.

All's fair in love and war perhaps, but so much about both goes unknown. Even as Cornwallis moved his forces around Point Comfort, he had no idea French warships sailing downwind across the Atlantic for the Caribbean had changed course for the Chesapeake Bay. By late summer, they were off the Virginia Capes, challenging the British Navy's control of the gateway to the colony. Receiving word of Cornwallis' movements and the new French naval presence off the coast, Washington pulled most of his forces out of New York and headed south.

On September 26, a united force of six thousand Continental Army troops, three thousand Virginia militiamen, and six thousand French troops converged by land and water on the James River site of the first permanent British outpost in America: Jamestown. From there, Washington and Lafayette rolled their massive force fifteen miles to Yorktown, trapping

Cornwallis against the tides. There would be no British ships for evacuation or resupply; the French fleet saw to that. The Franco-American allies dug trenches, built breastworks, and rained down cannon fire on the British, who watched their food and ammunition dwindle and their casualties mount over the next three weeks of siege.

On October 19, 1781, pinned against the water and outnumbered two to one, Cornwallis surrendered. His entire army—some seven thousand redcoats—marched out in formation across a windswept field at Yorktown and stacked their weapons one last time while a British band played an old familiar tune, "The World Turned Upside Down." The Revolutionary War was, for all practical purposes, over. From its ruins, a new nation arose. And after 174 years, the British Empire in America had come to an end, just fifteen miles from where it began.

8

RIVER OF DREAMS

LYNCHBURG—Cool water the color of jade rippled against the hull of the *Nelson County Rose* as the broad, oaken beam of the flat-bottomed bateau nestled against a narrow shelf of silt and sand along the shaded shore. Atop a brick–and–cast-iron hearth near the center of the boat, gray smoke drifted from a large, black skillet, the smell of bacon mixing with the earthy scent of the river on a morning in June. And from the captain's seat—a wooden crate filled with burlap sacks of onions, potatoes, and oatmeal—Greg Schluge straightened his straw hat and gazed downstream, contemplating the seven-day journey to Richmond. "It's dangerous," he allowed, running thick, calloused fingers through a salt-and-pepper beard. "I broke three ribs going through Shipwreck Falls about eight years ago. We eventually hit a rock. That's why we have a new boat."

Crafted by hand from two tons of white oak and pine, the *Rose* is a forty-two-foot reproduction of one of the thousands of bateaus that plied the system of canals and native stretches of the James that linked Richmond to this port town in the Blue Ridge foothills in the early nineteenth century, when rivers were the gateways to the deep interior of the fledgling nation. The semitrailers of the era, the wide-bodied transports helped to set in motion a great migration west and to knit the economic and social fabric of a new nation, one bateau trip at a time. "This," Schluge explained, "was the beginning of commerce in the United States."

In 1791, this central Virginia ferry crossing 150 miles upstream from Richmond got its first tobacco warehouse, a pungently profitable symbol of the westward expansion that nurtured American growth at its infancy. That same year, the United States Congress approved the Bill of Rights, essentially completing the federal Constitution the new nation had ratified three years before. Over the next century, shallow-draft riverboats like the *Nelson*

217

County Rose transported passengers and cargo from the western reaches of the state and across the gently rolling piedmont farmland to the growing market, manufacturing, and shipping center at Richmond, then hauled woolen and cotton cloth, molasses, coffee, nails, and other goods, along with migrants, back upstream to riverside port towns as far west as Buchanan, fifty miles upstream from Lynchburg.

Each June, that golden age of river travel returns to life for one week, when Schluge and several dozen other devotees of the James River bateau culture reprise the run from Lynchburg to Maidens, a landing just west of Richmond, on hand-built boats of vintage design with names like *The Lord Chesterfield*, *Tobacco Row*, and *The Ladyslipper*. "I always feel like my little square of air is from 1700, and I'm bringing it to people," said Lauren Schnyer. A seventeen-year-old history major at the College of William and Mary, Schnyer is a volunteer crew member aboard the *Rose* on a journey that takes her far from the world of dorm life, e-mail, and iPods. "After the first two days," she said, "you get real used to it."

Just downstream from Lynchburg, the James begins wandering through a dreamlike world of forested banks and high bluffs of Precambrian marble, a smooth and shimmering cake batter of white stone walls stirred through with cloudlike swirls of pink and blue. Drifting undisturbed past wilderness passes, rounding a bend to see a great gray heron take flight off the bow, or crashing through boiling, rock-strewn rapids as the river drops steadily down the great tilted table of the Virginia Piedmont, the crew of the *Nelson County Rose* senses much the same kind of exhilaration the river must have inspired in the first generation to inhabit the newly founded United States. For free people on the move, the bateau line opened a world of opportunity—manufacturing and migration, travel and trade—that embodied the mood of optimism sweeping the fast-growing country and the spirit of liberty at the heart of its revolutionary constitution.

In the decade following the American victory at Yorktown, the Constitution mapped out the path of American democracy, largely as construed in the mind of James Madison. A man dubbed "the father of the Constitution" by his contemporaries, the diminutive and deliberative Madison lived on a twenty-seven-hundred-acre estate about two hours by horse from Monticello, the home of his close friend Thomas Jefferson. There, near the banks of the Rivanna River, the architects of the Constitution and the Declaration of Independence lived just twenty miles from each other.

Madison didn't draft the Constitution in the literal way Jefferson authored the Declaration. As a member of the Continental Congress in 1787, however, Madison wrote the so-called Virginia Plan, which became the blueprint for the Constitution. After a year of debate, revision, and compromise, delegates agreed to a federal government with a bicameral legislature at its core, divided into a House of Representatives and a Senate, with separate executive and judicial branches set up to provide checks and balances on the powers of each. In naming the first president of the United States, delegates turned to the Revolutionary War commander in chief, George Washington, who quickly defined the office in the loftiest of terms. "The preservation of the sacred fire of liberty and the destiny of the republican model of government," Washington said in his first inaugural address, were "staked on the experiment entrusted to the hands of the American people."

Much of the constitutional debate centered on the question of slavery and the inevitable tug of war between state powers and federal authority. As a compromise, the Constitution protected the slave trade for twenty years, after which, many of the founders assumed, a new generation of statesmen would find a way to end it. Virginia's George Mason summed up the contradiction inherent in founding a nation based on the rights of man while one American in every five was enslaved. "Every master of slaves is born a petty tyrant," Mason wrote during the Constitutional Convention debate, warning that "Providence punishes national sins by national calamities." The heart of the federal authority question was when, and under what circumstances, federal sovereignty might trump states' rights. The Constitution provided imperfect answers to the questions of slavery and states rights, strains that would eventually lead to the very national calamity Mason tragically foresaw.

The Constitution was never meant to settle for all time every imaginable dilemma the U.S. government might confront. Its genius was, and is, that it allows each generation of Americans to resolve its own issues. It was designed to be a living document, showing the way for government to evolve with the times, while remaining true to those principles upon which the nation was founded and still holding inviolate the rights of the people as sovereign, goals the document sets forth in its opening lines: "We, the People of the United States, in order to form a more perfect union, establish justice, insure domestic tranquility, provide for the common defense, promote the general welfare and secure the blessings of liberty to ourselves and our posterity do ordain and establish this Constitution for the United States of America."

As early evidence that the Constitution itself was a work in progress, Madison led the congressional efforts to approve no fewer than ten amendments as a freshman member of the House in 1789, during the first U.S.

Congress convened under the terms of the new constitution. Known as the Bill of Rights, those amendments made explicit the individual protections and liberties commonly associated with constitutional law: the freedom of the press, speech, and religion; the right to peaceably assemble and to bear arms; the prohibition against cruel and unusual punishment and unreasonable search and seizure; the right to a fair and speedy trial by a jury of one's peers; and the prohibition against the forced quartering of troops. Now regarded as part of the essential birthright of all Americans, the set of explicit freedoms, individual rights, and constraints on government Madison helped set in place echoed the long litany of colonial abuses that led to the American Revolution. The Bill of Rights, though, also harkens back to the similar document of the same name enshrined in English law a century before, as well as to the Virginia Declaration of Rights penned by George Mason—with help from Jefferson and Madison—in the spring of 1776.

"But these libertarian ideas also had their limits," David Hackett Fischer and James Kelly wrote in *Bound Away, Virginia and the Westward Movement*. "Most ideas of freedom in Virginia coexisted with slavery," they wrote. "Meanwhile, the words 'all men are created equal,' though not meant for black ears, stirred black souls and worked powerfully on black minds."

A ROUGH FORM OF FREEDOM

One such soul who was deeply stirred was born in Richmond in the very year the Declaration of Independence was penned. Twenty-four years later, in the prime of his life and at the dawn of the new century, he led his own revolutionary struggle in the cause of liberty, organizing one of the farthest-reaching slave insurrections in American history. It did not earn him a bust of alabaster alongside the founders in democracy's pantheon; he wound up swinging from the end of a rope. His name was Gabriel, and he lived on in myth and legend that would inspire generations of black Americans yearning to be free.

Gabriel was born in 1776 on a Richmond tobacco plantation called Brookfield, owned by a planter named Thomas Prosser. Gabriel might have been called Henry, Jefferson, or Washington, as many slave children were at that time. He was named instead for an angel of God. Raised in the shadows of the American Revolution, Gabriel grew into a charismatic figure and skilled blacksmith. He married a slave woman, could read and write— Thomas Prosser's wife taught Gabriel to read the Bible—and was looked to as a natural leader by the fifty-odd other slaves at Brookfield. In his lifetime, Gabriel saw Richmond grow from a tobacco and buckskin town of perhaps six hundred people into a thriving capital and commercial hub with ten times that many residents. Fully half of them were black. Of those, at least three hundred were free blacks, managing their households, raising their families, and earning a living off the very sorts of artisan skills Gabriel possessed.

Gabriel lived near the outer edges of slavery's bounds, as did hundreds of other slaves in the booming capital. Enslaved blacks had long struggled to find ways to augment the hardscrabble lives most led on the tobacco plantations, tending small garden plots in the slave quarters, fishing in the rivers, backwaters, and streams, and raising or snatching up the odd pig here and there, some of which could be encouraged to stray from their owners' pens with a little urging from a determined slave.

By the late 1700s, large numbers of African Americans had acquired important skills working on the plantations, where slaves had become the masters of the trades. They were the carpenters, tanners, weavers, tailors, cobblers, cooks, boat builders, butchers, and watermen. The American Revolution was partly a commercial war, and boycotts of British-made goods sparked an explosion in demand for locally produced candles, rope, clothing, quilts, shoes, nails, and scores of other goods, all of which slave artisans produced, along with hogsheads, bricks, lumber, and staves. Slaves and free blacks alike worked in the coalfields west of Richmond, on the bateaus that shipped the fuel downstream, and in the ironworks at Westham, where they learned to smelt ore, cast iron, and bore cannon barrels.

In such an economy, a good blacksmith like Gabriel was worth his weight in gold, making everything from horseshoes and harness fittings to shovels and ploughs, even gun parts, using jealously guarded craft secrets learned from years on the job. Owners often hired out their slaves, especially skilled ones like Gabriel, to neighboring planters, wharf merchants, or manufacturers. Many slaves managed to work out arrangements that enabled them to earn modest amounts of cash on the side, which some saved to purchase their freedom or to provide as they could for their families.

Such opportunities weren't limited to those with skills. Raising tobacco, wheat, and corn were seasonal ventures. There was little work to be done between the autumn harvest and spring planting. At those times, slave owners found they could hire out their slaves as laborers to businessmen who needed the help. Arrangements varied, but typically the slave owner was paid—by an employer or by agents who brokered such deals—for a worker's services, and the laborer often received a small stipend as well, a cash incentive for reliable work during plantation downtime.

Among the free blacks were many with professional skills. One, Peter Hawkins, was both preacher and dentist, or, as he was known in the pre-fluoride era, a tooth-drawer. "As a preacher, he drew the fangs of Satan, with his spiritual pullikins, almost as skillfully as he did the teeth of his brother sinners on week days, with his metallic ones," the author Samuel Mordecai recalled in his nineteenth-century memoir, *Richmond in Bygone Days.* "His strength of wrist was such that he would almost infallibly extract, or break, a tooth, whether the right or the wrong one," wrote Mordecai, speaking from hard experience. "Peter's surgical, but not his clerical, mantle fell on his son, who depletes the veins and pockets of his patients, and when he has exhausted the latter, the former are respited."

As the eighteenth century sped toward the next, Richmond was a boomtown, its own prosperity mirroring that of the young and growing nation. In 1790—the first year of the official U.S. census—there were 3.9 million people in the United States. Nearly one in every five lived in Virginia, the country's most populous state, and about 40 percent of all Virginians were slaves. An economic miracle was unfolding in Richmond, where the river wedded mostly white management and investment to black and white labor and skills in a way that tied Piedmont farmers and Tidewater planters to the wealth of great ports around the world. Jobs were plentiful; demand for workers was intense as everywhere, it seemed, vast projects were being built.

In 1784, work began on a grand vision to dig a canal running alongside the river west from Richmond so that bateaus and packet boats could travel to and from the town without having to risk broken ribs—or worse—navigating the seven-mile stretch of fall line rapids running through the town. The James River Canal Company hired hundreds of slaves from area planters to work alongside Irish immigrants and other laborers on one of the great engineering marvels of its time. Together, these workers dug out the canal, fitting it with a system of granite and timber locks to staircase the boats upstream and a three-acre deepwater basin to accommodate oceangoing ships at the canal's Richmond terminus.

While not free by any stretch, the slaves who built the canal led a very different life from that of plantation field hands. Typically hired out for months at a time, and often for a full year, the canal workers lived together in boardinghouses or labor camps. They ate together, sometimes at cash eateries geared to the trade. And many could look forward to a Saturday night of gaming, singing, and dancing in the taverns and roadhouses that sprang up near the Richmond tobacco warehouses and wharves.

Along the riverfront, slaves and free blacks worked side by side with whites in factories where tobacco was processed, sorted, and cured, then twisted into flavored plugs for chewing or packed into hogsheads and crates to be shipped out for export aboard the oceangoing ships that pulled into Richmond just below the falls. Tobacco was the backbone of James River exports, but other products—salted fish, lumber, and beef among them— were shipped out as well. Opposite Richmond on the south bank of the river were mills that harnessed the power of falling water to spin raw cotton and wool into cloth. Joseph Gallego built one of three huge mills that ground wheat and corn floated down to Richmond from upland farms into flour sold in Europe, Australia, and South America. Great ships with tall masts sailed upriver to Richmond from Caribbean and Latin American ports carrying loads of coffee, sugar, bananas, and rum, adding tropical flavors to the pan-American bazaar that grew up along the banks of the James.

Distributing these products up and down the river employed a huge fleet of schooners, barges, sailing ships, and bateaus, crewed and piloted by whites, free blacks, and slaves, in jobs that required them to journey far from their owners for weeks or months at a time, getting to know others along the river while camping along its banks at night or socializing once they arrived in Richmond. "The entire urban riverfront developed stores, landings and patterns of social relations that offered Black Virginians unusual levels of autonomy," University of Texas historian James Sidbury wrote in *Ploughshares into Swords: Race, Rebellion, and Identity in Gabriel's Virginia.* "It was down along the James River and the canal that residents and visitors developed new urban norms to govern interaction between people of different status and racial background."

Rising above it all, from a commanding hilltop overlooking the river, was the construction site of the most majestic building in eighteenth-century America: the graceful Virginia Capitol that Jefferson designed while serving as Washington's envoy to Paris. Modeled after a Roman temple in Nimes in the south of France, the Capitol was Jefferson's sweeping bow to Rome. In the balance and symmetry of the ionic-columned Capitol, he traced the origins of citizenship, his architectural footsteps echoing down the marble-floored chambers of the senate and forum of the ancient democratic city-state that brought government by the people—well, some of them at least—to the classical world. "It is very simple," Jefferson wrote of the model for the Capitol in a letter to Madison, "but noble beyond expression."

Much like the grand Roman edifice Jefferson sought to emulate, his temple to Virginia democracy was largely built by slaves—like those who dug the canal, fired the bricks, ground the grain, and cast the iron upon which the economy grew. While white Virginians dominated the service sectors with managers, lawyers, auctioneers, financiers, doctors, merchants, and brokers, it was black Virginians who lent much of the sinew essential to success in a world where human toil remained an essential locomotive of prosperity. "Slaves provided the labor for nearly all aspects of Richmond's economic, urban and industrial growth, from cultivating and manufacturing tobacco and wheat to building supporting industries and creating the physical structure of the city," Fairhaven College historian Midori Takagi wrote in *"Rearing Wolves to Our Own Destruction": Slavery in Richmond, Virginia, 1782–1865.* "Richmond slaves were not ordinary field hands but craftsmen, ironmakers, blacksmiths, tailors and, of course, tobacco processors," wrote Takagi. "Many of these workers were accustomed to traveling alone, negotiating their work contracts and receiving cash payments for their labor."

Such a man was Gabriel, whose marketable blacksmithing skills and literacy placed him well above the status of common chattel. "Though he was still a slave in the eyes of the law," Douglas Egerton wrote in the *Journal of Southern History*, "he enjoyed a rough form of freedom."

The fluid and increasingly nuanced relationships between owners and slaves made for a changing society in Richmond. From the outside, the rules weren't always apparent or easy to comprehend. Ultimately, that led to the matter of the purloined pig and Absalom Johnson's left ear.

Johnson, a slave overseer, moved in 1799 to Richmond, where he rented a thirteen-hundred-acre plantation with two dozen slaves next door to Prosser's Brookfield. That September, he caught Gabriel and two other slaves trying to steal a pig from his property and, unwisely it turned out, confronted them. A fight ensued, and Gabriel, a big man steeled by years spent swinging a hammer in the blacksmith shop, bit off the better part of the overseer's left ear.

There's no record as to why Gabriel, who almost certainly could have afforded to buy a pig, chose instead to risk punishment to steal one. It may well have been for sport or even to taunt a new neighbor who didn't quite get it when it came to getting along with Richmond's blacks. Once caught, though, Gabriel had the option of simply handing the pig over, enduring a bit of verbal abuse, and either submitting to punishment or offering to provide money or services to make up for his offense. Instead, he attacked Johnson, knowing that to do so, under Virginia's harsh slave code, was a capital offense. Either Gabriel hated the overseer, wanted to teach him a lesson about how skilled blacks expected to be treated in Richmond, or was so taken aback by Johnson's reaction to the pig prank that he simply flew into a rage. Either way, Gabriel was convicted by the special slave tribunal provided for under Virginia law—the courts of oyer and terminer, a panel of five justices of the peace, with no jury and no appeal other than to the governor—and sentenced to be hanged for assaulting a white man.

As a first-time offender, Gabriel was able to take advantage of a provision in Virginia law that allowed him to avoid hanging and have his sentence reduced by showing remorse and reciting a Bible verse as proof of a Christian heart. Instead of being hanged, he received thirty-nine lashes at the whipping post. He was also branded on his thumb with a cross, indicating that he had already received the one second chance that the benefit of clergy accorded to felonious slaves in late eighteenth-century Virginia.

It was, for Gabriel, an intolerable insult. He was a highly skilled and somewhat educated Virginian, living what was, in many ways, the life of a middle-class black man in a town where one black in five was free. And here he was being publicly whipped and branded like livestock for what appears to have begun as a mischievous pig grab. Freedom, however rough, remained elusive. Gabriel was yet a slave.

But there was more than that to Gabriel's complaint. White Virginians regarded themselves as the high apostles of freedom, people who had, in Jefferson's words, pledged "our lives, our fortunes and our sacred honor" to establish and preserve what Washington called "the sacred fire of liberty." In the weeks it took for Gabriel's wounds to heal, the embers of that sacred fire smoldered within his soul no less than in the hearts of the founders. The next year, he was primed to strike his own blow for freedom.

"When men are tied as slaves," the Anglican priest Richard Hakluyt had counseled two centuries before, "all yell and cry with one voice liberty, liberty, liberty." In the summer of 1800, Gabriel used his extensive network of contacts to unite Richmond-area blacks around that common quest, organizing a massive and carefully planned insurrection plot that shook the American South to its core. By late August, more than five hundred blacks were part of a conspiracy Gabriel and a band of lieutenants had painstakingly stitched together, ingeniously making use of the mobility blacks had gained through their jobs as bateau pilots, mail couriers, and wagon drivers. His coconspirators, slave and free, ranged as far downriver as Norfolk and as far west as Charlottesville.

From reading Richmond newspapers, Gabriel knew that Gov. James Monroe had ordered new muskets for Virginia militia units and directed troops from around the state to send their aging weapons to Richmond, where they were stored in the Capitol powder magazine to be serviced. He knew also that in that election year the state was rife with political division, leaving Monroe's government vulnerable to additional pressure and short on allies in a pinch. Against that background, Gabriel masterminded a plan for slaves to gather at the Brookfield blacksmith shop and the bridge over nearby Brook Run, a Chickahominy River tributary, on Saturday night, August 30. From there they were to head down the Brook Road leading into Richmond from the north, armed with daggers and swords he and other blacksmiths pounded out of scythes and other farm implements. The group was to march on Richmond and split up, set fire to the warehouse district, seize the weapons in the powder magazine, take control of the governor's mansion, hold Monroe hostage, and demand freedom for Virginia slaves. "As far as I understand, all the whites were to be massacred, except the Quakers, the Methodists and the Frenchmen, and they were to be spared, on account as they conceived of their being friendly to liberty," Ben Woolfolk, a key conspirator in the plot, later testified. There was one thing more. Gabriel, the slave general, planned to carry with him a silk banner bearing a slogan that lent voice to his cause: "death or liberty."

History has sometimes dismissed Gabriel's plan as the desperate product of a radical mind. Gabriel was a radical, to be sure, and, just as certainly, he was desperate. But he had witnessed in his lifetime the unlikely defeat of a British monarch by a scrappy band of backwoods hunters and East Coast patriots. He had been raised on the rhetoric of revolution in his own country and had heard, and perhaps read, of Toussaint L'Ouverture's leading a slave rebellion that turned back French colonization in Haiti. It was by no means far-fetched to think a thinly defended town of merchants and planters might be brought to heel through a surprise attack in the dead of night by five hundred armed and determined black men, quickly joined by hundreds of other blacks and poor white sympathizers. And the ease with which black workers had slipped into Richmond's flexible labor market left little doubt in the minds of Gabriel and his followers that freedom for blacks was not only a moral imperative but it also made economic sense.

The winds of fortune, however, blew against him—quite literally. On the night of August 30, with all the pieces of the carefully choreographed insurrection in place, a tropical storm slammed into Richmond, washing out bridges, flooding low-lying spreads, and turning roads into impassable mixing bowls of mud. As a handful of rain-soaked stalwarts gathered near Gabriel's blacksmith shop, they bowed to nature's caprice and scrubbed the mission, spreading word that it would be carried out the next night. By then, though, it was too late. A pair of conspirators named Pharaoh and Tom got cold feet and spilled the beans to a planter named Mosby Sheppard. He immediately disclosed the plot to Monroe, who in turn called out the militia to start rounding up suspects.

By the time the militia arrived at Brookfield, Gabriel was gone. He had made his way down the steamy Chickahominy and hid out along its swampy banks. After two weeks on the lam, Gabriel took a risk, asking to board a James River schooner that turned out to be run by a former overseer who had gotten religion. Capt. Richardson Taylor had converted to Methodism just in time to offer Gabriel a berth to Norfolk. A slave crewman named Billy, though, had his eye on Gabriel—and on the $300 cash reward Monroe had offered for his capture. Once in port, Billy, a Hampton slave with a Richmond wife, informed local authorities, who arrested Gabriel, locked him in chains, and took him back to Richmond under heavy guard.

Gabriel was the leader of several dozen slaves, who were tried in one of the most captivating hearings of his age, a series of courtroom dramas that unveiled to white Virginians just how close they had come to a bloody massacre that might have overturned their world. He was found guilty of conspiracy and insurrection and sentenced, once again, to be hanged. On October 10, 1800, Gabriel walked up the rickety wooden steps to the public gallows on a steep hillside near 15th and Broad streets. Near the narrow channel of Shockoe Creek at the foot of the hill lay the pauper's graveyard, the final, rock-strewn resting place for most of the city's blacks. Atop the hill rising from the shore of the creek, the skyline was pierced by the small bell tower of St. John's Church, where Patrick Henry stood the year before Gabriel was born and fanned the flames of American independence with his immortal call for liberty or death. And two blocks south, cresting the slope where he would die, Gabriel could have seen the Virginia Capitol, Jefferson's magnificent white-columned temple to ancient rights and self-evident truths, very possibly the last thing Gabriel ever saw.

When men are tied as slaves, all yell and cry with one voice. It was Gabriel's calling to unite that voice and to ensure that it was heard. Its echoes were to ring in the lives of two babies born that same year: Nat Turner and John Brown. Decades later, Gabriel's mission lived large in the memories and minds of Virginia slaves and of abolitionists black and white. In his antebellum novel *Blake, or the Huts of America*, the African American nationalist Martin Delany describes the "sacred reverence" in which Gabriel is held by a fictional community of runaway slaves who have taken refuge in Virginia's Dismal Swamp. A primal, snake-ridden bog, the swamp was an Underground Railroad sanctuary where communities of so-called maroons did, in fact, exist from the 1600s. In Delany's novel, a runaway slave named Maudy Ghamus has lived for three decades in the swamp, feeding on fish, wild onions, and turtle eggs and conjuring up visions of his one-time cohort, "General Gabriel," whom the old man regards as a talisman.

"What Gabriel and his movement represented was the insistence, by at least the children of African people who had been sold into Virginia, that Virginia was as much theirs as it was white Virginians,'" Sidbury, the

University of Texas historian, said in an interview. "That's a kind of a strain of black protest. It's one of the earliest major expressions of it. It's one of really seizing and laying claim to his people's right to what had been created in Virginia." Those rights were summarily denied to Gabriel and twenty-five of his fellow conspirators; all were hanged for their alleged roles in the insurrection plot of 1800, a plan foiled by a tempest before it began. In a final nod to the primacy of state over slave, the courts of oyer and terminer set a dollar value on the life of each executed slave and paid that amount to compensate slave owners for their loss. The court decided a slave named Martin was worth $300 just before he was carted off to the gallows in a procession flanked by a company of Governor Monroe's uniformed militiamen. The court settled on $400 for Jack Ditcher and just $110 for Dabney Williamson, who was aged and partially lame.

The hanging might not have ended there but for concerns raised by the vice president of the United States, who happened to be a former Virginia governor, Thomas Jefferson. "There is a strong sentiment that there has been hanging enough," Jefferson wrote to Governor Monroe, who had sought his friend's advice. "The other states and the world at large will forever condemn us if we indulge in a principle of revenge, or go one step beyond absolute necessity." As morally conflicted over slavery as ever, Jefferson stopped short of endorsing Gabriel's cause. He noted that American and foreign observers alike would not lose sight of "the object" the rebels had hoped to achieve, by which he meant their freedom. Jefferson's chief concern, though, appears to have been preserving the carefully cultivated image of his native state as a bastion of liberty. He seemed far less troubled that Virginia had executed twenty-six men for having the temerity and courage to lay down their lives in pursuit of a truly radical ideal, the belief that all men are created equal.

EMPIRE OF LIBERTY

The next year, Jefferson was inaugurated as the third president of the United States. While modern presidents often draw inspiration gazing out from the White House upon his marble image in the domed memorial just across the Tidal Basin, Jefferson was not universally revered in his own time. He won the office, in fact, by the skin of his teeth. In one of the closest and most contentious presidential elections in American history, he was picked by a sharply divided House of Representatives, which had already voted thirty-five times without a conclusive result before choosing him on the thirty-sixth ballot. His razor-thin margin of victory was a telling barometer of the difficulty Jefferson would face maintaining domestic support through two presidential terms. His greatest domestic achievement, in fact, would stem not from a populist base but from his foreign policy instincts.

Earlier, Jefferson had been thrown into the bare-knuckled world of great power diplomacy, much like the young country itself, with little training or experience. His curious nature, liberal education, and decorous style, however, combined with his reputation as the author of the American Revolution to make for sound credentials when he went to France as Washington's envoy to the country's closest and most important ally. After four years in Paris, Jefferson returned home to oversee the entirety of the U.S. foreign policy portfolio as Washington's secretary of state.

Combining his diplomatic prowess with his lifelong passion for western exploration, President Jefferson managed to repeat for the map of the country what he had already done for the soul of the state, enlarging both beyond all expectations on the strength of his vision and will. Ever the surveyor's son, Jefferson was never one to pass up a good land deal. Almost immediately after becoming president, he began secret diplomacy aimed at securing the territories the French claimed west of the Mississippi River from the cash-starved government of the Emperor of France, General Napoleon Bonaparte.

In an age when rivers were the vital arteries of advanced civilizations, even as they had once bound the Virginia Indians to the James, the U.S. president understood that control of the Mississippi and Missouri rivers was essential to western expansion. These rivers also held the strategic keys to countering rival powers for control of the American heartland. As Jefferson took office, the country was bordered to the south and west by the Spanish, who were already established in present-day Florida, Texas, Arizona, New Mexico, California, and Nevada; to the north by Canada's British, who had their own designs on the American West Coast; and to the far northwest by Russia. The continent's major western river systems, in Jefferson's view, were natural conduits for whichever global power might seize them first. They posed at once a golden opportunity for American enlargement, an invitation to the young nation's rivals, and a mortal threat to Jefferson's expansionist vision. "Rivers dominated Jefferson's thinking about North America," historian Stephen Ambrose wrote in *Undaunted Courage*, his tale of the expedition Jefferson launched to explore the western territories. "He was determined . . . to prevent the West from breaking away from the United States." Beyond that, Jefferson was chasing the same dream that had led Columbus to America three centuries before, hoping to find an inland waterway to link the Atlantic Ocean to the vast Pacific and the lucrative Asia trade routes beyond. After two years in office, Jefferson pieced together the continental picture and the larger global setting to grasp a historic shot at nation building.

By 1803, Bonaparte's forces were sliding toward defeat in the long war of attrition L'Ouverture's slave rebellion had opened in Haiti a decade before. It was an especially bad time for France to be losing the rich sugar and coffee revenues of its Caribbean colony. Bonaparte was in the midst of the Napoleonic wars. Over the course of a decade, virtually every major power in Europe had been pitted against him, including, at various times, British, Russian, Austrian, Prussian, Dutch, and Spanish forces. With Haiti slipping through his fingers, Bonaparte decided to jettison French holdings in America altogether, before he was stretched too thin to defend them, and try to consolidate his position back home. Thus, after two years of quiet and meticulous statesmanship led by Jefferson's Blue Ridge neighbor and secretary of state, James Madison, officials from France and the United States finalized the Louisiana Purchase in the summer of 1803. It's often called the greatest real estate bargain ever struck. For $15 million, Jefferson's administration took title to most of the American West, some 828,000 square miles. With interest, it wound up costing U.S. taxpayers about a nickel an acre. Jefferson had the news announced in the *National Intelligencer* on the Fourth of July. Exactly twenty-seven years after the Continental Congress adopted his Declaration of Independence, Jefferson had doubled the size of the United States.

"Except in imagination, he himself never got farther west than the Warm Springs Valley of Virginia at any time in his long life," University of Virginia historian Dumas Malone wrote in his six-volume biography of Jefferson. "But his vision extended farther and comprehended more than that of anybody else in public life," Malone concluded. "In few things that he did as president was he more in character than as a patron of exploration, and he could well afford to leave his performance in that role to the judgment of posterity. One may doubt if any successor of his ever approached it." The Louisiana Purchase redefined the country. Onto a montage of former British colonies, it grafted a broad mosaic of Midwestern heartland and Rocky Mountain terrain extending to the mouth of the Columbia River and the Pacific Ocean beyond. In a single stroke, Jefferson had widened the United States across an uncharted, though not uninhabited expanse of fertile prairies, rolling rivers, and sweeping plains.

More than simply redrafting the boundaries, the Louisiana territories changed the way Americans saw themselves and their new nation. People who had watched their parents break the shackles of British control suddenly saw the old territorial constraints that bound them to the eastern seaboard shattered as well. Americans, wrote *Bound Away* authors Fischer and Kelly, "had begun to identify themselves with their destinations rather than their origins." The opening of the western territories widened their ambitions as it broadened their reach, triggering a century of westward migration by people willing to risk all they had to chase the opportunities unleashed in a nation of no apparent bounds. It was to become, Jefferson promised, an "empire of liberty," a rich and fruitful new republic reaching from sea to shining sea, no matter what, or who, might stand in its way. For while Jefferson readily acknowledged Napoleon's claims—and paid him to relinquish them—he ignored altogether indigenous people who had actually lived on the land for millennia.

In securing the Louisiana Purchase, neither Jefferson nor anyone else had much of an idea what he had done. He knew the Mississippi River bisected the continent some two thousand miles east of the Pacific Coast but had little idea of what lay in between. To help figure it out, Jefferson turned to Meriwether Lewis, a U.S. Army captain and Albemarle County neighbor whose family had known Jefferson's for nearly a hundred years. Lewis was a planter, hunter, and explorer whose Welsh ancestors had come to the foothills of the Blue Ridge Mountains in the first half of the seventeenth century. Born in 1774 at Locust Hill, a plantation an hour by horse from Monticello, Lewis attended the Charlottesville school for boys founded by Jefferson's former teacher Rev. James Maury. For the first two years of Jefferson's presidency, Lewis served as his personal secretary.

As his own assistant for the expedition, Lewis chose army lieutenant William Clark, a Virginia native whose ancestors had settled on the James River around 1630. The two men selected three dozen soldiers, scouts, and river men to accompany them in the Corps of Discovery that would conduct the Lewis and Clark Expedition. In one of the most epic journeys of exploration in history, the corps traveled nearly nine thousand miles in a three-year American odyssey traversing territory touching on seventeen present-day states from Pennsylvania to Washington.

At the end of August 1803, Lewis set off from Pittsburgh in a custom-built keelboat, heading down the Ohio River, past its confluence with the Kanawha River at the port of Point Pleasant and on to the town of Clarksville, across the Ohio River from Louisville, Kentucky. At Clarksville,

Lewis met up with Clark. The two drifted down the Ohio to the Mississippi River, then pressed upstream to its confluence with the Missouri. There, near St. Louis, they wintered, before setting out the next spring on their journey to the great Northwest.

In the summer of 1804, Lewis and Clark arranged to send a dozen Osage Indian men and two boys from present-day Missouri to Washington to meet with Jefferson. There, greeting them at the White House—known then as simply the President's House—Jefferson laid out his vision of U.S. citizenship for Native Americans and a future of cooperation based on mutual trust and respect between the white man and the red. "It is so long since our forefathers came from beyond the great water, that we have lost the memory of it, and seem to have grown out of this land, as you have done," Jefferson began. "We are all now of one family, born in the same land and bound to live as brothers."

Having defined Native Americans and former colonists as part of the same sweeping stroke of history, Jefferson went on to describe a future of peaceful relations between the two. Following the pattern set by English settlers along the James River two centuries before, however, Jefferson proposed a paternalistic peace on the white man's terms, expecting Native Americans to acquiesce in the impending loss of their sovereignty and lands. "The Great Spirit has given you strength, and has given us strength, not that we might hurt one another, but to do each other all the good in our power," Jefferson concluded. "Tell your people that I take them all by the hand; that I become their father thereafter."

Two years later, the expedition complete, Jefferson reveled in the territorial gains he had secured and the treasure trove of geographic and biological discovery Lewis and Clark reported upon their return. They had been stymied in their efforts to explore the Southwest by hostile Native Americans and Spanish. And their reports of the Rocky Mountains made clear there would be no easy river route to the Pacific. Jefferson, though, was ecstatic over what they had found. The little boy who'd learned a love of land and exploration on his father's knee by the banks of the James had grown into the U.S. president who launched a second wave of migration across the United States, opening the vast expanse of the American West to a restless new generation of settlers.

BAPTISM OF POCAHONTAS

At the dawn of the American movement west, the sun was setting on another epic migration from the east. In 1808, the Constitution's twenty-year reprieve on the transatlantic slave trade expired. By an act of Congress, the trade was outlawed that year, ending government acquiescence in a trade that had forced between five and six hundred thousand Africans into the United States. Over the next half-century, scores of thousands of enslaved Africans would be smuggled into the country illicitly. As a legally functioning institution, though, linking Europe, Africa, and the United States, the transatlantic slave trade was dead.

Slavery, however, was not. In 1810, the United States was a fast-growing nation of seven million Americans, one in seven of whom was enslaved. From its beginnings along the James River two centuries before, slavery had grown with the nation slaves helped to build. And while there were 174,339 free blacks in the country, there were six blacks in chains for every one who was free.

The new lands to the west beckoned Virginians at a welcome moment. Two centuries after John Rolfe initiated the transatlantic tobacco boom, enormous tracts of Virginia farmland had been worn out by the ravenous leaf. The invention of Eli Whitney's cotton gin in 1793 had revolutionized that industry, creating an insatiable demand for laborers to carve out and tend fields from the rich bottomlands opening up along the vast plains and fertile deltas draining the Mississippi and Missouri rivers. And the formal end of the transatlantic slave trade had driven up the value of what had become, for white Virginians, a rich resource: the next generation of slaves. With the importation of slaves from Africa at an end, children born to Virginia slaves could be sold into the new territories at premium prices. For scores of aging Virginia plantations, the breeding and selling of slaves bound for the new frontier became a new export industry, a way to raise money needed to reduce debts or pay taxes on land depleted by long years of tobacco farming.

Together, those trends created a storm that blew Virginians westward by the hundreds of thousands. Packing up their families, and often their slaves, they flocked to Ohio, Indiana, Illinois, Kentucky, Missouri, and Tennessee. Virginia became the single largest source of migrants headed west, the main thrust of a larger migration that would lead about a million people, black and white, out of Virginia over the next half-century or so. Suckled from its infancy by the fertile waters of the James, Virginia had become what the mid-nineteenth-century scholar Henry Ruffner would call "the Grandmother of States." By 1850, U.S. Census data showed nearly four hundred thousand native Virginians living in other states. That number, naturally, didn't include at least that many Virginians, and probably more, who had migrated westward and were no longer living by then; "nor did it embrace their children and grandchildren, who were reckoned in millions by 1850," Fischer and Kelly wrote in their book on Virginia's westward movement.

Many journeyed up the James, loading their families aboard wooden packet boats or bateaus and entrusting their lives and prized possessions to the skills of river pilots who worked their way upstream. By the mid–nineteenth century, the James River and Kanawha Canal enabled travelers to journey from Richmond 225 miles upstream to the port town of Buchanan. From there, they could go overland two hundred miles to the Kanawha River and travel that waterway to its confluence with the Ohio River, then head from there to the Mississippi. A person could board a boat in Richmond, in other words, and journey all the way to New Orleans, St. Louis, or Chicago, for that matter, traveling mostly by water.

Traversing the perilous cataracts or raging floodwaters of the James, though, wasn't the most complex piece of the puzzle. Virginia's great migration westward lay at the heart of the two central conflicts that defined nineteenth-century America: the white settlers' takeover of traditional Indian lands and the new nation's fight over slavery. From the moment the wide-eyed English sailed their wooden ships up the James, the Native Americans were thrust upon the horns of a dilemma, forced to choose between war with the *tassantassas* or peace on the invaders' terms. American expansionism translated into expulsion or annihilation for hundreds of thousands of native people. Jefferson's White House admonition that American Indians and westward settlers not "hurt one another" did little more to change that harsh dynamic than the Virginia Company's instructions two centuries before that the settlers should "have great care not to offend the naturals." And so, after Little Turtle, chief of the great Miami tribe, turned back early attempts by Virginians to settle into Ohio in 1791, a large U.S. military force returned three years later to defeat him. Little Turtle's people were forced off land their ancestors had roamed, in Native American terms, forever.

It isn't known how many Indians were in North America before the European settlers arrived. Most historians use an estimate of one million, but anthropological and ethnological studies have put the number as high as eighteen million. The difference remains a source of heated dispute even today. It is known that by the middle of the nineteenth century, only about half a million remained. The rest, however many they were, were gone, victims, largely, of combat with the advancing occupiers or the ravages of disease, settler-borne illnesses such as smallpox, against which the Native Americans had no natural immunity.

Despite the aversion to standing armies the Americans inherited from their British forebears, wars with the Ohio Indians convinced the Congress to build a permanent military force. Future U.S. president William Henry Harrison, raised at Berkeley, his family's James River tobacco plantation, traveled to the Indiana territory to lead the 1811 defeat of the powerful Shawnee chief Tecumseh, crushing his attempt to build a national alliance of Native Americans to confront the white trespassers. Three years after that, another future president, Andrew Jackson, defeated Creek Indians in Alabama. On and on it went, with white warriors relying on generally superior force and firepower to subjugate, relocate, decimate, or exterminate Seminoles in Florida, Chickasaw in Georgia, Chocktaw in Mississippi, Cherokee in the Carolinas, Seneca in New York, and dozens more tribes elsewhere in a decades-long campaign some historians have labeled genocide.

As the moral weight of the bloodshed descended upon the new Americans, it glanced without a shudder across the easel of Virginia artist John Gadsby Chapman. With the blessings of the U.S. Congress—and the body's $10,000 commission—Chapman reached back to the young nation's beginnings on the banks of the James River, dipped his brush into the rich allegorical palate of Virginia history and holy scripture, and painted an incandescent American myth. He called it the *Baptism of Pocahontas*.

The year was 1840. Harrison stood before the U.S. Capitol on a bitter cold day and gave the longest inaugural speech on record. A month later, he was dead of pneumonia, his long-winded rhetoric having contributed to the shortest presidential term in history. Harrison was succeeded by his vice president, John Tyler, his James River neighbor from nearby Sherwood Forest plantation.

At the core of the new capitol was a grand neoclassical rotunda of sandstone and marble. Designed to echo the Roman Pantheon, the rotunda was meant to be precisely what it has become, the spiritual epicenter of the American republic, a sort of national echo chamber of memory and myth where the political soul of the state might reside. Like the Roman temple it mimicked, the rotunda was to be a place where the essential national narrative was enshrined, a place to remind visitors and elected lawmakers alike of the sacrifice, virtue, and ideals laid before the altar of democracy by those who had gone before. It was for precisely that purpose that the rotunda's architects left open eight panels—each one eighteen feet wide and twelve feet high—for a collection of grand paintings Congress would commission to tell the dramatic story of the nation's beginnings in the broadbrushed romantic style of the day.

By 1824, four paintings were hanging in the rotunda depicting key scenes in the forging of the republic: the adoption of Jefferson's Declaration of Independence in Philadelphia, the British surrenders at Saratoga and Yorktown, and Washington resigning his commission in Annapolis as the army's commander in chief. Congress ordered that the final four be centered on European colonization: Columbus coming to America, the Pilgrims headed for Plymouth Rock, the discovery of the Mississippi River, and Chapman's *Baptism of Pocahontas*.

Precious little is known about her actual baptism, which took place in the spring of 1614. Most likely, it was a small affair. Alexander Whitaker was the Anglican minister who baptized the Virginia Indian princess with the Christian name Rebecca. John Rolfe, her future husband, is thought to have been there, as, perhaps, was the military governor of the struggling colony, Thomas Dale, who consented to her induction into the Anglican Church as a necessary prerequisite to the teenager's marriage to Rolfe a few days or weeks later.

A cultural wedding was more like what Chapman and Congress had in mind, with stakes that went far beyond matrimony for the first Anglo-American couple. Like the other grand paintings Chapman's masterpiece was to share space with in the hallowed hall of the rotunda, the *Baptism of Pocahontas* was art with a mission. The message Congress wanted to convey in 1840 was clear: Indians who turned from their own culture and adopted the white man's ways would be welcomed into the American fold. Those who would not willingly abandon the faith, customs, and land they believed had been handed down to them by their sacred creator at the dawn of time would face the righteous judgment of the bayonet tip and hot musket ball.

In a propaganda classic that would make Mao Tse-tung blush, Chapman turned the religious conversion of the spirited Pocahontas into a plea for American Indians to lay down their arms and a dark warning to those who refused. He transformed the rustic wilderness chapel at Jamestown into a Disney-style woodlands temple replete with timbered columns rising from an altar of oaken stairs. At that point, Chapman dismissed her actual baptism entirely and fused that event with her wedding to Rolfe. The historical composite has the effect of turning the baptism service into a kind of national wedding, a grand invitation by the English for the native Virginians and, by extension, their High Plains kin, to become part of the Anglo-American family—or perish.

Powhatan never visited Jamestown and thus skipped his favorite daughter's wedding to the English trespasser. As a matter of protocol and Powhatan pride, he sent her uncle, Opechancanough, to represent the tribe, along with two half-brothers who could be counted on not to raise the indelicate subject of her likely first husband, Kocoum. Whether the wedding was presided over by Whitaker or by Rev. Richard Bucke, parish minister for the Jamestown church, simply isn't known.

Chapman portrayed Whitaker in a long, flowing robe with his left hand extended like Jesus, blessing the masses before a sanctuary of about three dozen English and Native American guests. Kneeling before him, eyes closed and hands obediently folded in prayer, Pocahontas bows her head, bathed in sunlight that turns her diaphanous white gown into an almost effervescent symbol of God's favor. The light falls from the trail of her gown to the intrigued face of one of her half-sisters, who is seated cross-legged on the floor, suckling a baby. The young mother's sunlit bare shoulders and red-tinted skin form a vision of the continent's native beauty and promise, while at the same time making clear the potential the young republic held out for a new generation of American Indians willing to play by the white man's rules.

The alternative was, literally, in the hands of Dale. He looks on, tense fingers clutching his sheathed sword, casting a wary gaze at the gaggle of Indians on the opposite side of the room. One of the bride's half-brothers, Nantaquoud, stands haughty and proud, deliberately rejecting the union of red and white by turning his face away. Seated on the floor, cast in dark shadow and looking off toward the viewer is a brooding Opechancanough, the warrior chief who presided over the coordinated Indian attacks on the James River settlers in 1622 and 1644.

As if the painting's stark symbolism might conceivably be lost, Congress commissioned pamphlet to accompany the work, making explicit the meaning Chapman had already made clear. Pocahontas, Chapman wrote in the pamphlet, was the embodiment of what Congress hoped the American Indian might be: embracing of American culture, religion, values, and laws, in a way that married the white men and women with the Indians—figuratively speaking, of course. "With the purest simplicity she united the kindest heart, and to the timidity of a spotless virgin she joined a sagacity of mind, a firmness of spirit, and an adventurous daring," wrote Chapman, outlining the example Pocahontas had set for other Indians long before. "She stands foremost in the train of those wandering children of the forest who have at different times—few, indeed, and far between—been snatched from the fangs of a barbarous idolatry, to become lambs in the fold of the Divine Shepard. She therefore appeals to our religious as well as our patriotic sympathies, and is equally associated with the rise and progress of the Christian Church, as with the political destinies of the United States."

Church and the American state have seldom been more closely wed than on the pages of Chapman's pamphlet or the canvas of his brush. Here was a congressionally mandated appeal for Indians everywhere to seek salvation in the "fold of the Divine Shepard" or remain forever lost to the "fangs of a barbarous idolatry," a condition that not only justified the waging of war but, indeed, seemed somehow to invite it. In Chapman's world, the choice Pocahontas made couldn't have contrasted more sharply with that of her troublemaking uncle, Opechancanough. "The sullen, cunning, yet daring Opechancanough shrunk back," wrote Chapman, "and probably even then brooded over the deep laid plan of massacre which he so fearfully executed years after, when that spotless Indian girl had gone to reap her reward in heaven." By God, the artist is saying, if any Indian dares raise a tomahawk against the United States of America or its agents coast to coast, he will have bought his own destruction. Here then, was the great gift, heaven-sent, being offered by the United States Congress to wandering children of the forest everywhere: repent of your idolatry, kneel before the irrepressible advance of the American nation, and with you the fruits of our labors we'll share. Turn back to the shadows of your heathen ways, and you'll be trampled beneath the hooves of the U.S. cavalry.

Far from some avant-garde notion tossed from the artistic fringe, Chapman's painting expressed the prevailing mainstream sentiments of a nation seized with its own identity. Americans saw their republic as one blessed by God, a new kind of nation-state endowed with special purpose and what magazine editor John O'Sullivan called in 1845 America's "manifest destiny to overspread the continent allotted by Providence for the free development of our yearly multiplying millions." More than just an exquisitely pigmented palliative to salve the national conscience, the *Baptism of Pocahontas* conveyed a promise kept across the broad and expanding girth of the country's great middle. The threat of harsh judgment leapt from the canvas on the rotunda's stone wall to take its place in a bloodstained line that would eventually run from the James River villages of the Powhatan all the way to Wounded Knee. At the raging confluence of American art, journalism, and politics, a new force had been christened. Manifest Destiny would become the cause and the justification for a new American crusade that would spread the white man's world across the continent while driving native people to the edge of extinction.

A HOUSE DIVIDED

As the new Americans pressed westward on the gilded wings of Manifest Destiny, thousands took their slaves with them. Thousands more exported slaves up and down the new frontier, marching them in chains by the score or the hundreds in forced mass movements that resembled the tortuous slave herds African mercenaries ran. By the time the *Baptism of Pocahontas* was unveiled in the Rotunda in 1840, there were 182,000 slaves living in Kentucky alone, according to U.S. Census data. An additional 183,000 were in neighboring Tennessee. Most had come from Virginia, part of a larger black movement westward that was epic in scope. Between the late 1700s and the mid-1800s, more than half a million blacks are estimated to have gone west from Virginia, on par with the number who were shipped into the entire country from Africa during the two centuries of the transatlantic slave trade. "Large numbers were carried south and west by slave traders; many others emigrated with their masters," wrote Fischer and Kelly. "Altogether, the magnitude of African-American emigration from Virginia to other parts of the United States was much larger than immigration from Africa to British America."

Like the passage out of Africa, the journey westward from Virginia was a punishing affair. Gangs of up to three hundred slaves were chained and force-marched over primitive roads, the crack of the whip used to keep the walking freight train staggering forward over arduous journeys of hundreds of miles. Beatings and other forms of corporal punishment aside, being torn from their families, marched from their homes, and sold into faraway and unfamiliar surroundings was among the most terrifying of fates that could befall a slave. Few could read or write, so they had no way of staying in touch with family or lifelong friends once separated from them. To be sold "down the river" and freighted off to the slave markets of Charleston, Vicksburg, or Atlanta was to be cast into a harsh and uncertain future, severed forever from the people and places a slave had known for his or her entire life.

In his 1853 novel *Clotel*, the former slave William Wells Brown tells the story of just such a woman, the title character, who watches through tears as her mother and fourteen-year-old sister are auctioned like livestock in a Richmond slave market. In Brown's story, they are then forced to march eight days across the state as part of a gang of forty slaves, then shipped down the Ohio River to the Mississippi and to New Orleans, where they are sold again. "Laughing, joking, swearing, smoking, spitting and talking kept up a continual hum and noise amongst the crowd, while the slave girl stood with tears in her eyes," Brown wrote in describing the Richmond slave sale. "What words can tell the inhumanity, the atrocity, and the immorality of that doctrine which, from exalted office, commends such a crime to the favor of enlightened and Christian people? What indignation from all the world is not due to the government and people who put forth all their strength and power to keep in existence such an institution?

Nature abhors it; the age repels it; and Christianity needs all her meekness to forgive it."

Brown knew his subject well. A light-skinned Missouri slave fathered by a white man, Brown spent a year hired out, against his will, to a Mississippi River slave trader who bought blacks up and down the river and sold them in New Orleans. Brown watched in horror as the trader broke up families, in one instance ripping a crying baby from his mother's arms and leaving the infant at a roadside house as a "gift" to the slave trader's host for the night. Brown had heard tales of slaves exchanging hands as chits in riverboat card games. He had seen young slave women [forced to] become mistresses to the lowest sort of white men, including the slave trader he served for a year. After the threat that Brown himself was to be sold prompted him to flee to the North, Brown helped other runaways escape along the Underground Railroad, taking note of the personal stories he heard from those who passed his way.

One Virginian caught up in the great exodus west was a slave named Dred Scott. His flight from Virginia was the first step in a journey that would eventually lead him to the United States Supreme Court and a judicial ruling so contentious it set the stage for war. The year before Gabriel was hanged in Richmond, Scott was born on a plantation in Southampton County just a few miles south of the James, where the great river spreads out across Tidewater flatlands of black-water tributaries that slither across sandy channels, then disappear into a Maudy Ghamus world of cypress-studded shallows and deciduous dreams. It was in that county that the slave Nat Turner led his 1831 insurrection. Turner and his followers killed fifty-five whites before being stopped by militia and hanged, after which the heads of several of Turner's backers were severed as a warning to other slaves and posted on pikes along a backwoods passage known to this day as Black Head Road.

Some months before Turner's rebellion, Scott's owner, Peter Blow, moved his family to the Midwestern hub of St. Louis and sold Scott to a U.S. military surgeon named John Emerson. Over the next dozen years, Scott traveled with Emerson, based out of the free state of Illinois, before Emerson moved back to St. Louis. After Emerson died, Scott sued for his freedom. He won before a Missouri court, which ruled that he was no longer a slave, owing to the time he'd spent living in the free state of Illinois. The Missouri Supreme Court overturned that decision. In 1854, Scott, then held as a slave by yet another owner, appealed to the U.S. Supreme Court.

Missouri by then had become a symbol of the growing American divide between North and South over the issue of slavery. In the seventeen years since Jefferson's Louisiana Purchase, debate had grown heated over whether the new territories could enter as slave states. In 1820, members of Congress from the North and South struck the so-called Missouri Compromise. It allowed Missouri to come into the Union as a slave state and Maine to come in as a free state so as not to upset the congressional balance between the two sides. Beyond that, Congress agreed that no new slave states could come into the Union north of a line running west along Missouri's southern border—thirty-six degrees and thirty minutes north latitude—to a point just south of present-day San Francisco.

The precedent prompted furious debate after the United States invaded Mexico, touching off two years of war that ended in 1848 with the expansion of Texas, a slave state, and the U.S. acquisition of territory that would eventually become Arizona, New Mexico, California, Utah, Nevada, and parts of Colorado and Wyoming. With the fate of those territories up for grabs, a sharply divided Congress agreed to a series of acts that together formed the Compromise of 1850. California was admitted as a free state, and the rest of those territories didn't attain statehood until slavery was no longer an issue. Nevada joined the Union in 1864, Utah in 1869, Colorado in 1876, Wyoming in 1890, and Arizona and New Mexico in 1912.

If there were to be states in the Union where a slave might go free, the slave owners in the South wanted some assurance that their own property couldn't simply wander off in the night and melt away into the vast North. And so the Compromise of 1850 would include a new tool, the Fugitive Slave Act. One of the farthest-reaching uses of federal power ever ordered by Congress, the act mandated that federal marshals and their deputies hunt down runaway slaves anywhere in the country, free states included, and return them to their owners. Until then, there had been no federal law addressing the fate of runaway slaves. It was left to the individual states to determine what to do with those slaves who used the Underground Railroad or other means to make their way to freedom. Precious few managed to do so. Of the 3.2 million enslaved Americans that year, 1,011 managed to escape. That number comes from U.S. Census data drawn from the actual claims of slave owners, who had every incentive to report those gone missing.

One who did make it out was Henry "Box" Brown, the slave who famously arranged to have himself packed into a wooden crate—two feet by three feet and marked "this side up with care"—and shipped by rail in 1848 from Richmond to Philadelphia, where waiting accomplices unpacked their human cargo and Brown stepped out a free man. Not so lucky, though, was a James River slave named Shadrach, who escaped from Norfolk to Boston only to become the first runaway captured and returned to his owner under the provisions of the 1850 Fugitive Slave Act. No longer did states have the prerogative of determining the fate of runaway slaves; the federal government mandated their return—and the use of taxpayer-supported federal marshals and their deputies to force free blacks back into chains. The act infuriated abolitionists and galvanized their movement. Many who had long advocated nonviolence began to sing a different tune.

Four years later, in 1854, Congress was again divided over the issue of slavery in the western territories. At issue were statehood efforts by Kansas and Nebraska, two states located north of the no-slave line drafted in 1820. There were already slaves, though, in those territories, brought there by owners from Virginia and other slave states. No surveyor's line had stopped that; nor did the 1820 agreement prevent slave owners from demanding the right to retain their property. At the urging of Sen. Stephen Douglas of Illinois, Congress responded by passing the Kansas-Nebraska Act, the essence of which was to repeal the Missouri Compromise, erase the no-slave line, and allow the residents of each new territory to decide whether to permit slavery. Under a concept Douglas hailed as "popular sovereignty," the federal role in regulating slavery was to be diminished. It was a measure he touted as a constitutional solution to the vexing question of whether Congress should condone the spread of slavery. Less publicly, he hoped it would help him build Southern support for a future presidential bid.

It was in the midst of that bubbling stew of national politics and sectional strife that the U.S. Supreme Court handed down a 7–2 ruling against Dred Scott in 1857. In an opinion written by Chief Justice Roger Taney of Maryland, the court found that slaves were private property, no matter what state they were in, and, in any event, lacked standing as citizens to sue in federal court. Blacks, wrote Taney, were "so far inferior, that they had no rights which the white man was bound to respect." Blacks "are not included, and were not intended to be included, under the word 'citizens' in the Constitution," wrote Taney. "On the contrary," he added, blacks were considered by the authors of the Constitution to be "a subordinate and inferior class of beings who had been subjugated by the dominant race, and, whether emancipated or not, yet remained subject to their authority."

Taney's view, agreed to by six of the other eight justices, electrified the national debate over slavery, even as it further polarized the institution's backers and foes. Abolitionists wondered aloud how they could support a system in which the highest court in the land could disenfranchise an entire race in a single stroke. There were, by then, nearly four million slaves in the United States. If the Supreme Court could obliterate their rights, what might that imply for the future of the nearly half a million American blacks who were free?

The Dred Scott decision added fuel to the fire already ablaze in the heart of a messianic white abolitionist named John Brown. Born in Connecticut, the son of a tanner, Brown learned his father's craft, tried his hand at farming, then studied to become a minister, before finding his true calling in the moral wilderness between American slavery and freedom. By the time Taney drafted his opinion, Brown had already become a legendary conductor on the Underground Railroad and a veteran of bloody conflict over slavery in Kansas. Aided and funded by a clique of Northerners who agreed with Brown that peaceful means would never end slavery, he hatched a plot so outrageous and risky that not even his friend the famed black abolitionist Frederick Douglass would go along with it. Brown's plan was to create an armed state of free blacks across the thinly populated western reaches of Virginia and the Carolinas, banking on the demonstrated difficulty federal troops would have imposing order upon the mountains and hollows of Appalachia. Like Gabriel before him, Brown planned to start by securing weapons from the government arsenal. His target was the U.S. armory in Harpers Ferry, the railroad and port village at the mountainous confluence of the Shenandoah and Potomac rivers. With five free blacks and sixteen white men behind him, Brown led a raid on the night of October 16, 1859, quickly seizing the federal armory, arsenal, and rifle works and cutting the area telegraph wires.

More idealist than tactician, Brown had little in the way of a plan beyond that. Rather than making off with weapons, he dispatched a patrol to gather hostages and spread the word among area slaves to come join his party. Along the darkened railroad trestle near the armory, one of Brown's guards killed—of all people—a free black man named Heyward Shepherd, a railroad baggage agent who wandered too close to the raiders' operations. By morning, word of the raid had spread through Harpers Ferry and, via the same late night train Shepherd had turned out to service, all the way to Washington. Local militiamen and townsfolk struck back, driving Brown, his party, and several hostages into a brick-walled firehouse.

Jammed into the vaultlike structure with thirteen hostages and about as many of his own men, several of whom were wounded, Brown's fevered mind may well have echoed with the warnings he'd received from Douglass, who had called Harpers Ferry a "steel trap" and told Brown he would never get out alive. Indeed, Brown's escape options were slim. To one side of the firehouse were the treacherous rapids of the Shenandoah; to the other, those of the Potomac. Beside both were towering banks of granite that rose behind the town's narrow streets and nearby farms and disappeared from there into dense forest. In any event, Brown couldn't contemplate safe passage from the firehouse, which was surrounded by local residents sniping with rifles and squirrel guns at anything that moved.

As the hours passed without food, water, or medical aid for the wounded, Brown's condition slipped from desperation to abject despair with the arrival that night by train of a company of U.S. Marines led by a fifty-two-year-old cavalry officer, Lt. Col. Robert E. Lee. A West Point graduate and veteran of the Mexican War, Lee was a product of two Virginia dynasties—the Carter and Lee families—and the James River plantation culture. Ancestors of Lee's mother, Ann Hill Carter, and his father, Henry Lee, were both living on the James River by 1639. His mother was raised at Shirley, one of the largest and wealthiest tobacco plantations on the James. Still operated as a family farm, Shirley is, to this day, the oldest family business in America. Built on land deeded in 1613 to Thomas West, Lord De La Warr, and titled the "West and Sherley Hundred," Shirley was a thriving tobacco plantation owned by Edward Hill in 1638. Hill's great granddaughter, Elizabeth Hill, married John Carter, part of another wealthy Virginia planter family, and Shirley has remained in the Carter family ever since. Robert E. Lee's father, Henry Lee, was a legendary Revolutionary War officer, nicknamed "Light Horse Harry" for his cavalry exploits. After the war, the elder Lee served in the Virginia House of Delegates and was later elected to three one-year terms as governor. It was Henry Lee who, at the request of the U.S. Congress, eulogized his friend George Washington as "First in war, first in peace and first in the hearts of his countrymen." Two of Henry Lee's cousins, Richard Henry Lee and Francis Lightfoot Lee, signed the Declaration of Independence, the only brothers to do so.

Robert E. Lee was born in 1807 in the stately brick manor house at Stratford, his family's Rappahannock River tobacco plantation. By the time Lee was born, his father had squandered much of the family's wealth on bad investments. He wound up in debtor's prison, was beaten nearly to death by a Baltimore mob, and died a largely broken man. Young Lee moved with his family to the Washington suburb of Alexandria, where his mother provided for herself and her children using money from her family's Shirley estate. While Lee grew up visiting the grand plantation, his own upbringing was modest by comparison. Eschewing the planter's life and the land speculation that had ruined his father, Lee followed the path that had brought Henry Lee his greatest success, a military career. Robert E. Lee graduated second in his class at the U.S. Military Academy at West Point, was commissioned in the engineering corps, transferred to the cavalry, and distinguished himself in the Mexican War as an aide to Gen. Winfield Scott, who wrote that Lee was "the very best soldier I ever saw in the field."

He arrived at Harpers Ferry on the night of October 17 with his lieutenant, a young cavalry officer named J. E. B. Stuart. Lee may well have sympathized with at least some of John Brown's goals. Just three years before, Lee had denounced slavery as "a moral and political evil in any country." Lee, though, owned slaves himself, through the family of his wife, Mary Anne Randolph Custis. And, whatever his views on Brown's objectives, Lee was under orders to subdue the rebellion at Harpers Ferry.

At dawn the next day, Lee sent Stuart bearing a white flag to offer surrender terms to Brown and his men. With a carbine in one hand, Brown opened the fire house door a crack and began arguing with Stuart. When the young lieutenant concluded that Brown intended no surrender, he stepped aside of the door and waved his hat, a signal for the marine assault to commence. Within minutes, Brown's thirty-six-hour rebellion was over. He had lost ten of his men, including two of his sons. Five others had escaped. Lee's men captured Brown and his six remaining followers and sent them to the nearby town of Charleston, where all were found guilty of treason and sentenced to hang. In his report, Lee chalked up Brown's act as "the attempt of a fanatic or madman." To his Northern supporters, though, Brown was a hero.

"I deny everything but what I have all along admitted—the design on my part to free slaves," Brown testified at his dramatic three-day trial. "Had I so interfered in behalf of the rich, the powerful, the intelligent, the so-called great . . . every man in this court would have deemed it an act worthy of reward rather than punishment," Brown averred. "Now, if it is deemed necessary that I should forfeit my life for the furtherance of the ends of justice, and mingle my blood further with the blood of my children and with the blood of millions in this slave country whose rights are disregarded by wicked, cruel and unjust enactments, I submit; so let it be done!" With that, Brown was convicted of murder, treason, and inciting slave insurrection and sentenced to hang on December 2. Letters streamed into the office of Virginia governor Henry Wise. Some writers endorsed the sentence, while others demanded that Brown be pardoned. Wise received death threats and vows that his state would be invaded if he allowed the hanging to go forward.

On the day Brown went to the gallows in Charleston, church bells tolled in abolitionist strongholds throughout the North, where Brown became a martyr, eulogized in sanctuaries and meeting halls and lionized in newspaper editorials. The reaction to Brown's raid and execution further polarized the nation North and South, with citizens in the slave-holding states feeling increasingly under threat by abolitionists who openly condoned bloody revolt to end slavery. The U.S. Senate impaneled the Select Committee to Investigate John Brown's 1859 Raid on the U.S. Arsenal at Harpers Ferry, Virginia. The panel held months of hearings and issued a 255-page report of its findings. More enduring than any sermon, editorial, or committee brief, however, were the words penned in Brown's honor two years later by Julia Ward Howe as "The Battle Hymn of the Republic": "Mine eyes have seen the glory of the coming of the Lord; He is trampling out the vineyards where the grapes of wrath are stored; He hath loosed the fateful lightning of His terrible swift sword: His truth is marching on."

As Brown's legacy bloomed to sainted status across the North, the Southern voice in Congress was being steadily diminished. Senate and House members from nineteen free states advocated against the perceived interests of the fifteen-state caucus of slave-holding states. Increasingly, Southerners saw the Northern states as a threat to their economic welfare, their way of life, and their rights. Some began murmuring of secession, insisting that the Constitution provided states with the right to join or to leave the Union at their discretion. Sen. Stephen Douglas sought a national mandate for his message of popular sovereignty, taking it before the American people in the presidential elections of 1860. He was opposed by a gangly, six-foot-four-inch Republican, a man Douglas had already defeated for the U.S. Senate just two years before in their home state of Illinois. The contender's name was Abraham Lincoln, and he set about making clear his contention that the country could not withstand the sectional stress slavery imposed on the Union. "A house divided against itself cannot stand," Lincoln said in accepting his party's presidential nomination. "I believe the government cannot endure permanently half slave and half free."

Not a single Southern state supported Lincoln, who received only 39 percent of the popular vote that November. In a four-way presidential race, though, that was enough. On March, 4, 1861, Lincoln was sworn in as the sixteenth president of the United States. He was very nearly the last. By the time Lincoln took the oath of office on March 4, 1861, the country was coming apart at the seams. Seven Southern states—South Carolina, Mississippi, Florida, Alabama, Georgia, Louisiana, and Texas, in that order—had already seceded from the Union. They formed the Confederate States of

America and vowed to take up arms to fight for their independence from the United States.

The American founders had bequeathed to the sons and daughters of the revolution a majestic engine of self-governance. For all of that, the adolescent republic's democratically elected leaders were not able to resolve the question of slavery through the Congress, the presidency, or the courts. The country's leaders, diplomats, and body politic, North and South, each weighed in on the thorny matter. They all failed. For all the potential contained in the sacred promise of government by the people, this dispute would be settled the old-fashioned way, as if the age of enlightenment and the lessons of the nation's own hard history had all been forgotten and just swept away. The essential question of the rights of man would be decided on the battlefield, in the bloodiest and costliest reckoning in the nation's history.

During Lincoln's first six weeks in the White House, the opening shots in the Civil War were fired, and four other states—Virginia, Arkansas, Tennessee, and North Carolina—joined the Confederacy. The Confederate capital was moved from Montgomery, Alabama, to Richmond, a scant hundred miles from Lincoln's bedroom. It would become, for him, the longest hundred miles in history. Four years later, with 620,000 Americans dead, a war-weary Lincoln, with a week left to live, would watch the Confederacy collapse on the banks of the James, a hundred miles from Washington and just upstream from the marshy spit of sand where the country had begun two and a half centuries before.

9

A NEW BIRTH OF FREEDOM

CITY POINT—Campfires flickered behind Union lines, their reflections scattered like amber jewels against the smooth, taut throat of the James. The distant voices of soldiers skipped over the water like flakes of stone and trailed off into the night. From the decks of the navy flagship anchored in the broad channel of a sweeping bend, the muffled rumble of faraway cannon fire faded into the starry void like the thundering tail of a retreating storm. It was the third night of April 1865. One month into his second term as president, with less than two weeks to live, Lincoln drew in the cool night air and gazed out across the ship's bow. Upstream lay the objective of four years of war, the capital of the Confederacy, ground to ruin and swallowed in flames. "It is certain that Richmond is in our hands," Lincoln wrote that evening. "I will go there tomorrow."

Lincoln steamed upriver to the smoldering heart of the Confederacy the next morning, against the advice of his secretary of war, Edwin Stanton, who telegraphed his concerns from Washington. "Allow me respectfully to ask you to consider whether you ought to expose the nation to the consequence of any disaster to yourself in the pursuit of a treacherous and dangerous enemy like the rebel army," Stanton wrote on April 3. "Commanding generals are in the line of their duty in running such risks. But is the political head of a nation in the same condition?" Caution, by then, had been brushed aside by Lincoln's determination, against all prudent counsel, to confront in the flesh the defeated seat of the struggle that had shattered the nation, defined his presidency, and would, within days, end his life. For the man who led his country through the bloodiest war in its history, Lincoln's journey to Richmond marked the symbolic completion of an epic odyssey. It put a human face on the end of a conflict that had saved the

Union, freed the slaves, and reaffirmed American purpose. It was, for Lincoln, no mere pursuit of a rebellious foe; it was a pilgrimage. "The war had become for him by then a mysterious and deeply spiritual struggle for freedom," said University of Texas historian James Sidbury. "It makes perfect sense to me that he would have needed to go down and see the place where slaves had been whipped and killed and see what had been overcome and what all of the blood had been spilled to achieve."

Lincoln's journey to Richmond had begun the week before, when he set off from Washington with his wife, Mary Todd Lincoln, and their youngest son, Tad, aboard a chartered steamboat named the *River Queen*. Escorted by a fast U.S. Navy gunboat named the *Bat*, the presidential paddle wheeler churned its way down the muddy Potomac River through an afternoon squall on March 23. Lincoln spent that night coursing through rough waters down the Chesapeake Bay, tracing the route his top com-

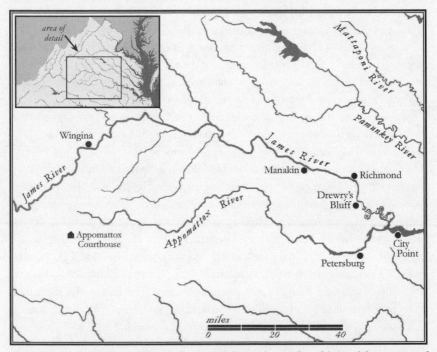

The strategic set-piece of the Civil War, Richmond was the object of four years of Union offensives culminating in ten months of siege by Grant, who set up his headquarters at City Point. Lincoln journeyed up the James to Richmond the day after its fall, the symbolic end of the war one week before Lee's surrender at Appomattox. Map drawn by Rebecca Wrenn.

mander, Gen. George McClellan, had taken three years before, when he opened the army's first earnest effort to capture Richmond.

A DULL AND DREAMY STILLNESS

It had once seemed easy to dismiss the Confederacy as the foolish pipe dream of hotheads, the sort who had gathered along the Battery by the harborside mansions in Charleston on the morning of April 12, 1861, and opened fire on Fort Sumter. Attacking a federal military outpost, however, was not some bachelors' quarters drinking prank, especially coming from one of the largest slave markets in the country. The attack hardened attitudes, North and South. "The last ray of hope for preserving the Union peaceably expired at the assault upon Fort Sumter," Lincoln wrote in the State of the Union Address he delivered to Congress the following December. "The Union must be preserved," he wrote, going on to make clear that "the struggle of today is not altogether for today, it is for a vast future also."

On paper, it had looked like a certain and not altogether difficult win for the North. Of the 31.2 million Americans counted in the 1860 Census, the eleven Confederate states had just 9.1 million, one-third of whom were slaves. Virginia alone, with 1.6 million people, accounted for nearly 20 percent of the Confederate population. Together, the North's three most populous states—New York, Pennsylvania, and Ohio—had as many people as the entire South.

Economically, the Confederate States of America was essentially a third world nation. It depended almost entirely upon the production of agricultural commodities: tobacco, cotton, indigo, and rice. Most of those raw materials were shipped north for processing or exported in exchange for manufactured and finished goods. Of the $1 billion worth of capital investment in American manufacturing facilities at the outset of war, just $96 million, a mere 10 percent, had been invested in the South. With $190 million worth of factories and assembly plants, Pennsylvania alone had twice the manufacturing capacity of the entire Confederacy. Even on a per capita basis, the investment gap was stark. Pennsylvania and New Jersey, for example, had each invested the equivalent of $65 in manufacturing equipment for every person in their two states. Virginia, at the top of the Southern scale, had invested $17 per capita, about one-quarter as much. In Georgia the figure was $10.30, in Texas it was $5.40, and in Arkansas it was $3, according to U.S. Census data.

The South was invested in slaves. Of the 4 million enslaved Americans in 1860, 3.5 million lived in the Confederate states. Most of the remaining half-million were scattered across Kansas, which entered the Union three months before the outbreak of war, and Kentucky and Maryland, slave states that remained in the Union. For decades, some Southern observers had bemoaned the region's lack of industrial development. Henry Ruffner, president of Washington College in Lexington, Virginia, even suggested that the unnatural reliance on slaves had bred troublesome "signs of stagnation or of positive decay" across the South. "Instead of the stir and bustle of industry," he wrote in an antislavery pamphlet in 1847, "a dull and dreamy stillness" had set in across the land. The manufacturing gap, though, was more than a numbing cultural feature. It would soon create a decisive difference in the way Confederate and Union forces were funded, equipped, and supplied.

Militarily, the North began the war with yet another advantage. It had a force in place—the United States Army and Navy—trained, organized, and equipped. The South would have to build both from scratch. The U.S. Army, though, was heavily dependent upon Southern officers for the backbone of its leadership. Each had sworn to "bear true allegiance to the United States of America," to defend those states "against all their enemies," and to "observe and obey the orders of the President of the United States." Of the 1,080 active U.S. Army officers who had taken that oath, about one-third turned their backs on it, leaving the Union to join the Confederacy. Nearly two hundred of those were West Point graduates; one was Robert E. Lee.

As the country listed toward war in the opening weeks of his presidency, Lincoln signed a commission promoting Lee to full colonel, with the command of a cavalry regiment. Days before, Lee had been offered a commission as brigadier general in the Confederacy. His wooing by opposing armies on the eve of war was merely the outward sign of an excruciating inner conflict as both Lee's native state and the country he'd sworn allegiance to confronted mortal peril. With the stroke of a pen, Lincoln called for seventy-five thousand fresh recruits to help subdue the Southern rebellion: he quickly got one hundred thousand. Hoping to keep Virginia from seceding, Lincoln wisely courted Lee, offering him the post of field commander over the entire U.S. Army, reporting directly to Gen. Winfield Scott, his old commander in the Mexican War. It might have been, for Lee, the capstone of a dutiful career. The gesture, for Lincoln, was less about military acumen than politics: if the courtly Southern colonel stayed with the Union, so might his native Virginia.

Lincoln had cause to be hopeful. Virginia was as divided over slavery and secession as the country at large. The state's wartime governor, John Letcher, had signed Ruffner's antislavery pamphlet a decade and a half before the war began. Owners of small family farms, with few if any slaves, in the western part of the state countered the interests of the Tidewater plantation owners who depended upon the labor of blacks. Indeed, when Virginia finally did secede, residents on the far side of the Allegheny Mountains opted to stay with the Union, breaking off to form a new state, Kanawha, later named West Virginia.

Even Virginia's mainstream political leaders resisted secession for months. "I am now, and have ever been, a friend to the Union of the States," Letcher had told the general assembly in his 1860 inaugural address. "I appreciate its value, ardently desire its preservation and would not rashly hazard its existence." Letcher spoke for many Virginians, perhaps even the majority. For if they were divided over slavery and secession, they were firmly united as to whom they believed had built the United States of America. And there was little question, in Virginia at least, as to exactly whose country it was. "The founding fathers of whom the state was so proud were masters of compromise, and the majority of Virginians still believed, or hoped, that some compromise could preserve the Union," author and journalist Ernest Furgurson wrote in *Ashes of Glory*, a vivid portrait of Richmond at war. "They were not eager to abandon what their grandfathers had done, the nation they had conceived. Rich and poor, they were proud of it."

Few were more proud than Lee, whose family roots in Virginia by 1861 already stretched back more than two centuries. The son of a Revolutionary War hero, the first cousin (twice removed) of two signers of the Declaration of Independence, and himself a West Point graduate and veteran of the Mexican War, Lee may have been as deeply vested in the United States as any man alive. Like Letcher and many other Virginians, he had hoped he might never have to make the personal choice between his nation and his state. After Fort Sumter, though, and Lincoln's subsequent call to arms, Lee viewed the U.S. mission as more than one to preserve the Union: it was an assault on native land he felt honor-bound to defend. "If the Union is dissolved and the government disrupted, I shall return to my native state and share the miseries of my people and, save in defense, will draw my sword on none," was Lee's reply to Lincoln's envoy, Francis Blair, the kitchen cabinet adviser assigned to offer Lee the command of the U.S. Army. "Though opposed to secession and deprecating war," Lee later explained, "I could take no part in an invasion of the Southern States."

With the outbreak of war, Lee, then fifty-four, tendered a one-line letter resigning his U.S. Army commission, boarded a train to Richmond, took a room at the Spotswood Hotel, and began helping to build a Southern military force to confront the army he'd served for three decades. "His resignation was not prompted by passion, nor did it carry with it resentment against the Union," wrote Lee's biographer, Douglas Southall Freeman. "On the contrary, if there was any resentment, it was against the authors, Northern and Southern, of the consummate wickedness of bringing about division within the Union. There was a pang and a heartache at the separation from brother officers. He was willing to defend Virginia, whatever her allegiance, but he did not desire to fight against the flag under which he had served."

OF WOODEN SHIPS AND IRON

Lee spent most of the first year of the war serving as military adviser to Confederate president Jefferson Davis, helping to plan and coordinate the recruitment, training, and organization of a rebel force.

Richmond was a Southern anomaly, an indigenous manufacturing, transportation, banking, and government center that was home to the largest foundry in the South. Harnessing canal and river power, the Tredegar Iron Works, on the banks of the James, used coal and iron ore brought down the river from the mountainous west to make products ranging from chain links and cannon to steam locomotives and rails. The single largest source of armaments for the Confederacy, the Tredegar works were a strategic necessity for the outgunned rebel forces.

It was that collection of assets, along with its powerful symbolism as the capital of the most populous state in the South and the oldest in the country, that prompted the Confederates to move their capital from Montgomery, Alabama, far from the threat of Union forces, to Richmond, at the Union's back door. From the moment that happened, the city that grew up at the falls of the James was in the Union crosshairs. It became the primary target of the North, the political and economic hub of the Confederacy, and the strategic epicenter of the war. "From 1861 to 1865, to a great extent, the eyes of the world were on Richmond," said Charles Bryan, president of the Virginia Historical Society. "It was the great symbol of the Confederacy, it was the great target of the Union forces from the beginning, and it took four bloody years to get there."

Few thought it would ever take that long, least among them George McClellan. A brilliant general who graduated second in his class at West Point and was decorated for his service in the Mexican War, McClellan left his job as president of the Ohio & Mississippi Railroad to take the U.S. command that Lee had turned down. His eye for logistics led McClellan to advise Lincoln early on that capturing Richmond would strike "directly at the heart of the enemy's power." Richmond's collapse, he wrote, would place in Union hands "the capital, the communications, the supplies of the rebels." Indeed, concluded McClellan, once Richmond fell, "all Virginia would be in our power."

McClellan wasn't alone in studying the map of the Confederacy and deducing that it could be defeated by strategic strangulation more readily than by battle. For while the coastal and riverine topography had nourished Virginia and much of the rest of the South through two centuries of growth, it had also left the region vulnerable in war. The contours of the South's agricultural economy and its heavy reliance on river travel had set the region far behind the North in the building of roads and the laying of rail, essential lines of transport and communications. And the Confederacy's dependence on oceangoing trade was quickly seen as its Achilles' heel. With no deepwater navy to speak of, the Confederacy struggled from the early part of the war with a highly effective Union blockade of a coastline stretching some thirty-five hundred miles, from the Gulf of Mexico to the mouth of the James. Throwing a naval blanket over the ports of Norfolk, Wilmington, Charleston, Savannah, Mobile, New Orleans, and Galveston enabled the Union forces to all but put out the lights on the Southern economy. That crippled the Southern states' ability to raise cash through exports to European or South American markets, to collect taxes through customs duties, or to import badly needed weapons and gear.

Gen. Winfield Scott, in fact, argued that Lincoln could bring the South to its knees by simply walling off the region from international trade, gaining control of its rivers one by one—in the West as well as the East—and steadily squeezing the economic life out of the region. Southern hotheads would cool, Scott reasoned, and Confederate leaders would negotiate to return to the Union, once plantation profits turned to loss and rebel widows tired of substituting peanut grinds for coffee and dining on sorghum-soaked corncakes each night. While Scott's approach was meant to reduce the need for major battles and their appalling human toll, it was ridiculed as an "anaconda" strategy his critics viewed as more costly and time-consuming than necessary to bring the South to heel.

Scott's measured strangulation eventually became crucial to the Confederacy's defeat. For all the North's advantages, the South would not collapse as quickly as his critics had hoped. The Union loss at Manassas in the first summer of the war had shocked Lincoln's advisers and emboldened the South. By the end of Lincoln's first year in office, hopes of a quick knockout blow to the Confederacy had dimmed. In January 1862, Lincoln issued General War Order No. 1, commanding General McClellan to lead a massive assault aimed at cutting off the head of the foe by capturing Richmond.

Lincoln ordered the deployment to begin on February 22, and he strongly urged McClellan to move his army overland the hundred miles due south from Washington to the Confederate capital. In a twenty-two-page rebuttal, McClellan argued for an amphibious assault that would take the entire Army of the Potomac, a massive force some 118,000 strong, down the Chesapeake Bay. There, troops would land at Ft. Monroe, the brick citadel U.S. forces had built at Point Comfort. They would use the fortress as the staging ground for a march up the narrow peninsula between the York and James rivers and directly to Richmond. Like British General Cornwallis eight decades before, McClellan could see it all before him, his enemy collapsing like a house of cards as his army swept across the former heartland of the Powhatan Indians.

It would take a month, McClellan noted, to assemble the canal boats, barges, schooners, and steamships needed to transport his forces down the Chesapeake. It would be a small price to pay, he predicted, "if, at the expense of 30 days delay, we can gain a decisive victory which will probably end the war." McClellan would soon learn, as Cornwallis had, how much could go wrong on that bloodstained peninsula. Both men had assumed that their navies would control the mouth of the James, giving them the river access needed to support their troops up the narrow neck of land. The French Navy disrupted those hopes for Cornwallis. For McClellan, the assumption was torpedoed, for a time at least, by an odd-looking boat that made history as the flagship of the tiny Confederate Navy's James River Squadron. The Confederates called the ship the CSS *Virginia*; the Union forces knew it by its earlier name, the USS *Merrimack*.

A forty-gun frigate powered by massive coal-fired boilers, the USS *Merrimack* was left behind in flames when a thin Union contingent was forced by rebels to abandon the port at Norfolk in the opening weeks of the war. With few ships to work with, the Confederates salvaged the heavily damaged craft and converted it into a warship some saw as invincible, armoring it with iron plates two inches thick produced at Tredegar. The *Merrimack* became the Confederates' first ironclad warship. The ship's weight pushed its entire hull beneath the waterline, leaving for a target only its squat and angular top, a floating artillery battery with ten heavy guns on a low-lying armored platform. When enemy cannon balls hit it, they generally just bounced off.

Reincarnated as the Confederate ship *Virginia*, the ironclad steamed into the chilly waters at the mouth of the James on March 8, 1862, to challenge the Union blockade at Hampton Roads. Striking the Union's wooden ships with virtual impunity, the ironclad rammed and sank the USS *Cumberland*, ran the USS *Minnesota* aground, and set the USS *Congress* on fire, while the rest of the Union fleet scrambled to get out of harm's way before the iron demon put back to port at Norfolk for the night. It had been a day of terror for Union seamen and the high-water mark, it turned out, for the Confederate Navy.

That night, by coincidence, the first U.S. ironclad, the USS *Monitor*, put into the bay, pausing en route to blockade duty off the coast of North Carolina from New York, where it had been commissioned just two weeks before. The next morning, when the *Merrimack* cruised out for a planned day of sinking Union ships, it was met instead by the *Monitor*, another strangely configured ship with a circular rotating turret that made the craft look like a floating cheese box. As spectators watched from Norfolk, Hampton, and Ft. Monroe, the two ironclads fought a four-hour duel, which marked the beginning of the end for the wooden warships that for centuries had ruled the waves. The shootout ended in a draw, and both ships limped back to port. It was a victory, though, for the Union Navy, which had ensured the protection of the blockade by neutralizing the *Merrimack* the day after its trial run as the first ironclad ship in combat.

Later that spring, when McClellan's army forced the Confederates out of Norfolk, departing rebels burned the port. They had hoped to take the *Merrimack* upriver, but the heavy craft drew too much water to make it past the sandy shoals upstream. After stripping off much of the craft's armor and even jettisoning its coal in an effort to lighten the ship, Confederates were forced to abandon the craft on marshy Craney Island, where the Elizabeth River pours into the broad mouth of the James. There they set the ship on fire with more than ten thousand pounds of gunpowder in its hull. The destruction of the *Merrimack* left the lower James virtually open to Union naval forces.

YOU HAVE DONE YOUR BEST TO SACRIFICE THIS ARMY

It was late March when McClellan landed his men at Ft. Monroe. By the time they moved out in early April, Confederate troops under Maj. Gen. John Magruder had dug into an old line of defense stretching across the narrow neck of land with a concentration at Yorktown. There, digging out and improving upon trenches left over from the last major battle of the Revolutionary War, Magruder managed with fewer than fifteen thousand troops to bog down McClellan's men for another month, in a prelude to what would become, for Lincoln, one of the most exasperating chapters of the war.

The telegraph introduced to war immediate communications between the front lines of fighting and the White House. Lincoln received almost constant dispatches detailing the positions of cannon and infantry, casualty assessments, weather reports, and updates on road conditions, troop morale, and even the outcome of minor skirmishes. His response, at times, was to try to micromanage the war from the White House. "You are probably engaged with the enemy," Lincoln wrote to McClellan on the morning of June 1, going on to offer the helpful suggestion that he "stand well on your guard—hold all your ground, or yield any only inch by inch and in good order."

Being in telegraph contact, though, wasn't the same thing as being in touch. As Lincoln proffered his war counsel, McClellan's forces were locked in mortal combat that began with cannon fire and ended with bayonets. "We have had a desperate battle," he telegraphed Lincoln at noon, still midway through a day of fighting, near the Chickahominy River at a place called Fair Oaks, that involved about forty thousand men on each side. "Our loss is heavy, but that of the enemy must be enormous." McClellan was correct on both counts. By day's end, nearly eight hundred of his men were dead, and forty-four hundred were wounded. Federal forces had killed one thousand Confederates and wounded fifty-seven hundred more.

"During the night began the ghastly procession of wounded brought in from the field," Richmond resident Constance Cary Harrison wrote of the battle's grim aftermath. "Every vehicle the city could produce supplemented the military ambulances." Searching for a cousin reported wounded the following day, she described looking into the bandaged and blood-caked faces of stricken and dying men, their wounds drawing swarms of flies. It was the beginning of a long and deep descent into the horrors of war for the debutantes and matrons of Richmond, who were quickly given over, Harrison later recalled, to the emergency care of an ever-rising tide of rebel soldiers. They arrived, she wrote, "in every stage of mutilation, lying waiting for the surgeons upon bare boards, with haversacks or army blankets, or nothing, beneath their heads."

Far from the carnage, Lincoln felt confident enough to assure McClellan that he needn't fret. His forces had drawn near enough to Richmond to hear church bells ring out from the hilltop belfries. "I think," the president consoled McClellan, "the hardest of your work is done." Lincoln, though, was wrong.

Confederate general Joseph Johnston was wounded twice at Fair Oaks. He was replaced by his friend and West Point classmate, Lee, who took control of the Army of Northern Virginia, the command that would become Lee's legacy. Over the next three weeks, Lee ordered line after line of trenches to be dug east of Richmond, where armchair generals belittled the new commander as "the king of spades" in the opening round of home front second-guessing that he was to endure throughout the war. The threat from McClellan, though, was real. The Confederate Army drafted contingency plans for the evacuation of Richmond, calling for rebels to torch the tobacco in the warehouses along the riverfront to deny the valuable commodity to the enemy in the event that they had to be abandoned. By the time McClellan's forces were prepared to attack, an entrenched Confederate force of ninety thousand troops had assembled to block his way.

McClellan spent much of June begging Lincoln for more troops in the mistaken belief that Lee had two hundred thousand men at his command. Besieged by similar requests from Union forces fighting as far afield as Memphis and constrained by the need to protect Washington, Lincoln insisted that he had no fresh forces to send. On the night of June 25, McClellan sent a telegraph to Stanton, complaining that his pleas for additional troops had been ignored and warning that, as a result, his entire army was poised for disaster in fighting "which will probably occur tomorrow." Indeed, the next day Lee struck hard. In the weeklong campaign that followed, the Seven Days Battles, McClellan lost nearly sixteen thousand men—dead, wounded, or missing. Lee's troops suffered twenty thousand casualties.

In the eighty years since the British surrender at Yorktown, tactics, strategy, and field maneuvers had changed little in comparison to the improved lethality and extended range of rifled artillery and musket fire. On the narrow neck of swampy land between the James and York rivers, both sides had witnessed the horror of modern war at a moment of clashing eras, when large groups of men in regimented formations sallied forth in the open into a new kind of combat, one in which a skilled sharpshooter could cut a man down at one thousand yards, then vanish into the brush, regular infantry was deadly within three hundred yards, and charging units could be annihilated in minutes from half a mile away by exploding cannon shells and the grape-sized buckshot fired from canister rounds. The result was battle after battle that each left more dead and wounded than the ten thousand Americans killed or hurt in the entire Revolutionary War.

Midway through the bloodshed on June 28, McClellan sent Stanton a blistering rant, lamenting the casualties and blaming the administration for leaving him shorthanded in the fray. "Had I 20,000 or even 10,000 fresh troops to use tomorrow, I could take Richmond," McClellan railed. Instead, he began a strategic retreat, fearing that to do otherwise would put his army at risk. "If I save this army now, I tell you plainly that I owe no thanks to you or any other persons in Washington. You have done your best to sacrifice this army," McClellan wrote to Stanton, in a passage deemed so incendiary that the military telegraph aide in Washington deleted it from the text forwarded to Lincoln's secretary of war.

With a staggering thirty-six thousand Americans killed, wounded, or missing in seven days of fighting over the very land once contested by Powhatan Indians and the English settlers, the chance for a quick capture of Richmond, and perhaps an early end to the war, was gone. So, too, was the illusion that the war might be a short-lived conflict of minimal losses. As those grim realities sank in through McClellan's desperate correspondence, Lincoln sent out an appeal on July 1 for three hundred thousand volunteers. Within weeks, he was forced to begin drafting them.

On the night of July 1, McClellan, exhausted by a week of battle and enraged by the bloodshed he'd witnessed, withdrew to Berkeley Plantation, known then as Harrison's Landing. Supplied by Union ships that controlled the river's tidewater reaches, his force set up quarters along the lush riverside. With some 144,000 men based there, Berkeley vied with Richmond that summer as the most populous place in the South. In the second week of July, Lincoln visited the sprawling camp himself. Traveling by boat down the Chesapeake Bay and up the James, he delivered new uniforms to McClellan's troops as a morale booster and pressed the general to advance on Richmond. He never did.

On a warm evening that month at Berkeley, one of McClellan's brigadier generals, Daniel Butterfield, whistled a doleful tune, when something about it caught his ear. He sent for a bugler and there, at Butterfield's tent, Pvt. Oliver Norton of Pennsylvania blew out the notes to the mournful dirge later titled "Taps." Its haunting strains carried across the James to where Confederates were encamped along the southern shore. A rebel picked up his own bugle and reprised the sorrowful tune in a melodic salute to his foe. And, in the stillness of the summer night, battle-scarred armies opposed in war reached across the water through the music of shared sacrifice, in the debut of the ballad of honor and loss that has signaled day's end for American soldiers ever since.

IF I COULD SAVE THE UNION

Three years later, on the morning of March 24, after its overnight passage down the Chesapeake Bay, the *River Queen* arrived at Ft. Monroe to take on fresh drinking water before heading up the James. A president who repeatedly invoked the power of linking the past to the land, Lincoln may well have reflected there at Point Comfort on the day when the first Africans arrived in chains at that very place two and a half centuries before. He may well have wished he had been there that day to turn back the Dutch man-of-war and the thousands of slave ships that were to follow in its wake. "If slavery is not wrong, nothing is wrong," he wrote in an 1864 letter to Albert Hodges, editor of the Frankfort, Kentucky, *Commonwealth*.

And yet, if Lincoln's personal views were clear, his ability to act on those views as president was more ambiguous. His job, he wrote, was to protect the Constitution and to preserve the Union, not to impose personal beliefs, no matter how strongly felt, upon the American people. "If I could save the Union without freeing any slave, I would do it; and if I could save it by freeing all the slaves I would do it; and if I could save it by freeing some and leaving others alone I would also do that," Lincoln wrote to New York *Tribune* editor Horace Greeley in August 1862, after Greeley assailed him in print for not doing more to make explicit that the war would end slavery. "What I do about slavery, and the colored race, I do because I believe it helps to save the Union," Lincoln continued. He closed by drawing a distinction between what he called his "official duty" as president and "my oft-expressed personal wish that all men everywhere could be free."

By then, Lincoln had already drafted and shown his cabinet a copy of his Emancipation Proclamation, declaring freedom for slaves in the Confederate states. It would not become official policy, though, until the next month, September 1862; it would be several months more before it took effect; and it could not be implemented until the Confederacy's defeat. One of the biggest gambles of Lincoln's high-stakes presidency, freeing the slaves virtually ruled out any chance that he might yet persuade the Southern states to return to the Union without protracted war. He had agonized over the question of how to deal with the slaves, and even privately wondered how God himself might handle the crisis, before deciding that freeing the slaves would be linked to the essential war aim of preserving the Union. However Lincoln settled the matter in his heart, he justified his decision to the nation in existential terms. "In giving freedom to the slave, we assure freedom to the free," Lincoln wrote in his State of the Union Address to Congress in December 1862. By staying true to those ideals, or breaking faith with them, he concluded, "We shall nobly save, or meanly lose, the last best hope of earth."

As the *River Queen* rounded Point Comfort, passing through Hampton Roads, the president saw to his left the Union-occupied port of Norfolk, where the last British governor of Virginia, Lord Dunmore, had proclaimed freedom for slaves who would abandon their plantations and take up arms to fight for King George III. Freedom and tyranny, despots and slaves, these formed an ugly commerce wedded as one along the very waters through which Lincoln now steamed and across which Dunmore's emancipation bid still echoed, even as Lincoln issued his own decree to free the slaves. "As a fit and necessary war measure for suppressing said rebellion," he declared in his Emancipation Proclamation on January 1, 1863, "I do order and declare that all persons held as slaves within said designated states, and parts of states, are, and henceforward shall be free."

Lincoln's presidency was dominated by unrelenting arguments, among his cabinet members, among his generals, and among the public at large, over how best to preserve the Union. In the summer and fall of 1862, Lincoln had been driven to invoke the draft, declare martial law, and suspend the writ of habeas corpus. "I felt that measures, otherwise unconstitutional, might become lawful, by becoming indispensable to the preservation of the Constitution, through the preservation of the nation," he later explained in his letter to the Kentucky editor Hodges. "I could not feel that, to the best of my ability, I had even tried to preserve the Constitution, if, to save slavery, or any minor matter, I should permit the wreck of government, country and Constitution all together."

Taking a page from Dunmore's playbook, Lincoln went one step further. He urged slaves seeking freedom to join the army, the navy, or the vast corps of laborers who supported the war effort by digging trenches, building forts, mending railroads, preparing food, chopping wood, and performing scores of other tasks required to maintain a fighting force. "I was, in my best judgment, driven to the alternative of either surrendering the Union, and with it, the Constitution, or of laying strong hand upon the colored element," Lincoln wrote to Hodges. "I chose the latter."

By the time Lincoln steamed past Norfolk in the spring of 1865, one million blacks, a quarter of the slave population, had escaped slavery by crossing the Union lines. Two hundred thousand served as soldiers, seamen, or military laborers and engineers. Scores of Northern relief agencies emerged to provide education, aid, and Christian ministry to the former slaves and to help build farms on plots of Union-occupied land across the South in a wartime prelude to the creation of some of the region's first black colleges after the conflict ended.

Still, simply proclaiming emancipation, Lincoln understood, would not ensure it. Before that could be accomplished, the bodies of the dead and wounded would be strewn across the shell-shattered land. Place-names forever bound in horror ran through his fevered mind like blood across a map aflame: Shiloh. Antietam. Fredericksburg. Chancellorsville. Gettysburg. "We cannot dedicate, we cannot consecrate, we cannot hallow this ground," he had said at that Pennsylvania town, in words he might have spoken at any place the battles raged. "The brave men, living and dead, who struggled here have consecrated it far above our poor power to add or to detract." Our poor power. He had thought it over and over again, this man who bore the burden of carrying the nation through this unforgiving trial, restoring faith when little was left, igniting determination from fading embers, this poor power to rise, to endure, and to prevail at all cost on the belief that, truly, this was that last best hope of earth, and it was his to lose or save.

"Four score and seven years ago," Lincoln began in his address at Gettysburg, "our fathers brought forth on this continent a new nation, conceived in liberty and dedicated to the proposition that all men are created equal." Exactly eighty-seven years before the American calamity that was Gettysburg—where forty thousand men were wounded or killed and eleven thousand more went missing—Jefferson had framed that proposition. In reaching back for the country's beginnings, Lincoln deliberately chose that moment, that document, the Declaration of Independence, and its most essential and self-evident truth, to date the founding of the American nation. "Now we are engaged in a great Civil War," said Lincoln, "testing whether that nation, or any nation so conceived and so dedicated, can long endure." Lincoln saw the conflict transformed. It was no longer a war about Union, no longer a war about slaves. It was a war about the fate of the nation, about the strength of its guiding ideals. It was a war to determine for all time and all people what it meant to be an American, bound to repay, every day, the debt that each owes. "From these honored dead," he concluded, "we take increased devotion to that cause for which they gave the last full measure of devotion, that we here highly resolve that these dead shall not have died in vain; that this nation, under God, shall have a new birth of freedom; and that government of the people, by the people, for the people shall not perish from the earth."

In its purity of expression and the clarity of its ideals, Lincoln's Gettysburg Address was the closest the country might ever come to a national prayer. He may well have prayed it once more on that afternoon two years later aboard the *River Queen*, when he passed within whispering distance of one of the oldest totems of national memory, gazing out across his starboard bow at the sandy banks of Jamestown. "I think a number of things were on his mind," said Princeton University historian James McPherson, author of *The Battle Cry of Freedom*, a masterpiece of Civil War scholarship. "The planting of English colonists at Jamestown in 1607 was the first step in a long journey that is often characterized as a journey toward greater liberty and freedom," McPherson said in an interview. "And, of course, that journey was marred along the way—and nowhere marred more than along the James River—by slavery. He must have been thinking about that too."

He could hardly have avoided thinking about it as he gazed through the twilight upon the manor house at Westover, the once-proud brick monument to privilege and wealth accrued on the backs of slaves in accordance with the laws nailed to the door of every church. "I am not much of a judge of religion," Lincoln had written the December before, "but that, in my opinion, the religion that sets men to rebel and fight against their government, because, as they think, that government does not sufficiently help some men to eat their bread on the sweat of other men's faces, is not the sort of religion upon which people can get to heaven." If he permitted himself a smile at that thought, Lincoln might have cringed before the broad poplars of Westover faded from sight, recoiling at the thought of tyranny by another name, the aristocracy of plantation owners who clung to the delusion that freedom and slavery could be reconciled with enough whips and chains. Lincoln may well have pondered the many thousands gone whose forced labor had carved out rich estates along the James. These dead too, he must have told himself, shall not have died in vain, and all, henceforward, shall be free.

THE ALTARS OF SACRIFICE

Darkness had fallen on a near-moonless night by the time the *River Queen* reached City Point, the tiny corner of southern riverbank jutting into the James just below its confluence with the Appomattox. It was 9 p.m. on

March 24. Had he rounded the broad bend upstream, he would have seen on the opposite shore the ghostly outlines of a grand mansion, the ancestral home of Lee.

Lincoln professed no personal dislike for Lee, though he'd sought for four years to destroy him. In the manor house at Shirley Plantation, though, from where Lee's maternal line long hailed, Lincoln could have seen the brick-and-mortar vestiges of the great rebellion he sought to quell. "Fondly do we hope, fervently do we pray, that this mighty scourge of war may speedily pass away," Lincoln had said just three weeks before, standing in front of the U.S. Capitol on March 4, 1865, for his second inaugural address. If peace even yet would not come, Lincoln would press the fight and press it hard. The manor at Shirley and every tobacco barn, thrashing shed, icehouse, smokehouse, and outhouse around it could crumble to sand and wash to the sea, in Lincoln's view, if that's what it would take to prosecute the war to its bitter end. "If God wills that it continue, until all the wealth plied by the bondman's two hundred and fifty years of unrequited toil shall be sunk, and until every drop of blood drawn with the lash shall be paid by another drawn with the sword," Lincoln continued, turning to scripture, "as was said three thousand years ago, so still it must be said, that 'the judgments of the Lord are true and righteous altogether.'"

Whether righteous or true, the judgment of the sword had long ago been placed by Lincoln in the hands of his most trusted warhorse, Ulysses S. Grant. Like Lee, he was a West Point graduate and veteran of the Mexican War. General in chief of U.S. forces, Grant had turned tiny City Point into the headquarters for his siege of Richmond, which had ground into its tenth month by the time Lincoln arrived. Base of operations for a Union force one hundred fifty thousand strong, City Point—the town of Hopewell is there today— had become a massive military depot, a place of hastily built warehouses brimming with ammunition, clothing, food, and medical gear from the North's whirling factories. Fresh supplies came upriver daily aboard the schooners and steamers that choked the broad channel there. Emptied of their cargo, the ships returned downstream, bearing by the hundreds the wounded and ill and the simple pine coffins of the Union dead.

From his log cabin billet atop a tall bluff, Grant walked down to the wharf where the *River Queen* tied up to welcome his commander in chief and to offer his personal congratulations on Lincoln's second inauguration just three weeks before. A few days shy of his twelfth birthday, Lincoln's son, Tad, strolled out into the starlight with his father's bodyguard, hoping to stretch his legs and get a good look at the troops. The two were turned back, though, by sentinels grown wary from the hazards of war at the front.

Ten miles to the west, at Petersburg, Lee's tattered forces formed the southern terminus of a defensive line that stretched some thirty miles, all the way to Richmond. Through four years of war, Richmond's beleaguered residents had come to know too well "the tramp of rusty battalions, the short, imperious stroke of the alarm bell, the clash of passing bands, the gallop of horsemen, the roar of battle, the moan of hospitals, the stifled note of sorrow, all the Richmond war sounds, sacred and unforgettable," as Constance Cary Harrison recalled. By the spring of 1865, hope had faded and turned to dread. "Starved, nearly bankrupt, thousands of our best soldiers killed in battle, their places filled by boys and old men," she wrote, "the besieged dwellers of Richmond" could "feel the death-clutch at its throat." With no more than fifty thousand poorly equipped and half-starved troops, Lee's army was a spent force on the brink of collapse. For four years it had defended Richmond from attack, battling Union forces that had tried to sweep into the capital along every conceivable route. Still they came, ever stronger, always more, and beyond their lines, still others stood ready to step into the breech.

Since January, when his men huddled in frozen trenches with threadbare horse blankets and scraps of carpet as shelter against the cold, Lee had warned Confederate president Jefferson Davis that Richmond might fall. It was the Confederate Army's Valley Forge, a time when skirmishes gave barefoot rebel survivors the chance to scavenge a pair of boots or a coat or gloves from the still-warm corpse of a fallen foe. The coming of spring held only the promise of more Union forces better able to attack once the rains let up and the muddy roads dried enough to allow wagons and cannon to pass.

From Union armies to Lee's south and west, Grant could bring to bear, within weeks, another one hundred thousand seasoned and well-equipped men. Lee could muster another thirteen thousand, at best, and that only by somehow joining forces with Confederate troops to the south. By the middle of April, early May at the latest, Lee could be surrounded by a well-fed and heavily armed Union force four times the size of his famished and war-ravaged army.

Desperate measures had been a part of Lee's battle plan since the opening months of the conflict. With the weight of war closing in on all sides, he held one final card. He decided to play it on the morning of March 25. Two hours before dawn, as Lincoln lay asleep on the *River Queen*, rebel forces eight miles away blitzed across the one-hundred-fifty-yard-wide no-man's-land between their paper-thin lines and the Union positions at Ft. Stedman. It was part of a military Hail Mary for the sinking South. Against the longest of odds, Lee hoped his troops might sever Grant's lines and leave part of the Union forces stranded from their City Point supply depot. The rebels would then abandon Richmond to escape the steel vice Grant had erected around it and cut south to join Confederate forces in North Carolina, taking the fight elsewhere and perhaps making it through one more summer. Hours after Lee's troops took Ft. Stedman, though, Union forces rallied a massive counterattack, led by heavy artillery fire followed by disciplined infantry. Lee's forces fell back, leaving behind some thirty-five hundred men, who were killed, wounded, or taken prisoner in fighting within earshot of the president.

That morning, as he ate breakfast aboard his riverboat, Lincoln was briefed on the battle by his son, U.S. Army captain Robert Lincoln. The two walked up to Grant's headquarters for an update on the fight. When Grant was satisfied that the president could venture forth with minimal danger, Lincoln visited the battlefield. On a rickety rail spur Union engineers had laid to link City Point to Petersburg, the president chugged slowly past the battle-torn and still-bleeding landscape. Never before or since has a sitting American president followed so closely on the boot heels of battle. Surgeons were yet operating in the field on the wounded, some moaning or writhing in pain. Burial parties tended to the dead. And prisoners filed past by the hundreds, close enough for Lincoln to look into the Confederate faces and eyes, sunken portraits of despair and defeat.

After seeing the corpse of one man shot through the head and another with both arms blown off, Lincoln teared up when an aide approached him from the battlefield with an empty canteen. He had given a red-haired boy in a rebel uniform a drink of water, before the youth, shot in the head, stammered out his last words, "Mother, mother," and died. "This was where Lincoln first saw close up the results of desperate combat on more than a small scale," the Illinois poet Carl Sandburg wrote in his majestic biography of Lincoln. "On the soil where Union countercharges began Lincoln saw the dead in blue and gray and butternut lying huddled and silent, here and there the wounded gasping and groaning," Sandburg wrote. "He had seen the altars of sacrifice wet and red."

Lincoln was ready for the sacrifice to end. Two days later aboard the *River Queen*, he presided over a war council with the two men he most trusted to bring it to a close: Grant and General William Tecumseh Sherman. Another West Point graduate from Ohio who had served in the Mexican War, Sherman had just concluded a seven-month orgy of destruction and plunder across the South. After sacking Atlanta in September 1864,

Sherman led a force of some sixty-two thousand Union troops on his infamous "march to the sea," laying ruin to Georgia farms, plantations, railroads, and towns along a sixty-mile-wide swath all the way to Savannah. After a brief rest there, Sherman took his forces north, laying waste to much of the Carolinas on a path that swept through Columbia and Fayetteville to Goldsboro and Raleigh. Damage in Georgia alone was estimated at $100 million—it would be worth at least twenty-five times that amount in today's dollars—and the destruction surpassed anything the country had ever experienced. Sherman's march aroused the enduring hatred and resentment of the Southern people, tens of thousands of whom were left homeless and destitute by his army's ruinous run. Sherman justified the destruction of property, though, as a way to break the will of the South and destroy its means of support in order to hasten the end of a war that had already taken more than half a million lives. Whatever he may have thought of Sherman's scorched-earth tactics, Lincoln fully supported the result: a deep South no longer able to wage war in any effective way.

The next morning, the three men gathered with Admiral Horace Porter, commander of the Union naval forces on the James, in the upper deck saloon of the *River Queen*. Weary and worn, deep lines etched into his craggy face and dark circles beneath his eyes, Lincoln laid out the road ahead. The rebels were a beaten bunch; the president had seen it for himself. His priority, he told the high command, was to get the Confederates to return to the Union. That cause wouldn't be advanced by gratuitous attacks on civilian property or a punitive approach to the foe. Lee must be defeated, Lincoln left no doubt, whether next week or the week after that. And any surrender must make clear that all Confederate states were to return unconditionally to the Union and that slavery would immediately end. Once those terms were agreed to, however, no further retribution would be tolerated, and punishment was to be avoided wherever possible. Rebel soldiers should be allowed to take home their horses and even their hunting guns, Lincoln stressed, so they might have some start on rebuilding their shattered lives. He even hinted that it might be best if Confederate president Jefferson Davis be allowed to escape. That way Lincoln wouldn't be confronted with the dilemma of having to make the Confederate president a martyr by hanging him for treason or sparing his life and appearing to critics to be soft on the defeated insurrectionists.

Sherman left to return to his troops near Goldsboro. The next day, Grant rode off for the front. And from his Petersburg headquarters, Lee mapped out the South's desperate endgame.

THE TERRIBLE SPLENDOR OF RICHMOND

Jefferson Davis stepped out of the White House of the Confederacy in the brilliant spring sunshine on the morning of April 2, walked the six blocks to St. Paul's Episcopal Church, and took a seat in his family pew. Part way through the service, he was tapped on the shoulder and handed an urgent telegram sent by Lee from the front. "I advise that all preparation be made for leaving Richmond tonight," it read. "I will advise you later, according to circumstances." The circumstances, for Davis, were clear enough. He rose quietly, left the church, walked across the street to the Capitol grounds, and began to shut down the Confederacy.

Before the toll of church bells announced the end of services that day, word was all over town. Lee was abandoning Petersburg, the last brick in the crumbling dike that had held back the sea of blue-coated troops besieging Richmond. By early afternoon, soldiers, politicians, and bureaucrats were scrambling on horseback, in wagons, on carts, and by train to set in motion the shrieking machinery of evacuation, while puzzled and panicked residents looked on in dismay as the day of reckoning came unwound in a furious spin.

Having read accounts of Sherman's exploits and heard tales from refugees of his ravaging march, men and women alike had ample cause to fear the worst. Thousands jammed what family treasures and necessities they could into baskets and trunks and made their way across the Mayo Bridge in carts, on skeletal mules, or on foot. Others joined a clattering stream of humanity wandering west along the canal towpath in a confused mass exodus of the capital on the eve of its fall. Still others hunkered down in their homes, gathering family and close friends for last suppers and prayers, hiding heirlooms in attics and burying dinner plates and silverware in backyards.

Wagons under heavy guard took the last of the gold from the Confederate Treasury and loaded it onto a freight car at the Richmond & Danville Railroad depot downtown, leaving behind bales of worthless Confederate currency among the equally meaningless reams of government records and documents strewn across the Capitol floors. Mayor Joseph Mayo called the city council to an emergency session to tell them Richmond was being abandoned to Union forces. With the war a lost cause, Mayo sent word to Gen. Richard Ewell, commander of Confederate defenses of the capital. There was no longer any need, Mayo exhorted, to put the city at risk by setting fire to the tobacco warehouses, repositories for what little of value the city might be able to use in the aftermath of its surrender. Ewell never got the message.

That night, after Davis and his fugitive government had rumbled out of town and across the river on the last Confederate train to Danville, Ewell ordered the warehouses set afire, spawning a blaze that quickly spread through the business district, destroyed Richmond's waterfront and gutted more than six hundred homes and businesses along a path thirteen blocks long and up to seven blocks wide. Flour mills, merchant houses, and residences were consumed as flames worked their way north to the edge of the Capitol grounds and spread west along the river as far as the Tredegar works.

Bridges, too, were put to the torch by Confederate forces as they fled. Ewell assigned Capt. Clement Sulivane to oversee the destruction of the last bridge standing, Mayo's Bridge, stretching over the base of the rapids of the James at 14th Street. Working through the night, Sulivane had barrels of flammable tar and canisters of kerosene spaced at intervals across the wooden bridge. Ordered to hold the structure at all costs until the last Confederate troops left town, Sulivane positioned a single cannon in the middle of the bridge, loaded it with grapeshot, and aimed it straight up 14th street. "This done, I had nothing to do but listen for sounds and gaze on the terrible splendor of the scene," he later wrote, recalling a city that was "like a blaze of day amid the surrounding darkness."

As the flames roamed at will, they spread to warehouses full of ammunition that exploded with concussions that shattered windows up to two miles away. Sulivane watched in horror from his post atop the bridge like a spectator at some Dantesque funeral pyre. "Three high-arched bridges were in flames; beneath them the waters sparkled and dashed and rushed on by the burning city," he wrote. "Every now and then, as a magazine exploded, a column of white smoke rose up as high as the eye could reach, instantaneously followed by a deafening sound. The earth seemed to rock and tremble as with the shock of an earthquake, and immediately afterward hundreds of shells would explode in air and send their iron spray down far below the bridge. As the immense magazines of cartridges ignited, the rattle as of thousands of musketry would follow, and then all was still for the moment, except the dull roar and crackle of the fast-spreading fires." Just before dawn on April 3, there was an explosion downstream that eclipsed anything Sulivane had yet heard. Rebels had set afire ships at the naval yard, blowing up the last vessels of the Confederate Navy.

As the Confederate government plunged through its tailspin, law and order crumbled beneath the weight of the collapsing state. Guards at the penitentiary left their posts, unleashing upon the chaos more than three hundred convicts. By daybreak, thousands of people—women and children mixed with criminals and thugs—formed an ungoverned knot around a riverside warehouse where the government had put up emergency stores. From his perch several blocks away, Sulivane could see the flame-lit scene. "The depot doors were forced open and a demoniacal struggle for the countless barrels of hams, bacon, whisky, flour, sugar, coffee etc., etc., raged about the buildings among the hungry mob," he wrote. Troops were ordered to break open casks of liquor to keep a drunken mob from wreaking further havoc on the city, though some devoted revelers were undeterred. "The gutters ran whisky," wrote Sulivane, "and it was lapped as it flowed down the streets, while all fought for a share of the plunder."

Shortly after daylight, Sulivane saw Confederate cavalrymen, their swords drawn against the unruly mob, galloping down 14th Street and leading a rollicking caravan of ambulance wagons taking the wounded toward Mayo's Bridge. A thin, bearded officer reigned in his horse. It was Gen. Martin Gary, a Harvard law school graduate from South Carolina, leading the last Confederate soldiers out of Richmond. "My rear guard," he hollered down to Sulivane with a touch to the brim of his hat. "All over, goodbye, blow her to hell."

The general sat upright in his saddle and trotted his horse over the bridge as if on parade. Sulivane and two aides picked up pine knot torches and set the tar barrels and kerosene buckets ablaze. Turning back from the south side of the bridge, Sulivane saw through the smoke and flames a solid line of blue-coated cavalry racing up Main Street and turning down 14th Street toward the bridge. The Union forces fired a few parting shots at Sulivane and his men, who disappeared into the morning haze.

Just east of the city, along the old market road, Mayor Joseph Mayo and five other city fathers rode a rickety wagon fitted with an odd white flourish. Realizing they had no truce flag to fly, the men had torn off their shirttails and tied them together to craft a homespun surrender banner. "To the General Commanding the United States Army in front of Richmond," read the letter the mayor presented to the Union officers he met.

> The Army of the Confederate Government having abandoned the City of Richmond, I respectfully request that you will take possession of it with an organized force, to preserve order and protect women and children and property.
> Respectfully, Joseph Mayo, Mayor.

Grant's ten-month siege of Richmond had succeeded at a staggering cost: seventy thousand Union and Confederate men wounded, dead, or missing. In a sense, though, Richmond had been under siege for the better part of the war. From the Seven Days Battles to the horrific fights at Fredericksburg, to Chancellorsville, Cold Harbor, and the Wilderness, all told no fewer than two hundred thousand Union and Confederate men had been killed or wounded or were missing in the desperate quest for the ashen-faced prize. "I can't think of two enemy capitals in the history of the world that have been as close to each other as Richmond and Washington," said the Virginia Historical Society's Bryan. "As a result, the land between Richmond and Washington became the bloodiest ground in the Western Hemisphere," he said. "And Lincoln had been staring down that bloody road."

FOR A VAST FUTURE

Admiral Porter rose early on the morning of April 4 and readied the USS *Malvern*, flagship of the Union Navy on the James. He ordered every craft in the fleet to be made to look sharp. On the decks of gunboats, transports, schooners, steamers, and barges, men stood at full salute as the *Malvern* got underway. On its deck, they could see their impossibly tall president acknowledge their service with a tip of his trademark black stovepipe hat as he passed by and headed upstream.

The river was running fast and high, and its muddy torrents bore the flotsam of Richmond's fall: charred and broken timbers, bits of warships blown apart, the bloated corpses of dead horses. As the *Malvern* neared the ruined capital, deeper dangers loomed. The Confederates had distinguished themselves with their development of underwater mines. Naval engineers had already cleared dozens of them along Lincoln's route that morning, but more remained concealed. Torpedoes lay strewn about the banks of the James, Porter later recalled, "like so many queer fish basking in the sun." And beneath the waters lurked sunken hazards: ships the Confederates had scuttled in the channel to deter naval assault.

Nearing the still-smoldering city, Lincoln could smell the acrid smoke of rebel defeat. Rounding the gentle bend just east of town, he saw the towering bluff of Chimborazo Hill and, atop it, the sprawling hospital compound that treated seventy-eight thousand wounded and sick Confederates, thousands of whom never left alive. Moving further upstream, he gazed out at the hilltop church of St. John's, perhaps with the words Patrick Henry once delivered there—liberty or death—ringing in his ears.

On shifting shoals in the unfamiliar waters, the big ship ran aground. Lincoln and Porter disembarked in midstream, transferring to a barge towed by a tug, which, in turn, developed engine trouble. And so, it was not in the majesty of a conquering giant that Lincoln arrived at Richmond but aboard a small wooden boat rowed by a dozen sailors and marines, a craft more fitting for a day of fishing than for the landing of a commander triumphant. Even that boat hung up in the rapids, before drifting back to a finger of sand. There, just downstream from the crackling carcass of Mayo's Bridge, out climbed the president of the United States, less like Caesar, it seemed to some, than like Christ. "Bless the Lord, there comes the Messiah," exclaimed a black man who was repairing a footbridge over the canal nearby. "There is Mister Abraham Lincoln, sure enough!"

Within minutes, Lincoln and his tiny entourage were descended upon by dozens of African Americans who had been born into slavery and had, only that morning, awakened as free men and women for the first time in their lives. "Thank you, Jesus," one woman cried out. "Glory Hallelujah!" A black man followed by several more bowed down before the leader they credited with their first taste of freedom. "Don't kneel to me, that is not right," said Lincoln. "You must kneel to God only, and thank him for the liberty you will hereafter enjoy."

Picking his way through the rubble of the burned district, Lincoln walked uphill toward Main Street. Near Lee's former quarters at the Spotswood Hotel, a woman wore a U.S. flag draped over her shoulders, as the crowd of onlookers grew to a throng. Blacks sang out hymns and praises, a few whites nodded and smiled, but much of Richmond was numbed by the scene, in shock over the destruction of their city and the collapse of the Confederacy. For if some saw Lincoln as a savior, others regarded him as the devil incarnate, an unyielding tyrant blinded by hubris and intoxicated with the power of an imperial presidency, a man who led the bloodiest war in the nation's history to invade, subdue, and impose his will upon sovereign people in independent states, especially the one that considered itself the mother of the nation. When one white Virginian ran excitedly toward Lincoln, Porter drew his sword, anxious over the security nightmare he had suddenly inherited, before the onlooker pulled up short and faded into the crowd without incident.

Protected by just a dozen sailors and marines with bayonets, Lincoln was besieged by a crowd of hundreds—some accounts suggest thousands— as he walked more than a mile through the conquered city, his life in imminent danger every step of the way. "The blinds of a second story window of a house were partly opened, and a man dressed in gray pointed something that looked like a gun directly at the president," Lincoln's bodyguard, William Crook, later recalled. "I was sure he meant to shoot." Perhaps the mysterious tube-shaped device was a telescope. As Crook would remember it, however, "it was nothing short of miraculous" that, in a city so recently defeated, no one tried that day to attack Lincoln.

A warm sun was high in the sky by the time the president arrived at the former White House of the Confederacy, where the commanding general, Godfrey Weitzel, had set up headquarters for the Union occupation.

"Could I please have," Lincoln asked, "a drink of water?"

It's hard to know just what passed through Lincoln's mind as he sat in the parlor occupied over the past four years by his longtime political nemesis, Jefferson Davis. Hot and bone-weary, Lincoln rested in his enemy's chair, drank his water, and let it sink in. "He looked far off with a serious, dreamy expression," Porter later wrote. What was behind that look, historians can only guess. "I think a number of things were on his mind," said McPherson, the Princeton historian. "Great satisfaction with the news he had received. He was also continuing to think about the question of what next—once the war is over, how are we going to incorporate these enemies, now fellow citizens, back into the Union." The weight of history, the power of symbols, and the links between past and place could not have been far from Lincoln's thoughts. "He had talked about a new birth of freedom," said McPherson. "Freedom is an ongoing process, it's a work in progress, in different times at different places. And the history of the James River, with these landmark events—1607, 1776, and then 1865—these are landmarks in the ongoing determination of freedom and of who we are as a country."

Surely all of that and more was on Lincoln's mind later that afternoon, when he climbed the marble steps of Jefferson's ionic-columned temple to democracy, the Virginia Capitol, over top which, for the first time in four years, the stars and stripes waved once more. Before him, festooned with onlookers, was Thomas Crawford's masterful monument to Washington, unveiled on the first president's birthday three years before the outbreak of war, with the Revolutionary War general seated astride a great horse, bronze statutes of Jefferson and Henry at his feet. The master of the moment, rhetorician extraordinaire, Lincoln looked at those proud memorials to the men who gave force, reason, and voice to the American Revolution. He gazed out over the thousands of people before him, white and black, citizens, soldiers, daughters, and sons. He raised his tall hat in the afternoon heat and said . . . nothing. "I almost wish he had, standing there on the steps of the Capitol, with the flag flying above it and the Washington monument there, this is the time to do it," said Mike Gorman, a National Parks Service historian and guide who traced Lincoln's historic footsteps through Richmond on a warm, sunny day. "Maybe it's better he didn't say anything."

Whether he said it or not, Lincoln left little doubt as to what he was thinking. "With malice toward none; with charity for all; with firmness in the right, as God gives us to see the right, let us strive on to finish the work we are in; to bind up the nation's wounds; to care for him who shall have borne the battle, and for his widow, and his orphan—to do all which may achieve and cherish a just and a lasting peace, among ourselves, and with all nations." Those were Lincoln's words before Congress on March 4, 1865, one month to the day before he stood on the Capitol steps at Richmond and looked out upon a people who were at once the oldest Americans and, suddenly, among the newest.

On his way out of town that afternoon, Lincoln paused by a final sad symbol of war, the infamous Libby Prison, a former warehouse along the James where thousands of Union prisoners scraped by on near-starvation rations. "Pull it down," someone hollered out, but a somber Lincoln preferred to leave it standing as an enduring reminder of the price the country had paid over four years of battle that had left 620,000 Americans dead from combat or war-related disease.

Likely inflamed by hard memories, Weitzel used the moment to ask Lincoln for direction on the treatment of the Richmonders now under his thumb. Lincoln, though, had seen suffering enough. "If I were in your place," he said, "I'd let 'em up easy. Let 'em up easy."

It was an exhausted, if exhilarated, Lincoln who collapsed that night aboard the *Malvern*, finally docked at the deepwater wharf at Rockett's Landing. The next morning, April 5, he left.

Four days later, Lee bowed to what had become inevitable, surrendering his army, and what was left of the Confederacy, just eighty miles to the west, at Appomattox. Six days after that, Lincoln was dead, shot through the head on Good Friday. His assassination on the day Christians mourn the crucifixion of Christ formed an almost biblical coda to the life of a man millions regarded as a secular, yet nearly sanctified, disciple of American democracy.

"I have seen him in the watch-fires of a hundred circling camps; they have builded Him an altar in the evening dews and damps; I can read His righteous sentence by the dim and flaring lamps; His day is marching on." Lincoln was very much alive in 1861, when Julia Ward Howe penned those lines of the "Battle Hymn of the Republic." She was in Washington at his invitation when she wrote them, and they endure as part of his eulogy even now.

Martyrdom, though, was not on Lincoln's mind as the *Malvern* untied at Rockett's that day. Doggedly, he had pressed a war that preserved the Union and set free the slaves at a horrifying cost to the nation, North and South. After so much grief and pain and loss, he felt the nation's best days surely lay ahead. With malice toward none, Lincoln breathed in the cool air and dared at last to imagine the unbound possibilities of a new birth of freedom. "Not altogether for today," he had promised the Congress four tortuous years and an eternity ago, but rather "for a vast future also."

It was a morning in April. The sun lifted the mist off the river, and Lincoln drifted downstream toward the sea, borne away by ancient waters and the spirit of the James.

EPILOGUE

Undimmed by Human Tears:
American Identity for the Next Four Hundred Years

WASHINGTON—On the last Sunday in October 2005, half a century after her refusal to give up her seat to a white man on an Alabama bus helped to galvanize the national civil rights movement, the body of ninety-two-year-old Rosa Parks was carried in a plain mahogany casket and left to lie in state in the rotunda of the U.S. Capitol. It was the first time the life of either a woman or a black person had been honored in that way, left to pause, in a sense, between this world and the next in the hallowed chamber that symbolically enshrines the unity and political soul of the nation.

Had she been able to open her eyes one last time, Parks could have looked across the cool marble floor of the rotunda and gazed upon John Chapman's masterpiece, *Baptism of Pocahontas*, flanked by a bust of the Rev. Martin Luther King Jr. and a statue of Thomas Jefferson holding the Declaration of Independence. Four centuries after Native Americans, English, and Africans first came together along the banks of the James, the icons memorialized in the rotunda still speak to each group's role in the imperfect forging of the nation's founding ideal and the enduring struggle to give it meaning for all Americans.

"I have a dream," King declared in the 1963 speech that seared the American conscience with a renewed sense of purpose in the vision that Parks and so many others worked to advance, "that one day this nation will rise up and live out the true meaning of its creed: 'We hold these truths to be self-evident, that all men are created equal.'"

All created equal.

It was, wrote Jefferson, a self-evident truth. And yet, as a slaveholding statesman helping to build a new nation from the flames of revolution on land taken from people who had lived there for centuries, Jefferson knew this was more of a promise. It was a promise that, by 1963, had become, in King's mind, a dream. Somewhere near the heart of American identity for the next four hundred years lies a haunting question: which is it? "I think it's an evident truth, it's a promise, and it has turned out to be a dream," said Julian Bond, chairman of the National Association for the Advancement of Colored People (NAACP), the oldest and largest civil rights group in the country. "I'd like to see the promise made real and hope it wouldn't take four hundred years."

TOWARD A COMMON REMEMBERING

Four centuries ago, when the English first came to Jamestown, geography was destiny for a world of nation-states built around physical boundaries and regional clusters of kith and clan. Over the next four hundred years, borders and ethnicity will matter far less than national identity—the national story, shared inheritance, and common purpose that gather a people as one.

Few things have the power to define a nation's identity as much as its national story, the collective understanding of a nation's past. No earthquake or flood has ever sculpted a landscape the way the quiet force of remembering can shape the unyielding topography of the human mind. Part of what binds us so strongly as Americans is that we got our mythology down early; one thing that divides us so bitterly is that we got so much of it wrong. For myth is more than memory; it's the shards of memory we choose to believe, to repeat to ourselves, and to embellish with time. And it's the untold stories of the larger parts we just as willfully choose to neglect.

"There's nothing more important than what I would call the burning need to tell a more complete and accurate story about our nation's history," Richmond mayor Douglas Wilder told the National Press Club in Washington, D.C., in a 2006 speech. The grandson of slaves, Wilder was elected governor of Virginia in 1989, the first black person ever elected chief executive of a U.S. state. He's embarked on a mission to build a new museum devoted to the history of slavery in America, from its beginnings along the banks of the James to emancipation. "Even some 400 years later," he said, "there's still a blot on our national conscience."

No American is proud of slavery. What troubles Wilder is that so many people—black and white—would prefer to ignore it entirely. In doing so, he said, the country overlooks an essential part of its national story, an essential part of American identity. "It's not understated, it's unstated and it's unrecognized," Wilder said in an interview in his City Hall office, "and the obliteration of that aspect of our history, as such, it robs Americans of that knowledge of who we are as a people."

To stroll the placid grounds and immaculate gardens of the James River plantations, places like Berkeley, Westover, and Tuckahoe, is to wander through a historical illusion. The plantations were not idyllic set pieces from some romantic play. They were working farms, corporate endeavors with bottom-line demands and legions of enslaved laborers. What's missing from the plantation showcases of today is the slaves—not only the treatment they were forced to endure but their partnership in the creation of that riverside world.

It was that world that generated the wealth that helped to underwrite the birth of the country, its fight for independence, and the national effort to knit together these united states from a fragmented collection of colonies. Building that world was more than a contribution; it was an achievement as grand in its own way as the creation of the democratic republic, a triumph of the human spirit far less celebrated, yet every bit as heroic, as the endurance of the soldiers at Valley Forge.

"When people talk about America's founders, they mention the likes of Washington and Jefferson and Franklin and Adams. Too often they ignore another group of founders—men and women and children who did not come to America of their free will, but in chains," President George W. Bush told participants in the NAACP's 2006 convention in Washington. "These founders literally helped build our country. They chopped the wood, they built the homes, they tilled the fields and they reaped the harvest." Wilder and Bush are leaders in a larger movement urging the nation to peer back at its beginnings through a widening lens, to reach beyond the roles played by a few great men and to recognize the vital contributions of millions more. "That's a part of the story," said Wilder. To tell it faithfully, he said, "we need more voices."

Historians have searched out those voices in recent decades, taking note of the achievements of a vast array of farmers and artisans, cowards and shills, liars and carpenters, seamstresses and suffragettes, servants and slaves. This broader portrait of the American past, the commonplace as well as the heroic, has produced a far richer narrative than the country had before. It has invigorated the national conversation about where we have come from and who we are. As some see it, though, we have only begun, as a nation, to undertake the honest reckoning of our national voyage that will set us on the course toward a truly common remembering.

"You go over the landscape of this country, and it's all the monuments to the Europeans," said government professor Alan Lichtman of American University in Washington. "But if you're a native American, and you went through that same landscape, it would have utterly different meaning, every place would have utterly different meaning. If you're an African American in the South, every place would have utterly different meaning. And the more we understand that, I think, the more we can work to enrich each other with the capacity of a diverse people to live together harmoniously and not just to tolerate each other but to benefit from that diversity," said Lichtman. "That's the great hope and challenge of America."

FOR ALL OR FOR NONE

In October 2005, several weeks before Rosa Parks died, Secretary of State Condoleezza Rice journeyed to her native state to speak at the University of Alabama at Tuscaloosa. With Americans mired in a grinding war against Islamic jihadists, Baathist holdouts, Iranian proxies, and garden variety thugs in Iraq, Rice traveled south to draw the line connecting this country's own tortured beginnings with the difficulties Iraqis now face in trying to build democracy in their own country.

"When the founding fathers said 'We the people,' they didn't mean me," said Rice, the first African American woman ever to serve in the post first held by Jefferson. "Make no mistake," she continued, "citizenship was not a gift that was given to black Americans. It was a right that was won through the courage and sacrifice of many impatient patriots, weary of hypocrisy, whose demand was 'Freedom Now.'"

It's little wonder, then, that not all Americans regard the four-hundredth anniversary of Jamestown as a celebration. To Native Americans, it is a bitter reminder of lands taken away, cultures swept aside, and lives, families, and entire communities destroyed. To African Americans, it recalls the beginning of the horror that was American slavery. Even to many white Americans, it conjures up thoughts of brutality and grief.

And yet, if not all Americans have shared equally in the sacrifice and loss it took to build the country or in the fruits of the nation's success, all do now share a common inheritance. "Our common inheritance as a nation of diverse people is, as Abraham Lincoln said, a government of the people, by the people, and for the people," said Lichtman, who teaches a course on what it means to be an American. "This was always the great American dream, that sovereignty in America would rest ultimately with who we are, not by birth, but by our shared sense of common democratic and humane values."

Jefferson and his fellow founders owned slaves, yet they wrote of inalienable rights, defining for their age, and every age since, the essence and spirit of personal liberty. They penned the philosophical blueprint for the first nation in history to be created for the explicit purpose of ensuring and safeguarding the rights of the individual within the framework of a government accountable to the people it served. Despite their shortcomings, the founders "dug the well of democracy deep in America," said Rice. They put in place the means for the country to mend its flaws; they could not guarantee that it would do so.

"Our chosen form of government is not in itself a cure for all that ails the human spirit," Rabbi Michael Panitz of the Temple Israel of Norfolk reminded the Virginia senate during prayers opening a session in March 2006, "but rather a structure resting on a base of values." It was those values, said Rice, that ultimately cried out with one voice that no American could ever be truly free until all Americans were free. "Either the principles of our nation's creed were true for everyone, or they were true for no one," Rice told the students and faculty in Alabama. "If these truths were self-evident, if all men really were created equal, then it was America that had to change, not America's democratic ideals." Those changes, the struggle and sacrifice they required, and the country's enduring capacity for continuing change, said Wilder, lie at the heart of our common inheritance. "America would not have been what it is today without the ridding of slavery and the abolition of slavery and the war that it took to do it," he said. "That's why it's so important for us to be continually examining who Americans are and who made America and what is America."

In asking those questions, some indeed find much that all can celebrate. "The thing that sets the United States apart, and its great contribution to the world, is that human freedom is a birthright, and that means each individual is worthy of these liberties and to be treated with dignity," said Richmond attorney Frank Atkinson, chairman of the federal commission formed to oversee the four-hundredth anniversary commemoration of Jamestown. "If you want to trace the roots of this, John Smith said, 'You may be a gentleman, but over here, if you don't work, you don't eat, and over here, we've begun something new.'" What began at Jamestown was the imperfect miracle of democracy in America, a powerful force ever flowing downstream, constantly testing and renewing its banks, correcting its course and adjusting to the rocks it finds itself in. "In each generation, with toil and tears, we have had to earn our heritage again," President Lyndon Johnson reminded Americans in 1965, when a prosperous nation was bitterly divided by racial tensions and the Vietnam War. "If we fail now, then we will have forgotten in abundance what we learned in hardship: that democracy rests on faith, that freedom asks more than it gives," said Johnson. "If we succeed it will not be because of what we have, but it will be because of what we are; not because of what we own, but rather because of what we believe. For we are a nation of believers. Underneath the clamor of building and the rush of our day's pursuits, we are believers in justice and liberty and in our own union. We believe that every one must some day be free. And we believe in ourselves."

No democracy anywhere can ever be stronger than free people insist that it be. Left to drift unattended, it will naturally extend increasing power and influence to those who are already powerful and influential, those who, like those early James River landowners, have the access and means to game the system to their exclusive advantage in a way that penalizes, and ultimately tyrannizes, the rest. The founding fathers understood this, for they had seen it at work in their midst. They knew that wedding democratic governance to free enterprise had the potential to create the most powerful engine in history for converting human instincts into wealth and might. They warned that human impulse could not be trusted, that the country's political and economic machinery must be based on the rule of law, constantly fine-tuned to prevent its power from being harnessed to the purpose of tyranny. And they left to future generations the constitutional tools to keep the engines of governance whirring for the common good. "The history of America is one of constant renewal," Bush told the NAACP. "We must continue to work for a new founding that redeems the promise of our Declaration and guarantees the birthright of every citizen."

In July 2006, the week after he addressed the NAACP, Bush took his own place in that continuing process, signing into law legislation that extended to a new generation of American minorities the protections enshrined in the Voting Rights Act of 1965. The act grew out of modern racist violence that shocked the nation, when vigilante citizens with clubs and whips and police with attack dogs viciously struck a group of peaceful and unarmed civil rights activists as they marched across the Edmund Pettus Bridge in Selma, Alabama, to demand an end to discrimination at the ballot box. "The right of ordinary men and women to determine their own political future lies at the heart of the American experiment," Bush said during a White House ceremony, as he signed the voting rights extension on a steamy summer morning in the Rose Garden. "America began with a declaration that all men are created equal," said Bush. "In four decades since the Voting Rights Act was first passed, we've made progress toward equality, yet the work for a more perfect union is never ending."

As much as Americans like to prick and probe their own identity, sometimes there's no substitute for the view from afar. In one of those amusing tricks history loves to play, it recently fell to a British leader, Prime Minister Tony Blair, to clarify the common inheritance all Americans share. "Don't ever apologize for your values," Blair admonished a joint session of Congress in July 2003, when the country was under criticism from many leaders abroad for launching the invasion of Iraq four months before. "Tell them why you're proud of America," said Blair. "Tell them when 'The Star Spangled Banner' starts, Americans get to their feet—Hispanics, Irish, Italians, Central Europeans, East Europeans, Jews, Muslims, whites, Asians, blacks, those who go back to the early settlers and those whose English is the same as some New York cab drivers I've dealt with, but whose sons and daughters could run for this Congress. Tell them why Americans, one and all, stand upright and respectful. Not because some state official told them to but because, whatever race, color, class or creed they are, being American means being free. That's why they're proud."

AMERICAN VOICES, AMERICAN DREAMS

George Whitewolf has wrestled with it for years, and he still can't get some folks to understand why it's important to get the colors right. Everyone agrees on what the colors are—red, white, yellow, and black—but when it comes to setting them down on an emblem, on a flag, or a spot on the floor, the result is invariably division and pain.

Traditional American Indians say yellow must always be east, as it represents the rising sun. White, it follows, is the snow from the north, black is the darkness of night when the sun sets in the west, and red is the color of the earth when the rains from the south wash away the rich top of the soil. What Whitewolf can't seem to get some folks to understand is that all of that changed a long time ago. The old meanings no longer hold. "Some of us know who we are," he explained, shaking his head, a sinking sun casting his frame in long shadow across a grassy field where Virginians of Native American ancestry gather each autumn near the Pamunkey River. "Some of us think we know who we are. And some of us don't have any idea who we are."

Part Monacan Indian, part Caucasian, a Maryland native who lives in the mountains at the western edge of the Virginia Piedmont and vows he'll die there, a plumber by trade, shopkeeper by vocation, and Souian spiritual and cultural leader by choice, Whitewolf is in many ways the archetypical twenty-first-century American. At sixty-three, he is a man whose identity is blurred but whose mission is clear, a curious and unrepentant half-breed who can't seem to slip the gravitational pull of his own ethnicity and wanders instead in urgent search of his place within the racially ambiguous landscape of a nation that sometimes seems destined to struggle forever with the question of how to get the colors right.

For decades, Virginia refused to recognize its native groups as distinguishable Indian tribes, as though their very ethnicity had vanished the way riverside villages of wood and clay melt into the forest and disappear. Now, Whitewolf's generation is struggling to recreate its past, to resurrect a native identity by studying Indian ways, holding regional powwows and pressing for such public recognition as comes with legislative resolutions and place markers on historical roadside signs. Much as the quest for a more perfect union is ever a work in progress, so too is the search for a national identity predicated upon common purpose.

"This is something I think about all the time, because I have this amazing experience of listening to America call in unfettered," said Brian Lamb, founder, president, and chief executive officer of the popular cable network C-SPAN. For nearly three decades, Lamb has sat at the electronic crossroads of America, listening as people phone in from around the country to weigh in on issues ranging from the federal budget deficit to the quest for a constitutional amendment that would ban gay marriage. C-SPAN has become the ultimate American civics class, not only because it broadcasts live and uninterrupted proceedings before the House, the Senate, and countless government agencies and think tanks, but also because of the public participation Lamb deliberately promotes by inviting Americans to call in on live television with their questions and comments on events of the day. If Walt Whitman heard America singing, Lamb gets to listen when America rants. "We don't try to muzzle that," Lamb said in an interview at C-SPAN headquarters in Washington. "Everybody feels very strongly that they have something to say, and they're going to say it. You hear this all the time: 'It's a free country, and I'm going to tell you what I think.' I can hear people put the phone down and say, 'Yeah! I just got my say in. I'm equal to everybody else, and I can say what I want to say.'"

Four centuries into this country's experiment with government by the people, C-SPAN provides a daily glimpse into the founding ideal, an ethereal venue where Jefferson's promise of equality has been made real for all, a raw and sometimes rowdy arena where voices compete on an even mat, a kind of televised mirror of American democracy. "I say often to myself, it's a miracle that it all works," said Lamb. "There's such a diversity of views, some days you feel, 'How do we ever get together? How do we get an election? How do we ever decide on anything?'"

The wonder of Lamb's rough and tumble democracy is not that it spools together people who share a common view, but rather the role it plays in the much higher calling of distilling a common view from the cacophonous whole, part of the political alchemy through which collective decisions emerge from individual thought. "We are free to say what we think," said Lamb, "and the more opportunity we have for voices the better off we are." Americans sometimes take that for granted. Perhaps we shouldn't. For the great plague of the modern world is not some endless war or mysterious disease. More often it's our old-fashioned inability to fathom and to value the wealth of diversity within the human race and to build common ground amid divergent views. In the Balkans, in Darfur, in the Middle East and elsewhere, ethnic, cultural, and religious differences remain a source of strife, not strength.

It's hard work anywhere to make diversity a virtue, to build systems of governance where the majority rules without running roughshod over the minority, to form national communities that recognize individual differences as strengths to be nurtured, not frailties to be feared. Four hundred years after its own beginnings at the confluence of three disparate and ancient ways of life—African, English, and Native American—the United States still struggles with all of that. The stakes have since become global, and so is the struggle.

The rise of militant Islam has forced Americans to begin to grapple with what the Pentagon warns could be a generational conflict against the kind of terror groups that struck this country on September 11, 2001. To prevail in what the Defense Department has termed the "Long War" against such groups, the United States must not only combat the militants, it must keep their ranks from growing. Ultimately that will require a new kind of relationship that promotes and widens durable partnerships between this country and the Islamic world. In a way, the two groups have embarked on a kind of modern mission of discovery, with strains and even conflicts echoing those that similar encounters have wrought throughout history.

Capt. John Smith and Chief Powhatan were products of separate worlds. Just physically connecting one to the other required months of hard sailing on uncertain seas. Even then, ignorance on both sides bred prejudice, hatred, suspicion, and fear that undermined their ability to build partnerships or even to communicate, whether across the ocean or across a smoke-filled lodge. They understood little and misunderstood much about the needs and aims of their people. And by that misunderstanding untold opportunities and lives where lost.

Four centuries on, physical distance has been all but erased by the jumbo jet, Christiane Amanpour, the satellite phone call, and the Internet. Old World divisions no longer exist. But has the map of the human mind kept pace? Can this country take the lessons its forebears learned in the hardest of ways and use them to help avert the clash of civilizations some analysts believe may have begun already between the Islamic world and the West? Will Americans find new ways to grasp the aspirations and fears of 1.4 billion Muslims and to translate a coherent American vision to them in a way that keeps faith with American ideals? "To me, ultimately what the United States does represent is human rights, democracy, the ideals of the founding fathers," Akbar Ahmed, a former Pakistani diplomat who is chairman of Islamic studies at American University, testified before the Senate Foreign Relations Committee in July of 2006. "That is the vision and the dream we constantly need to come back to and share with the Muslim world."

ALL OF ITS PEOPLE

It was a dream more audacious than empire, fueled by the radical belief that it might be possible to build a nation where all men and women actually were created equal, treated with equality, and given equal opportunity to rise to their potential, whatever that might be. The odds were very much against it, from the moment bold spirits set forth to cross the sea in leaking wooden boats driven by the wind and guided by the stars. It was never inevitable that they would succeed. In some ways, they fell short of their own ideals. But many millions have lived believing in that dream and died that it might one day come true. They left behind far more than a vision. They have left us a national story, a shared inheritance and a common purpose. They have left us an American identity as rich and as sturdy as we the people are varied. After four hundred years, a nation that began with a trickle and followed its dreams downstream has taken on the collective strength of all its tributaries.

"What has made America great is its people," said Wilder. "All of its people." The four-hundredth anniversary of this nation's beginnings gives all of its people the chance to look closely at who we are and all that has brought us together as one. Doing so may be the best birthday present the country could give itself. For in embracing our differences, we pay tribute to our past, we honor the natural order of the world, and we play to our greatest strength. That is, in many ways, what this country and its people have been struggling from the very beginning to learn. Perhaps when we fully grasp that, when we sweep aside the misbegotten notions of our national myth, we might finally come to understand that we are strong as a nation not because Americans make up some chosen race but because we are all Americans, regardless of race.

As borders recede in importance, as ethnic origin melts away, that enduring and unifying truth links Americans to the people of every nation everywhere in the world. That is the heart of our national story. That is the inheritance we share. That is our common purpose. And that, our history tells us, is what will guide this audacious dream for the next four hundred years.

In the hours Rosa Parks lay still in the rotunda, a vast cross section of America passed by. There were senators, congressmen, and senior government officials, as well as tourists from all walks of life. Parents of every station and color stood in line for hours so they and their children might pay their final respects to this slight, but powerful, woman who transformed the most common of acts, that of simply sitting on a public bus, into an affirmation of democracy and a clarion call, demanding that this country make good on its founding promise that all are created equal. As they walked past in reverent silence, some gazed up at Constantino Brumidi's lavish fresco on the inside of the great Capitol dome, a hundred and eighty feet above her casket. There, in brilliant colors and swirling brushstrokes depicting the apotheosis of George Washington, a pair of heavenly bodies clutched a banner. "E Pluribus Unum," it reads, the Latin motto of the United States: out of many, one.

BIBLIOGRAPHY

"A Quaint Consideration." *William and Mary College Quarterly Historical Magazine* 5, no. 2 (October 1896): 112.

Adovasio, J. M., and Jake Page. *The First Americans: In Pursuit of Archaeology's Greatest Mystery*. New York: Modern Library, 2002.

Ambrose, Stephen E. *Undaunted Courage: Meriwether Lewis, Thomas Jefferson, and the Opening of the American West*. New York: Touchstone, 1996.

American Heritage Dictionary. 4th ed. New York: Dell, 2001.

Anderson, Fred, ed. *George Washington Remembers: Reflections on the French and Indian War*. Lanham, Md.: Rowman & Littlefield, 2004.

Andrews, Matthew P. *The Soul of a Nation: The Founding of Virginia and the Projection of New England*. New York: Scribner's, 1944.

Appleby, Joyce, Lynn Hunt, and Margaret Jacob. *Telling the Truth about History*. New York: Norton, 1994.

Appomattox Court House. Division of Publications, National Park Service.

Aptheker, Herbert. *American Negro Slave Revolts*. New York: International, 1943.

Axelrod, Alan, and Charles Phillips. *What Everyone Should Know about the 20th Century: 200 Events that Shaped the World*. Holbrook, Mass.: Adams Media, 1995.

Ayers, Edward L., and Bradley C. Mittendorf, eds. *The Oxford Book of the American South: Testimony, Memory, and Fiction*. New York: Oxford University Press, 1997.

Barbour, Philip L. *The Complete Works of Captain John Smith*, 1580–1631. Chapel Hill: University of North Carolina Press, 1986.

——— . *The Three Worlds of Captain John Smith*. London: Macmillan, 1964.

Bartels, Emily C. "Othello and Africa: Postcolonialism Reconsidered." *The William and Mary Quarterly*, 3rd Ser., 54, no. 1 (January 1997): 45–64.

Basler, Roy P., ed. *The Collected Works of Abraham Lincoln*. Vol. 3. New Brunswick, N.J.: Rutgers University Press, 1953.

——— . *The Collected Works of Abraham Lincoln*. Vol. 5. New Brunswick, N.J.: Rutgers University Press, 1953.

Berlin, Ira. *Generations of Captivity: A History of African-American Slaves*. Cambridge, Mass.: Belknap, 2003.

——— . *Many Thousands Gone: The First Two Centuries of Slavery in North America*. Cambridge, Mass.: Belknap, 1998.

Billings, Warren M. *A Little Parliament: The Virginia General Assembly in the Seventeenth Century*. Richmond: Library of Virginia, 2004.

——— . *Sir William Berkeley and the Forging of Colonial Virginia*. Baton Rouge: Louisiana State University Press, 2004.

Blackburn, Robin. "The Old World Background to European Colonial Slavery." *The William and Mary Quarterly,* 3rd Ser., 54, no. 1 (January 1997): 65–102.

Bondurant, Agnes M. *Poe's Richmond*. Richmond: Edgar Allan Poe Museum, 1978.

Boorstin, Daniel J., ed. *An American Primer*. New York: Meridian, 1966.

——— . *The Americans: The Colonial Experience*. New York: Random House, 1958.

Boyer, Paul S., ed. *The Oxford Companion to United States History*. New York: Oxford University Press, 2001.

Breen, T. H., ed. *Shaping Southern Society: The Colonial Experience*. New York: Oxford University Press, 1976.

Brewer, James H. "Negro Property Owners in Seventeenth-Century Virginia." *The William and Mary Quarterly,* 3rd Ser., 12, no. 4 (October 1955): 575–80.

Brown, Katherine L., and Nancy T. Sorrells. *Virginia's Cattle Story*. Staunton, Va.: Lot's Wife, 2004.

Bruun, Erik, and Jay Crosby, eds. *Our Nation's Archive: The History of the United States in Documents*. New York: Black Dog and Leventhal, 1999.

Campbell, Charles. *Life of Isaac Jefferson of Petersburg, Virginia, Blacksmith. William and Mary Quarterly,* 3rd Ser., 8, no. 4 (October 1951): 566–82.

Cannon, John, ed. *The Oxford Companion to British History*. New York: Oxford University Press, 1997.

Carson, Jane. *Bacon's Rebellion: 1676–1976*. Jamestown, Va.: Jamestown Foundation, 1976.

——— . "Bacon's Rebellion, 1676–1976." *The William and Mary Quarterly,* 3rd Ser., 35, no. 2 (April 1978): 417–18.

Chapman, John Gadsby. *The Picture of the Baptism of Pocahontas Painted by Order of Congress, for the Rotundo of the Capitol*. Washington, D.C.: Peter Force, 1840.

Chase, Owen. *The Wreck of the Whaleship Essex: The Riveting Life-and-Death Saga of Man against the Deep that Inspired the Writing of* Moby Dick. New York: Harcourt, Brace, 1965.

Conrad, Robert E. *In the Hands of Strangers: Readings on Foreign and Domestic Slave Trading and the Crisis of the Union*. University Park: Pennsylvania State University Press, 2001.

Cook, Chris, and John Wroughton. *English Historical Facts*. Totowa, N.J.: Palgrave Macmillan, 1980.

Copeland, David A., and Carol S. Humphrey. *The French and Indian War and the Revolutionary War*. Westport, Conn.: Greenwood Press, 2005.

Coski, John M. *Capital Navy: The Men, Ships and Operations of the James River Squadron.* Campbell, Calif.: Savas Woodbury, 1996.

Coward, Barry, ed. *A Companion to Stuart Britain.* Oxford: Blackwell, 2003.

Cullen, Joseph P. *Richmond Battlefields: A History and Guide to Richmond National Battlefield Park.* Washington, D.C.: National Park Service, 1961.

Dabney, Virginius. *Richmond: The Story of a City.* Garden City, N.Y.: Doubleday, 1976.

——— . *Virginia: The New Dominion.* Charlottesville: University Press of Virginia, 1971.

Davis, Burke. *To Appomattox: Nine April Days, 1865.* New York: Rinehart, 1959.

Davis, David B., and Steven Mintz. *The Boisterous Sea of Liberty: A Documentary History of America from Discovery through the Civil War.* New York: Oxford University Press, 1998.

Delany, Martin R. *Blake or the Huts of America.* Boston: Beacon, 1970.

——— . *The Condition, Elevation, Emigration, and Destiny of the Colored People of the United States and Official Report of the Niger Valley Exploring Party.* Amherst, Mass.: Humanity Books, 2004.

Dorman, John F., ed. *Adventures of Purse and Person: Virginia 1607–1624/5.* 4th ed. Vol. 1. Baltimore: Genealogical Co., 2004.

Douglas, Marjorie S. *The Everglades: River of Grass.* Sarasota, Fla.: Pineapple Press, 1997.

Dowdey, Clifford. *The Great Plantation: A Profile of Berkeley Hundred and Plantation Virginia from Jamestown to Appomattox.* 6th ed. Charles City, Va.: Berkeley Plantation, 1988.

Duke, Maurice, and Daniel P. Jordan, eds. *A Richmond Reader: 1733–1983.* 3rd ed. Chapel Hill: University of North Carolina Press, 1983.

Egloff, Keith, and Deborah Woodward. *First People: The Early Indians of Virginia.* Richmond: Virginia Department of Historic Resources, 1992.

Eifert, Virginia S. *Of Men and Rivers: Adventures and Discoveries along American Waterways.* New York: Dodd, Mead, 1966.

Ekirch, A. Roger. "Bound for America: A Profile of British Convicts Transported to the Colonies, 1718–1775." *The William and Mary Quarterly,* 3rd Ser., 42, no. 2 (April 1985): 184–200.

Ellis, Joseph J. *American Sphinx: The Character of Thomas Jefferson.* New York: Vintage, 1998.

——— . *Founding Brothers: The Revolutionary Generation.* New York: Vintage, 2002.

Eltis, David. *The Rise of African Slavery in the Americas.* Cambridge: Cambridge University Press, 2000.

Faust, Patricia L., ed. *Historical Times Illustrated Encyclopedia of the Civil War.* New York: Harper and Row, 1986.

Fischer, David H., and James C. Kelly. *Bound Away: Virginia and the Westward Movement.* Charlottesville: University of Virginia Press, 2000.

Frye, Keith. *Roadside Geology of Virginia.* 7th ed. Missoula, Mont.: Mountain Press, 1986.

Furgurson, Ernest B. *Ashes of Glory: Richmond at War*. New York: Knopf, 1996.

Fuson, Robert H. *The Log of Christopher Columbus*. Camden, N.J.: International Marine, 1987.

Gallivan, Martin D. *James River Chiefdoms: The Rise of Social Inequality in the Chesapeake*. Lincoln: University of Nebraska Press, 2003.

Gallivan, Martin D., Thane Harpole, David A. Brown, Danielle Moretti-Langholtz, and E. Randolph Turner III. *The Werowocomoco (44GL32) Research Project: Background and 2003 Archaeological Field Season Results*, 2–100. College of William and Mary Department of Anthropology. Richmond: Commonwealth of Virginia Department of Historic Resources, 2005.

Gates, Henry L., Jr., and Nellie Y. McKay, eds. *The Norton Anthology: African American Literature*. New York: Norton, 1997.

Gleach, Frederic W. *Powhatan's World and Colonial Virginia: A Conflict of Cultures*. Lincoln: University of Nebraska Press, 1997.

Goodwin, Doris K. *Team of Rivals: The Political Genius of Abraham Lincoln*. New York: Simon & Schuster, 2005.

Gordon, Ann I. "Will of Ann Isham Gordon." *William and Mary College Quarterly Historical Magazine* 14, no. 3 (January 1906): 211–13.

Greenblatt, Stephen. *Will in the World: How Shakespeare Became Shakespeare*. New York: Norton, 2004.

Greene, Jack P., and J. R. Pole, eds. *A Companion to the American Revolution*. Malden, Mass.: Blackwell, 2004.

Gupton, Oscar W., and Fred C. Swope. *Trees and Shrubs of Virginia*. Charlottesville: University of Virginia Press, 1981.

Haile, Edward W., ed. *Jamestown Narratives Eyewitness Accounts of the Virginia Colony: The First Decade: 1607–1617*. Champlain, Va.: Roundhouse, 1998.

Hale, Horatio. *American Language Reprints: The Tutelo Language*. Vol. 23. Bristol, Pa.: Evolution, 2001.

Hatch, Charles E., Jr. *The First Seventeen Years: Virginia 1607–1624*. Charlottesville: University Press of Virginia, 1957.

Hecht, Irene W. D. "The Virginia Muster of 1624/5 as a Source for Demographic History." *The William and Mary Quarterly*, 3rd Ser., 30, no. 1, Chesapeake Society (January 1973): 65–92.

Hitchens, Christopher. *Thomas Jefferson: Author of America*. New York: HarperCollins, 2005.

Holton, Woody. *Forced Founders: Indians, Debtors, Slaves, and the Making of the American Revolution in Virginia*. Chapel Hill: University of North Carolina Press, 1999.

Horn, James. *A Land as God Made It: Jamestown and the Birth of America*. New York: Basic, 2005.

Horton, James O., and Lois E. Horton. *Slavery and the Making of America*. New York: Oxford University Press, 2005.

Hranicky, Jack, ed. *Indian Stone Tools of the Commonwealth of Virginia*. Alexandria: Virginia Academic Press, 2002.

Hudgins, Carter C. "Old World Industries and New World Hope: The Industrial Role of Scrap Copper at Jamestown." *The Journal of the Jamestown Rediscovery Center* 2 (2004).

Ingram, Bruce. *The James River Guide: Fishing and Floating on Virginia's Finest.* Corvallis, Oreg.: Ecopress, 2000.

Istanbul and Northwest Turkey. 4th ed. New York: Knopf, 1993.

The James River Basin: Past, Present and Future. Richmond: Virginia Academy of Science, 1950.

Jefferson, Thomas. *Autobiography of Thomas Jefferson.* Mineola, N.Y.: Dover, 2005.

———. "The Letters of Thomas Jefferson to William Short." *William and Mary College Quarterly Historical Magazine,* 2nd Ser., 12, no. 4 (October 1932): 287–304.

Keegan, John. *Fields of Battle: The Wars for North America.* New York: Knopf, 1996.

Kelso, William M., and Beverly A. Straube. *Jamestown Rediscovery: 1994–2004.* Richmond: The Association for the Preservation of Virginian Antiquities, 2004.

Keneally, Thomas. *Abraham Lincoln.* New York: Penguin, 2003.

Kennedy, Paul. *The Rise and Fall of the Great Powers: Economic Change and Military Conflict from 1500 to 2000.* New York: Random House, 1987.

Kneebone, John T., ed. *Dictionary of Virginia Biography.* Richmond: Library of Virginia, 1998.

Kricher, John. *Eastern Forests: A Field Guide to Birds, Mammals, Trees, Flowers, and More.* New York: Houghton Mifflin, 1988.

Lacey, Robert, and Danny Danziger. *The Year 1000: What Life Was Like at the Turn of the First Millennium: An Englishman's World.* Boston: Little, Brown, 1999.

Lankford, Nelson. *Richmond Burning: The Last Days of the Confederate Capital.* New York: Viking Penguin, 2002.

Larson, Chiles T. *Virginia's Past Today.* Charlottesville, Va.: Howell, 1998.

Leonard, Joan de Lourdes. "Operation Checkmate: The Birth and Death of a Virginia Blueprint for Progress 1660–1676." *The William and Mary Quarterly,* 3rd Ser., 24, no. 1 (January 1967): 44–74.

"Letter of Don Diego De Molina, 1613." *American Journeys Collection* (2003): 217–24. Wisconsin Historical Society Digital Library and Archives.

"Letter of John Rolfe, 1614." *American Journeys Collection* (2003): 237–44. Wisconsin Historical Society Digital Library and Archives.

Leuchtenburg, William E., ed. *American Places: Encounters with History.* New York: Oxford University Press, 2000.

Levy, Andrew. *The First Emancipator: The Forgotten Story of Robert Carter, the Founding Father Who Freed His Slaves.* New York: Random House, 2005.

Lincoln, R. J., and G. A. Boxshall. *The Cambridge Illustrated Dictionary of Natural History.* Cambridge: Cambridge University Press, 1987.

"List of Colonial Attorney-Generals." *William and Mary College Quarterly Historical Magazine* 10, no. 3 (January 1902): 165–67.

Loth, Calder, Jessie B. Thompson, Addison B. Thompson, Jessie Ball, T. Krusen, and Richard T. Couture. *Tuckahoe Plantation.* Tuckahoe Plantation Enterprise, Va., 1997.

Mallios, Seth, and Beverly Straube. *1999 Interim Report on the APVA Excavations at Jamestown, Virginia*. Richmond: Association for the Preservation of Virginia Antiquities, 2000.

Malone, Dumas. *Jefferson and the Rights of Man*. Boston: Little, Brown, 1951.

——— . *Jefferson the President: First Term 1801–1805*. Boston: Little, Brown, 1970.

——— . *Jefferson the Virginian*. Boston: Little, Brown, 1948.

Mann, Charles C. *1491: New Revelations of the Americas before Columbus*. New York: Knopf, 2005.

Mapp, Alf J., Jr. *The Faiths of Our Fathers: What America's Founders Really Believed*. Lanham, Md.: Rowman & Littlefield, 2003.

McCartney, Martha W. *A Study of the Africans and African Americans on Jamestown Island and at Green Spring, 1619–1803*. Williamsburg, Va.: Colonial Williamsburg Foundation, 2003.

McCusker, John J., and Russell R. Menard. *The Economy of British America: 1607–1789*. Chapel Hill: University of North Carolina Press, 1991.

McIlwaine, H. R., ed. *Journals of the House of Burgesses of Virginia: 1659/60–1693*. Richmond: Colonial Press, E. Waddey Co., 1915.

——— . *Minutes of the Council and General Court of Colonial Virginia*. 2nd ed. Richmond: Virginia State Library, 1979.

McPherson, James M. *Battle Cry of Freedom: The Civil War Era*. New York: Oxford University Press, 1988.

Middlekauff, Robert. *The Glorious Cause: The American Revolution, 1763–1789*. New York: Oxford University Press, 2005.

Miller, Randall M., and John D. Smith, eds. *Dictionary of Afro-American Slavery*. Westport, Conn.: Praeger, 1997.

Mordecai, Samuel. *Richmond in By-Gone Days*. Richmond: Dietz Press, 1946.

Morgan, Edmund S. *American Slavery, American Freedom*. New York: Norton, 1975.

Morton, Oren F. *A Centennial History of Allegheny County Virginia*. Dayton, Va.: J. K. Ruebush, 1923.

Morton, W. S. "Letters to Hugh Blair Grisby." *William and Mary College Quarterly Historical Magazine*, 2nd Ser., 9, no. 2 (April 1929): 118–22.

Mulligan, Tim. *Virginia: A History and Guide*. New York: Random House, 1986.

Murphy, Bruce, and William R. Benet, eds. *Benet's Reader's Encyclopedia*. 4th ed. New York: HarperCollins, 1996.

Nash, Gary B. *Red, White, and Black: The Peoples of Early North America*. 5th ed. Upper Saddle River, N.J.: Prentice Hall, 2006.

——— . *The Unknown American Revolution: The Unruly Birth of Democracy and the Struggle to Create America*. London: Viking, 2005.

The Negro in Virginia. Winston-Salem, N.C.: John F. Blair, 1994.

Nepo, Mark, ed. *Deepening the American Dream: Reflections on the Inner Life and Spirit of Democracy*. San Francisco: Jossey Bass, 2005.

Nicolson, Adam. *God's Secretaries: The Making of the King James Bible*. New York: HarperCollins, 2003.

Niles, Blair. *The James: From Iron Gate to the Sea.* New York: Farrar and Rinehart, 1939.

"Observations by Master George Percy, 1607." *American Journeys Collection* (2003): 3–23. Wisconsin Historical Society Digital Library and Archives.

"Occaneechee Island." *William and Mary College Quarterly Historical Magazine* 11, no. 2 (October 1902): 121–22.

Oxford Encyclopedia of World History. New York: Oxford University Press, 1998.

Pagan, John R. *Anne Orthwood's Bastard: Sex and Law in Early Virginia.* New York: Oxford University Press, 2003.

Page, Jake. *In the Hands of the Great Spirit: The 20,000-Year History of American Indians.* New York: Free Press, 2003.

Parent, Anthony S., Jr. *Foul Means: The Formation of a Slave Society in Virginia, 1660–1740.* Chapel Hill: University of North Carolina Press, 2003.

Partridge, Eric. *Routledge Dictionary of Historical Slang.* London: Penguin, 1937.

Powars, David S. *The Effects of the Chesapeake Bay Impact Crater on the Geologic Framework and the Correlation of Hydrogeologic Units of Southeastern Virginia, South of the James River,* 1–53. Washington, D.C.: Hampton Roads Planning District Commission, 2000.

Price, David A. *Love and Hate in Jamestown: John Smith, Pocahontas, and the Heart of a New Nation.* New York: Knopf, 2003.

"Proceedings of the Virginia Assembly, 1619." *American Journeys Collection* (2003): 247–78. Wisconsin Historical Society Digital Library and Archives.

Quitt, Martin H. "Immigrant Origins of the Virginia Gentry: A Study of Cultural Transmission and Innovation." *The William and Mary Quarterly,* 3rd Ser., 45, no. 4 (October 1988): 629–55.

Rainbolt, John C. "The Alteration in the Relationship between Leadership and Constituents in Virginia, 1660 to 1720." *The William and Mary Quarterly,* 3rd Ser., 27, no. 3 (July 1970): 411–34.

"The Randolph Family." *William and Mary College Quarterly Historical Magazine* 7, no. 3 (January 1899): 195–97.

Randolph, Isham. "Brick-Making in Goochland." *William and Mary College Quarterly Historical Magazine* 5, no. 2 (October 1896): 109–10.

Ransome, David R. "Wives for Virginia, 1621." *The William and Mary Quarterly,* 3rd Ser., 48, no. 1 (January 1991): 3–18.

"The Relation of the Lord De-La-Ware, 1611." *American Journeys Collection* (2003): 207–14. Wisconsin Historical Society Digital Library and Archives.

Rountree, Helen C. *Pocahontas, Powhatan, Opechancanough: Three Indian Lives Changed by Jamestown.* Charlottesville: University of Virginia Press, 2005.

Rourke, Constance. *American Humor: A Study of the National Character.* New York: New York Review Books, 1931.

Rouse, Parke, Jr. *The James: Where a Nation Began.* Richmond: Dietz Press, 1990.

Royster, Charles. *The Fabulous History of the Dismal Swamp Company: A Story of George Washington's Times.* New York: Vintage, 1999.

Ryan, David D. *The Falls of the James*. Richmond: William Byrd Press, 1975.

Sandburg, Carl. *Abraham Lincoln: The War Years*. New York: Harcourt, Brace, 1939.

Salmon, John S., comp. *A Guidebook to Virginia's Historical Markers*. Charlottesville: University of Virginia Press, 1994.

Schama, Simon. *Rough Crossings: Britain, the Slaves and the American Revolution*. New York: HarperCollins, 2006.

Segal, Ronald. *The Black Diaspora*. London: Faber and Faber, 1995.

Shorto, Russell. *The Island at the Center of the World: The Epic Story of Dutch Manhattan and the Forgotten Colony that Shaped America*. New York: Vintage, 2004.

Sidbury, James. *Ploughshares into Swords: Race, Rebellion, and Identity in Gabriel's Virginia, 1730–1810*. New York: Cambridge University Press, 1997.

Simpson, Paige S., and Jerry H. Simpson, Jr. *Torn Land*. Lynchburg, Va.: J. P. Bell, 1970.

Smith, John. *A Map of Virginia: With a Description of the Countrey, the Commodities, People, Government and Religion*. Wisconsin Historical Society, Digital Library and Archives, 2003.

———. "A True Relation by Captain John Smith, 1608." *American Journeys Collection* (2003): 27–71. Wisconsin Historical Society Digital Library and Archives.

Southern, Ed, ed. *The Jamestown Adventure: Accounts of the Virginia Colony, 1605–1614*. Winston-Salem, N.C.: John F. Blair, 2004.

Spelman, Henry. *Relation of Virginia*. London: Chiswick Press, 1873.

Stanard, W. G. "Randolph Family." *William and Mary College Quarterly Historical Magazine* 9, no. 3 (January 1901): 182–83.

Stephenson, Richard W., and Marianne M. McKee, eds. *Virginia in Maps: Four Centuries of Settlement, Growth, and Development*. Richmond: Library of Virginia, 2000.

Stewart, Richard W., ed. *American Military History: The United States Army and the Forging of a Nation, 1775–1917*, 2–5. Vol. 1. Washington, D.C.: Center of Military History, 2005.

Strachey, William, comp. *American Language Reprints: A Dictionary of Powhatan*. Vol. 8. Southampton: Evolution, 1999.

———. *The Historie of Travell into Virginia Britania*, ed. Louis B. Wright and Virginia Freund. Nendeln, Liechtenstein: Kraus Reprint Limited, 1967.

Straube, Beverly, and Nicholas Luccketti. *1995 Interim Report*, 4–61. Richmond: Association for the Preservation of Virginia Antiquities, 1996.

Swift, Earl. *Journey on the James: Three Weeks through the Heart of Virginia*. Charlottesville: University Press of Virginia, 2001.

Sydnor, Charles S. *American Revolutionaries in the Making: Political Practices in Washington's Virginia*. New York: Free Press, 1952.

Takagi, Midori. *"Rearing Wolves to Our Own Destruction": Slavery in Richmond, Virginia, 1782–1865*. Charlottesville: University Press of Virginia, 1999.

Taylor, L. B., Jr. *The Ghosts of Richmond . . . and Nearby Environs*. Williamsburg, Va.: L. B. Taylor, 1985.

Tekiela, Stan. *Birds of Virginia Field Guide*. Cambridge, Minn.: Adventure, 2002.

"Three Notable Indian Battles." *William and Mary College Quarterly Historical Magazine* 13, no. 3 (January 1905): 194.

Totty, Dale. *Maritime Richmond*. Charleston, S.C.: Arcadia, 2004.

Trout, W. E., III. *The James River Bateau Festival Trail: A Guide to the James River and Its Canal, from Lynchburg to Richmond*. Richmond: Virginia Canals and Navigations Society, 2002.

———. *The Upper James Atlas: Rediscovering River History in the Blue Ridge and Beyond*. Richmond: Virginia Canals and Navigations Society, 2004.

Trout, W. E., III, James Moore III, and George D. Rawls, eds. *Falls of the James Atlas: Historic Canal and River Sites on the Falls of the James with a Special Supplement on the Tuckahoe Creek Navigation*. 2nd ed. Richmond: Virginia Canals and Navigations Society, 1997.

Tyler, Lyon G. *The Cradle of the Republic: Jamestown and the James River*. Richmond: Whittet and Shepperson, 1900.

———. "Isle of Wight County: Papers Relating to Bacon's Rebellion." *William and Mary College Quarterly Historical Magazine* 4. no. 2 (October 1895): 111–15.

Varon, Elizabeth R. *Southern Lady, Yankee Spy: The True Story of Elizabeth Van Lew, a Union Agent in the Heart of the Confederacy*. New York: Oxford University Press, 2003.

Vickers, Daniel, ed. *A Companion to Colonial America*. Malden, Mass.: Blackwell, 2006.

Virginia: A Guide to the Old Dominion. Work Projects Administration in the State of Virginia. Richmond: Virginia Center for the Book, 1992.

Washburn, Wilcomb E. "The Governor and the Rebel: A History of Bacon's Rebellion in Virginia." *Ethnohistory* 5, no. 2 (spring 1958): 176–80.

———. "The Humble Petition of Sarah Drummond." *The William and Mary Quarterly*, 3rd Ser., 13, no. 3 (July 1956): 354–75.

Washington, James M., ed. *A Testament of Hope: The Essential Writings and Speeches of Martin Luther King Jr.* New York: HarperSanFrancisco, 1986.

Waugh, John C. *Reflecting Lincoln: The Battle for the 1864 Presidency*. New York: Crown, 1997.

Weisman, Steven R. *The Great Tax Wars: Lincoln–Teddy Roosevelt–Wilson How the Income Tax Transformed America*. New York: Simon & Schuster, 2002.

Wertenbaker, Thomas J. "Give Me Liberty: The Struggle for Self-Government in Virginia." *The Mississippi Valley Historical Review* 45, no. 3 (December 1958): 492–93.

Wilkins, Roger. *Jefferson's Pillow: The Founding Fathers and the Dilemma of Black Patriotism*. Boston: Beacon, 2002.

Wills, Gary. *Lincoln at Gettysburg: The Words That Remade America*. New York: Simon & Schuster, 1992.

Winchester, Simon. *The River at the Center of the World: A Journey up the Yangtze, and Back in Chinese Time*. New York: Picador, 1996.

Winik, Jay. *April 1865: The Month that Saved America.* New York: HarperCollins, 2001.

Wittkofski, J. Mark, and Theodore R. Reinhart, eds. *Paleoindian Research in Virginia: A Synthesis.* 2nd ed. Shacklefords, Va.: Archeological Society of Virginia, 1989.

Wood, Betty. *Slavery in Colonial America: 1619–1776.* Lanham, Md.: Rowman & Littlefield, 2005.

Wood, Gordon S. *The Radicalism of the American Revolution.* New York: Vintage, 1991.

Woodlief, Ann. *In River Time: The Way of the James.* Chapel Hill, N.C.: Algonquin Books of Chapel Hill, 1985.

Wright, Kai, ed. *The African American Archive: The History of the Black Experience through Documents.* New York: Black Dog and Leventhal, 2001.

Wyatt, Francis. "Letter of Sir Francis Wyatt, Governor of Virginia, 1621–1626." *William and Mary College Quarterly Historical Magazine,* 2nd Ser., 6, no. 2 (April 1926): 114–21.

In addition to the sources listed this bibliography, I found the following Internet websites useful:

The Colonial Williamsburg Foundation maintains an educational resource site at www.history.org/history.

The Library of Congress maintains historical collections at http://memory.loc .gov/ammem/index.html and selected manuscripts at www.loc.gov/rr/mss/ ammem.html.

Cornell University maintains an online digital library called "The Making of America" at http://library8.library.cornell.edu/moa.

The University of Virginia Library maintains an online Historical Census Browser drawn from U.S. census data at http://fisher.lib.virginia.edu/collections/ stats/histcensus/index.html.

The College of William and Mary maintains the Omohundro Institute of Early American History and Culture site at www.wm.edu/oieahc and a separate site on research at the Powhatan village of Werowocomoco at http://powhatan .wm.edu.

The Virginia Council on Indians maintains an informational and educational site at http://indians.vipnet.org.

The Wisconsin Historical Society maintains online digital manuscripts of early American explorers at www.americanjourneys.org.

The U.S. Army Center of Military History's site is located at www.army.mil/cmh-pg.

The Encyclopaedia Britannica Premium Service is located at www.britannica.com.

Lawrence H. Officer, professor of economics at the University of Illinois, maintains an online historical currency converting calculator http://eh.net/hmit/ ppowerbp.

INDEX

ABOUT THE AUTHOR

Bob Deans is a national correspondent for Cox Newspapers. A Virginia native, he started out in the news business when he was ten years old, delivering his hometown paper, the *Richmond Times-Dispatch*. His first newspaper-reporting job was with the *Charleston Post and Courier* in South Carolina. From there he joined the *Atlanta Journal-Constitution* before becoming the chief Asia correspondent, based in Tokyo, for the paper's parent company, Cox.

In 1992 Deans moved to Washington, D.C. where he has covered foreign policy, national security, economic affairs, and the White House. He was president of the White House Correspondents Association 2002–2003. He lives in Bethesda, Maryland, with his wife, Karen, and their three children.